Television Times
A Reader

Edited by

John Corner
Professor, School of Politics and Communication Studies,
University of Liverpool

Sylvia Harvey
Reader in Broadcasting Policy, School of Cultural Studies,
Sheffield Hallam University

ARNOLD

A member of the Hodder Headline Group
LONDON • NEW YORK • SYDNEY • AUCKLAND

First published in Great Britain in 1996 by
Arnold, a member of the Hodder Headline Group
338 Euston Road, London NW1 3BH
175 Fifth Avenue, New York, NY 10010

Distributed exclusively in the USA by
St Martin's Press Inc.,
175 Fifth Avenue,
New York, NY 10010

British Library Cataloguing in Publication Data
A catalogue entry for this book is available from the British Library

Library of Congress Cataloging-in-Publication Data
Television times : a reader / [compiled by] John Corner. Sylvia Harvey
    p.   cm.
  Includes bibliographical references and index.
  ISBN 0–340–65234–9 (hb).—ISBN 0–340–65233–0 (pbk.)
  1. Television broadcasting.   2. Television.   I. Corner. John,
1943–   . II. Harvey, Sylvia.
PN1992.15.T46   1966
791.45—dc20   96–5603

ISBN 0 340 65233 0 (Pb)
ISBN 0 340 65234 9 (Hb)

Typeset by Phoenix Photosetting, Chatham, Kent.
Printed and bound in Great Britain by J. W. Arrowsmith Ltd, Bristol.

In memory of Jo Li
(1949–1995)

'Not marble, nor the gilded monuments of princes . . .'

```
                    DATE DUE

  AUG   1 1998

  APR   7 1999

  APR  23 1999
  DEC  0 8 2000
  NOV  2 1 2000
  NOV  2 6 2001

  NOV  1 4 2001

        NOV 2 6 2002
        APR 2 4 2004
```

GAYLORD   PRINTED IN U.S.A.

Contents

Acknowledgements

The editors and publishers would like to thank the following for permission to use copyright material in this book: The Centre for Contemporary Cultural Studies, University of Birmingham, for extracts from Stuart Hall, 'Television as a medium and its relation to culture', Part 4 of a four-part report to UNESCO entitled *Innovation and decline in the treatment of culture on British television* (1971), pp. 89–97; the authors for extracts from Charlotte Brunsdon and David Morley, *Everyday television: 'Nationwide'* (British Film Institute, 1978), pp. 58–70; Kevin Robins and Les Levidow, 'The eye of the storm: reviewing the Gulf War', *Screen* 32(3) (autumn 1991), reprinted by permission of Oxford University Press, *Screen* and the authors; Sage Publications for extracts from Christopher Campbell, 'Traditional racism', *Race, myth and the news* (1995), pp. 42–56; the author for Justin Lewis, 'Decoding television news', from P. Drummond and R. Paterson (eds.), *Television in transition* (British Film Institute, 1985), pp. 205–16, 232–4; the British Film Institute for extracts from John Hill, 'Television and pop: the case of the 1950s', from John Corner (ed.), *Popular television in Britain: studies in cultural history* (Arnold, 1991), pp. 90–8; extracts from Philip Schlesinger and Howard Tumber, 'Fighting the war against crime: television, police and audience', *British Journal of Criminology* 33(1) (Oxford, winter 1993), pp. 22–8, 30–2 reprinted by permission of Oxford University Press and the authors; Routledge for extracts from Andrew Goodwin, *Dancing in the distraction factory* (1993), pp. 132–42, 149–55; Blackwell Publishers for extracts from Christine Geraghty, 'The aesthetic experience', *Women and soap opera* (1991), pp. 25–38; Routledge and the author for extracts from Hilary Hinds, '*Oranges Are Not the Only Fruit*: reaching audiences other lesbian texts cannot reach', from Tamsin Wilton (ed.), *Immortal invisible: lesbians and the moving image* (1995), pp. 52–69; the authors for extracts from Andy Medhurst and Lucy Tuck, 'Situation comedy and stereotyping', from Jim Cook (ed.), *Television situation comedy* (British Film Institute, 1982), pp. 43–5, 49–52; University of Minnesota Press and University College London Press for Paul Giles, 'History with holes: Channel 4 films of the 1980s', from Lester Friedman (ed.), *Fires were started: British cinema and Thatcherism* (1993), pp. 70–91; the authors for extracts from Mica Nava and Orson Nava, 'Discriminating or duped? Young people as consumers of advertising/art', *Magazine of Cultural Studies* 1 (1990), pp. 15–21; Indiana University Press for extracts from Lynn Spigel, 'Television in the family circle', from Patricia Mellencamp (ed.), *Logics of television* (British Film Institute, 1990), pp. 80–9; University of Pennsylvania Press for Margaret J. Heide, 'Gender and generation: the case of *thirtysomething*', from *Television culture and women's lives: 'thirtysomething' and the contradictions of gender* (1995), pp. 2–9; Sage Publications for John Fiske, 'Radical shopping in Los Angeles: race, media and the sphere of consumption', *Media, Culture and Society* 16(3), pp. 471–7, 484–5; Manchester University Press for John Corner, 'Mediating the ordinary: the "access" idea and television form', from M. Aldridge and N. Hewitt (eds.), *Controlling broadcasting* (1994), pp. 20–33; the author for Thérèse Daniels, 'Programmes for black audiences', from S. Hood (ed.), *Behind the screens: the structure of British television in the nineties* (Lawrence & Wishart, 1994), pp. 65–81; Sage Publications for extracts from Klaus Bruhn Jensen, 'Reception as flow: media constituents of social semiotics', *The social semiotics of mass communication* (1995), pp. 108–17; the author for extracts from Sylvia Harvey, 'Channel 4 television: from Annan to Grade', from S. Hood (ed.), *Behind the screens: the structure of British television in the nineties* (Lawrence & Wishart, 1994), pp. 102–29; Westview Press for extracts from William Hoynes, 'Public television: the historical and political context', *Public television for sale: media, the market, and the public sphere* (1995), pp. 1–23, 103–5, 108; the British Film Institute for extracts from Roberto Mader, 'Globo village: television in Brazil', from T. Dowmunt (ed.), *Channels of resistance: global television and local empowerment* (1993), pp. 67–89; the Independent Television Commission for extracts from 'Diversity and quality in television', from *Invitation to apply for a Channel 3 licence* (1991), paragraphs 103–6; 'Advertising and children', from *Code of advertising standards and practice* (1993), Appendix 1, paragraphs 1–11; 'Impartiality', from the *Independent Television Commission programme code* (1995), sections 3.2, 3.3, 3.5 and 3.8; the British Broadcasting Corporation for extracts from *Producers' Guidelines* (1993), Chapter 8, section 6, and Chapter 13, sections 1–6; the Independent Television Network Centre for 'Guidelines for drama-documentary', *Statement of best practice: factual drama on television* (1994); St Martin's Press and the author for Newton Minow, from the Introduction to E.G. Krasnow and L.D. Longley, *The politics of broadcast regulation* (1973); the author for extracts from 'Author's note', from N. Minow, *Equal time: the private broadcaster and the public interest*, edited by L. Laurent (Atheneum, 1964), pp. vii–x.

The editors would also like to thank Pam Hibberd and Sue Bragg at the Centre for Media and Communities Research at Sheffield Hallam University for most welcome administrative support during the production of this book.

Introduction

The box in the corner of the living-room, the small screen with its strange light and flickering pictures, is a relative newcomer to human society and culture. However, this newcomer, born before the mid-point of the twentieth century and emerging as a popular form in the wake of the Second World War, has embedded itself so deeply into the routines of daily life that it has taken on the character of a landmark: a sign of social unity and of social division, much loved, much attacked and likely to remain with us for a long time to come. In many respects, then, these are 'television times', however variable the manifestations of the medium and however unresolved the debates about its specific powers and effects.

It is difficult for us today to imagine the strong new sense of social connectedness and of domestic pleasure which followed the arrival of broadcasting in the home. With the beginning of radio services in the 1920s, the feeling of a radical shift in public communication and in the relationship between what was 'public' and what was 'private' was quickly established. Here was a medium which could transmit speech and music across vast distances, could bring the voices of favourite entertainers and leading public figures directly to the living-room and could describe major events, including sporting occasions, 'live' as they happened. Radio installed itself rapidly into the heart of everyday life and its schedules became a national rhythm. In the late 1940s and early 1950s television built on this earlier achievement but here the degree of wonder was still stronger. For tele-vision (literally 'seeing at a distance') seemed even more miraculously to bridge the gap between world and home, opening out a corner of the home on to a range of changing vistas, recorded and live, in a way which initially had all the allure of magic. Like radio, it too was a 'sociable' medium, often addressing the viewer as a member of a known community, sometimes perhaps as a friend.[1] However, it was the 'sights' which television offered – variously mundane, extraordinary, intimate, grand, informative and thrilling – which gave it its distinctive identity and force as a cultural technology.

This book brings together a selection of writings about the economic, social and cultural phenomenon of television – as system, as medium and as communicative process – which we hope will help students who are starting to think about it and discuss it. The items are drawn from a wide range of sources and they ask questions of different aspects of television from a number of perspectives.

In this introduction we want first of all to comment on the general character of television systems and to note significant shifts and differences in their organization over the years. We then want to reflect briefly on the nature of television study, noting some of the issues, and indeed the challenges, which present themselves in the mid-1990s.

Already, in the first fifty years of its existence, the little box in the corner has undergone a host of changes: from exclusively live transmissions to the preparation of programmes pre-recorded on videotape, from black and white to colour, from single-channel to multi-channel reception and from being 'free at the point of reception' (through advertiser, licence fee or public funding) to the possibility of 'pay per view' systems. In the richer parts of the world a multi-channel environment has been made possible by the development of cable and satellite – acting as adjuncts to the older systems of *broad*casting – and this has put pressure on the existing giants, the network providers used to reaching and holding a large proportion of the audience. Specialist, 'niche' services have emerged as alternatives to the mass-market generalist channels which, historically, have offered a varied and cross-generic diet of fact and fiction, information and entertainment. Investors in the newer technologies (with varying degrees of support from politicians) have been largely successful in creating a new interest, a new need and a new market, and this has changed existing viewer loyalties and patterns of viewing, having a major impact upon broadcasting practices and policies.

Meanwhile, the forms of television have continued to develop across the genres – news, documentary, situation comedy, serial drama, variety show and game show being joined by a whole range of newer forms, including, for instance, a growth of programmes based on dramatized reconstruction and new formats for talk shows and for audience participation programmes. Technological innovation together with new conventions of programme design have facilitated this development. Through-out, the importance of cinema films to the schedules has been sustained and, with the arrival of 'movie channels', intensified.

These various shifts and developments in the mass (and now sometimes not-so-mass) medium show no sign of diminishing – far from it – and they continue to be shaped by human actors whose imperfectly realized objectives and priorities determine the economic, political and social contexts of change. In many countries television celebrates its first half-century of existence by having displaced its large-screen sister, the cinema, only to confront a new rival in the small screen of the home computer. An extraordinary and ever-changing feast of sights, sounds and symbols now awaits those households with the spare cash needed to buy subscription television services, personal computers, CD-ROMs and the telephone line rental and services connecting the small screen to the world-wide information Internet. Though faced with such a feast of audio-visual and information plenty some cultural critics have posed questions about how such riches might be used, and have pointed to the coincidence of 'glut' and of 'famine' as those that 'have' get more, while those that 'have not' remain impoverished. As one American critic has put it, describing the proliferation of new media services rooted in private investment decisions and oriented to maximum profitability, 'the communications revolution will probably enhance inequality in the population'.[2] Clearly, though, there are other, and more optimistic, views about the social role and potential of the small-screen-based services of the future.

As we noted earlier, unlike its elder sister cinema, television manifests its richness of symbolic goods primarily within the private, domestic space of the home. Born out of the conjunction of scientific invention with commercial and political interests, it has proved itself to be an economical and effective system for communicating with millions of people, meeting needs, creating markets, attracting investors and awakening both the enthusiasm and the suspicion of politicians. For if the small screen offers entertainment and sometimes escape from the worries of everyday life, connecting back to the much older recreational histories of circus and music-hall and producing its own vast new culture of leisure, it is also part of a machine for moving around information and ideas at great speed and to large numbers of people. It is this second potential which, despite television's apparently private mode of address, has made it a fundamentally public form of communication. It is also this potential that has most directly attracted the attention of politicians and generated what is now almost half a century of debate about the social role of the medium: servant of public interest or of corporate profit, agent of enlightenment or of trivializing distraction, creature of the powerful or enabler of democracy?

The 1980s, last decade of the Cold War between West and East, capitalism and communism, saw an intensification of these debates about the role of broadcasting. In the United States and in Britain the governments of Ronald Reagan and of Margaret Thatcher embodied a new and vigorous defence of the principles of free markets and free enterprise, and sought to advance the interests of private business, to cut public spending and to reduce the provisions of the welfare state. In sometimes marked tension with the European social democratic tradition which seemed still to accept a large measure of collective planning in the public interest, the Reagan–Thatcher strategy sought to minimize public regulation and to maximize the freedoms and opportunities open to competitive entrepreneurs. In this deregulatory climate various nationalized utilities were returned to the private sector, and public service broadcasting (the BBC in Britain, the still fledgling public television service in America) was subjected to increasing pressure.

However, in Britain the principle of public service broadcasting, seen as a major enabler of democratic debate as well as a provider of low-cost but well-resourced entertainment services, was deeply embedded and widely accepted. This view had encouraged relatively strong forms of public regulation: of content, of structure and of ownership. In the United States, by contrast, a private ownership and private interest model for broadcasting has tended to dominate since the 1920s, and the rights of proprietors have been preferred over any extensive public or governmental regulation. The model of individuals and of corporations competing freely in the market-place of ideas has been advanced against the argument that the state, acting in the public interest, might function in support of the rights of citizens to engage in public debate and dialogue.

These differences in cultural history and orientation are vital for any understanding of the differences between national television systems. The American emphasis on business interests and private ownership, and the almost exclusively market-based forms of broadcasting provision which have prioritized entertainment over informational functions, compared with the long tradition of public interest interventions in European broadcasting, may help to explain the very different rhetorics around television developed by public figures on the two continents. The observation by one of President Reagan's appointees to the Federal Communications Commission that television is 'just an appliance, like the toaster'[3] may, with its apparently striking disregard for the cultural and social role of the medium, help to crystallize some of these differences.

If television has become a kind of cultural landmark, celebrated and derided though seldom ignored, at best a facilitator of public debate, at worst a conduit for the numbing of emotions and the neglect of reason, how significant is it in *global* terms at the end of the twentieth century?

The picture is rapidly changing and this will require constant revisions to any assessment of the social role and function of the medium. Inevitably, debate about television and study of it are most developed in those countries where there are most television sets. For the time being, we can pose the question of significance more precisely if we survey the global distribution of television sets as a percentage of the population. The United Nations Educational, Scientific, and Cultural Organization (UNESCO) provides us with some comparative figures for 1992. These figures show wide variations for different countries, from 0.2 per cent in Tanzania to 82 per cent in the United States; from 3 per cent in China to 61 per cent in Japan. The 3 per cent continental average for Africa masks considerable differences between, for example, Angola at 0.6 per cent and Egypt at 12 per cent, while the European continental average of 38 per cent covers a spectrum from 8 per cent in Albania to 44 per cent in Britain and 56 per cent in Germany. Note that these figures do not indicate percentage 'reach' to populations, which in all cases will clearly be much higher.[4]

In its heartland areas of North America, Europe and Japan, television is present in between 97 per cent and 98 per cent of households, and the sheer weight and extent of its presence is recorded by the available statistics. In Britain, for example, the average weekly viewing figure in 1993 was 25 hours.[5] In the United States the figure is significantly higher, with one estimate indicating that television sets are 'turned on' in the home for 49 hours a week.[6] However, this very reference to the television being 'turned on' raises questions about whether anyone is watching it, and with what degree of pleasure or of serious attention. It is at this point that vigorous disagreements begin within television studies concerning the extent of the social impact of the medium.

For some commentators television is viewed as highly significant, exercising a determining influence on everything from clothes and lifestyle to beliefs, values and voting intentions. At the other end of the scale are two very different views which none the less share a common scepticism about relative social significance. In the first group are critics who tend to dismiss television as a medium of entertainment, largely disconnected from and irrelevant to the world of ideas and of official politics; this view almost certainly underestimates the part that entertainment plays in reflecting and shaping the viewer's sense of identity and of individual and social values. In the second group are the more sophisticated critics of 'media-centricity' who emphasize the ways in which viewers, journalists and screenwriters all draw on sources other than television in forming their view of the world, in telling stories and in assessing actions and values. The role of family and of peer groups, of educational institutions, the world of work and gossip, oral histories and direct 'experience of life', may be as important as television in this respect, although we should not underestimate the extent to which television permeates into these areas too.

It is in reviewing the spectrum of responses to the perceived social importance of television that the inadequacy, or even the misleading nature, of certain generalities about the medium become apparent. At different times and in different countries, all, some or none of the above views might be persuasive. For television varies considerably in its effects because it differs in form and content, in modes of ownership and control, in 'reach' and, crucially, in the extent to which it is regarded as credible in different parts of the world. Examples from Russia, from eastern central Europe and from South Africa, in the period since 1989, may demonstrate the considerable variations in types of broadcasting systems, the speed with which they can change and the variations in viewer response: from apathy and disbelief to passionate concern and energetic engagement.

It would be a mistake to think of television in Western Europe and in the United States as entirely free of governmental and political control, but for the most direct forms of state and indeed of party political control, we have to turn to the former Soviet Union (USSR) and its satellite states in Eastern Europe prior to 1989, and to the example of South African broadcasting before 1994. The principle of *glasnost* or 'openness' encouraged by Mikhail Gorbachev in the USSR attained a legal basis in the critical area of the mass media only with the passing of a new media law in 1990. This law began the process of ending monopoly party control, prohibited censorship and gave journalists new reporting rights. Prior to the new mood of openness, surveys had shown that the Russian audience was simply bored by its television service, becoming apathetic and inattentive and finding its output increasingly incredible as the gap between perceived reality and television report grew.[7] It has been the gradual phasing out of the 'official' state or party voice that has begun to re-engage the viewers – although in Russia, as in other parts of Eastern and central Europe, the situation has remained extremely volatile, and governments or presidents have retained direct control of key appointments and of budgets for national television services.[8]

Developments in Romania in the late 1980s offer us examples of an audience both actively disengaging from a national programme service viewed with disbelief and even contempt, and subsequently taking action in defence of a new service. The presidency of Nicolae Ceauşescu was marked by intense and sometimes bizarre forms of social repression, with strict and monolithic party control of ideas and of behaviour, and the routine interventions of a numerous and active secret police. And yet, despite the levels of control, from the mid-1980s a large number of new TV aerials started to appear on the rooftops as people became determined to pick up television signals from neighbouring countries. A contemporary commentator has noted the speed with which 'forests of antennae grew on the roofs all around the country' and argued that the significance of this phenomenon was 'the transition from hidden to open disobedience ... which finally inflicted upon the dictatorship its first public defeat'.[9] When the wave of protest and radical change which had swept through Eastern Europe reached Romania, journalists working at the national television station turned against their erstwhile political masters, broadcasting live coverage of the demonstrations that led to the fall of Ceauşescu. The government threat of military intervention at the television station brought an appeal for public support by the broadcasters, and within a few hours the building was surrounded by well-wishers whose sheer force of numbers protected the station and its staff.

In South Africa the changes to a national broadcasting system, reflecting radical changes in the political system, came about a little more slowly. In the period before the first free elections in 1994 the apartheid government had retained firm control of national broadcasting in support of white minority rule. The vast majority of the population had been as culturally disenfranchised in relationship to television as they had been disenfranchised in the political realm. This was to change in the months leading up to the elections as various procedures were agreed between the government and the African National Congress, designed to ensure full and impartial coverage of issues during the election period. As a result the identity of the South

African Broadcasting Corporation was radically transformed, from mouthpiece of apartheid to forum for debate in the new multiracial society.[10]

In all these examples it is clear that television cannot take its audience for granted, and that the scope of its power is dependent not only on the energy and intelligence of its creative personnel but also on the broader social and political context.

THE STUDY OF TELEVISION

Given its emerging character as the principal means of public communication in modern societies, as one of the main arteries of citizenship as well as a transforming agency of domestic entertainment, it is not surprising that television has attracted widespread academic attention. Nor is it surprising that much of this attention, from the 1940s onwards, has displayed a high level of *anxiety*. How television might influence, for instance, political process, social perceptions, attitudes to violence and the desire for consumer goods has provided much research with its agenda of enquiry, an agenda which has often received generous funding from bodies that have had various interests in the findings.

Anxiety about influence has, internationally, encouraged a form of television study which draws on the concepts and methods of the social sciences. The aim has been to produce 'findings' which, in however tentative a way, might inform either public policy or the corporate policies of the television industry itself. Even work which has not directly engaged with questions of influence, but which has looked, for instance, at the institutions of television, at its routines and conventions of production or at its programmes, has often worked with assumptions about influence as part of the whole rationale for undertaking such study. That is to say, television – across its whole range of aspects and dimensions – has been seen as a justified object of academic investigation precisely in so far as it is perceived to be politically, socially and culturally powerful.

Although the dominant mode of television research remains that which draws on the social sciences – notably on sociology and social psychology – it has in the past twenty years or so been joined by a developing strand of enquiry within the arts and humanities. Here the emphasis has been placed much more on television as a cultural process, a system of visual and speech conventions whose political and social impact lies in the distinctive symbolic forms it employs. Although not wanting to ignore those features of television organization and process which have so concerned social scientists, researchers from the humanities have seen attention to the complexity of television's ways of meaning-making as holding the clue to its power. Rather than sociology or social pyschology, it has been linguistics, literary criticism and studies of cinema which have been most influential in shaping the approach here.

This broad difference of focus, with its related ideas of what questions are the most important to ask and *how* they might best be asked, continues to trouble television research and television studies. It does so despite the quite considerable degree of convergence and agreement which has occurred in the researching of particular topics and which can be seen in many of the items selected for this book. Partly, this continuing tension is the reflection of more general differences in approach between humanities and social science enquiry, differences still reinforced by the institutionalized pattern of academic work, with its strong sense of the borderlines between the disciplines and its consequent feelings of separateness and even of rivalry.

So over the past few years there has been intensive work on the television industry and its economics, on policy and production, on the many different kinds of programme content and form, on the ways in which audiences make sense of and use what they see and hear, and on the ways in which television might exert an influence – behavioural, attitudinal or ideological – over them. There have been studies that have focused on particular national systems and their histories, and studies that have tried to engage with aspects of television globally, registering the new technological developments in production and distribution which, as we noted above, are inevitably changing television's social identity. There is no doubt that much study has been undertaken with a high degree of ignorance about work lying outside the specific field of interest receiving attention. As the bright spotlight of enquiry has been placed on one 'part' of television, so other 'parts' have been plunged into darkness. This has often led to a kind of essentialism in which general pronouncements about the state of television *per se* have been made on the basis of very limited analyses. So, for instance, we have had studies of production which show little interest in the form of programmes themselves, critical analyses of certain programmes which show no interest in other kinds of programme and frequently no concern whatsoever for the interpretations made by the viewers who make up the intended audience, and studies of audiences which show not the slightest awareness of the economic and institutional contexts within which specific viewing opportunities are made possible. We observed that there are signs that such mutual ignorance and 'narrowness' is now starting to be replaced by a real concern to make connections and to locate the study of television in a larger, cross-disciplinary landscape of overlapping interests. If it is not simply to consist of loose generalities (and there have been some studies of this kind too!), any analysis of television needs to be selectively focused, but that should not stop it from being informed by, and then in turn informing, a wider set of ideas and arguments about the medium.

It would perhaps be useful to say something here about the large role which 'theory' of different kinds has played in the television study of the last two decades. Although it is often used rather carelessly as an impressive synonym for 'ideas', the term 'theory' indicates a connected set of propositions and/or hypotheses about how something works. Necessarily, such propositions are highly abstract, operating well above the level of local description and analysis in order to make claims about the larger picture and about causes and consequences.

Nearly all the social science and humanities disciplines have seen an intensification of theoretical work in recent years. This has been largely due to increased debate, internationally, about the procedures by which academic knowledge is produced, but it also follows from a sharpened sense of the complexity and contradictoriness of social organization, social phenomena and cultural process. Television has attracted a good deal of theorizing from different perspectives because, as we have suggested, it has been seen as a key feature of late modernity (such that phrases like 'television culture', 'the television society', have been regularly used). It has also been regarded as pivotal in the shift towards distinctively new forms of political and cultural order, a shift which many commentators have judged, with varying degrees of optimism or pessimism, to be both current and profound (the term 'post-modernism' has been widely used to indicate this sense of general transition).

Quite a lot of theorizing about television in the 1970s and 1980s drew on Marxist ideas, providing analysis with a rich and often dense critical vocabulary about television, addressing both capitalist economic relations and 'ideological reproduction'. This latter notion points to the strategic installation within society of certain ideas as 'common sense' at the same time as other ideas are marginalized or excluded altogether. Some of our extracts show work of this kind but others show how there is now a good deal of debate about the adequacy of Marxist explanations of economy and culture. This debate has given rise both to attempts at theoretical revision and to counter-theories. The question of television and of what role it has to play in the renewal of democracy (or, as some would claim, the destruction of democracy) has inevitably been caught up in these developments.

There is some agreement now that, although we need fresh thinking about television, thinking which engages with emerging political and cultural ideas at a proper level of abstraction, much previous theory was insufficiently connected to specific analysis. When theoretical developments disconnect themselves entirely from enquiry into the historical and the particular, their ability both to yield explanatory models and to develop rapidly declines. In the future, thinking about television will need to keep up a dialogue with 'lower'-level analysis. It will need to be more explicit about its precise aims than it has often been in the past, and it will also need to be clearer; the sheer obscurity of much theoretical writing on television has put off many readers, as well as minimizing the potential influence of academic thought upon public decision-making.

It is not only at the most general levels of conceptualization that study of television faces a challenge and the need for revision and innovation. There is still much to be done in developing our understanding of just how the images and words of television's formats operate as signs, converted into meanings (variously constitutive of realities and fictions, knowledge and pleasure) by viewers' interpretative activities. This entails a closer appreciation of television's expressive range (drawing in part on the critical vocabulary of film studies) but it also requires a more self-consciously social mode of enquiry – alert to television's sensitive positioning within the circulation of 'looks and sounds' within a society and able to recognize the ways in which production, distribution and viewing have a bearing on the construction of 'texts'. Many of the extracts which follow show the directions in which such enquiries might go and some of the ideas with which they might wish to work.

Television times has been assembled in the belief that the study of television has produced a body of work having intellectual worth and social significance and that it is currently undergoing a period of revision and growth internationally. This period will be an exciting one for students and researchers and it is likely to produce accounts which are of interest to policy-makers and broadcasters themselves as well as to the academic community.

Our main criterion in selecting material for this book has been clarity of argument and suggestiveness for discussion among groups who may have done little previous reading in the field. We have largely excluded material which is primarily descriptive in favour of work which opens up debates by a pointed piece of analysis or the putting forward of ideas. With such a vast range of possible items, any selection is bound to involve difficult decisions both as to what topics to cover and by what pieces to represent them. We have worked to our own sense of priorities and balance in the space available, drawing on programme analysis, policy debate, production studies and audience research.

Television in Britain or the United States is the subject of most of the items, but there is an address to global factors too. Throughout, we have tried to select items which, in different ways, bring out the *specificity* of television in the process of connecting it with other social and cultural factors. We have selected with the knowledge that others may well identify areas which they see as 'omissions'. Of course, it is precisely a part of the design of a volume like this that it should be used in conjunction with other readings, supportive and complementary. The volume is divided into four main sections to aid use in teaching, moving from the more textual to the more contextual concerns, but it is clear that firm categorization here is impossible. The sections are offered merely as loose groupings, indicating where it seemed to us that the most useful interconnections between approaches and topics were located. We have included a final section of industry documents, drawn from British and United States sources, which give the reader a sharper and more direct sense of the policy and regulatory issues referred to in a number of the main items.

Each of these main items is introduced by a commentary. This sets the piece in context, introduces its principal concerns and offers a little preliminary explanation for any terms or specific references which might otherwise cause difficulty for the student reader.

Items are presented in the formats used in first publication. In all cases we have indicated in full the source from which we have taken material, including an indication of material omitted. Omissions within the extracted text are indicated conventionally by three dots enclosed in square brackets [. . .]. In some cases, we have provided extracts with a new title which better fits their specific content than the title of the book or article from which they were taken.

Below, we offer an annotated bibliography of those books which we think might prove most helpful as initial further reading.

NOTES

1. The domestic novelty of early broadcasting receives commentary in a number of studies. *See* Paddy Scannell and David Cardiff's *Social history of British broadcasting*, vol. 1 (Oxford, Blackwell, 1991) for detailed documentation and discussion.
2. Robert W. McChesney, *Telecommunications, mass media and democracy: the battle for the control of US broadcasting, 1928–1935* (New York and Oxford, Oxford University Press, 1993), p. 259.
3. Cited in Douglas Kellner, *Television and the crisis of democracy* (Boulder, CO, Westview Press, 1990), p. 92.
4. UNESCO, *Statistical yearbook 1994* (Paris, UNESCO, 1994). Table 9.2 of the *Yearbook* deals with broadcasting and lists the number of television receivers and/or licences per 1000 inhabitants for each country. The figures given here are extrapolated from this source and generally rounded up to the nearest decimal point.
5. André Lange (ed.), *Statistical yearbook: cinema, television, video and new media in Europe*, edition 1994–5 (Strasbourg: European Audiovisual Observatory, 1994), pp. 29 and 148.
6. Kellner, *Television and the crisis of democracy*, p. 1.
7. *See* Brian McNair, *Glasnost, perestroika and the Soviet media* (London and New York, Routledge, 1991).

8. *See* the special issue of *Media, Culture and Society*, 'The Media after Communism', 16(2) (April 1994).
9. Pavel Campeanu, 'The Romanian TV: from image to history', paper presented to the International Television Studies Conference, London, 1991, pp. 4 and 6.
10. Ruth Teer-Tomaselli, 'Moving towards democracy: the South African Broadcasting Corporation and the 1994 election', *Media, Culture and Society* 17(4) (1995), pp. 577–601.

A SELECTIVE BIBLIOGRAPHY

ALLEN, Robert (ed.). 1995: *To be continued: soap operas around the world*. London: Routledge.
This is an impressively large collection of essays on what is perhaps the most popular form of television internationally. Studies on aspects of soap opera, from many countries, provide an excellent resource for further study.

ALLEN, Robert (ed.). 1992: *Channels of discourse reassembled*, 2nd edn. London: Routledge.
A collection of overview articles on different kinds of approach to television study. The contributions are of variable quality but many of them give a good sense of current research and debate, particularly from arts and humanities perspectives.

CORNER, John. 1995: *Television form and public address*. London: Arnold.
An attempt to look closely at the communicative organization of a number of staple forms, including news, documentary and advertising, and at key debates about influence, interpretation and quality.

CORNER, John (ed.). 1991: *Popular television in Britain: studies in cultural history*. London: British Film Institute.
A collection of essays on television in the 1950s and early 1960s, when the television system was in the process of generic formation, related to changes both in the technology and in production conventions.

CURRAN, James and GUREVITCH, Michael (eds.). 1996: *Mass media and society*, 2nd edn. London: Arnold.
The second edition of a valuable collection of articles on media analysis. Work on television appears alongside analysis of press and the new electronic media and the overall approach emphasizes sociological studies.

DAHLGREN, Peter. 1995: *Television and the public sphere*. London: Sage.
A survey of those television studies which have tried to assess the medium's political impact, particularly that of its journalism. The book ends with a detailed assessment of the possibilities for more democratic uses of television.

ELLIS, John. 1992: *Visible fictions*, 2nd edn. London: Routledge.
A closely argued account of cinema and television as social and cultural media. The comparison made between the two sometimes fails to recognize the generic range of television but the clarity of exposition and the regular use of examples make the book a valuable aid to study.

FISKE, John. 1987: *Television culture*. London: Routledge.
Perhaps the single most influential book on television of the last decade. Clear exposition of the 'cultural' approach to analysis, backed up with examples. Some of the theoretical positions informing the book have become more subject to questioning and debate since its first publication.

LIVINGSTONE, Sonia and LUNT, Peter. 1994: *Talk on television*. London: Routledge.
A provocative and generally positive account of the new 'talk shows', which mixes close analysis of participant talk with investigation of audience interpretations and assessments. An attempt is made to put new developments in televised talk within a political context.

MORLEY, David. 1992: *Television audiences and cultural studies*. London: Routledge.
A collection of essays on audience interpretation by the scholar whose early work was decisive in shifting the agenda of television research towards 'ethnographies' of reception.

NEWCOMB, Horace (ed.). 1994: *Television: the critical view*, 5th edn. Oxford: Oxford University Press.
An excellent collection of articles on television, well balanced and edited. The emphasis is on

textual criticism rather than sociological approaches. Most of the contributions concern North American examples.

SCHLESINGER, Philip. 1987: *Putting 'reality' together: BBC news*, 2nd edn. London: Constable.
A classic study of the production of television news. The analysis engages with questions of instititutional practice and sets these within the larger framework of the national political system. Several excellent case-studies.

SILVERSTONE, Roger. 1994: *Television and everyday life*. London: Routledge.
A critical survey of the ways in which television as a technology has 'colonized' everyday life. Impressively synoptic in the range of sources drawn on and concerned with the question of television's future identity and social uses.

TULLOCH, John. 1990: *Television drama*. London: Routledge.
A sustained examination of the forms of television drama, which relates dramatic forms both to the practices of scriptwriting and direction and the various expectations of audiences. Wide-ranging in its examples and its discussion of other studies.

WILLIAMS, Raymond. 1974: *Television, technology and cultural form*. London: Fontana.
An important volume in the development of television studies in Britain. Inevitably rather dated in some of its analysis but with sections on technology and influence which still repay attention. Williams's sense of the interconnectedness of the different aspects of television remains persuasive.

Section I

TEXTS

1

Technics of the medium

Stuart Hall

From Hall, Stuart 1971: Television as a medium and its relation to culture, Part 4 of a four-part report to UNESCO, *Innovation and decline in the treatment of culture on British television*. Birmingham: Centre for Contemporary Cultural Studies, 89–97. (The original organization and numbering of the text has been preserved here.)

Hall's discussion is taken from Part 4 of a 1971 report to UNESCO on aspects of British television and culture. In this section, Hall gives an account of television discourse and the types of transformation which it works upon its 'raw materials'. It is interesting to note how early this document comes in the development of media studies and media research in Britain; for instance, it was written three years before Raymond Williams's influential *Television: technology and cultural form*.

Hall's is a very clear discussion and, 25 years later, can be understood without much need for contextualization. Although a great deal has changed in the nature of British television in the intervening years, the basic points which Hall wishes to establish remain valuable and applicable. For instance, he suggests a division between those forms of television which work to 'relay' anterior, pre-televisual events and those forms of television whose content is specifically produced for television, on television's terms. Such a rough distinction can be seen in the schedules today. But, importantly, Hall also notes the increasing interplay between these forms and the way in which, even when it appears to be most clearly involved in 'straight relaying' (of sport for example, or of an outside broadcast from some major public occasion), television's transformative effects are still at work. Television is, says Hall, a 'thoroughly manipulated medium' – a judgement which is primarily descriptive of its essential nature as representational practice but which also carries a criticism of the specific political uses to which Hall thinks it is presently being put. This linking of the analysis of television's depictive conventions to a more general, pessimistic judgement on the medium's political character was referred in the Introduction to this book and is echoed in several other contributions. Rarely, however, is the attention to communicative process as lucid and thoughtful as here.

It is useful to apply the terms of the analysis to newer forms of television. In the 1960s sports magazine programme, *Grandstand* (BBC), Hall sees an example of an interesting 'hybridity' – the mixing together of various kinds of programme element which might in earlier television have been kept separate. In the 1990s, hybridization has been a major factor both in the commercial development of programmes as attractive commodities and (not always the same thing) in the attempts by many of those who work within television to open up new possibilities for the use of image and speech.

[...]

9. By technics we mean those qualities of the television medium which, though not belonging to the technical sphere *as such*, seem to be intrinsic to its nature, its use, and to its characteristic mode of communication.

10. Television is a *hybrid* medium. In part, this is because it is so extraordinarily heterogeneous in content and subject-matter. But, in terms of its formal properties, television also appropriates and cannibalizes a variety of forms and techniques from other sources, *including other media*. Its position as a highly advanced and socially specialized technology is marked by the degree to which it *combines* old and new media into a new medium. As Enzensberger has remarked (in his article 'The consciousness industry'): 'All new forms of the medium are constantly forming new connections, both with each other and with older media . . .'[1]

In the domain of culture, broadly defined, a good deal of television appears to be a relatively untransformed reproduction of presentational forms typical of other arts and entertainments: the cinema, the theatre, the concert hall, the circus, the stage show, the music hall, the cabaret, the public lecture, the after-dinner conversation, the seminar, the interview, etc. We stress the point *relatively untransformed*. It would be quite wrong to believe that these forms and contents come to us via the television screen *untransformed*. There is practically no unmediated or untransformed transmission on television [. . .] As Richard Dyer recently remarked, 'pure, straight transmission in television is a utopian category'.[2] Television *always* manipulates its raw material – it is, by nature, a 'dirty medium'. Though nature and actuality constantly *appear* before us on the screen *as if* transparently captured by the telecine, the images we see are constructions of or representations of 'the actual', not reality itself. This is the case even when television seems content simply to reproduce a theatre play in its original terms: the production has, in some way and to some degree, been rethought/reworked/realigned for television transmission. The *transparency* of the television screen is an illusion.

The most significant test case here is, perhaps, the cinema, which provides a product which can be fed into the transmission channels more or less direct, and which might therefore appear to be the perfect example of 'straight transmission' on television. Yet this is not the case. There is an important controversy in progress at the moment about the degree, nature and extent of *cuts* imposed by television on films transmitted on the television screen. The cutting is mainly of two kinds: (a) to tailor films of uneven length to the rigid requirements of television programme schedules, especially on ITV where an evening's viewing is composed of part-network, part-local programmes; and (b) to remove 'unsuitable incidents', especially though not exclusively violent incidents, during the viewing hours when children are watching. The average length of cuts made currently to films playing on ITV screens (the major offender) is seven minutes, according to a recent issue of *Films and Filming*. There is also the continuous selection process by which some films are chosen for television from what is generally available. Further, the transmission on the small screen of an image intended for the big screen crucially alters its form and impact. Film on television is, thus, on several levels, the product of small but significant *transformations*, made at different levels, as the product passes from one medium to another. Again, as Enzensberger reminds us, 'The most elementary processes in media production, from the choice of the medium itself to shooting, cutting, synchronization, dubbing, right up to distribution, are all operations carried out on the raw material. There is no such thing as unmanipulated ... filming or broadcasting.'

11. What makes television distinctive in this connection is (a) the relatively *low level* of the *type of transformation* which television operates on the great bulk of its contents; and (b) the very high proportion of cases in which the *raw material* which television transforms is itself *the content of another medium*. A great range of transformations of material for television transmission consists of minor cuts in film, slight alterations of angle, lighting and composition of theatre plays for more compact television camera movements, rearranging the seating at public occasions so that it offers a more orchestrated 'studio audience' for the performance being filmed, rearranging the order or length of acts so as to suit the requirements of the camera or the schedules, etc. Small changes can certainly have large consequences: one of the films recently cut in the London area of ITV was Howard Hawks' great masterpiece, *Rio Bravo,* from which one whole crucial scene was excised, though time was found to preview the following day's film presentation. But this is less important, in the long run, than the fact that the modifications made for transcribing a content from its indigenous medium or location to television involve transcriptions of a relatively *minor kind* in formal terms. The instances where television fundamentally modifies its subject-matter are far fewer than we might suppose. Television uses up – indeed, exhausts – the contents of other media and of everyday life: but it does not, characteristically, decisively *impose* its forms upon that material. In much of the transmission in the arts, the content which television is reworking is already *formed* in another medium or presentational mould. The weak character of its transformations is the source of what was called above 'the utopia of straight transmission'.

12. The question of forms seems inseparable here from contents. A fair proportion of television content is *actuality* – pictures of people, events and places in the 'real' world, transmitted to us via the medium of the set. A great deal of television material which is not live actuality is in the form of a report or *documentary*: that is, it tries to reproduce the forms of a 'live actuality'. Because television communicates in pictures, and is a rapid if not instant visualizer, a very high proportion of television is conceived in the *naturalistic* mode. Moreover, a good deal of television consists of visual reportage of *everyday life and events*. When the illusion of formal transparency is linked with the weight of naturalistic content in the medium, we can understand why television's *channel* functions *appear* to predominate so widely over its *medium* functions. The cinema, of course, is also a medium of visual realism, and the documentary film made for the cinema has many of the characteristics of a television programme – indeed, as a presentational form, *the documentary* is in general an ambiguous or intermediary zone between the two media. Many cinema documentaries are transferred straight from film to television, and vice versa. But characteristically, though the cinematic image has a fidelity or transparency to actuality, we have come more and more to think of the cinema as *exploring*, through its forms and language, the 'raw material' or actuality with which it deals. On the other hand we tend to think of television as *reproducing* the reality with which it deals.

Thus, in the domain of culture and the arts, the audience probably values television as much, if not more, for its ability to give us the artistic experience direct, in its original form, as it does television's capacity to *do something* in its own terms with that experience. Via television, we can be *in* the theatre, Covent Garden, the Festival Hall, the Talk of the Town, Barnsley Working Men's Club, the Variety, etc. This is television's *relay* function.

13. Television's power to 'capture reality' in visual terms, and transmit it into the living room is, then, at the present time, *its dominant function*. In technical terms, this is often conceived as coincidental with television when it is transmitting 'live' – as opposed to using film or video-tape. But more careful consideration suggests that there is a complex and shifting relationship between the channel/medium continuum in television and the live versus filmed/taped distinction. Television might transmit the last night of the Prom concerts on the night and at the time when the occasion is in progress: the technical link, then, is direct between the 'outdoor' cameras and the transmitting/receiver apparatus. But it might *film* the last night of the Proms, 'as it happened', and transmit it at a later time or date. In the first case, television is transmitting 'live'. In the second, it is transmitting filmed or *stored* images of an actual occasion: the feel of actuality is an illusion. But both types of transmission still belong, essentially, to television's channel functions. That is, in both cases, the presentational form is dictated largely by conditions *in the concert hall*: television only weakly imposes its own forms upon this already-formed material. The same is true, in reverse, when productions are mounted entirely in the television studio, and when the presentational forms and techniques have been worked out with television's requirements as the sole determinant. A studio television play may be transmitted 'live' or it may be filmed/videotaped and transmitted later: but in formal terms, this is television operating as a *medium*: the script has been prepared, acting positions and movements worked out in relation to camera positions and angles, etc. In some cases, we have a complex interplay of all the elements. For example, a Wednesday play with a strong documentary emphasis may be filmed *on location*, and transmitted at a later time. Its context and location then are very close to those of an 'actuality' transmission (this is indeed the illusion being sought in moving from studio to location). But it has been conceived formally in television terms, and probably edited, much as a film would be. Its mode of transmission is in the filmed/taped category, not in the 'live' category. In short, television's *channel* functions (where the imposition of television forms is weak) and its *medium* functions (where the imposition is stronger) make indiscriminate use of the technical *means of transmitting material*. The fact that much of television's 'canned' material *creates the illusion* of 'live actuality' is important: but this is an aesthetic and social matter – not a technical one. It has to do with television's innate naturalism, of form and content, and the developing body of practices and idioms in television, which tend strongly to *favour* and *exploit* that naturalism.

14. The occasions when television exploits its powers as a medium must be linked, essentially, not with the technical means of transmission, but with two types of *production*: *staged* performances, and *studio* production.

By *staged performance* we mean a television production which has been specifically mounted for television, whether it takes place in a studio or on location. In the area of culture with which we are dealing, a staged performance may be a play, concert, musical show, etc., which has been written, or devised for television: where camera angles, *mise-en-scène*, acting or performance are shaped and guided throughout by the technical limits and opportunities of the medium. Staged performances can make a 'mixed' use of the different modes of transmission – i.e. 'live' or 'canned'. The television play may be recorded earlier on tape and transmitted later, though in script-form and performance it has been wholly conceived in televisual terms. The acting performance before the cameras can be supplemented by *inserting* into the transmission sequences which have been filmed or taped at a different place and time. In some *Wednesday Plays*, for example, or in *Softly Softly*, the police series, the production is composed of mixed elements, some acted before the cameras, some fed in through tele-cine in taped or filmed form. There *does* appear to be a continuum or spectrum here which impinges directly on the domain of culture. It seems to be a general rule that the more serious, 'high brow' or 'high culture' in orientation the production is, the *less* it will be conceived *ex novo* for television – the more it will borrow from other media. The Shakespeare play will tend, on the whole, to be either a straight relay from the Stratford stage, or a production in studio which is subordinate in form, setting, acting technique, rhythm and staging to theatrical forms. The closer we get to the popular end of dramatic productions – popular plays, serials, series – the stronger will be the *medium* elements, the more distinct they will be from theatrical conventions.

15. The predominant way in which television operates as a *medium* (rather than as a relay) is in the great variety of *studio situations*.

Studio situations characteristically mix the modes of transmission. That is, in documentary and current affairs programmes, the programmes will be composed of sequences in the studio plus filmed inserts. Arts review programmes are similar – the compère or reviewer/anchor-man presiding 'live' before the cameras over a set of filmed or canned inserts. Discussion and interview programmes have little or no filmed/canned content: they are almost exclusively studio productions (again, transmitted 'live' or 'canned').

A great range of programmes – sports coverage around the country on Saturdays on both channels, the attempt to integrate the various regional news-magazine programmes into a single transmission in the late afternoons (*Nationwide*) or the arts magazine like *Review* or *Aquarius* – are sequences of filmed inserts presided over by a compère or presenter. The presenter in the studio provides, visually and verbally, a framework for the different, dispersed items (in the case of arts magazines, previously filmed excerpts; in the case of sports coverage, 'live' transmissions from different locations). He 'builds a programme' for the viewer in the studio out of these filmed and video-transmitted items. An edition of the sports programme *Grandstand*, for example, consists of (a) bits of 'live' video transmission from the race-track, rugby game, horse jumping competition, swimming, or athletics meeting, with the commentator on the spot providing a 'voice-over' commentary; plus (b) the tying together of these reports, 'in studio', by a resident compère, who administers the breaks between one event and another, smooths the transitions from one place or sport to another, and, occasionally, makes use of studio aids, charts, diagrams, superimposed captions, etc., to 'give an overall sense' of the results or state of the sporting world that afternoon. Now, in terms of the distinctions drawn above, the 'in studio' bits of that programme are formally strong in medium elements. No other medium, except perhaps radio (but without the visual element), can 'create' a programme of this kind out of discrete fragments. The filmed or video-transmitted elements are weak in medium elements: the form of the race-meet, the rugby game, etc., belong intrinsically to sport not to television. However, television has also transformed even these bits of actuality. It does not give us the whole rugby game, but edited highlights of it: it does not cover the whole field statistically, but moves cameras around, shifts angles and distances to *re-create* parts of the game for us in visual terms. So, *in both aspects*, the programme transforms its content.

16. Such a programme, which combines 'live studio' and filmed insert elements, is close to a television original. There is nothing *quite like it* in any other medium. Radio, as we have observed, comes close in some respects, because it too can integrate into studio transmission *taped* inserts. The filmed newsreel comes close to it in another sense, since it too can edit together bits of film taken on different occasions – though, unlike television, the newsreel rarely if ever makes use of the 'live' studio situation.

Such a television programme is itself a curious *hybrid*. If we break the programme down into its elements, we find studio sequences, filmed sequences, video-transmitted elements with commentary over, and so on. Intrinsically, the whole programme, as a programme unique to television, consists of the *assembling together* of these channel-originated and medium-originated materials into a single programme unit under the guidance/direction of a producer and a presenter. The presenter is responsible for imposing a unity over the different elements before the camera: the producer is responsible for transmitting this *constructed programme* to the viewer.

17. This *assembly role* of television is one of its unique properties. The degree of technical coordination required to effect these switches from place to place, event to event, 'live' to 'canned' material and so on is enormous. So are the social, communicative – indeed, *managerial* – skills required to effect smooth narrative transitions between studio, reporters, events, etc. The programme is an enormous feat of collective socio-technical coordination and control. But the effort to account for the programme as a whole in terms of a unified set of aesthetic criteria, or the attempt to derive such a coherent aesthetic from such programmes, is an extremely difficult, if not impossible, task. When the viewer is not totally absorbed into the 'raw material' of the programme, what he tends to notice most are aspects of this assembly and coordination process. He notices the mannerisms of the compère, his style or delivery, his encyclopaedic knowledge ... He notices *especially* when things go wrong *in the flow of production* – losses of contact with a commentator at the other end of the line, unrehearsed pauses as we 'lose' and 'regain' sound, references to play in the rugby game unaccountably followed by an insert from a boxing championship, and so on. That is, he notices *breaks* in the smooth assembly and coordination–integration of the elements, because *formally* this is what the programme *is*. The aesthetics of the medium, then, tend to be fragmented or serialized. It is difficult to see what common formal terms can be applied, overall, to a programme which consists of good or poor coverage of the rugby game, good or bad link-commentary or illustration provided in the studio, and good or poor continuity maintained by presenter/producer between these elements.

The predominance of the *assembly process* as a characteristic of television communication has, of course, crucial consequences. It highlights the role and performance of the presenter or compère – to the degree that the programmes become associated with the style, manner and personality of their presenters. These 'resident managers' imprint programmes with their personalities because the programmes themselves so centrally depend on the live execution of the skills of communication-management before the camera. But this, in turn, means that the vast bulk of television material is *mediated* to the audience through the techniques and personae of the presenter. Now this is of critical significance in the domain of culture, since what is important for this domain are the social values and attitudes invested in or overprinted on the cultural material itself. Television can almost never be the means by which the viewer gains access to the 'raw materials' of culture, free of the mediation of cultural–social values inherent in the presentational elements of the programme. Thus *Monitor* derived its strengths and weaknesses not simply from the range of cultural things it offered to the viewer, but because of the socio-cultural *package* in which the 'raw material' was integrated.[3] It was Wheldon-on-culture which *Monitor* offered us – and, through the presenter, a selective range of cultural attitudes were powerfully mobilized and transmitted. Because television so often consists of embedding one kind of content-form within another, the very form in which the links and connections are forged is itself an intrinsic and powerful formulative element of the programme itself. Just as the camera guides, selects and omits as it ranges over and around its material, so the presenter or producer guides/selects/omits/ stresses what has already been guided/selected, etc. The collective values and attitudes which structure and frame such processes of selection and assembly thus interpenetrate every content which television appears to 'present straight'. In short – whether to good ends or to bad – television is technically and socially a *thoroughly manipulated medium*. The utopia of straight transmission, or the 'naturalistic fallacy' in television, is not only an illusion – it is a dangerous deception.

18. The whole argument hinges around one of television's technical properties which has not yet been clearly pin-pointed. We speak of the 'television camera'; but we think of it as we think of a film camera. In the cinema the production/editing of the image and the distribution of the image are two distinct processes. We do not often take into account the fact that the television camera has a decisive *dual function*. It records and stores images: but it also transmits images. When equipped with film stock, the 'television camera' functions like a film camera: it stores content on the film stock itself. When equipped with video-tape, the camera can also store information and content for later transmission. But when, in studio, the 'camera' is *linked directly* to the transmitting apparatus, it stores nothing – it is a medium for passing the images directly into the channel and through to the receiver. In short, the television camera is itself a storing, an assembling and a transmitting device. The technical heart of the process is not the camera alone but the *link-ups from cameras to transmitting apparatus* – whether the link-up is made direct, from studio camera to the open channel, or indirectly from film camera on location through the studio link into the channel, or from filmed or canned inserts, via tele-cine machines, into the channel. Any single television programme can make use of these three functions. With the great expansion of

inter-continental television systems, the links through cameras to studio to receiver-channel are now world-wide.

NOTES

1. The English version of Enzensberger's influential essay on media and consciousness was published in a book of this title by the Seabury Press, New York, 1974. (Eds.)
2. Richard Dyer, now Professor of Film Studies at the University of Warwick, was a postgraduate student working with Hall at the Centre for Contemporary Cultural Studies at the University of Birmingham. The reference is to an internal discussion paper. (Eds.)
3. *Monitor* was a pioneering and popular arts review, produced by the BBC. Its presenter was Hugh Wheldon, whose introductions gave the series much of its identity. (Eds.)

2

Linking and framing in popular television journalism

Charlotte Brunsdon and David Morley

From Brunsdon, C. and Morley, D. 1978: *Everyday television: 'Nationwide'*. London: British Film Institute, 58–70.

Charlotte Brunsdon's and David Morley's 1978 study, *Everyday television: 'Nationwide'*, was a perceptive and influential attempt to examine the conventions of television journalism. It explored the ways in which one early evening magazine programme organized its stories and addressed its viewers. *Nationwide* (BBC) was a very successful programme, gaining its identity from a distinctively 'relaxed' way of reporting, its strategic address to family audiences and its extensive use of stories from the BBC's studios outside London, combining regional interest with a strong sense of nationhood. Brunsdon and Morley describe its typical contents as constituting a 'mosaic' of both 'serious' and 'entertaining' items, where linking between them in a way which retains viewer interest becomes crucial (Michael Barratt was the celebrity presenter at the time of this analysis).

In the extract we have chosen, the authors examine the way in which items are introduced, developed through the use of location footage and the speech of different interviewees, and then closed. They set out a typology of phases and then apply this to examples, paying particular attention to an item which is about the invention of a new drawing-board for the use of blind students. Both in this and the later examples in the extract, they are nicely alert to the way in which shifts of visualization and of speech involve shifts in the positions of knowledge available to the viewer. The degree of control exercised over viewer perceptions during filmed reports is seen to be continued in the way in which interviews are introduced and conducted, potential threats to the programme's own discursive plan being deftly avoided.

More recent studies of the television audience suggest a relationship between screen and viewer which is a good deal more open to variation and hazard than seems, at times, to be suggested here. Yet the authors' interest in devices of address and in the way in which topics and participants are managed by the use of implicit criteria, cultural and political, produces a lucid and still instructive commentary.

Note: the extract involves reference to items which have been identified earlier in their book. These include an item on a drawing aid for blind students, an item on a woman attacked by a lion in a safari park and an item about design students carrying out a 'survival' exercise using materials from a rubbish tip. There are also interviews with the US consumer rights campaigner Ralph Nader and with Patrick Meehan, a man recently released from prison after serving seven years of a life sentence for murder.

Everything is 'linked in'; an item cannot appear on *Nationwide* without having been firmly set in context. First, it will be introduced by being located in the structure of the programme text – it is made clear what part of the programme we are in (Regional/National *Nationwide*) and how the item relates to other parts of the programme. Second, it is made clear how it relates to our concerns in the social world.

This can usefully be seen as a four or five stage strategy:

(1) *Linking* –   performing the textual function, guiding us through the programme discourse ('now, over to . . .').

(2) *Framing* –   establishing the topic and its relevance to the concerns of the audience.

(3) *Focusing* –   establishing the particular angle that the programme is going to take on the topic.

If there are to be extra-programme participants a fourth stage is necessary:

(4) *Nominating* –   clueing the audience in as to the identity of extra-programme participants or interviewees; establishing their 'status' (expert, eyewitness, etc.) and their right/competence to speak on the topic in question – thus establishing their (proposed) degree of 'credibility'/authority within the discourse.

Nationwide members, of course, also have their 'statuses' continually marked and established within the discourse ('our reporter in Lakenheath. . .') but they are also pre-given as established figures, with an established competence (e.g. Barratt) and role in the programme.

Customarily there is a fifth stage of the process:

(5) *Summing-up* – drawing together the main threads of the item, its relevance and the context in which it is to be placed; done by the interviewer at the end of the item (internally), and/or by the linkman, before going on to introduce the next item.

If we look at the item on the blind students who have been able to learn to draw because of a new invention we can see this process in operation:

(1) *Link*:   'One of the things you   The link is given by the
                 wouldn't expect a blind   regional presenter; he links
                 person to be able to do is   its relevance back to the
                 draw . . . a picture like the   previous item (a child's
                 one we've just seen but   drawing of the weather)
                 things of course are   and frames/connects it with
(2) *Frame*:   changing all the time, and a   our social concern for the
                 new invention . . . could   blind.
                 change all that.'

He then introduces/nominates the reporter who is going to do the story:

'. . . a report now from Duncan Gibbons.'

who moves on to phase (3) of the process:

(3) *Focusing*: 'A class at . . . College for the Blind . . . these youngsters are working with a new device . . . giving them a remarkable insight into the world of the sighted person. The device is a new drawing-board . . .'

He focuses our concern with the topic onto the specific role of a new invention in helping blind people to produce 3-D drawings.

He goes on to explain a little how the device works and then moves to phase (4):

(4) *Nominating*: 'The man who invented the drawing-board is Mr Christopher Vincent, head of technical graphics at Birmingham Polytechnic . . . he adapted it from a perspective grid . . . hopes to introduce the device into other colleges for the blind . . .'

He thus nominates the first extra-programme participant – he introduces him and explains his status as expert/inventor, and thus his competence to speak on the topic.

The inventor is then interviewed, and afterwards two of the students who are using the invention. At the end of the interview with the students we move out to a film report of them walking cumbersomely out of the college, arm in arm, and the reporter, in voice-over, sums up:

(5) *Summing-up*: 'Soon 3-D maps will be developed using drawings from the board. Then blind youngsters like . . . [these] will be able to find their way around much more easily.'

The summing up contextualises the item in terms of its social use-value; the invention will help to produce maps which will practically improve the lives of the blind students.

This item, then, displays a recurring *Nationwide* structure:

(L	F	(N)	Fo	N	(. . . .)	F)
(Link	Frame	(Nominate)	Focus	Nominate	(. . . .)	Frame)

The structure contains (in both senses: includes, and holds within its limits) the independent-authentic contributions of the extra-programme participants. That is, it defines and determines the structure of how, where and what the extra-programme participants can contribute. Of course, the items appear to ground, witness and authenticate themselves, outside the programme, in the 'real world' through these 'extra-programme' contributions. This process of authentication is supported and realised by the forms in which the participants' accounts are signified: that is, participants are shown 'in their own person' on film; what they are said to be doing is witnessed to by our seeing, in the visuals, that they are indeed doing it; and they are shown and heard, speaking 'in their own voice'. But this apparent transcripted reality is itself framed by the encoding structure of the item, which establishes its own over-determining 'reality'; and, through the visual and verbal commentary, encodes, as its privileged reading, a specific interpretation of what they are saying and doing. The discursive work of linking and framing items binds the divergent realities of these different items into the 'reality' of the programme itself – reconstitutes them in terms of their reality-for-the-programme. Over against the divergent times, histories and locations of these different items, the linking work establishes its own privileged continuity – incorporates them into the 'natural' *Nationwide* flow, into *Nationwide* time. Essentially, *Nationwide* as a programme is articulated through these two axes: the axis of *difference* (different items, different topics, different participants – each with its own register, its own point of interest, contributing to the panoramic *variety* which is *Nationwide*'s manifest stock-in-trade, its claim to be a magazine topicality programme); and the axis of *continuity and combination*, which binds, links and frames these differences into a continuous, connected, flowing 'unity'. But the linking discourse has a determining primacy in the hierarchy over the other discourses, which are actively subordinated to it through certain specific discursive strategies.

It would be perhaps more appropriate to define the linking and framing discourse as the *meta-language* of the programme – that which comments on and places the other discourses in a hierarchy of significance, and which therefore actively constitutes the programme as a 'structure in dominance'.

As we move through any one item – from direct address, through filmed report and interview, to studio discussion – we move from that level of the discourse at which control is most directly in the presenter's hands, to that at which the structure is more 'open'. This movement, however, is paralleled by an increasing restriction of access as we move up the scale: only the *Nationwide* team have access to the level of the discourse in which frames and contextualisations for all the elements of an item are given. Extra-programme participants only have access to the lower levels of the discourse; and their contributions are always framed by the presenter's statements.

VERBAL AND VISUAL DISCOURSES: COMBINATIONS AND CLOSURES

The framing of items is also set by the relations of hierarchy established between the visual and verbal levels of discourse. The use of voice-over film reports – where the commentary 'explains' the meaning and significance of the images shown – is the most tightly controlled form in which the 'actuality' material is presented: here, the verbal discourse is positively privileged over the visual. It is important, analytically, to hold a distinction between these two, distinct, signifying chains. The visuals could, potentially, be 'read' by some section of the audience outside of or against the interpretive work which the commentary (voice-over) or meta-language suggests. But the dominant tendency – which the specific work of combination accomplishes here – is for the visual images to be 'resolved' into those dominant meanings and interpretations which the commentary is providing. This interpretive work is, however, repressed or occluded by the synchronisation of voice-over with images, which makes it appear as if the images 'speak for themselves' – declare their own transparent meaning, without exterior intervention. This synchronisation of discourses is the work of *coupling* – the accomplishment of a particular combination of discourses which has the effect of *fixing* certain privileged meanings to the images, binding the two signifying chains together in a specific relation of 'dominance'. Specifically, film used on *Nationwide*, although it may have its own faint sound-track (naturalistic background sound, for example), is invariably *voiced-over* for some part of an item, except where the *Nationwide* team itself (e.g. on the East Anglia boat trip) is the 'subject' of the item, providing the content of, as well as the commentary on, the report. In that situation, sound is relayed direct.

Thus, there is a repeating structure which is used for both the 'Blind' and the 'American' items:

(introduction – v/o film report)
(interview(s))
(conclusion – v/o film report)

As in the case of framing by direct address, v/o introductions set the frame and dominant meaning within which the content of an item or interview is set.

This structure can be seen at work if we look at the item on 'Blind students' – now with special attention to the visual discourse. Visually, this item has a complex form: we begin with v/o film report, showing the invention in use in a classroom – we see and hear students performing operations which we do not yet understand. The indeterminacy or unresolved nature of this visual 'clue' is sustained in the v/o commentary:

REPORTER: This/mysterious/clicking noise makes this a very special classroom.

This temporary 'suspense-effect' is quickly resolved, as the commentary begins to explain the meaning of these unintelligible visual messages. We then see film without commentary (in direct sound) of an obviously authoritative figure (this much is signified by his manner, dress, age, style of addressing and directing the students) moving around the classroom. After a few seconds – in which the visual resolution is, once again, temporarily suspended – the reporter's commentary identifies him:

REPORTER: The man who's patented the drawing-board is Mr . . .

We then move on to more film of the invention in use, with v/o commentary – this time, an internal commentary, provided by the inventor himself – and then to a shot of the inventor being interviewed, speaking now direct to camera.

In these sections of the item, visual sequencing reinforces (and also constitutes) the force of the meaning of the images: while the inventor is talking, explaining how the invention works and how he derived the idea for it, the camera gives us detailed close-ups of the use and workings of the invention: shots of hands moving along T-squares, etc.

When we move, however, to speak to the students themselves, the camera zooms in to a facial close-up, as soon as they begin to speak of the difference the invention has made to their personal lives. Here the emphasis is fixed, visually, on one student (on his facial expression) as he explains how the invention has changed his life. The use of visual close-up on the face – expressing in personal terms the essential human 'point' of the item – supports the displacement of focus from the technical to the experiential register.

For the final section of the item (third move in the structure), as we watch the blind students leaving the college, the students walk away from us out of the door, the camera moving back to allow us a more distanced/'objective' perspective – a concluding, rounding-out, closing shot. The reporter sums up and contextualises the significance of the item *as a whole*, in v/o commentary, over the 'closing' filmed images.

SETTING THE SPECTATOR IN PLACE: POSITIONS OF KNOWLEDGE

It is clear from this brief analysis that no permanent dominance is given to the visual in the hierarchy of discourses established in this item. Rather, we would have to say that, at the key points of transition in the item, a dominant interpretation is, if anything, 'privileged' by the signifying discourse of the commentary and v/o meta-language. However, certain key transitions *are* principally realised through the shift from one visual register to another – for example, the *technical* aspect of the item is 'shown' by the close-ups of hands manipulating the apparatus, before its 'workings' are explained by an internal commentary; the transition from the technical to the *experiential* register is principally accomplished by the camera movement to full-face visual close-up; the 'closure' of the item, and its 'human significance', is pointed principally by the camera pulling back to give us a more 'overall' view of what has been accomplished for the blind students, coupled, of course, with a framing commentary. What matters, then, is not the permanent primacy of the visual discourse, but rather the way the verbal-visual hierarchy of combinations is differently established at different moments or points in the item – the discursive work which each on its own and both together accomplishes and sustains.

The visual discourse, however, has a special significance in *positioning* the spectator, setting him/her in place in a set of shifting positions of knowledge with respect to the item. Even here, positioning ought not to be reduced to the specific technical movements of camera shot and angle, but must rather be understood as the result of the combined visual-verbal 'work' – sustained by and realised through the programme's discursive operations.

Thus, when we first 'look' at the invention being used in the classroom, we look at this scene with and through the 'eye' of the presenter. It is his 'gaze' which we follow, from a position – a perspective on the filmed scene – outside the frame, looking in on it. Here, paradoxically, we 'see' from an absent but marked position, which is where the presenter's *voice* appears to come from: 'this mysterious clicking noise . . .'

It is the 'gaze' of the presenter/spectator, outside the programme, which 'finds' the inventor, within the frame; which then picks up and follows (as the camera does) his 'glance'. The spectator's position is now, through a mirror-reciprocation, identified with that of the inventor's as we look at what he looks at – and he can now directly address 'us'; an identical line of vision, from inside the frame to 'us' outside the frame, has been established. This privileged giving-of-the-commentary over to a representative figure within the frame (operating along this line of vision) is sustained by the specific work of designation, presenter-to-inventor. That is, it is sustained by the *process* through which, progressively, the various positions of the viewer are established: the overseeing 'look' at the film, from a position outside its system of significations; the 'finding' of a position of identification for the spectator (outside), inside the film-space; the mirror-effect, which, having established 'us' at the centre of the film – seeing what is to be seen, through its glance – then enables the reciprocating look, back at us, through direct address, eye-to-eye. Our 'look' is now identical with 'his' (the inventor's). Hence, while, as he speaks, he looks down and around at the operations which he is explicating, 'we' follow his glance; we have been inscribed in it, and take the perspective of his look: close-ups of the invention, hands moving along T-squares, feeling their way . . .

The transition to the students speaking and imaged 'as themselves' returns us to a position outside the frame – but a privileged one; a point emphasised by the camera zoom, manipulating the distances, which 'takes us closer in' – but which is also a shift of focus in the other sense, obliterating the technical details of the classroom, and 'focusing' (or re-focusing) our 'look' on what is now the most important element – the expressive signifier of the face of the subject, in what has been abstracted/ emphasised (by the zoom) as the essence, the truth, the human point, of the item: technology changes lives; it enables the blind to 'see'; we 'see' that it does, because we see the intense (i.e. intensified, by the close angle) meaning-for-the-subject of what has already been shown.

The point once made, in its most intensified moment/point of registration, we are ready for the closure. Closure is signified here by re-positioning the spectator in the place of a now more-inclusive knowledge – in the enclosing, framing, gathering-together plenitude of our 'sense of a sufficient and necessary ending'. 'They' – the subjects of the item – are seen moving away from us, from our position of knowledge/vision; we, in turn, move back from this involvement (i.e. are moved back, as the camera retreats, from the point of intensity), to get a retrospective-circumscribing 'over-look' of the item: what it *all* means . . .

What we 'know' about the 'Blind' item is inscribed through the process of *how* we come to know – that is, the positions from which we see and hear what there is to be known about this item. That knowledge is constructed in part through the inscription of the spectator-as-subject in a series of positions – positions of vision, positions of knowledge – sustained by and realised in the discursive operations. These operations set us in place in a process of knowledge – from perplexed ignorance ('this mysterious clicking noise . . .') to completed, circumscribed understanding (what the item was *really* all about). The ideological effect of this item is not in any sense completed by this process of positioning – it includes, for example, what we 'come to know' about humane technology, about how lives are changed; but it depends, in part, on how the process of 'coming to know' is sustained through the programme's discursive work – constituting the spectator actively in the unity of the places in which 'we' are successively fixed and positioned.

SPEAKER STATUS AND THE STRUCTURE OF ACCESS: SUBJECT AND EXPERTS

Access to the discourse is controlled by the programme team. The question is 'access on what terms for whom?' and the crucial variable here is the extra-programme status of participants. Participants of 'low' status (a) will tend to be questioned only about their 'feelings' and responses to issues whose terms have already been defined, and (b) will tend also to be quickly cut short if they move 'off the point'. Those of 'higher' status conversely (a) would tend to be questioned about their 'ideas' rather than their 'feelings', and (b) will be allowed much more leeway to define issues in their own terms.

This distinction is formally supported by the tendency to move in for bigger close-ups of subjects who are revealing their feelings, whereas the set-up for the 'expert' is usually the same as that for the interviewer: the breast pocket shot. Both kinds of statused participants are 'nominated' by the reporters into the discourse, questioned by a member of the team, and have their contributions framed and 'summed-up'.

Thus, there is a clear differentiation in the discourse between those participants who appear, principally, as 'subjects' – something newsworthy has happened to them – and those who appear as 'expert' in some particular field. The distinction between the two types of participants is constructed through the interview questions.

Thus, in the case of those who appear as newsworthy subjects it is their feelings and experiences which are explored:

(1) to lady attacked by lion: 'How did you feel . . . when this attack took place? You must have literally thought it was your end, did you?'

(2) to blind students learning to draw: '. . . what sort of difference has this drawing system made to your everyday life?'

When we meet 'experts' of various kinds it is their ideas and explanations that are of interest, not their feelings as 'human subjects':

(1) to inventor of drawing system: 'Did it come as a surprise to you to learn that blind people had a perspective?'

(2) to Nader: 'What are your ideas, for instance, on industrial safety?'

Interviewees whose status is constructed as being low (either – in the case of Patrick Meehan – because of their background or – in the case of the lecturer who organised the 'rubbish/survival kit' project – because of a lack of clear legitimacy in their particular (in this case educational) field of practice) can be easily cut short if they go 'off the point'.

In the case of the lecturer, Tom Coyne as interviewer feels able to demand that he give an account of himself in a way that forces him to comply. Thus after a brief introduction to the item Coyne asks crisply:

What's it all about?

to which the lecturer feels bound to respond, half-apologetically:

LECTURER: Um, I think I should explain . . .

However, he fails to provide an explanation which meets Coyne's fundamental questioning of the validity of the project, and is cut short in favour of interviews with the students who 'actually went to the rubbish dump'.

When an interviewee is considered to have some more considerable status – as in the case of Ralph Nader in this programme – he will be allowed more time to develop his answers to questions; he cannot be cut short so brusquely and may even be allowed the 'space' to redefine the questions asked into his own terms. Greene [a reporter] questions Nader quite sharply on the legitimacy of his campaigning activity. Obviously Nader presents something of a troublesome figure for *Nationwide*; on the one hand he claims to stand for the 'rights of the consumer' much in the way that *Nationwide* does, on the other hand his activities have a 'maverick' quality. But, even when Greene presses the point, invoking what 'many people' think:

GREENE: Would you be unhappy if you were described, as many people have described you, as an agitator?

Nader is granted the space in his reply to redefine Greene's question and to answer it in his own terms:

NADER: Well you see any change involves agitation, King George found this out two hundred years ago and . . . of course, by definition, any improvement requires a change of the prior status quo, or displacement of it, and so I think that's a very important role for people to play because there's a lot of change needed in our world today.

CONTROLLING THE DISCOURSE: THE WORK OF NOMINATION

'Tonight we meet the person who . . .' is a characteristic *Nationwide* introduction, but the point is that although we may 'meet' a host of individuals in the course of the programme, we never meet them direct. The 'meeting' is carefully set up by the *Nationwide* team. Thus, we are told in the regional menu that we will:

TC (direct address) to camera: join the lady who was attacked by the lions in the Safari park as she goes back again to meet the lions.

After the first section of local news we cut again to Tom Coyne in his role as outdoor linkman. He first supplies the textual link, situating this item in the flow of the programme:

TC: Well, there's going to be more news of course later in the programme.

Then he moves on to introduce and frame this particular item, first linking it back to an earlier story covered by the programme:

TC: I wonder if you remember this dramatic picture we showed you a few weeks ago of Mrs Barbara Carter of Halesowen. She was attacked by lions in the West Midlands Safari park. Well, after an experience like that you'd hardly expect Mrs Carter to be keen on seeing lions again. But today she visited a farm near Stratford on Avon to do just that . . .

Mrs Carter's status and identity as a newsworthy person are established; her actions are situated in our frame of expectations – the focus is placed on her doing something 'you'd hardly expect' – breaking the frame of our everyday expectations and therefore being newsworthy (cf. introduction to 'Americans in England': 'let's hear from another part of East Anglia, from Suffolk this time although you *might think* it was a bit of America'). Coyne then nominates the reporter for the story:

TC: A report from Alan Towers.

At the end of the interview the newsreader moves momentarily out of his impartial role, to add a personal comment:

A much braver and a very determined person than I could ever be

before moving on to the next story – a report of a policeman attempting to rescue a woman from a fire. At the end of that item the newsreader's comment links it back to Mrs Carter's story:

Two stories of bravery.

Similarly, the interview with Ralph Nader is introduced by a statement which clearly 'statuses' the interviewee:

COYNE (d/a to camera):   You know America's leading campaigner on consumer affairs, Ralph Nader . . .

followed by a framing/introductory question:

. . . we hear of you on all sorts of controversial topics . . . what motivates you to get into all these different fields?

The introduction and the question thus tell us Nader's status and competence and establish the topic on which he is to speak: again in the interview with Patrick Meehan we find the two-stage introductory frame at work:

BARRATT (d/a to camera):   This afternoon, as you may have heard, Patrick Meehan was released from prison in Peterhead, so over now to David Scott in Aberdeen.

Barratt thus nominates the reporter, who continues:

SCOTT (d/a to camera):   Meehan was released from prison after seven years. Most of it had been spent in solitary confinement as a protest against his conviction . . .

The chain of nomination passes from Barratt, as presenter, to the regional reporter, and only then to Meehan – his appearance is by no means a direct access or meeting with the audience: it has been 'framed', we have been told who he is, what is remarkable about him and how long ago (two hours) he got out of jail. His status for-the-programme is pre-established.

At the end of the interview Barratt (speaking d/a to camera again) sums up the item in a way that contextualises it and thus attempts to encode it within a preferred interpretation:

BARRATT: Patrick Meehan, who of course has served seven years of a life sentence for murder – a conviction based *yet again* on identification evidence [his emphasis].

Here Barratt proposes a dominant framework for the interpretation of the events portrayed and retrospectively inserts the item into the frame; only he, as presenter, can authoritatively lay claim to the right to privilege one interpretation in this way. Meehan, on the other hand, can only speak *within* the frame set by the interviewer, which itself is within the frame set by the presenter.

Within the interview itself, *Nationwide* has a lesser degree of control over the discourse: thus Meehan repeatedly tries to 'break the frame' that has been set up for him – talking about the political issues behind the case rather than about his feelings while in prison:

MEEHAN: I think it's wrong that, er, when things happen in places like America that people over here should become all sanctimonious and criticise, little do they know that the same things are happening here and the whole system is geared to prevent these things coming to the surface . . .

Indeed, at the point where he claims that he was framed by British Intelligence *Nationwide* has to resort to the ultimate level of control (cutting the film) in order to maintain the dominant direction of the discourse.

Control, then, is not simply 'given' by the structure of the discourse; it has to be maintained, at times through an ongoing struggle, by specific discursive strategies, on the studio floor. In this interview Meehan repeatedly attempts to answer the questions that he would have liked to be asked rather than those he is asked: that is, he attempts to gloss or inflect the discourse in his favour:

the first thing I want to do is pursue the matter further, er, for a public enquiry, and, er, I hope that within the next few days I'll be back in court applying . . . for permission to bring an action against, er, certain, witnesses shall we call them, for perjury.

The interviewer is then faced with the difficulty of steering the discussion back to the realms of feelings and personal experience:

You sound quite bitter . . .
What was your daily routine in prison?

In this interview, then, we see a struggle being conducted over the very terms of the discourse. This is not a struggle about what 'answers' are acceptable – since, strictly speaking, the interviewer cannot precisely prescribe what his respondent will say; and he cannot directly contradict, counter or break off the interview after an 'unacceptable' reply without prejudicing or rupturing the protocol within which this type of interview operates. These interviews are based on an apparent equivalence between interviewer and respondent – equal parties to the conversation – and they are governed by the protocols which provide the 'rule' in all current affairs TV – the protocols of 'objectivity' (of the interviewer) and 'balance' (between interviewer and interviewee). But it *is* a struggle over the way items are framed – over which 'frame' is operating or dominant. The frame is the device which, though it cannot absolutely prescribe the content of a reply, does prescribe and delimit the *range* of 'acceptable' replies. It is an ideological strategy, in the precise sense that, when it works, it sustains a certain spontaneous circularity – the form of the answers being already presupposed in the form of the questions. It is also ideological in the sense that it sustains an apparent equality in the exchange, while being founded on an unequal relationship – since the respondent must reply to a question within a frame he/she does not construct.

In sustaining, through the exchange, the tendency to reply within this restricted limit, much depends on the 'rule' of acceptability: a reply must appear to be relevant to the question, while sustaining the sense of 'natural following-on', good conversational practice, flow, natural continuity. To make an 'unacceptable' reply, while maintaining coherence, relevance, continuity and flow, entails a very special kind of work – a struggle in conversational practice: first, to re-frame or re-phrase (e.g. to break the 'personal experience' frame, and to replace it with an alternative, 'political' frame); second, then to reply within the reconstituted framework. It is in this sense that interviewing and responding, within the dominant discursive strategies of this kind of programme, entail the work (for the presenters) of *securing* the dominant frame (for it cannot be taken for granted as unproblematically given), and sometimes also (for the respondents) of struggling against or countering the dominant frame (though these counter-positions are by no means always taken up).

3

The eye of the storm: reviewing the Gulf War

Kevin Robins and Les Levidow

From *Screen* 32(3), 324–8 (Autumn 1991)

The military use and adaptation of communication media has posed major ethical questions for those concerned not just with a history of media technologies but with some of the moral consequences of these developments for listeners and viewers and for the practice of journalism. A long-standing debate about the effects of war reporting, most notably in the case of American television coverage of the war in Vietnam, has raged over the competing propositions that images of war involve and mobilize or desensitize and render passive the civilian audience.

This article by Kevin Robins and Les Levidow on the ethical implications of media coverage of the Gulf War of 1991 revisits some of these debates, with some trenchant observations on the representation by the media of military surveillance and weapons guidance systems. 'Operation Desert Storm' had come to be referred to as the 'Nintendo war' after a popular games computer which allowed users to simulate the hi-tech activity of military engagement, targeting and destroying enemy installations.

Robins and Levidow describe the new 'smart bomb' technologies of the Gulf War which involved on-board camera guidance systems and the generation of images taken by these cameras as the weapons approached their targets in relays of planned and precise, 'surgical' strikes. The widespread military practice of making these images available for television news created a war which, they argue, implicated the viewer in the 'passionless' looking of the weapon, separating seeing from feeling and the visible target from the actual human consequences of pain and death. This activity of distancing viewers from the effects of bombing was necessary, they suggest, for establishing both the military and the moral superiority of the West in the war against Iraq. Only rarely, when 'the smart turned to hellish', did the audience receive images which might be construed as massacre and not as legitimate combat. Moreover, the language of reporting, often drawn directly from the military – the 'turkey shoots', the 'target-rich environment', the 'military surgery' – had an objectifying and desensitizing effect. This, along with the visual imagery, led to a paradoxically dispassionate partiality in reporting which, as the head of BBC News and Current Affairs subsequently recognized, was at times too like a *'Boy's Own* report' of 'amusement-alley warfare'.

The article raises important questions of ethics and point of view, reinvigorating a long-established tradition of debate about war reporting. However, it implicitly poses the problem that the meaning of particular media images, remembered and 'used' by viewers, may have as much to do with already formed views of the world and of politics as with the potentially manipulative power of the language of television.

Even before 'Operation Desert Storm' had ended, it had become a cliché to dub it, referring to an addictive computer game, the Nintendo war. The US military remote-controlled its attack through an array of surveillance, simulation and strike technologies. At the same time, tele-spectators could identify with the technology 'taking out' alien targets apparently without human consequences. Moreover, by evoking the computer-game comparison, in which the participant–viewer feels constantly under threat, the remote technology served to portray as heroic 'combat' what was mainly a series of massacres.

If Desert Storm was a screen-gazing war, its reality was at the same time screened out. That screening, in the dual sense, provided crucial support for the 'just war', epitomizing the West's claims for its superior morality. Thus the war against Iraq also involved a battle for 'hearts and eyes', as well as minds, here in the West. That perceptual conflict highlights the relation of vision to feeling and understanding, and to a problematic sense of humanity in Western culture.

During the Gulf War, the trend in military technologies became apparent. New global networks of sensors turned a whole country, conceptually speaking, into targeting information. The five months preceding the attack on Iraq in January 1991 involved laborious 'software work' to digitally map and plot strategic installations there. The networks were then used to keep track of targets in real time, to program and guide 'precision' long-range weapons, and then to undertake 'battle damage assessment'. The whole network formed a closed system, a kind of cybernetic input and feedback loop.

The role of vision and image technologies was crucial to the functioning of this system. Military strategy has always been about seeing and not being seen: about combining vision with stealth. It is the increasing automation and precision of this principle, however, that makes the new generation of weapons 'smart' and 'brilliant'. From the earliest days we were told of the American spy satellites orbiting over the Middle East. With their multiple ways of seeing – photography, radar imaging, infrared imaging – America's 'secret eyes in space' looked through night and fog, peering into Iraq's entire civilian and industrial infrastructure, dubbed 'Saddam Hussein's war machine'. Iraq was being surveyed from space and then pinned down for 'precise military surgery'.

In this war, we learned that the weapons of destruction had piercing electronic eyes, too. Aircraft like the American F-15E and the British Tornado were equipped with imaging systems that illuminate objects with infrared beams, allowing low-altitude flying and location of targets in the desert night. In the nose of the Apache helicopter was a forward-looking infrared navigation and targeting system that projected information onto screens in the visors of the crews' helmets. After the strikes had been launched, photo-reconnaissance aircraft would then sweep across the skies of Kuwait and Iraq, documenting the 'degradation' of hostile forces and feeding this photo-information back into the central intelligence computers.

The ultimate achievement was the Tomahawk cruise missile, which has been described as a 'brilliant' weapon, fired and then forgotten. For most of its journey the

Tomahawk navigates through a radar altimeter which compares the topography of its flight path against detailed terrain maps stored in its memory. As it reaches its 'terminal end point', a new guidance system takes over with a small digital camera comparing the view from the nose against a library of stored images. These images have been prepared from earlier satellite reconnaissance photographs of selected targets. It was through this vision guidance system that the missile was able to achieve the 'precision' penetration of a 'surgical strike' – 'down the air vent' or 'through the front door'. Of the first fifty-two Tomahawks fired, we are told, fifty-one hit their target.

These high-tech weapon systems dominated our perception of the war, creating a sense of technological euphoria. We saw them hit enemy targets, as if we were riding or guiding the weapons, though the video game images concealed what it meant to 'cleanse' or 'neutralize'. We thought even less about what these images were doing to us, the watchers. We came to see the war through the passionless eyes of these 'smart' weapons, through their surgical scan and their penetrative look. Through this missile-eyed perspective, we too came to look down on Iraq as a 'target-rich environment'. What this created, as Robert J. Lifton has suggested, was a kind of psychic numbing: 'the splitting or inner division of parts of the individual mind, in this case a separation of knowledge from feeling. We know that our weapons are murderous, but we cannot afford to feel the pain of death at the other side of them' (*Guardian*, 14 February 1991). In this war, combat was mediated and simulated through the screen. Soldiers and spectators alike were involved in a new kind of remotely-exhilarating tele-action; both were tele-present and tele-engaged in the theatre of war. And, as they were drawn into this image-space, home spectators, and even many soldiers, became detached from the bloody reality. When they could no longer remained detached, or when they could no longer easily experience their activity as military combat, soldiers devised a series of animal metaphors, such as 'turkey shoot', to detach themselves emotionally and morally from human death.

Launching his precision weapons, the soldier achieves a moral dissociation. His victims become psychologically invisible. Killing is done 'at a distance', through technological mediation, without the shock of direct confrontation and violence; it breaks the causal link between the firing button and the deaths that ensue. This kind of psychological insulation is generally enhanced if the victims are 'out of sight'. What is clear, however, is that moral invisibility is not necessarily undermined by optical visibility – or at least by certain kinds of mediated and remote visibility.

In the Gulf War, the vision of the long camera shot extended the moral distanciation of previous wars. The silent movie filmed from the bomb bay or from the nose of the missile had a similar numbing remoteness. In this war, however, the rationalization of vision was pushed further. Here we had an apparently greater visual proximity between the killer and the victim. Indeed, the missile-nose view of the target simulated a super-real closeness which no human being could ever attain. It was the ultimate voyeurism: to see the target hit from the vantage point of the weapon. An inhuman perspective. Yet this remote-intimate kind of watching could sustain the moral detachment of earlier military technologies. Seeing was split off from feeling; the visible was separated from the sense of pain and death. Through the long lens the enemy remained a faceless alien. Her and his bodily existence was de-realized.

Thanks to the cameras in their guided weapons, the Western military forces were able to replay their destruction of enemy targets to analyse the pinpointedness of their accuracy. Like football coaches, they could meticulously review the tapes to assess the success of the game plan. And through these replays they could reactivate the *frisson* of excitement: 'I am going to show you the luckiest man in Iraq on this particular day,' General Schwarzkopf boasted to the world's media as he showed them footage of an Iraqi vehicle passing through the crosshairs of a bomb sight shortly before the bomb 'took out' the bridge it had been travelling across. It was perhaps the costliest tracking shot ever. But to watch it, to linger over its slow-motion precision, was to identify with the technological supremacy underpinning the West's claims to moral superiority.

Meanwhile, back at home, other voyeurs could tele-consume the same images and exult in the same fantasies. At home, we could even listen to American generals giving voice-over commentary on the video bombing. The high-tech strikes were played over and over on the Western networks, watched and rewatched. Home viewers were encouraged to identify with the technical expertise of those who were scripting the war-game. Public acceptance of the war depended on the coexistence of remote engagement and moral detachment. As Tony Hall, Director of BBC News and Current Affairs, came to acknowledge, too many '*Boy's Own* reports' on the high-tech equipment conspired to create the image of a 'sort of amusement-alley warfare'. Through the evidential force of the images, we could know about the war, but it was a kind of de-realized war we were knowing. It was at once a way of seeing and a way of not seeing.

It was as if, drawn into the image, we were exempted from our responsibility as participants in a reality.

Even if we were delinked from it, the reality was always there, however. And there was always the danger that the images might eventually give access to that reality. Certain military videos were for private screening only. General Schwarzkopf did not want the world to see what the camera recorded on the driver's face as it was propelled into the cab of another Iraqi vehicle. And what of the night vision shots from Apache helicopter raids? 'Even hardened soldiers,' John Balzar reported, 'hold their breath as Iraqi soldiers, as big as football players on the television screen, run with nowhere to hide. These are not bridges or aeroplane hangars. These are men.' The Iraqi soldiers looked 'like ghostly sheep flushed from a pen – bewildered and terrified, jarred from sleep and fleeing their bunkers under a hellish fire. One by one, they were cut down by attackers they could not see' (*Guardian*, 25 February 1991). When smart turned to hellish, the images had to be censored. Although some troops reportedly enjoyed watching these video films over and over again, the audience back home had to be protected from images which might have presented 'combat' as massacre. Only long after the war did we see some of these images on television: they were all too eloquent records of the West's technological supremacy (or of the deadly expertise it calls supremacy, at least).

But not all 'disturbing' images could be screened out. As the war developed, the repressed reality did break through. On 13 February, at Baghdad's Al-Amiriya air-raid shelter, we saw the first real pictures of burning, mutilation and death. For the first time, we saw the faces and even heard the voices of the victims. Limited by their own technocratic vision, US officials were hard pressed to explain away the hundreds of shrouded corpses. They could respond only by insisting that surveillance pictures showed it to be a military installation, and that cameras on board American jets recorded a precise hit on a 'positively identified military target'. Expensive cameras don't lie: there was no way it could be a civilian refuge. 'I have no idea why there were civilians in the bunker at four in the morning – it belies logic,' commented General Neal.

And, for the first time since the start of the war, British television had to acknowledge its own acts of censorship. Television news felt that it was necessary to 'edit' these images because of their 'disturbing nature'. Close-up images of real death would disturb our unreal sense of video-game war without bloodshed, and would show how deadly precise precision weapons can be. Questions of 'taste' and 'sensitivity' made it desirable to shroud the killings in the 'fog of war' where no one sees clearly.

And again, 'apocalyptically', on the Basra road, reality threatened to spill over the images. After another massacre hit thousands of soldiers and civilians scrambling to escape Kuwait City, the carnage made a mockery of surgical strikes and Nintendo wars. 'Far from the smart bomb videos and "target-rich environment" jargon,' wrote one correspondent, 'the grim reality of war is a horror to behold.' He describes how an American intelligence officer 'lifted his camera to snap a photo of a cluster of blackened bodies. Then he let the camera drop' (*Guardian*, 11 March 1991). In the midst of slaughter, the blackened skulls stared back from their burnt-out sockets. Suddenly journalists were confronted by that thing they call the 'reality of war'.

From this final 'turkey shoot', we have an image, a charred mask of ash, that was once the face of an Iraqi soldier, a target sitting on top of a tank. Already it has been hailed as a classic war photograph: it has come to symbolize the 'reality of war'. Offered to several British Sunday papers, it was rejected by the *Sunday Times* as unsuitable for family viewing on a Sunday morning; but was published by the *Observer* (3 October 1991), captioned 'the killing fields of Kuwait', with an implied analogy with the Khmer Rouge holocaust against the Cambodian people. The accompanying report by journalist Colin Smith described the panicked retreat, 'more gypsy than military', as having undergone 'one of the most terrible harassments of a retreating army from the air in the history of warfare'. 'I wouldn't even call this a mopping-up operation,' said a US officer.

In the following week's *Observer*, Harold Evans wrote to explain why, despite having supported the war, he backed the newspaper's decision to publish. By dissolving the photo into a timeless horror of war, however, his defence served to detach the image from the journalist's report, which had questioned whether the attack could be called 'combat'. The picture was, says Evans, 'a necessary shock': 'It was a solitary individual in the transfixation of a hideous death. Before this, it had been possible to enjoy the lethal felicity of designer bombs as some kind of video game' (*Observer*, 10 March 1991). Here we were confronted with the consequences of our belief in this 'just war'. And here too, through this image, we could experience 'an elemental human sympathy'. 'The disputed photograph,' Evans writes, 'did something to redress the elusive euphoria of a high-tech war.' But did it? Could it? The reality, of course, was that this was, precisely, the outcome of the video-game war fantasy. What could the 'still silence' of this corpse tell us about post-heroic warfare? Of course, those who have seen this image 'will never forget it'. But what will they remember of its meaning? The contest over interpretation will determine whether we experience such disturbing images as symbolizing the unavoidable (and perhaps exceptional) horror of a 'just war' or, alternatively, a series of massacres presented as honourable combat.

Thus Desert Storm has highlighted what is potentially dehumanizing about the role of images in our society, in our culture of viewing. Through our vision technologies we were able to disavow the reality: that there were real people, other living beings, on the other side of the electronic images. We could see, but we were deaf to what we saw. 'Four or five times a day,' John Berger writes, 'the public received a TV lesson about how to become deaf to the voice of their memory, of their conscience or of their imagination.' There was a connection, he suggests, between this deafness and the high-tech arms that brought such a swift victory: 'Both operated as inhuman agents *at a distance*' (*Guardian*, 2 March 1991). Our deafness betrayed our inhumanity. We inflicted high-tech Armageddon upon a people we didn't even know. We never heard their voices or listened to their point of view. In his war poem, 'A Cold Coming', Tony Harrison focuses on what the charred man might have to *say*. It becomes necessary 'to find words for this frightening mask':

> So press RECORD! I want to reach
> the warring nations with my speech.
>
> Don't look away! I know it's hard
> to keep regarding one so charred.

Through our new vision and image technologies, we were able, almost at will, to zoom in on the action. We could come close, but we were looking in the wrong way, and in the wrong direction. The images engaged our identification with the lethal eye of the storm, while assisting our disengagement from its political purposes and human consequences.

4

Traditional racism

Christopher Campbell

From Campbell, C. 1995: *Race, myth and the news*. London: Sage, 42–56

News has remained both one of the most popular and one of the most contested areas of television programming. Impartiality if not objectivity is secured, it has been argued, on the basis of the ethical commitments of responsible journalists, and the financial resources of the television station ensure detailed and regionally, nationally or globally informed reports. These informational riches are increasingly presented in a crisp, exciting and occasionally humorous style.

But news is manufactured in many different forms and contexts, and this genre, at least as much as that of television fiction, reflects the conflicts and preoccupations, the priorities and the structured silences, of its surrounding society. Christopher Campbell offers us a detailed and textually specific analysis of three American news broadcast items. The first two are 'end-on' reports broadcast by a local station in the state of Mississippi in January 1993 on the official national day commemorating the life of Martin Luther King. African Americans make up nearly 30 per cent of the population of the two counties served by this station. The third item is from a station serving a much larger market in the Minneapolis area; here, Native Americans make up about 5 per cent of the population.

Drawing on the work of Roland Barthes and others, Campbell develops a detailed semiotic reading of the text, considering both its visual and its aural dimensions, the journalistic routines, practices and values that inform the story, and the broader social and 'mythic' implications, elucidating in the process the values and beliefs which are embedded in or structure the account. In the case of all three items Campbell concludes that there is both a lack of journalistic neutrality and a lack of sensitivity on racial matters which amounts to an implicit, and indeed what he calls 'everyday', form of representational racism.

The analysis of the first two linked items allows for the development of some useful comparative analysis. The first item deals with an apparently (as represented on the screen) exclusively black-supported parade celebrating the life of the great civil rights activist Martin Luther King. The events are covered by one camera with no on-the-spot interviews; the American flag imagery suggests for Campbell an idea or ideology of the post-civil rights South as a 'tolerant and progressive place'; the item is under 30 seconds long. The following item covers a celebration of the birthday of Confederate general Robert E. Lee – a figure representing the values of the old pro-slavery South. Campbell points out that this celebration is in fact being staged a day before the actual Lee birthday, perhaps to coincide with and provide a counter news item for the Luther King Day celebrations.

Although the journalists cannot be held responsible for this 'odd' but perhaps strategic retiming, they offer the Lee commemoration significantly better coverage: the item is twice as long as the one preceding it; a reporter as well as a camera crew are present; synchronized sound interviews are included; and a more lively sense of identification is offered with the figures filmed. By contrast, Campbell suggests, the African Americans represented in the King story are given no direct voice and are therefore perceived as 'other'; the 'myth of marginality' is thereby 'ritualized'.

'EVERYDAY' RACISM AND NEWS COVERAGE

Case 1: Mississippi celebrations

The first two stories to be analyzed come from the 6 p.m. news program broadcast on WDAM-TV, Monday, January 18. WDAM is an NBC affiliate located in Hattiesburg, MS, and serving the Hattiesburg–Laurel, MS, market – listed as the 164th 'ADI' (area of dominant interest) market in the United States (*Broadcasting*, 1992). Hattiesburg is a city of nearly 42,000, with an African American population of about 40 percent (US Department of Commerce, 1990). Laurel is a city of about 19,000, with an African American population of about 48 percent. Perhaps more representative of WDAM's audience, however, are the demographics of the two counties in which those cities are found. The total population of Jones and Forrest Counties is about 130,000. African Americans make up about 28 percent of that population.

On its January 18 broadcast, WDAM ran 12 news stories, ranging from 15 seconds to 2 minutes in length, as well as a weather forecast and a sports report. WDAM journalists who appeared on-screen included two white anchors, a white sports anchor, a white meteorologist and two white field reporters. Stories ranged from a murder in Laurel to problems with the Jones County jail to disaster relief for a tornado-damaged area. The broadcast also included two stories that will serve as the basis for this textual analysis. The first, which ran for about 27 seconds about 8 minutes into the program, described a parade in Laurel in honor of that day's Martin Luther King, Jr holiday. The second, which directly followed that story and ran for about 60 seconds, described a local tribute to Confederate general Robert E. Lee.

For now, I will ignore the peculiar juxtaposition of these two stories – one related to our nation's most prominent civil rights leader, the other to the commander of the Southern forces during the Civil War. Instead, I will first examine the King parade story in its own right, then the Lee tribute story. Following that, I will analyze the juxtaposition and compare the station's coverage of the two stories.

In semiotic terms, we can look at the stories on several levels of signification. Barthes (1972) analyzed images and words on many tiers, among them denotation, connotation and myth. He described denotation as the first order of signification; in this case, the words we hear and the images we see on the television screen can be described in their most overt terms.

On the denotative (or 'signified') level, the King parade story was handled as a 'reader' by anchor Bob Noonan; that is, as Noonan reads the story, the audience first sees a medium (chest-up) shot of the anchor, then 'actuality' footage from the parade. No reporter is seen at the parade site, and no interviews are conducted with participants. The audience is told that about 75 people participated in the march, and the long shot (from a distance – an 'establishing' shot) of the parade indicates that this is probably an accurate estimate. In the shots that follow we see that many of the marchers appear to be children, and all appear to be black. The audience is told that the parade organizers 'hope the commemoration will make young people more aware of [King's] legacy and bring blacks as well as whites together'.

On the second level of signification, connotation, the story takes on ideological meaning as well. The story could be 'read' as a symbol of the continuance of the civil rights movement, King's hopes for an integrated America, promises of an American future that does not discriminate, an end to bigotry. An honor guard leads the parade carrying an American flag, a symbol of this country's sense of freedom and justice. These connotations reflect what Campbell (1991) has described as a 'middle-American' mythology; in that way, the story reflects a commonsense notion – or, in Barthes's words, 'the naturalization' (p. 131) – of the American melting pot. The images could also be seen as a reflection of what Mixon (1989) describes as New South mythology, reflecting a sense of a post–civil rights era South that is a tolerant and progressive place where equality and fairness prevail, 'a land that [is] rich, just, and triumphant' (p. 1114). Hall (1980) would describe these readings as 'dominant' or 'preferred'; that is, from the point of view of WDAM's journalists and many of the station's viewers, the images here would reflect a majority culture understanding of those images.

But other connotations can also be read into the story, those that Hall would describe as 'negotiated' or 'oppositional'. An observer who rejects the coverage's 'preferred' codes might question the 'dominant' interpretation: If King's dream of racial unity is alive, why are all of the marchers black? And why are all of the WDAM journalists white? Although the script would indicate the journalists' commonsense acceptance of the value of 'bringing blacks as well as whites together', the fact is that Laurel, MS, and most other American cities are largely geographically and economically divided along racial lines. In the story, no African Americans are interviewed. With only white journalists on camera the station's coverage ritualizes the myth of marginality. Although nearly 30 percent of the viewers in WDAM's market are African Americans, the coverage suggests a sense of 'otherness' about the black people who are participating in the march, implying, as Hartley (1984) says, that 'what happens at the edges ... doesn't count' (p. 121). Or, as Essed (1991) describes one aspect of 'everyday' racism, 'Blacks can be tolerated as long as they remain marginal' (p. 196). The myth of the New South, writes Mixon (1989), 'fail[s] to reflect reality adequately' (p. 1114).

The commonsense/dominant culture mythology at work in the King parade story is more clearly evident in the Lee tribute story that follows. On the denotative level, we see a medium shot of anchor Whitney Vann, who offers this transition from King to Lee: 'While each of the fifty states honored the life and legacy of Dr Martin Luther King today, thousands of Southerners paid tribute as well to Robert E. Lee.' As she reads, we see a close-up of a portrait of Lee, a full (head-to-toe) shot of six men in Civil War uniforms firing guns into the air, a close-up of the base of a statue that reads 'TO THE MEN AND WOMEN OF THE CONFEDERACY', a full shot of five people who are apparently attending the tribute, a full shot of a woman in Civil War–era clothing placing a wreath at the foot of the statue, then a full shot of the sculpted soldier who is on top of the statue, possibly Lee.

Vann says that Lee's birth date is 'one of several special days including Confederate Memorial Day and Jefferson Davis's birthday observed nearly 130 years after the end of the Civil War.' She then tells the audience that 'a Hattiesburg member of the Sons of Confederate Veterans says Robert E. Lee is well deserving of the honor.'

Next we see a full shot of a man identified in a graphic as Rick Forte. He is seated on a couch, apparently in a room in his home that is filled with Civil War memorabilia. He wears a T-shirt that displays a Confederate battle flag. A full shot shows an unidentified reporter who is taking copious notes while seated on a chair next to Forte. A close-up of Forte speaking remains until the end of the story. He says, '[Lee] just stood for what a Southern gentleman stood for and what a soldier stood for – honor, you know, land, your home, honor, family. He stood for that.' Vann's voice-over concludes the piece: 'Rick Forte is the man who discovered skeletal remains designated and reburied in 1979 as the official unknown Confederate soldier.'

Mythic connotations can be read in both the language that is used in the story and in the images we see on camera. The anchor links King and Lee without acknowledging the obvious irony – King, the ultimate symbol of black America's push for equality; Lee, commander of the Southern army that fought to maintain the enslavement of black Americans. We are told that 'thousands' of Southerners paid tribute to Lee, and that 'for decades' this and other 'special days' are observed 'nearly 130 years after the end of the Civil War'. The anchor's commonsense explanation of the tribute to Lee and her introduction to the story's key source – 'a Hattiesburg member of the Sons of Confederate Veterans says Robert E. Lee is well deserving of the honor' – lend legitimacy to the middle-American/Southern values he espouses in his account of Lee's symbolic worth: 'He just stood for what a Southern gentleman stood for and what a soldier stood for – honor, you know, land, your home, honor, family. He stood for that.'

His words suggest that what he says is obvious, a truth that cannot be questioned: the 'just' in his 'he *just* stood for' implies an implicit acceptance of his explanation of Lee's symbolism. The 'you know' that is inserted in his list of the values he associates with Lee sounds less like a nervous hesitation than an appeal to the reporter who sits across from him, perhaps to the audience, that his interpretation is manifest: '*we* know'. The attributes he cites echo some of the 'enduring values' described by Gans (1979) – like ethnocentrism and small-town pastoralism – who argued that news supports a 'social order' (p. 61) of white, male hegemony. By tying together the concepts of the Southern gentleman and soldier with honor (which comes up twice in the list), land, 'your home' and family, Forte's version of Lee's symbolic value seems to preclude an understanding of these values outside of that realm. He conjures up a Southern myth of family life and rural existence that, as Sharp (1989) points out, hardly fits today's South:

> In recent years southern families have experienced much the same rates of change as families throughout the rest of the nation, with growing numbers of divorces, single-parent families, and two-income couples seeking childcare. Also, the region is no longer predominantly rural, residents are very mobile and most adults maintain frequent contacts only within the nuclear family and with parents and siblings.
>
> (p. 1105)

But Forte's version is authenticated by a sort of natural acceptance on the part of the two journalists who appear in the story, the anchor and the unidentified reporter. What Bobo (1988) calls the 'enduring cultural values and beliefs' that contribute to 'the ideology of bounded racial change' (p. 109) become the commonsense understanding of Lee's symbolism. In a final legitimization of Forte as a news source, the anchor concludes the story by describing Forte as 'the man who discovered skeletal remains designated and reburied in 1979 as the official unknown Confederate soldier'. In what Thornburn (1987) calls 'consensus narrative', the story reflects 'the wisdom of the community' (p. 170).

The images we see also contribute to that narrative. The soldiers firing rifles into the air in salute and the crowd watching as a wreath is placed at the foot of the Confederate memorial reflect community support. The Confederate flag that appears on Forte's T-shirt becomes a reflection of moral virtue; never mind the fact that it is the symbol of choice for white supremacists. A 'cutaway' shot shows the unidentified white reporter sitting next to Forte busily taking down Forte's words into his notebook, adding increased legitimacy to Forte's 'commonsense' perception of the tribute to Lee.

In running the King parade and Lee tribute stories side by side, and in linking them in the anchor's transition between the two, the program suggested a parallel: two stories about Americans celebrating the lives of American heroes. But a comparison of the coverage of the two stories raises further questions about the mythic nature of race and the news. Parks (1940) argues that news robs events of historical meaning, placing isolated events in a vacuum. In this case, the stories' lack of historical perspective dictates a very narrow, commonsense understanding of the events.

Semiological analysis allows for examination of these texts within a more immediate context of associations. As Seiter (1987) writes, 'Semiotics argues that the meaning of every sign derives in part from its relationship to others with which it is associated in the same sign system' (p. 36). Through paradigmatic (sets of similar signs) and syntagmatic (sign sequence) analysis, we can examine the two stories within the context of the 'sign system' of local television news. A paradigmatic examination of the stories calls for a look at the coverage in terms of language and visual imagery. The syntagmatic approach allows us to look at the juxtaposition of the two stories as part of a sequential, meaning-making chain.

Both stories ran on January 18, the day set aside as the national Martin Luther King, Jr holiday. Although it is not mentioned, the Lee tribute was actually a day early – Lee's birth date is January 19. On a paradigmatic level, the Lee tribute is granted more detailed and salient coverage, both in the language used to describe the events and in the allotment of the station's resources. The King parade story ran first, but only for about 27 seconds – less than half the time allotted for the Lee tribute story. The coverage indicates that the station sent only a camera operator to cover the King parade, but sent both a reporter and camera operator to cover the Lee tribute. No interviews are conducted by participants in the King parade, leaving only WDAM's white journalists to explain its significance. Although we are told that the parade was 'one of a series of holiday events in Laurel', this is the only one that we see. The parade, described as including 'about 75 participants' and illustrated primarily from a distant camera angle, looks small and somewhat disjointed.

In the coverage of the Lee tribute, we are told that 'thousands of Southerners paid tribute' to Lee, although we see a total of only about 10 on camera. There are no long shots of the tribute at the Confederate monument, so we never get a sense of the size of the crowd in attendance. What we do see is a series of full shots, one showing a rifle-firing salute, another showing a woman placing a wreath at the foot of a statue, another of five people in attendance. The impression that the crowd shot creates – coupled with the anchor's explanation that thousands of Southerners celebrated Lee's birthday (though she did not mention that they were a day early) – is that many more may also be in attendance. The interview with Forte that concludes the story grants it further prominence. A spokesperson for the 'thousands', Forte becomes the commonsense voice of middle America and the mythical South.

The anchor tells us that 'for decades' Lee's birthday has been 'commemorated throughout the South', evoking Old South tradition and legacy. The description of the King parade in small-town Laurel, MS, pales in comparison. The American flag carried in the King parade – perhaps a symbol of a New South, the integrated and open-minded place of contemporary Southern mythology – flutters in ironic contrast to the Confederate stars and bars on Forte's chest.

How is it that the coverage of the Lee tribute was granted more prominence than the celebration of the national Martin Luther King, Jr holiday? A cynic might wonder if the Lee tribute was a media event intentionally staged a day before Lee's birth date as a distinctly white celebration to counteract the impact of the commemoration of America's most prominent black leader.

A syntagmatic reading of the two stories fails to support a sense of journalistic neutrality about the coverage. The juxtaposition and coverage of stories about these two heroes certainly raises questions about the racial sensitivity of WDAM's journalists. Although both men may merit tribute for the contributions they made to their causes, the symbolic contradiction inherent in those two causes is a blatant one. It is likely that those journalists intended no offense. Research on contemporary racism describes the 'aversive' form of racism as one in which

> people who have developed a value system that maintains it is wrong to discriminate against a person because of his or her race, who reject the content of racial stereotypes, who attempt to disassociate negative feelings about blacks from their self-concepts, but who nonetheless cannot entirely escape cultural and cognitive forces.
>
> (Gaertner and Dovidio, 1986, p. 66)

So despite the best intentions of the white journalists, who may have seen the two stories as balanced and representative, their coverage reflects, at best, insensitivity and, at worst, overt racism that marginalizes African American life. In describing 'everyday' racism, Essed (1991) offers this possible explanation: 'Dominant group members usually lack sensitivity to racism in everyday life. They have little understanding of the problem because they are not confronted, on a regular basis, with critical views of race and ethnic relations' (p. 285).

Case 2: *Minnesota spearfishing*

KARE-TV is an NBC affiliate serving the Minneapolis–St Paul, MN, market – the country's 13th largest (*Broadcasting*, 1992). The twin cities total about 640,000 residents; whites make up almost 80 percent of that population, Native Americans about 5 percent (US Department of Commerce, 1990).

On its January 19 broadcast, KARE ran 14 news and feature stories as well as weather and sports reports. Eight KARE journalists – two anchors, four reporters, a meteorologist and a sports anchor – appeared on camera during the broadcast, all of them white. News stories covered topics ranging from a shooting in north Minneapolis to the attempted rescue of a farm accident victim to an increase in state gasoline taxes. KARE led off the newscast with its longest story of the evening, a 3-minute, 15-second account of a fishing rights controversy pitting Minnesota's sports fishermen against a Native American tribe; that story will serve as the basis for this chapter's final textual analysis.

On a denotative level, the story was handled as a news 'package' by the KARE crew; that is, the coanchors and a reporter contribute information, and we see 'actuality' videotape as well as 'live' coverage of the reporter at the Minnesota Capitol Building. The story unfolds like this:

First, we see a long shot of snow-covered Lake Mille Lacs in the daylight, then a cut to a medium shot of an unidentified man – apparently a Native American – spearing a fish from a boat at night. Anchor Paul Magers reads, 'A frozen blanket of ice covers the waters of Lake Mille Lacs, but this serene setting is the centerpiece of Minnesota's hottest controversy. The issue? Native American spearfishing.' Next we see coanchors Magers and Pat Miles on the set, and Miles explains that the agreement reached by state officials and a Chippewa Indian group is one that 'some anglers fiercely hate'. We are then sent to reporter Dennis Stauffer at the Capitol for 'the details'. He explains that the agreement is 'showing no signs of calming the controversy'.

Next we see videotape of two unidentified anglers – apparently white sports fishermen – one pulling a large fish out of a hole in the ice on a rod and reel while the other assists. Stauffer explains that Lake Mille Lacs is 'Minnesota's premier trophy fishing lake' and that the agreement, according to the commissioner of the Division of Natural Resources, will protect sports fishing. The white Department of Natural Resources (DNR) commissioner is then seen seated at the head table of a news conference; he sits next to a Native American man who apparently negotiated the agreement with the state. A graphic is shown to illustrate a 6000-acre 'treaty zone' that gives the Mille Lacs Indian reservation exclusive access to what appears to be about 8 percent of the lake. A second graphic outlines the terms of the agreement, which Stauffer describes. It allows for Indian netting and spearing of fish in the treaty zone, apportions the Indian harvest to the limit on the entire lake and calls for the state to pay the tribe $10 million and cede 7500 acres of state land to the tribe.

We then see the DNR commissioner at the news conference explaining that, without the agreement, the state could lose a lawsuit to the tribe: 'We could lose as much as half the fish in Mille Lacs Lake,' he says, 'and if that were the case I think it would have a tremendous impact on sport fishing, tourism and local economy.' We then see videotape, the same footage shown at the top of the story, that shows a fish being speared. Next Stauffer tells us that the DNR commissioner had cited a Wisconsin lawsuit that granted Indian tribes 50 percent of the fish in a lake that borders on Minnesota. A graphic shows that an 1837 treaty that was upheld in that case also covered the Mille Lacs Lake area.

Next we see videotape of a group of about 75 men who are apparently protesting the agreement, some holding signs reading 'No nets' and 'Governor Carlson – We need your help.' Stauffer tells us that 'critics, which include sports and tourist groups, say the Indians gave up their rights long ago under subsequent treaties and that Minnesota would win in court'. Next is a close-up of Bud Grant, the former head coach of the Minnesota Vikings football team. A long, low-angle shot of Grant shows that he is seated in front of a wall full of Viking memorabilia, most prominently the number 10 jersey of Fran Tarkenton, once the team's star quarterback. Stauffer tells us that Grant is the honorary chairman of the Save Mille Lacs Association. Grant says, 'I think there is a right and a wrong. Why should one group of people be allowed to do something another group of people cannot do? Why should they have exclusive rights?'

Finally, we see Stauffer again in the assembly room of the Capitol Building. He explains that both the Mille Lacs tribe and the state legislature will have to approve the agreement before it will become law. Then we see the coanchors back in the studio, watching Stauffer on a large monitor. Coanchor Magers asks Stauffer, 'Is the tribe happy with it as well?' Stauffer says the Indian negotiator had supported it, and that the tribe is more likely to approve the treaty than is the state legislature. Coanchor Miles then asks if the agreement has the potential 'to become the most controversial issue before the state legislature this year'. Stauffer tells her, 'It certainly has the potential to generate the most sparks around here.'

On a connotative level, the story takes on mythic meaning not unreminiscent of traditional 'cowboy and Indian' movies. The magnitude of the conflict between the Native American tribe and the white sportsmen (represented on camera by the ice fishermen, the protestors and spokesman Bud Grant) is accentuated in the words the journalists use throughout the story. The 'headlines' that preceded that evening's newscast made the first reference to 'the Lake Mille Lacs controversy'. In introducing the story, anchor Paul Magers calls the issue 'Minnesota's hottest controversy'. Coanchor Pat Miles then says the white sportsmen 'fiercely hate' the proposed agreement. Reporter Stauffer says the agreement shows 'no sign of calming the controversy'. The theme is repeated at the end of the story when Miles asks Stauffer if the issue is potentially 'the most controversial issue before the state legislature', and he says it 'has the potential to generate the most sparks'. The story's language draws clear battle lines.

The narrative continues to evoke Western film mythology by positioning the Indians as the 'bad guys'. A Native American source to offer the tribe's point of view is never heard, thereby marginalizing that point of view; as in the old movies, the audience is never asked to consider a nonwhite understanding of the story. Three white journalists report on the events, a white state official describes the agreement, a throng of white protesters represents the dissatisfaction of 'sports fishing' enthusiasts, and local hero Bud Grant, a white man, serves as the commonsense champion of their cause. 'There is a right and a wrong', he says.

The story's visual imagery further summons the film stereotypes of Native Americans. Trimble (1988) describes one stereotyped view of Native Americans as 'untamed, innocent ... pure lovers of nature' (p. 188). Twice in the story we see the same 'actuality' footage to illustrate spearfishing. No one is identified, but the tape – which lasts only about 8 seconds – would appear to be from the station's files because the water is not frozen. It is dark, and a man in a boat takes one poke with a long wooden spear into the water, which is illuminated by someone holding a flashlight. He pulls out the spear, on which is impaled a wriggling fish. Then we briefly see two men carrying their canoe to shore.

Both times we see it, we do not hear the sound on the tape. The first time it is shown, anchor Paul Magers is introducing the story as 'Minnesota's hottest controversy ... Native American spearfishing'. The second time we see it, reporter Dennis Stauffer is describing a lawsuit in Wisconsin that upheld Native American fishing rights. The only other Native American we see in the story is the tribe member who negotiated the agreement seated at the press conference. He is never identified, nor do we hear from him. In the absence of any other image of tribal life, the spearfishing videotape becomes the central characterization of Native American existence. Although it may seem appropriate (common sense) to use the tape to illustrate spearfishing, it also contributes to the kind of historical robbery described by Parks (1940) in which news coverage fails to place single events into meaningful context. The audience never is given a sense of why the Wisconsin court, in a similar case, upheld Native American fishing rights, which might go a long way in giving the story some historical perspective. And the audience never hears from a Native American who could articulate that perspective.

Syntagmatically, the spearfishing video also works as a binary opposite of the brief 'sports fishing' tape seen during the story. As Stauffer explains that Mille Lacs is 'Minnesota's premier trophy fishing lake', we watch as a large fish is slowly pulled by rod and reel from a hole in the ice by one man, as another bends down and grabs it. We briefly hear the sound on the tape, and a jolly angler shouts, 'There we go! Ha! Ho!' The contrast between spearfishing and 'trophy fishing' furthers the story's white, commonsense perception of the use and function of America's natural resources: the primitive ritual of spearfishing – seen in the darkness and without sound – is juxtaposed against the sportsmanship of 'trophy fishing' – a daylight enterprise undertaken by spirited hobbyists.

The lack of a tribal spokesperson further contributes to the film-myth narrative, evoking the caricature that Trimble (1988) describes as 'the silent Indian':

> The wooden cigar-store Indian, as he stands alone, staring off into space, saying nothing, is the notion of an Indian of many Americans.
>
> (p. 188)

Trimble points out that the film stereotype of the Native American 'good guy' is as merely a sidekick to the white hero: 'The character is inevitably inferior to whites, but slightly more sophisticated than other Indians' (p. 190). We never hear from the tribal leader who sits at the news conference table; rather, a white state official is called upon to explain the agreement. Although he appears to be in conflict with Bud Grant and the white protestors, his argument is not one that clarifies the Native American position, nor does it offer any historical perspective. He simply explains that without the agreement, the protestors stand to suffer a greater loss in the courts.

His reasoning is countered first by the images of the protestors on the Capitol Building steps, whose signs appeal to the governor for help and show the universal 'no' sign over the word 'nets'. (Interestingly, KARE's journalists play up the spearfishing angle, although netting appears to be just as much a part of the controversy.) Reporter Stauffer explains that the agreement's critics 'say that Indians gave up their rights long ago under subsequent treaties and that Minnesota would win in court'. Again, no historical perspective is provided that might explain that Native American treaties with the US government did not so much involve Indians 'giving up their rights' as having those rights taken from them.

The critics' position is further articulated by spokesman Bud Grant. Although he would not need an introduction to Minnesota viewers – he led the Vikings to three

Superbowls and, years before, was a star athlete at the University of Minnesota – the 'headlines' that ran before the news program had identified him. The anchor announced the agreement and explained, 'We'll get reactions from the number one crusader against the plan, former Vikings coach Bud Grant.' We briefly see a long shot of Grant standing at a microphone, surrounded by some of the protestors on the steps of the Capitol, smiling as he appears to be taunted by a Native American man. (Grant's smile seems to diminish the man's position, as if it is not to be taken seriously.) The 'headline' sequence seems out of step with the 'package' that follows. In the story, we do not see Grant with the protestors, nor do we see a Native American counterprotest. When interviewed, Grant is no longer on the steps, but seated in a room surrounded by football memorabilia. The Native American man whom we see so briefly does not appear in the story that follows.

In the story Grant is introduced as the honorary chairman of the Save Mille Lacs Association, but the Viking jerseys and helmets that hang behind him clearly link him to his status as a local hero. The long, low-angle shot, in fact, seems intended to connect the former coach with his football success; he is neatly framed next to the jersey of his star quarterback, Fran Tarkenton. Grant's explanation of the group's opposition to the treaty becomes the story's commonsense understanding: 'I think there is a right and a wrong.' He then asks what appear to be rhetorical questions: 'Why should one group of people be allowed to do something another group of people cannot do? Why should they have exclusive rights?' Without the presence of an on-camera respondent, Grant – a local legend, the voice of middle America – dominates the story's message. Answers to his rhetorical questions would possibly go a long way in explaining the tribe's view: There are plenty of historical reasons for why 'one group' should be allowed to do something 'another group' cannot. And there is certainly an argument for Native American 'exclusive rights', although we never hear it in this story.

The marginalization of the Native American position is furthered by the reporter's response when coanchor Paul Magers asks him toward the end of the story, 'Is the tribe happy with [the agreement] as well?' Stauffer replies that the tribe's negotiator, whom he describes as 'their sort of commissioner of the division of natural resources, if you please', was at the news conference, and that he had supported it. Stauffer's description of the negotiator implies that the man has either no official title or a title that a white audience might not understand. He offers the white counterpart's title in explanation, his 'if you please' compounding the story's sense of otherness about the tribe. Why we do not hear from a tribe member is never made clear, implying either that the Native Americans have nothing significant to add to the story or that they are incapable of articulating their position. Stauffer continues his response by explaining that the tribe will draft its own fishing regulations as part of the agreement, 'which they say will be consistent with state regulations and handled responsibly', implying that the tribe might somehow handle the regulations *irresponsibly*.

The KARE journalists who contributed to the coverage likely focused on the story's controversy to add a sense of drama and attempted to balance the coverage with white explanations of the tribe's position. But the narrative's persistent marginalization of a Native American perspective feeds what Trimble (1988) says is 'the prevailing image of the Indian as a dependent, helpless child' (p. 200). The journalists were simply offering their own perspective, attempting to cover the story as dutifully as possible. But their perspective is one that carries the weight of years of film and textbook stereotypes. As cultural critic bell hooks (1992) explains,

> Both African and Native Americans have been deeply affected by the degrading representations of red and black people that continue to be the dominant images projected by movies and television. Portrayed as cowardly, cannibalistic, uncivilized, the images of 'Indians' mirror screen images of Africans. When most people watch degrading images of red and black people daily on television, they do not think about the way these images cause pain and grief.
>
> (p. 186)

REFERENCES

BARTHES, R. 1972: *Mythologies* (Jonathan Cape Ltd, trans.). New York: Hill & Wang. (Original work published 1957.)

BOBO, L. 1988: Group conflict, prejudice, and the paradox of contemporary racial attitudes. In Katz, P.A. and Taylor, D.A. (eds.), *Eliminating racism*. New York: Plenum, 85–114.

CAMPBELL, R. 1991: *Sixty minutes and the news: a mythology for Middle America*. Urbana: University of Illinois Press.

ESSED, P. 1991: *Understanding everyday racism*. Newbury Park, CA: Sage.

GAERTNER, S.L. and DOVIDIO, J.F. 1986: *Prejudice, discrimination, and racism*. Orlando, FL: Academic Press.

GANS, H. 1979: *Deciding what's news*. New York: Pantheon.

HALL, S. 1980: Encoding/decoding. In Hall, S., Hobson, D., Lowe, A. and Willis, P. (eds.), *Culture, media, language*. London: Hutchinson, 128–38.

HARTLEY, J. 1984: Out of bounds: the myth of marginality. In Masterman, L. (ed.), *Television mythologies: stars, shows and signs*. London: Comedia Publishing Group, 118–27.

hooks, b. 1992: *Black looks: race and representation*. Boston: South End.

MIXON, W. 1989: New Southern mythology. In Wilson, C.R. and Ferris, W. (eds.), *Encyclopedia of Southern culture*. Chapel Hill: University of North Carolina Press, 1113–15.

PARKS, R. 1940: News as a form of knowledge: a chapter in the sociology of knowledge. *American Journal of Sociology* 45(5), 669–86.

SEITER, E. 1987: Semiotics in television. In Allen, R.C. (ed.), *Channels of discourse*. Chapel Hill: University of North Carolina Press, 17–41.

SHARP, S.A. 1989: Mythic South: family. In Wilson, C.R. and Ferris, W. (eds.), *Encyclopedia of Southern culture*. Chapel Hill: University of North Carolina Press, 1104–5.

THORNBURN, D. 1987: Television as an aesthetic medium. *Critical Studies in Mass Communication* 4(2), 161–73.

TRIMBLE, J.E. 1988: Stereotypical images, American Indians, and prejudice. In Katz, P., Katz, A. and Taylor, D.A. (eds.), *Eliminating racism*. New York: Plenum, 181–202.

5

Decoding television news

Justin Lewis

From Drummond, P. and Paterson, R. (eds.) 1985: *Television in transition*. London: British Film Institute, 205–16, 232–4

Justin Lewis's study of how sample viewers made sense of an edition of ITN's nightly news programme, *News at Ten*, offers an excellent way into questions about interpretation. These questions concern the interface between the significations, visual and verbal, out of which programmes are constructed and the understandings which viewers variously take from what they see and hear. To assume that the meanings of programmes are somehow 'fixed' and that therefore the only interesting issue for research is whether or not they have been 'got' by audiences has been regarded as a naive view for some time, one likely, among other things, to suggest too simplified a theory of media influence. Lewis carried out his research as part of an attempt to plot the ways in which 'understanding the news' is an active, constructive process, subject to variation. There are a number of routes one can take in exploring the variability and contingency of the meaning-making process. Lewis's puts tight emphasis on questions of perception, cognition and inference, and attempts to plot the relationship between specific signifying element and specific understanding.

His study is from a published article which was itself extracted from a longer paper. We have included at the start of our extract the summary offered by his original editors, Phillip Drummond and Richard Paterson. They indicate the broad terms of the research and also the five-category system by which he analyses the construction of viewer interpretations from what is on the screen. Lewis then provides a synopsis of the news material before going on to develop, in fascinating and significant detail, the variations which appeared in cited viewer 'decodings'. He pays particular attention to an item which involves a senior Cabinet politician making a speech. Lewis wants to know why the journalists' account so clearly failed to carry through into viewer understanding, why there was so much uncertainty and confusion. We have then extracted from his article a later section in which he offers a rewritten version of the item, a version which he thinks is less likely to suffer from this problem.

His focus on the tightly specific linkage between 'message unit' and 'sense' contrasts with the more recent tendency towards broader audience 'ethnographies'. His relative lack of interest in the *social differences* which lie behind (and may partly serve to determine) interpretative variation is also at odds with recent research emphases, although he shows himself to be well aware of this aspect of 'extra-textual context'. Some might also question the nature of his 'improved' version of the news. Nevertheless, he offers a very clear and provocative study in television's mediation of knowledge, producing valuable pointers some of which have yet to see substantial development. At the end of the extract, we include his own brief retrospective comments on the 1982 study. His more developed account of the issues involved is contained in his 1991 volume, *The ideological octopus* (London: Routledge).

———————

[In the longer version of this essay presented to conference, Justin Lewis contextualises his interest in the analysis of television news in terms of a convergence between text-oriented semiotics and an audience-oriented 'cultural studies' approach which has contributed to the development of notions of the encoding-decoding process, particularly through such initiatives as David Morley's work on *Nationwide*.

Lewis's project began with the selection of a British TV news broadcast – the thirty-minute ITN *News at Ten* broadcast of Friday, 26 March 1982. It went on to analyse the programme through a series of 54 detailed interviews with audiences of 'decoders'. The first four groups were used to develop specific lines of questioning, the remainder to provide the basis for the analysis. A variety of educational and occupational backgrounds was sought, as well as broad age-range and gender parity.

The 200,000 words of response were then codified by Lewis under five main categories. First, units of meaning as constructed by members of the audience were regarded as 'lexias', following Barthes's model in *S/Z*. Second, 'themes' were established in terms of the audiences' perceptions of news items as wholes. Third, 'narrative contexts' were identified, in the sense of 'a particular history that gives a news item (or parts of that item) meaning'. Fourth, a range of 'critical discourses' was identified, covering a spectrum from notions of media 'bias' to specific ideological responses to particular items. Fifth, the 'residual' category of 'extra-textual contexts' was established to designate meaning-systems or contexts, other than the 'narrative' or 'critical', whose origin lay outside the text – *Eds*.]

PROGRAMME SYNOPSIS: *NEWS AT TEN*, 26 MARCH 1982

The British Leyland item   This story began with news of a 'new deal' between management and unions at the Longbridge plant, but concentrated in its film report upon the increases in productivity brought about by the use of robots. A manager and two workers were interviewed, both enthusing about the productivity increases, despite the redundancies involved. The story finished with the reporter stressing that BL's future success could only be jeopardised by strike action.

The company car item   This was a brief reference to a 20 per cent increase in company car tax.

The pound/dollar item   A brief report dealt with the price of sterling against the dollar, in relation to American interest rates.

The West Bank item   This report concerned disturbances on the West Bank, with Israeli troops clamping down hard on rioting among the Palestinian population. These disturbances were said to follow the sacking of three Palestinian mayors by the Israelis. After film of the disturbances, an Israeli spokesperson, Menachem Milsom, was filmed justifying the sacking of the mayors and the Israelis' new hard-line approach. The reporter, Derek Taylor, then contextualised the story in terms of possible problems with the future Israeli withdrawal from the Sinai.

[*Advertisements*]

The El Salvador item   This was a report from El Salvador on the eve of their elections. We were introduced to the main candidates, Duarte and D'Aubuisson, and to the political complexion of them and the other candidates. We were then told that D'Aubuisson was now being considered a possible winner, that he was on the extreme right and had been linked to the death squads. The Americans, we were then told, had shifted their position in order to accept a possible D'Aubuisson victory.

The China/USSR item   This referred briefly to China's response to friendly overtures from the Soviet Union.

The drugs item   A fairly short item followed about the conviction of a Sussex University research student for the manufacture of an illegal drug (Bromo STP).

The Whitelaw item   Coverage was given to the Home Secretary's speech on law and order to a Conservative Party conference (see below for full transcription).

The jobs item   This made up part of ITN's weekly look at recent job losses, new jobs and new orders in Britain. The number of jobs, the firms and the places involved were given with accompanying graphics.

The Everest item   Following the summary of the headlines, there was a fairly serious film report on the progress of a British expedition to Tibet, to climb Everest by a 'totally new route'. The film revolved around rare shots of the British team in the Tibetan capital.

TRANSCRIPT OF THE WHITELAW ITEM

Burnet: The Home Secretary, Mr William Whitelaw, got a standing ovation today after a speech to Conservative Party activists at Harrogate. He spoke in a debate on law and order at an annual conference of the party's central council and, to judge from his reception, he has emerged triumphant again, after a week fending off his critics. From Harrogate, our political correspondent, David Rose.

Alastair Burnet (anchor) in studio. No logo.

Rose: Mr Whitelaw must have been worried about what sort of reception he'd get today. There had been rumblings from the party's grass roots, and he'd been given a rough time by the party conference on this issue last year.

Film of Whitelaw walking on to platform.
Rose captioned.
Shot of audience applauding.
Whitelaw sitting with colleagues on platform.

But in the event, every speaker except one supported him. Mr Whitelaw defended his record, and contrasted it with his predecessors' and opponents'.

Speaker below platform.
Whitelaw listening, smiling.
Audience listening.

Whitelaw: It was Labour Home Secretaries like Roy Jenkins who failed to provide the prison places, for whose shortage they now criticize us. I am tired of those, whether Liberal, Labour or SDP who, far from supporting the police, and encouraging the public to help, concentrate on criticism and complaint.

Whitelaw speaking (captioned).

Rose: He was clearly delighted by the way the debate had gone.

Zoom out, no sound.

Whitelaw: And may I once again thank you deeply for the support and help which you have given to me at a very difficult time. (Applause.)

Sound up again.

Whitelaw sits down.

Rose: And they rose to him. Afterwards Mr Whitelaw told me that he had been hurt by previous criticism, from within his own party. Many of these representatives from the Tory grass roots are worried by the crime figures – but today, few held the Home Secretary personally responsible.

Zoom out to reveal audience who slowly rise.

Zoom in to Whitelaw acknowledging applause. Audience clapping.

There's no doubt that Mr Whitelaw has received almost total support from the Conservative Party workers here at Harrogate. This time last week he feared what looked like a tough week of criticism: first on Monday, from Tory MPs; then in the House of Commons yesterday; then here from party workers in Harrogate. But tonight his position looks very much stronger. David Rose, *News at Ten*, Harrogate.

Rose, to camera.

THE AUDIENCE IN ACTION – A SUMMARY OF THE RESEARCH

The process of decoding

Two stages in the process of decoding can be identified:

1. The extra-textual contexts – particularly the narrative contexts – used by the viewer to understand and interpret a news item will significantly determine which lexias will be decoded and how they will be decoded. These meaning systems can therefore be understood as channels for access to the TV message.
2. The organisation and meaning of these lexias will then determine how the message as a whole will be read.

It should be emphasised that these two stages are separated for analytical purposes – they do not necessarily represent a chronology of the decoding process. The specific channels of access used by the viewer to understand an item may have been appropriated because of the way that item was constructed. In other words, in identifying a process in which two determinations interact, I am not suggesting which one of these determinations 'comes first'.

News at Ten's weekly item detailing the areas where jobs have been lost, or where new jobs have been created (the *Jobs* item), provides a simple but neat demonstration of this process. A majority of the decoders understood this item in relation to a story – or narrative context – about the level of unemployment and the economic climate in general. The programme's weekly report about jobs had, indeed, been created largely in response to the 'beginning' of this story – during the period when unemployment under Mrs Thatcher had begun to rise fairly dramatically. From that point on, rising unemployment became extremely newsworthy.

For these decoders, the relevant part of the *Jobs* item was the *ratio* of 'new jobs' to 'jobs lost' (rather than, say, which kinds of jobs had been gained/lost, or the areas/companies involved). In other words, the narrative context employed by these decoders gives them access to a *specific part* of the item, and gives those parts meaning. Accordingly, the item was seen to mean that: unemployment continues to rise (articulated by 15 decoders); unemployment continues to rise, but jobs are beginning to return (articulated by 9 decoders); or simply that jobs are beginning to return (articulated by 4 decoders). So, viewers using a certain narrative context to understand the *Jobs* piece are directed towards a certain part of that item, which then directs the viewer towards one of a limited range of meanings.

For those decoders who, on the other hand, used more complex narrative contexts to understand the item, the process of decoding produced quite different meanings. Some of the decoders (8 of the 50), for example, interpreted the item in terms of an extra-textual context identifying regional differences in unemployment levels (clearly a matter of some importance to people living in an industrial northern city like Sheffield). Accordingly, this opened up and made meaningful those parts of the item indicating *where* jobs were coming and going. During the interview/viewing sessions, therefore, every member of this group made references to *places* mentioned on the item. This, in turn, led them to construct meanings that either confirmed or denied regional trends in unemployment levels. In this instance, the ratio of jobs lost to new jobs became a less significant part of the item; for these decoders, it is *where* jobs are coming and going that is important in determining its meaning, rather than simply *how many*.

Another group of decoders (5 of the 50) were able to refer to a narrative context specifying the decline of jobs in manufacturing industry (as opposed to, say, the service industries). In these cases, the types of jobs lost or gained became significant. Once this happened, the viewer was forced to construct a meaning confirming the narrative context – in this case (because of the nature of the lexias involved) the item was seen as demonstrating the decline in British manufacturing industry.

The process of decoding that produces these meanings is not a matter of choice for the decoders. It is not a case of the viewer choosing, on the basis of his/her predilections, which part of the message he/she feels is important and then constructing a suitable meaning. This is a common conception of the audience to which the 'uses and gratifications' approach gave a great deal of credence. It is a comfortable model of the television audience that has provided both researchers and broadcasters with an easy and convenient view of the world – yet it is profoundly misleading. The viewer will, on the whole, have only a limited range of appropriate meaning systems (extra-textual contexts) to draw upon when watching a television news story. These contexts will give the viewer a specific form of access to certain sections (lexias) of the item, which will, in turn, force him/her towards a certain meaning (or set of meanings). Moreover, because these channels of access (as I have called them) will frequently open up only certain parts of the TV message, the nature of exactly *what* is being communicated is by no means predictable.

The news of Whitelaw's reception in Harrogate, for example, would appear, to both broadcasters and researchers, to have a fairly straightforward and clear meaning. The story was 'about' the favourable reception given to Willie Whitelaw by Conservative Party workers, following a period when he had been losing credibility with his own party's right wing. The story was, indeed, something of an anticlimax. After a series of attacks upon Whitelaw for his supposedly 'soft' approach to law and order – attacks which had become particularly vociferous during the 1981 Conservative Party conference – the broadcasting media sent teams up to Harrogate expecting the (then) Home Secretary to be given a rough ride. As one BBC news broadcaster put it, in one of the group discussions: 'We were there to see Willie Whitelaw get mauled, and he didn't. We'd expended all that effort, and so had they (ITN), so we still had to produce something out of it.' What resulted on *News at Ten* may not have been terribly newsworthy, but it was not, apparently, ambiguous. Not, at least, until we examine how it was decoded.

The *Whitelaw* item can be divided into three main stages. The first stage is a résumé of the story's narrative context by Alastair Burnet (briefly) and the reporter on location, David Rose. We are then shown a brief film clip of Whitelaw's speech, following the news that all the speakers in the debate, bar one, had supported him. The final part of the story sees a relieved Whitelaw receiving a standing ovation, with David Rose reporting that this support has made Whitelaw's position, within his own party, 'very much stronger'.

In terms of the story's *encoded* meaning, the second section of the item – the brief clip of his speech – was completely irrelevant. *What* he said, in terms of how the story was set up, was of little importance; what was significant was *how he was received*. The footage of Whitelaw's speech was intended to signify nothing more than 'here is Whitelaw speaking'. Despite this, of the three sections, it was Whitelaw's speech that made the greatest impact upon the decodings. Of the 50 decoders, 41 incorporated references to the speech into their readings, 38 incorporated references to his reception and only 12 incorporated references to the story's context (i.e. the fact that he had been having a difficult time in his own party recently). Although the fact that Whitelaw received support at Harrogate was signified throughout the item (verbally by Alastair Burnet, David Rose and Willie Whitelaw, and visually by shots of his audience applauding or giving him a standing ovation), several decoders were unable to identify the origin of this support, or its significance. Of the 38 decoders who referred to this support, for example, 8 suggested it came not from members of the Conservative Party, but from people in general. Of the 41 decoders who referred to Whitelaw's speech, on the other hand, a large number – 31 – mentioned at least one of the two points he made, despite the irrelevance of these points in relation to the encoded meaning of the story (he begins by criticising former Home Secretaries for not building enough prisons, and then refers to the need to support the police and the opposition parties' failure to do this).

I shall deal with the relative impact of these two sections of the item in more detail later. Suffice to say at this point that, for many of the decoders, Whitelaw's speech was actually seen as the focal point of the story. This was made possible by the decoders' failure to incorporate the item's introduction into their readings. Without knowledge of the context of events in Harrogate, it is impossible to understand the significance of Whitelaw's good reception. This, in turn, forces the decoder to shift his/her attention towards what Whitelaw actually said.

If the decodings are analysed in more detail, we can see that the ability to absorb the item's introduction into a reading is fairly dependent upon the decoder *already knowing* about the narrative context to which the introduction refers. Of the 12 decoders referring to the item's résumé of Whitelaw's problems in his own party, 9 had detailed prior knowledge of Whitelaw's recent trials, and 3 a vague knowledge of them. (There were, on the other hand, 10 decoders who referred neither to Whitelaw's previous position nor the support given him at Harrogate, and none of these had any knowledge of the story's narrative context.) In other words, the first section of the item became meaningful only for decoders with access to the narrative context to which it referred. For the majority of the decoders without access to this narrative context, the broadcaster's encoded meaning *was simply not communicated*.

For the smaller group who already knew about Whitelaw's problems, the process of decoding worked thus:

1.   The decoders were able, on the basis of this narrative context, to make the opening lexias, the item's introduction, meaningful;
2.   The introduction to the story therefore related to subsequent parts of the item, giving *them* specific meanings;
3.   These meanings then combined to create a range of readings around the central theme – that Whitelaw, after criticism from within his own party, was now enjoying support.

For the larger group of decoders who did not already know about Whitelaw's problems, the process of decoding worked like this:

1.   The decoders were not able, on the basis of narrative contexts (or other extra-textual contexts) available to them, to make the item's introduction meaningful.

They were, on the whole, able to construct readings around Whitelaw's speech and the support he received on the basis of various discourses about law and order and politicians in action.

2. This gave Whitelaw's speech and/or his enthusiastic reception a certain range of meanings in relation to one another (or in isolation, depending on the extra-textual contexts available to the decoder). Without knowledge of the item's introduction, for example, the meaning of his enthusiastic reception is constructed in relation to the speech, i.e. it is specifically *what he has just said* that has earned him a standing ovation.

3. These meanings then combine around a range of themes: Whitelaw supported by his party for his handling of certain law-and-order issues (constructed by 3 decoders), Whitelaw speaking about law and order (constructed by 9 decoders), Whitelaw gaining general support for his measures (constructed by 4 decoders) and so on.

Decoding narrative

It has already been indicated how the *Whitelaw* item worked in terms of two narratives: one with Whitelaw's speech as its focal point, one directing the viewer towards the reception he received. This seems a useful place to begin, as it allows three important points to be made. First, the *Whitelaw* item demonstrates, lest we forget, that narrative structure is a product of the process of decoding. However powerful a narrative structure may be in directing the viewer's interest and concern, that power is ultimately dependent upon the availability of appropriate extra-textual contexts. Second, the two conflicting narratives present in the *Whitelaw* story reveal a great deal about the nature of narrative in television news. In their introductions, both Alastair Burnet and David Rose cite the story's introduction and attempt to direct the viewer past Whitelaw's speech towards his reception. Burnet begins with the most 'newsworthy' element of the story:

> The Home Secretary, Mr William Whitelaw, got a standing ovation today, after a speech to Conservative Party activists in Harrogate.

He then refers briefly to the speech – *without mentioning its content* – before returning to the main point:

> ... to judge from his reception, he has emerged triumphant again, after a week fending off his critics.

David Rose then proceeds to fill out the context in more detail and, in so doing, strengthens the emphasis on Whitelaw's *reception* rather than his speech:

> Mr Whitelaw must have been worried about what sort of reception he'd get today. There had been rumblings from the party's grass roots, and he'd been given a rough time by the party's conference on this issue last year. But in the event ...

As has already been indicated, these attempts to construct a narrative, moving from a 'worried' to a 'triumphant' Whitelaw, are surprisingly unsuccessful. There are a number of reasons for this (which will be dealt with in this essay when appropriate), but perhaps the most revealing is the way this narrative conflicts with the conventions of news narrative.

These conventions instil various expectations into the TV viewer. Where a news story contains a fairly brief sequence of actuality film (preceded by a newsreader's and/or a reporter's introduction), the viewer can usually expect that sequence to signify the focal point of the story. This is the case, for example, with the *West Bank* item, where the actuality film of the Arab–Israeli disturbances is not only the 'newsworthy' focal point of the story, but is also perceived as such by the decoders.

Given these expectations, the *Whitelaw* item contains two possible focal points: the speech and Whitelaw's reception (these being the only two 'events' communicated during the film report). For the majority of decoders (who were not guided by the encoded narrative towards his reception), the second is necessarily seen as a 'reaction' to the first. The traditional format of television news therefore encourages a reading based upon the least significant (insignificant in terms of the news value encoded into it) part of that item.

A slightly different example of a traditional format producing certain expectations amongst viewers of TV news occurred during the decoding of the *pound/dollar* item. Nearly all the decoders were aware that the level of the pound against the dollar was a piece of information that cropped up fairly regularly on the news. The common feature of this brief but regular financial news item is the level of the pound, i.e. whether it rose or fell. This information, rather than the news about American interest rates or Chicago money markets (news that, on this *News at Ten*, gave meaning to the information about the level of the pound), therefore provided the focal point for most decoders' readings of it – even though many failed to recall whether the pound had actually gone up or down. The decoders had learnt a specific structure of response. What is significant is that these responses do not necessarily facilitate an understanding of a news story, or the ability to structure it into a coherent narrative.

The third point raised about narrative by the *Whitelaw* item is perhaps the most interesting. It refers to a code of narrative identified by Roland Barthes in his analysis, in *S/Z*, of Balzac's short story 'Sarrasine'. It is a narrative code that structures the relation between lexias, defined by Barthes as the hermeneutic code:

> Let us designate as hermeneutic code all those units whose function it is to articulate in various ways a question, its response, and the variety of chance events that can either formulate the question or delay its answer; or even, constitute an enigma and lead to its solution.[1]

The hermeneutic code, then, is a way of establishing links within a narrative. It is, moreover, perhaps the most powerful link in televisual communication. The hermeneutic code, more than any other, draws the viewer into the narrative: once the viewer has become interested in the question, the enigma, he/she has become 'hooked'.

The code of enigma works on a number of levels. It can refer to the straightforward posing of a question, such as the one that opened the *News at Ten* under study (seen by the decoders): after the first chime of Big Ben, we were asked of Roy Jenkins, 'Is he now the alternative prime minister?' It can also refer to implicit suggestions about the future *of the narrative*, the kind of enigma/resolution structure that characterises most TV or cinematic fiction, but which is embodied most obviously in the continuous serial like *Coronation Street*. As Christine Geraghty writes,

> The apparent multifariousness of the plots, their inextricability from each other, the everyday quality of narrative time and events, all encourage us to believe that this is a

narrative whose future is not yet written. Even events which would offer a suitable ending in other narrative forms are never a final ending in the continuous serial: a wedding is not a happy ending but opens up the possibilities of stories about married life and divorce . . .[2]

The qualities that Geraghty attributes to narratives like *Coronation Street* are, in a number of ways, appropriate to TV news. All of the main items on *News at Ten* are episodes of stories of which the viewer will, if he/she wants, hear more. The *Hillhead* item, in resolving one narrative (the Hillhead by-election) opens up others: the future of Roy Jenkins, the leadership of the SDP and the Alliance and, ultimately, the whole future of parliamentary politics. The *British Leyland* item very obviously finishes with an enigma: will strikes disrupt the progress now being made at Longbridge? The viewer is therefore referred to the future of BL, in terms of both productivity and industrial relations. The *West Bank* story refers specifically to the future of the Sinai withdrawal, and more generally to future Arab–Israel relations and international relations; the *Whitelaw* piece, in signifying harmony, suggests the possibilities of disruptions in the future, and so on. We are witnessing the plot of history. Despite this, the continuous serial is one of the most compelling forms of television while, for most people, TV news is the least. As Patterson writes, the audience of TV news programmes is often 'an inadvertent one – which, in large proportion, does not come purposefully to television for news, but arrives almost accidentally, watching the news because it is "on", or because it leads into or out of something else. . . .'[3] Why is this?

If a programme-maker were asked to produce a narrative form that, by subverting or ignoring the hermeneutic code, failed to capture or sustain the viewers' interest, he/she might have come up with a TV news programme. Apart from occasional instances during opening headlines (like the question about the alternative prime minister), TV news pre-empts the development and resolution of enigma. It does this in two ways.

First, it orientates the news item around a focal point or series of focal points. These focal points, be they disturbances on the West Bank, or reactions of senior politicians to the Hillhead by-election, are almost never presented as resolutions or developments or enigmas/questions. When the history of an event is referred to, the enigmatic quality of that history – what would be the reaction of the Palestinians to the sacking of their mayors? what were the circumstances of Jenkins's win at Hillhead, and what are the consequences? – is absorbed into the event/focal point itself. During the film report from the West Bank, reference is made to the mayors *after* the disturbances have (on the film) begun, while the Hillhead by-election itself is covered *after* reactions to it have been given (the circumstances of Jenkins's victory are not mentioned at all).

Second, on the rare occasions when the history of an event *is* presented as an enigmatic prelude to the focal point of the story, any enigmatic quality it may have is subverted by the newsreader's introduction to the story. This is precisely what happens during the *Whitelaw* item. David Rose attempts to set up an enigma, thereby guiding the viewer towards Whitelaw's reception (rather than his speech): 'Mr Whitelaw must have been worried about what sort of reception he'd get today. There had been rumblings from the party's grass roots...' This attempt has, however, already been pre-empted by Burnet's introduction: 'The Home Secretary, Mr William Whitelaw, got a standing ovation today, after a speech...' The hermeneutic code could have worked here to shift the decoders away from the speech towards Whitelaw's reception. The newsreader's introduction robs the enigma of its power.

The role of the introduction on television news is not to set up or contextualize the subsequent report, but to summarize it. The 'main points' of the story are given before the story is properly told. If the 'main points' of *Coronation Street* or the FA Cup Final were given at the beginning of the programmes, only the most enthusiastic viewers would be inclined to continue watching.

TV news is not, of course, alone in suppressing the hermeneutic code. Print journalism operates in much the same way, although there is a suggestion that the tabloid newspapers are beginning to move towards a more narrational style of reporting. What makes the denial of enigma on TV news so significant is that it is virtually the only form of television to subvert this narrative structure. Even a programme like *Top of the Pops* attempts to introduce the hermeneutic code into its narrative, via the chart run-down (who will be where in the charts this week?) and the presenter's reluctance to introduce the acts other than immediately before they appear (who else will be on this week's show?).

Examples of the hermeneutic code on *News at Ten* are, therefore relatively few and far between. It is important, nevertheless, to understand *where* and *how* the code operates in relation to decoding narrative [. . .]

A PRACTICAL RECOMMENDATION

It seems appropriate to end with a brief example of what some of those recommendations might look like in practice. Even if the news values adopted by *News at Ten* are more or less accepted, the news stories it contains can be rewritten to overcome many of the problems of communication revealed by the research. The *Whitelaw* item demonstrates these points.

The main problem the decoders had with the *Whitelaw* story was a difficulty in understanding its significance. The narrative context of the story was clearly crucial to the communication of its particular meaning. Although the reporter, David Rose, referred to the appropriate narrative context (i.e. the difficulties Whitelaw had been having in placating the party's right wing on the law-and-order issue), this was missed by most of the decoders – apart from those who were already familiar with that narrative context. Partly because of this, and partly because of its position in the narrative and its verbal/visual impact, the decoders attributed undue significance to Whitelaw's actual speech. This speech, in terms of the story the *News at Ten* team were trying to put over, was entirely inconsequential.

The failure of the *News at Ten* team to get its message across to the majority of decoders is, as has been demonstrated, due not so much to absences in the news item, as to the way that item was constructed. Most importantly, the three-stage narrative – Whitelaw's problems in his own party, his reception at Harrogate, the meaning of that reception – was not read off by most decoders for three main reasons:

1.   The subversion of the hermeneutic code, i.e. the question implied by the narrative context – 'how will Whitelaw be received at Harrogate?' – was answered before it was asked.

2. The summary of the item's narrative context was further weakened because it was not supported by any accompanying visuals.
3. The speech itself was made to appear as the item's focal point rather than its reception).

All these problems have been avoided in the following version of the *Whitelaw* story.

Burnet: Speculation about the future of Mr William Whitelaw was brought to a head today, at a Conservative Conference in Harrogate. Mr Whitelaw has had a difficult few months coping with hardliners in his own party – David Rose reports from Harrogate.	Burnet in studio.
Rose: (Over background noise from the 1981 Conference.) Since his rowdy reception at last year's Conservative Party Conference, Home Secretary Willie Whitelaw has had a tough time fending off criticism from right-wingers in his own party.	Film of Whitelaw speaking to 1981 Conference, with graphics indicating time and place.
Both in and out of the House of Commons, Conservatives to the political right of Mr Whitelaw have been saying that the solution to the rising crime figures lies in taking tough action against offenders. They have attacked the Home Secretary for his more liberal approach to law and order.	David Rose, in the conference hall, to camera.
In the face of this criticism, the response of Conservative Party workers in Harrogate today was seen as a crucial test.	Film of Whitelaw walking on to the platform.
In the event, the party workers rallied round to give him their full support. During the debate, every speaker bar one supported him. As the party representatives rose to give him a standing ovation, Mr Whitelaw was clearly relieved.	Film of the debate.

Film of Whitelaw receiving a standing ovation. |
| *Whitelaw*: And may I once again thank you deeply for the support and help which you have given to me at a very difficult time. | Film of Whitelaw speaking. |

Rose: There is no doubt that, after his reception tonight, Mr Whitelaw's position in his own party looks very much stronger. David Rose, *News at Ten*, Harrogate.	Film of Whitelaw acknowledging applause.

Burnet's introduction merely refocuses the viewer's attention towards the issues at stake in the subsequent report. David Rose is then allowed space to set up the narrative context of the story, accompanied by a direct visual link. Having developed this context, Rose then firmly establishes the enigma: what will happen at Harrogate? The enigma is then resolved, Whitelaw expresses his relief and, as the applause fades away, Rose briefly confirms the significance of what has taken place. This significance has already been symbolized verbally and visually by the story's structure, moving as it does from Whitelaw under attack to Whitelaw receiving support. Pictures of the 1981 conference are replaced by pictures from Harrogate. The story, for the time being, is complete.

NOTES

1. R. Barthes, *S/Z* (London, Jonathan Cape, 1975), p. 17.
2. C. Geraghty, 'The continuous serial – a definition', in R. Dyer *et al.*, *Coronation Street* (London, British Film Institute, 1981), p. 11.
3. T. Patterson, *The mass media election* (New York, Praeger, 1980), p. 57.

AFTERWORD (1995)

Since this is both a brief and an early version of my research on news and narrative, let me offer a couple of retrospective comments. While the research can be read as a recommendation for news editors to improve what is, in the traditional sense, an extremely poor method of communication, that is not my main intention.

My concern is with the role TV news plays in the construction of ideology. It is, in this sense, important to understand those moments of news that are likely to remain with most audiences and those that do not. The failure of serious news programmes to use narrative to engage viewers means that news constructs fairly basic, unsophisticated patterns of meaning that bear no straightforward relation to its overall content. These meanings are clustered not around a series of historical relationships but, like advertising, through repetition and simple associations (e.g. Pepsi = youth and exuberance, Saddam Hussein = Hitler).

It has been suggested to me that we should be thankful for anything that decreases the power of TV news. That may be so, but my research does not suggest that TV news influence is *limited* by its failure to communicate. On the contrary, those fragments that do get through – that ideologically resonate with audiences – become the informational building-blocks of political opinion. But if only certain fragments are being heard, we need to know which fragments they are and what role they play in the formation of contemporary ideologies.

J.L.

Section II

GENRES

6

Television and pop: the case of the 1950s

John Hill

From Corner, J. (ed.) 1991: *Popular television in Britain: studies in cultural history*. London: Arnold, 90–8

As other material in this Reader suggests (see item 8), the relationship between popular music, with its attractions for the young, and television, with its need for good ratings and a strong advertising profile, has developed in a number of different ways.

John Hill examines the formative period of televised pop in Britain. In the extract we have chosen, he focuses his attention on the BBC's *Six-Five Special* and then ITV's *Oh Boy!*. The first of these programmes began in the early 1950s and was in effect the start of a whole line of programmes, sometimes in competition with each other. *Oh Boy!* was the first major competitor (devised by the orginator of *Six-Five Special*, who had been tempted to leave the BBC, like many other talented producers of the period), starting in 1958. However, Hill's analysis is not just about popular music and television; it also concerns the development of television programme production – the building of a particular 'assembly' (see Hall, item 1) of live and recorded materials into an entity which would attract young viewers. The new popular music programmes of the 1950s were seen by both the BBC and ITV companies as playing an important part in the weekend schedule – screened as they usually were at around tea-time on a Saturday. Hill looks at the way in which the programmes were constructed visually and also at the way in which they were presented (initially involving a compromise between the need to appeal to teenagers and yet also to appear acceptable to their parents).

At this relatively early stage in the development of the medium, some of the transitions required in the programme challenged both the technology and conventional studio practice. It was soon recognized that pace and variety were going to be essential features of a successful pop programme, and Hill examines how the 'hectic' look was initially constructed and how it was rethought in response to social change and consequent shifts in cultural and musical style.

Among other things, Hill's piece gets across very well the interaction between television as 'industry' and television as 'cultural form', catching the search for innovation and market success, the factors of planning as well as the factors of chance, at a specific and significant historical moment.

While the Postmaster General (PMG) may seem an unlikely candidate for a place in the history of rock'n'roll he did, nonetheless, make a small but important contribution to its advance in the 1950s. Under the terms of the Television Act of 1954, which had paved the way for commercial television, the PMG was responsible for the allocation of television hours. Up until 1957, the most striking consequence of this arrangement was the closed period on television between 6 and 7 p.m. Known colloquially as the 'toddler's truce', it was designed to allow parents to put their children to bed free of the distractions of television. When ITV was launched in September 1955, the commercial companies had complied with this requirement but, in the face of financial losses the following summer, had petitioned the then PMG, Charles Hill, for the ban's removal. Hill, who felt 'it was the responsibility of parents, not the State, to put their children to bed at the right time', was sympathetic and persuaded the Government to agree to a change, with the result that the 'toddler's truce' on Mondays to Saturdays was formally ended on Saturday 16 February 1957.[1] At 6 p.m. that evening, the BBC broadcast a five-minute news bulletin, followed by a new programme aimed at young people and featuring live music. *Six-Five Special* was born and a small piece of both television and rock'n'roll history was made.

Although *Six-Five Special* is often regarded as a watershed in television's treatment of pop music it was not, of course, without precursors. The growth of the record industry during the 1950s and the compilation of the charts on the basis of record sales, rather than sales of sheet music, had already aroused television interest. The BBC itself had launched its own version of the US TV show *Hit Parade* in 1952 and revived it in October 1955. This consisted of a selection of songs from those currently featuring in the Top Twenty as well as one 'standard'. The songs were not performed by the original artists, however, but by a team of residents, led by Petula Clark and Dennis Lotis, who not only sang, but also acted out the songs in an appropriate setting ('dramatic, humorous, tearful or sentimental').[2] *Hit Parade*'s producer, Francis Essex, was also responsible for the BBC's *Off the Record* launched in May 1955. This attempted to deal with various aspects of the record industry, providing news, 'behind the scenes' interviews and even small features (such as a 'Life of a Disc' profile recorded at EMI). The bulk of the show, however, was devoted to a varying roster of singers and bands performing in the studio, introduced by the veteran bandleader Jack Payne. These included, in the first show, Max Bygraves, the Four Aces (then in the charts with their version of 'Stranger in Paradise'), Ronnie Hilton and Alma Cogan (performing her subsequent No. 1, 'Dreamboat'). As these performers and titles suggest, both shows, although linked to the charts, were showbiz in orientation and tied to the popular music traditions of Tin Pan Alley.[3]

This was also true of ITV's first venture into the field, ABC TV *Music Shop*, which appeared on their third day of transmission. This too consisted of current recording stars performing in the studio, although with more of an emphasis on US performers than in *Off the Record* (Teddy Johnson, Pearl Carr and Josh White, for example, all put in an early appearance). The bias of these shows, however, was hardly surprising. Although Bill Haley and the Comets had entered the British charts as early as January 1955 with 'Shake, Rattle and Roll', it was not until relatively late the following year that rock'n'roll was to make major inroads into the British Top Twenty. As a result, it was not until the end of 1956 (31 December, in fact) that the first show to register this musical shift appeared.

Made for Associated-Rediffusion, *Cool for Cats* was initially only to be seen in the London region, first on Mondays at 7.15 p.m. and then on Thursdays. The idea for the programme belonged to the Fleet Street journalist Ker Robertson, who not only selected the records to be played, but also presented the opening shows. However, the fact that he was 'balding, bespectacled and middle-aged' was not, perhaps, the ideal qualification for the host of 'a teenage disc show' and by the end of the first month he had handed over to the marginally more youthful Kent Walton (aged thirty-eight).[4] The show itself was short – only fifteen minutes – and consisted of the presenter's comments on the discs plus visual interpretations of the music, devised and directed by Joan Kemp-Welch. These usually consisted of dance sequences, employing a regular troupe of dancers choreographed by Douglas Squires, but they could also be more abstract in nature. 'Sometimes I'll use just hands miming,' Kemp-Welch told the *TV Times*, 'or close-ups of bowls of flowers for a sentimental number.'[5] The show proved sufficiently successful to be nationally networked twice a week in June 1957 and continued to run, in one form or another, until December 1959.

Cool for Cats' lead in the televising of pop was, however, short-lived. *Six-Five Special* followed it only six weeks later and quickly established itself with an audience of between six and seven million. Although the programme soon became a corner-stone of the BBC's Saturday evening schedule, its appearance was largely fortuitous. The Corporation had actively opposed the ending of the 'toddler's truce' and, when it became clear that the ban would end anyway, sought to delay its implementation. Failing to do so, their response was to look for stop-gap programmes which could be mounted both quickly and cheaply. Thus, *Six-Five Special* was intended to run for only six weeks (on a budget of £1,000 per show), and was still at a relatively early stage of planning at the end of January 1957. *Tonight*, the news magazine programme called upon to fill the gap on Mondays to Fridays, was still without a title a week before its launch.[6]

The benefit of this haste, however, was that it not only created openings for young programme-makers (Jack Good, the co-producer of *Six-Five Special* was only twenty-six while *Tonight*'s producer, Alasdair Milne, was twenty-seven), but also allowed them a relative freedom to experiment with new programme ideas. It was thus with some surprise that both programmes were greeted by the press. 'Yes, it was BBC, not ITV,' observed one review of *Six-Five Special*, 'just the kind of thing, in fact, you might have expected from ITV.'[7] The irony, in this case, was that ITV had shown none of the same enterprise and had opted instead for an episode of *The Adventures of Sir Lancelot* followed by a repeat of a short play, *The Stolen Pearl*. That the BBC had apparently stolen a march on their commercial rival, however, was less the result of competitive vigour, at a time of falling audience figures, than the unexpected by-product of an initial reluctance to change.

But, while the association of pop on television with six o'clock on Saturday was largely coincidental, it did have a significant influence on the way televised pop developed in the 1950s. The ending of the 'toddler's truce' had forced broadcasters to anticipate the kind of viewer who might watch at this hour. Thus, the magazine format of *Tonight* was orientated towards those returning home from work and who might be expected to 'switch on at any time'. This would not be the case on a Saturday and here a programme aimed at young people seemed the natural choice to fill the gap between children's television in the late afternoon and proper 'grown-ups' TV in the evening.

However, it was also unlikely that only teenagers would be watching at this hour and any programme occupying this slot could not afford to be too exclusive in its appeal, especially given the importance of the hour for 'catching' the audience for the evening (one of the possible titles for *Six-Five Special* was, in fact, 'Start the Night Right').[8] In the cinema, 'teenpics' could be successfully targeted at the increasingly important youth audience, but television, with only two channels, had to make more of an allowance for the domestic and familial context in which it was received and hence the more heterogeneous nature of its audience.[9] This was especially true, perhaps, of what the press had dubbed 'tea-time TV', with its implied image of the family gathered around the television set while eating. With the launch of *Six-Five Special*, it was also Saturday tea-time when pop music was most likely to be seen on TV in the years which immediately followed. As a result, the programmes called upon to fill this slot were engaged in a balancing act, attempting to satisfy a specifically teenage audience on the one hand, and a more generally adult one on the other. It was thus with some pride that the BBC were able to report in their annual handbook that while 'primarily designed for a teen-aged audience', *Six-Five Special* had become, nevertheless, 'a national institution equally enjoyed by the parents'.[10]

This desire to cater to both young and old was already implicit in the show's early billing as the 'bright "new look" programme' aimed not simply at young people but 'the young in spirit of all ages'.[11] It was also evident in the show's format, which was much more of a mix than is commonly remembered. This took the form of a cross between a variety show and a magazine programme, in which musical acts, of various kinds, were interspersed with comic turns and special items. This mixture was designed not only to broaden the show's appeal, but also to temper, in the appropriate Reithian manner, the programme's offerings of entertainment with small doses of information and education. The programme's design, in this respect, is often regarded as something of a compromise between the show's main inspiration and co-producer, Jack Good, and the BBC. Whereas Good wished to bring the excitement and energy of rock'n'roll to television, the BBC management were clearly reluctant simply to indulge what it still regarded as no more than a passing fad. Only a month after the programme's start, for example, the Assistant Head of Light Entertainment, Tom Sloan, was anticipating rock'n'roll's demise and warning the show's producers that, 'as Rock and Roll diminishes it is important to introduce ... more items of general interest'.[12]

The nature of this compromise was well illustrated by the very first show. This was presented by Pete Murray and the show's co-producer, Josephine Douglas. Like so many pop programmes before and after, both hosts, and especially Douglas, were too 'old' and too obviously 'professional' to be entirely convincing to a teenage audience. 'Several viewers ... suggested that neither was really suitable, either in age or personality, for this particular job,' the BBC's Audience Research Department subsequently reported. 'In their opinion a programme for teenagers should be introduced by teenagers.'[13] However, Douglas, middle class and smartly dressed, did provide the show with a sensible presence, reassuring older viewers that they were not excluded from the programme and that it was unlikely to get out of hand. Her role, in this respect, was well brought out by her opening exchange with Murray, in which the programme's twin forms of address were clearly presented:

PETE: Hi there, welcome aboard the Six-Five Special. We've got almost a hundred cats jumping here, some real cool characters to give us the gas, so just get with it and have a ball.

Jo: Well I'm just a square it seems, but for all the other squares with us, roughly translated what Peter Murray just said was, we've got some lively musicians and personalities mingling with us here, so just relax and catch the mood from us . . .[14]

This judicious balancing of young and old, the entertaining and educational, was also apparent in the show which followed. The musical numbers, for example, were deliberately varied and designed to provide a balance of pace and style. Kenny Baker and his jazz band played the show in and out, while the singer Michael Holliday contributed a couple of ballads. The rock'n'roll meanwhile was provided by Bobbie and Rudy and the King Brothers. The most unexpected musical item, however, was undoubtedly the appearance of the classical pianist, Pouishnoff, performing a selection from Beethoven and Chopin. Although a member of the audience was enlisted to voice her approval ('It doesn't matter what sort it is . . . if the music's good I like it'), it was evident that, whatever the desire of the programme to provide musical uplift, classical music did not really fit the bill. The programme persevered with a classical item for a few more weeks, but then it was quietly dropped.

Other regular features were also begun. There was a film extract (Little Richard in *Don't Knock the Rock*) and a 'Star Spotlight' featuring a light-hearted interview with the film actress Lisa Gastoni. More unusually, the boxer Freddie Mills was recruited to present a sports item featuring lesser-known activities. This began somewhat comically with a demonstration by two Hungarian musclemen, the Herculean Balancers. 'If you're going to rock'n'roll properly you need to have your muscles in pretty good shape,' Freddie Mills explained, after he had been carried in by the two Hungarian heavyweights.

Finally, the programme included a filmed feature profiling the Brady Boys' Youth Club choir, who performed a selection of folk songs. Along with the sports spot (which subsequently featured judo, swimming and boxing), it was the filmed feature (usually narrated by Josephine Douglas) which was most characteristically dedicated to educating the audience or encouraging them to more active and sensible pursuits. These could, however, give the impression of being rather artificially grafted on to the show. In one edition (31 August 1957), for example, the bandleader Ray Anthony was encouraged to demonstrate the new 'American dance sensation', the Bunny Hop. This he proceeded to do before leading his fellow dancers in a conga-like bunny hop around the studio. No sooner had this rather bizarre activity been concluded, however, than the programme was off to Wales to join a climbing expedition.

It was, however, the music which was the show's most important feature. Although this was varied, four main types of music tended to predominate: rock'n'roll, skiffle, traditional jazz and ballads. The show, in fact, developed a particularly strong association with skiffle – its eventual theme tune was performed by the Bud Cort skiffle group, Lonnie Donegan, Chas McDevitt and Willie McCormick all made regular appearances and the show even launched its own skiffle competition – but it was its links with rock'n'roll for which the programme became most famous. It was only a few months before the start of the programme that rock'n'roll had really arrived in Britain. Elvis Presley had enjoyed his first British hit with 'Heartbreak Hotel' in May 1956, *Rock Around the Clock* had reached the cinemas in September, while Britain's first native rock'n'roller (and an early guest on *Six-Five Special*), Tommy Steele, had entered the charts for the first time with 'Rock Around the

Cavemen' in October. And it was precisely because rock'n'roll was so new in Britain that *Six-Five Special* was able to play such an important role in its growth.

This was evident both in the programme's ability to influence record sales (The Diamonds' 'Little Darlin', for example, was an early beneficiary) and to provide an important stepping-stone to success for individual artists. Partly because of the show's budget and partly because so few American rock'n'rollers were visiting Britain (Presley refused to come at all), the show was heavily dependent on British talent. As, at this stage, few enough British rock'n'roll acts existed, or were established, the show became an important launching-pad for new discoveries. The programme's power, in this regard, was quickly demonstrated by the case of the hapless Terry Dene, Britain's first rock'n'roll star after Steele but also its earliest casualty.[15] Appearing on *Six-Five Special* in April, he entered the charts shortly afterwards with his cover of Marty Robbins' 'A White Sports Coat'. More hits and even a film, very loosely based on his career, *The Golden Disc*, were to follow. Other singers were also to benefit. Jim Dale, who subsequently became the show's presenter, and Marty Wilde were two of the best known, but there was also a string of *Six-Five* regulars, such as the King Brothers, the Mudlarks and Don Lang, who were to achieve chart success as a result of appearing on the show.

However, for at least one reviewer it was not these performers but the teenage audience who were 'the real stars of the show'.[16] For central to the show's conception, and an important part of its appeal, was not just the live music but the dancing in the studio. This idea was not entirely new. In Philadelphia, *Bandstand* (subsequently *American Bandstand*) had already used teenage dancing to good effect.[17] However, in the context of British television the innovation was striking and, if Palmer is to be believed, the source of some consternation at the BBC, which initially opposed Good's plans for scenes of 'wild abandon'.[18] If this was the case, the objections quickly dissolved and by the time of the programme's anniversary the Controller of Programmes, Kenneth Adam, was even lamenting the loss of time devoted to watching the audience, the very feature, he observed, which had 'put the programme on the map in the first place'.[19]

The appeal of the studio audience, in this respect, was not just their contribution to the informal party atmosphere enjoyed by many viewers, but also their role as unofficial guides to the latest fashions in clothes, haircuts and, above all, dancing. The programme encouraged this last interest, in particular, by running dance competitions (offering LP vouchers to the couple who could 'cut the coolest capers' in the first show) and recruiting 'experts' to demonstrate the latest dance crazes (or, as in one show, the difference between 'rock'n'roll' and 'jive dancing'). Dancing was also integral to the show's presentation of the music. The bands generally performed on slightly raised rostra while the audience danced in front. During musical numbers the cameras would cut between the performers and the dancers, who were usually shot either from above or by cameras roving the studio floor. Singers would also join the dancers and occasionally perform surrounded by members of the audience while having, as one viewer put it, to 'fight their way towards the cameras'.[20]

In order to maintain the energy levels of such scenes, rehearsals for the show were kept to a minimum. There would be a band-call on Friday morning but, apart from that, all the rehearsal took place on the Saturday. The various acts would be rehearsed during the day, followed by a preliminary session – 'more of a try-out than a run through' – at 3 p.m.[21] A final run through then took place at 4.30 p.m., leaving half an hour to spare before the actual show. This schedule became even more exhausting once the show began touring. The programme's normal home was Lime Grove, subsequently the Riverside studios, in London, but the programme also took to the road at an early stage, broadcasting a special, for example, from Glasgow in May 1957.

The most famous of the programme's outside broadcasts, however, was undoubtedly its trip to the 'birthplace' of British rock'n'roll, The Two I's Coffee Bar in Old Compton Street on 16 November. With cameras placed both upstairs and in the basement, performers, audience and crew cheerfully jostled for position. Owner Paul Lincoln dutifully defended rock'n'roll against its detractors, Terry Dene was seen in a clip from *The Golden Disc* and teenagers hand-jived happily. Meanwhile, an assortment of *Six-Five* regulars and Two I's residents belted out a succession of numbers, culminating in a version of 'Rockin' at the Two I's' by the unlikely combination of Two I's favourite Wee Willie Harris, the King Brothers and Mike and Bernie Winters. Even the Deputy Director, Cecil McGivern, was aroused. 'This edition,' he wrote the following Monday, 'was not only extraordinary but extraordinarily good. It was first class television as well as first class entertainment.'[22]

Ironically, this show was also destined to be one of Jack Good's last. Good and the BBC had never seemed entirely at ease with each other and it was possible that the arrival of a new co-producer, Dennis Main Wilson, in November (following the decision of Josephine Douglas to go freelance) had been the source of some friction. The immediate cause of Good's departure, however, appears to have been his decision to proceed with a *Six-Five Special* stage show against the wishes of the BBC, and, on 9 January 1958, the Corporation announced that it was not renewing Good's contract. Duncan Wood was brought in to replace him and share production duties with Main Wilson. Billy Cotton Jr joined them later.

The BBC's attitude towards Good's departure was surprisingly complacent. Only days after Good's dismissal, the Controller of Programmes, Kenneth Adam, announced that he had been concerned about the way in which the programme had been developing anyway, mentioning, in particular, its excessive reliance on rock'n'roll, and called for a review of the programme's policy.[23] Once this was completed, he felt happy that the change in producers had been made 'only just in time'.[24] Subsequent events, however, were to prove him badly wrong. Once Good had left, the show never regained its full momentum, despite (or perhaps, because of) a succession of changes in personnel and format. More importantly, Good himself was subsequently to join the opposition and it was his new show, *Oh Boy!*, which was finally to deal a death-blow to the programme he had once created.

Oh Boy! was made for ABC and began with a trial run in the Midlands in June 1958 (not long after The Crickets had enjoyed a three month run in the charts with the song 'Oh Boy'). It was nationally networked from 12 September and scheduled in direct competition with *Six-Five Special* at 6–6.30 p.m. The programme represented, in some regards, what Good had wanted all along. Apart from the occasional piece of comic knockabout courtesy of the show's two hosts, Tony Hall and Jimmy Henney, *Oh Boy!* discarded all of *Six-Five Special*'s variety acts and magazine features in favour of non-stop music. The programme was broadcast live each week from the Hackney Empire and, whereas *Six-Five Special* had tried to recreate a party atmosphere, *Oh Boy!* sought to generate the excitement of a live stage show. Its central tactic, in this regard, was speed. Billed in the *TV Times* as 'an explosion of beat music', the programme aimed to pack as many musical numbers into each show as possible (managing seventeen in twenty-six minutes in the very last one) and nothing was allowed to interrupt the flow.

This was particularly noticeable in the case of the presenters, who were allowed none of the limelight enjoyed by Pete Murray and Josephine Douglas in *Six-Five Special*. They generally appeared at the beginning and end of the show but were otherwise kept out of sight. Their introductions to the acts, if they existed at all, were simply heard. Instead, the cameras cut, without pause, from one act to the next, or a singer would just appear and take over the microphone almost before the previous song was completed. This rapid succession of numbers also left no time to dwell on the audience, who rarely appeared in front of the cameras as they had in *Six-Five Special*. A shot of a group in the balcony was used to accompany the opening titles, but after that, bar the very occasional view from the stage, the audience remained unseen. They were, however, heard. A constant barrage of applause and screaming carried on throughout the programme and did much to add to the overall sense of frenzy.

The music itself was provided by a mix of guests and resident performers. The residents were led by the show's musical director, Harry Robinson, and his band. Lord Rockingham's XI (whose constant appearances on the show helped them to a No. 1 hit with the novelty number, 'Hoots Mon'); The Vernons Girls, a song and dance troupe originally recruited from employees of the pools company; and The Dallas Boys (in fact, a five-piece from Leicester) also provided regular support. Although the show, like *Six-Five Special*, was obliged to make the odd concession to musical variety (the occasional ballad, comic number or song and dance routine), the emphasis was firmly on rock'n'roll. *Six-Five* veteran Marty Wilde was also a resident and many of the new acts with which the show became associated – Billy Fury, Dickey Pride, Vince Eager, Cuddly Dudley – were drawn, like Wilde, from the Larry Parnes stable of rock'n'rollers.

The show's greatest discovery, however, was undoubtedly Cliff Richard. He appeared on the very first show and within two weeks had entered the charts with 'Move It'. He joined the show as a regular and quickly moved to top billing in the *TV Times*, originally having come last. Good himself took a keen interest in the youngster and reputedly helped to groom him for stardom.[25] But, important as the show was in breaking individual acts, it was in its ensemble playing that it really excelled. The resident musicians not only performed their own numbers, but also played together and with most of the guests (the groups were the usual exception). Guests, moreover, were not merely provided with backing, but were also incorporated into productions involving other members of the cast. This was particularly true of the show's opening number, or medley, which would characteristically begin as a solo but end as a rousing ensemble.

The drama of such numbers was increased by an appropriately striking visual style. Although broadcast live, the programme aimed to do more than simulate the appearance of a live concert, and staged its numbers and conceived of its effects specifically in terms of the television cameras. The casual camerawork and general air of informality which had been a feature of *Six-Five Special* was thus dispensed with and replaced by a carefully choreographed and visually arresting use of cutting, light and composition in depth. The design of the stage itself was kept simple, with the band to the right, steps and rostra at the back and a central microphone at the front. It was usually only at the end of the big ensemble numbers, however, that the camera would pull back to reveal the whole set and most of the performers were shot in either close-ups or mid-shots.

A typical number would, therefore, begin with shots of a singer at the microphone before the rest of the performers were revealed on both sides of the rostra behind. This would be done either by cutting directly between different parts of the set or, more strikingly, by cutting to a new shot of the original singer (usually a slightly angled mid-shot) to enable the artists who were behind to be seen. The same effect could also be achieved by a movement of the camera or, more commonly, a change of lighting. Without any resort to cutting, singers could be dramatically brought into view through the introduction of light. They could then, just as readily, be plunged back into darkness or transformed into silhouettes. And while most of the numbers relied on a combination of quick cutting and lighting changes, the show could also dispense with both and present a whole song (usually a slow number) in one simple and unbroken close-up. It was a striking and visually accomplished achievement which the press was quick to acknowledge. 'The three-dimensional sets, clever lighting and fast, exciting atmosphere of *Oh Boy!*,' observed the *Daily Herald*, have 'confirmed Jack Good as ITV's most imaginative producer of "pop" shows.' The BBC, on the other hand, would 'have a nerve to show *Six-Five* again'.[26] [...]

NOTES

I am indebted to a number of people and institutions for their assistance in the preparation of this article. My thanks to Debbie Whittaker of the BBC Written Archives Centre, Caversham, Reading, for her help with written material and to Simon Radcliffe of the BBC for arranging screenings. Thanks also to the staff of the National Film Archive, London, and the Weintraub-Pathé Film Library, Elstree for their help with screenings. My thanks too to Noleen Kennedy for her typing. My thanks, in particular, to Pamela Gibson for her help and advice on the writing of this article.

1. Lord Hill of Luton, *Both sides of the Hill* (London, Heinemann, 1964), p. 170. The ban on Sunday broadcasting at this time was to continue until March 1958 when programmes of a religious nature were permitted to be broadcast. For a survey of the debates over television hours, see Bernard Sendall, *Independent television in Britain*, vol. I: *Origin and foundation, 1946–62* (London, Macmillan, 1982).
2. Anon., 'At the top of the list', *Radio Times*, 14 October 1955, p. 21.
3. *Off the Record*, which carried on until 1958, did begin to include some rock'n'rollers, although these were introduced with some disgruntlement by Payne. With respect to vocabulary, I am using the term 'popular music' to refer to the Tin Pan Alley tradition of 'light' music and the term 'pop music' to refer generally to the new styles and techniques of youth-orientated music which first began to emerge in the 1950s. In this respect, I am using 'rock'n'roll' in its specific sense (as a species of 'pop' music) rather than as a general category synonymous with 'rock'.
4. David Griffiths, 'Ker's no kitten – but he's real cool', *TV Times*, 14 June 1957, p. 27.
5. Griffiths, 'Ker's no kitten', p. 27.
6. For details, see Gordon Watkins (ed.), *Tonight* (London, British Film Institute, 1982).
7. *Birmingham Mail*, 18 February 1957.
8. Other titles considered included 'Hi There', 'Live It Up', 'Take It Easy' and 'Don't Look Now'. 'Six-Five Special' was preferred because of the popularity of allusions to trains in

'jazz-parlance'. Memo from Josephine Douglas to Assistant Head of Light Entertainment, Tom Sloan, 2 January 1957, BBC Written Archives Centre (WAC), File index number T12/360/3.

9. The importance of television's 'familial' viewer is discussed in more theoretical terms by John Ellis, *Visible fictions* (London, Routledge & Kegan Paul, 1982) and Jane Feuer, 'The concept of live television: ontology as ideology', in E.A. Kaplan (ed.), *Regarding television* (Los Angeles, American Film Institute/University Publications of America, 1983). Simon Frith's discussion of the importance of 'hearth and home' to radio light entertainment also suggests a parallel; see 'The pleasures of the hearth: the making of BBC light entertainment', in *Formations of pleasure* (London, Routledge & Kegan Paul, 1983).

10. *BBC Handbook* (London, British Broadcasting Corporation, 1959), p. 99.

11. *Radio Times*, 22 February 1957, p. 4.

12. Memo to Josephine Douglas and Jack Good, 18 March 1957, WAC T12/360/3.

13. Audience Research Report on *Six-Five Special*, 5 April 1957, WAC T12/360/6.

14. As no copy of this particular edition appears to have survived, this quote is taken from the script for the show held at the BBC Written Archives Centre. Despite the programme's reputation for apparent spontaneity, the show was rigid in its adherence to a script and it is unlikely that the broadcast show deviated significantly from the agreed script (Pete Murray's speech is, in fact, quoted as it appears in the script in the *Sunday Times* review of 17 February 1957). All subsequent quotes, from this edition only, also derive from the script.

15. The rise and fall of Terry Dene is eloquently recalled in Nik Cohn, *Awopbopaloobopalopbamboom: pop from the beginning* (London, Paladin, 1970).

16. *Punch*, 3 April 1957.

17. Unlike *Six-Five Special*, however, most of the performances on *Bandstand* were mimed. For the details of the programme, see Michael Shore (with Dick Clark), *The history of American Bandstand* (New York, Ballantine Books, 1985). This famous American show is not, of course, to be confused with the half-hour jazz programme, *Bandstand*, launched by ITV in September 1959.

18. According to Tony Palmer, Good was obliged to resort to subterfuge for the first show and had 'a set constructed for the show that looked harmless and was approved by management'. The set, however, was on wheels and, during rehearsals, 'the entire set was quickly moved around so that the audience for the show was in front of the cameras as Good had planned'. See *All you need is love: the story of popular music* (London, Futura, 1976), p. 215. Internal BBC memos, however, suggest that the BBC management were less distressed by the show than this story implies. The Head of Light Entertainment, Ronald Waldman, for example, wrote to Douglas and Good following the second programme and praised them for 'a good show'. His concern was less with the studio audience than the contrivance of the star spotlight interview, the over-exposure of Josephine Douglas and the rough and ready nature of some of the camera-work (memo, 25 February 1957, WAC T12/360/3). The Deputy Director of Television Broadcasting, Cecil McGivern, wrote, in turn, to Waldman about the seventh show, an 'exuberant programme' which he apparently enjoyed. Once again, he was unhappy about the camera-work but was mostly put out by Ian Carmichael's use of a 'chamber pot' in a comedy sketch (memo, 1 April 1957, WAC T12/360/7). The issue of the audience did arise later in the year when the Television House Manager complained about their 'generally rude and aggressive behaviour' (memo to Light Entertainment Organiser, Television, 25 September 1957, WAC T12/360/3). This complaint was referred to Good and Douglas, who were informed by the Assistant Head of Light Entertainment, Tom Sloan, that 'the actual nature of this programme' could not be regarded as an 'excuse for bad manners on the part of the audience' (memo, 25 September 1957, WAC T12/360/3).

19. Memo to Head of Light Entertainment, 7 February 1958, WAC T12/360/4.

20. Cited in BBC Audience Research Report on *Six-Five Special*, 1 January 1958, WAC T12/360/12.

21. Rowan Ayers, 'The studio was jumpin'', *Radio Times*, 5 April 1957.
22. Memo to Head of Light Entertainment, 18 November 1957, WAC T12/360/9.
23. Memo to Assistant Head of Light Entertainment, 13 January 1958, WAC T12/360/4.
24. Memo to Head of Light Entertainment, 7 February 1958, WAC T12/360/4.
25. George Melly, indeed, blames Good for turning Cliff into 'acceptable family entertainment' by removing his guitar and sideburns and suggesting a new repertoire of arm, leg and hip movements: see *Revolt into style: the pop arts* (New York, Anchor, 1971), p. 56 (orig. London, Penguin, 1970). This is undoubtedly overstated. Good did make changes to Cliff's image but, as his appearance on the final *Oh Boy!* indicates, these were not designed to make him appear wholesome so much as to add an air of insolent, if somewhat studied, sexuality. Indeed, according to Chris Welch, Cliff was attacked for 'obscenity' after appearing on the show in December. See 'Rock '58', *The history of rock, No. 11* (Orbis, 1982), p. 205.
26. Mike Nevard, *Daily Herald*, 15 September 1958.

7

Television, police and audience

Philip Schlesinger and Howard Tumber

From Schlesinger, P. and Tumber, H. 1993: Fighting the war against crime. *British Journal of Criminology* 33(1), 22–8, 30–1.

This extract is taken from an article by Philip Schlesinger and Howard Tumber examining the highly successful BBC series *Crimewatch UK*, which began transmission in 1984. Programmes in this series are based on the dramatic reconstruction of crimes, which then become the subject of appeals for information. In a way which has become indicative of a whole new tendency in television, the series thus has a strong 'entertainment' value at the same time as it appears to serve the public good in aiding the police. As the authors point out in a section before the one we extract here, the model for *Crimewatch UK* was in fact taken from the German channel ZDF, which had run a successful dramatized reality series, *Case XY . . . Unsolved*, since 1967.

In the principal extract we have chosen, the authors look first at the identity of the series, citing comments from a number of sources about the 'rules' by which police interests and television interests are combined. They then offer an analysis of the format and resourcing of the series, with its distinctive mix of dramatization, broadcaster presentation and police involvement (by way both of interview and direct address). The appeal for information is a central part of the programme idea, established visually in the banks of police-manned telephones on the studio set. It also provides continuity and development of the programme idea by leading to 'update' items (and, indeed, a separate update programme).

We have also included here the authors' general conclusions. As we have indicated above, these have a relevance which goes beyond an assessment of the specific material under analysis. 'Infotainment' formats uneasily bridge (and sometimes perhaps blur over) the gap between different public communication functions and models. In fact, as the authors suggest, *Crimewatch UK* also risks falling victim to a problem which has been distinctively that of British public service television: deference to official definitions.

As new formats appear – some of them modelled on US precedents, others developed from within national channels – the kind of sociology of aims and functions which Schlesinger and Tumber undertake here will become an important complement to critical analysis.

The emergence of *Crimewatch* in the mid-1980s dovetails neatly with the accentuated concern with 'law and order' politics that characterized Mrs Thatcher's governments and which has remained a prominent public preoccupation. Peter Chafer summed this up as follows. 'Ten or fifteen years ago I don't think it would have worked because ... then we were very concerned as a society about what it was we were doing to people to make them criminal ... In the last three or four years we've suddenly said to ourselves, "To hell with the criminal, what about the poor bloody victim?" ' The rise of law and order politics has brought the police into the forefront of public attention and, as we have demonstrated elsewhere, they have become increasingly sophisticated in their media strategies (Schlesinger *et al.*, 1991; Schlesinger and Tumber, 1992). It would be difficult to envisage the present level of police–broadcaster co-operation without such prior developments. Unlike such programmes as *Out of Court* and *Rough Justice*, *Crimewatch* is *constructed* on the basis of assumptions that unambiguously support the fight against crime. It poses no difficult questions about the effectiveness of the police nor about their methods in achieving results, although these have become major issues of public concern.

Within this overarching framework of identification with crime-fighting, police co-operation with *Crimewatch* is based upon a set of mutual understandings with the BBC. On the BBC's side, apart from deciding to steer clear of political crime, a number of other rules of the game have been established. Thus, the *Crimewatch* team is careful to stress its relative distance from the police. The programme's presenters observe that one problem 'has been to ensure that our professional relationship with the police does not become so embracing that it puts in jeopardy the independence of the BBC' (Ross and Cook, 1987, p. 156). Elaborating on this, Peter Grimsdale, successor producer to Peter Chafer, observed to us: 'We are television programme-makers who use the police and offer police opportunities to appeal for information on crimes they're investigating. At the end of the day we have editorial control, and that's that, really.'

Much hangs on how independent 'editorial control' is interpreted in practice, especially in reconstructing major crimes. In effect, there is an 'exchange' or bargain: an unusual measure of access to information on the part of the broadcasters is traded for publicity required by the police to help solve specific crimes (cf. Tunstall, 1971). According to the journal *Police Review*,

> concern about the use of dramatic reconstruction to jog the public's memory and at the same time 'entertain' the majority was allayed by the mutual formulation (by ACPO and *Crimewatch*) of two basic ground rules: first, that anything filmed would be embargoed and could not be used again unless the force involved gave its permission; and second, that the police must reveal all the known facts and their suspicions to the *Crimewatch* team – then the two parties make a mutual decision about what is to be shown to the public.
>
> (Diggins, 1986, p. 187)

In principle, therefore, the police have ultimate control over the filmed material screened, although, so far as we have been told, once the process of making a reconstruction has been initiated no embargo has ever been applied.

This arrangement implies very close collaboration between the programme team and the police in the making of reconstructions. Usually, a director, a researcher, and a production assistant are allocated to the story; then

> police officers now have to be persuaded to unlock all their secrets ... Detectives who have learned to mistrust the media with some vigour sometimes find this rather hard. It

is equally difficult for our journalists whose instinct is to publish anything that's fit to print, and more besides. So far each side has seen the sense in extending confidentiality and the mutual trust has never broken down.

(Ross and Cook, 1987, p. 32)

The broadcasters must attempt to safeguard themselves from being used by the police. Over and above the need to know as much as possible about a given case in order to make a credible reconstruction, their insistence on being privy to the details tests whether or not a public appeal is really genuine. As Peter Grimsdale observed:

> The thing is, we don't want to be seen to be fitting people up: it would call the whole programme into question then. And we also have to be careful because if the case came to court and the defence were to argue in such a way that their client had been tried by *Crimewatch* then we might find ourselves having to go off the air.

The rule of thumb, therefore, is that there should be no major leads or suspects.

PROGRAMME FORM

Crimewatch has a well-established formula. It runs for forty minutes; after the opening sequence, the two BBC presenters introduce the programme as giving the public a chance to do something about crime and then (in the style of a news programme) offer a menu of the main items to follow. Next comes the first main 'reconstruction' of a serious crime, followed by 'Incident Desk', a round-up of several less serious incidents by the two police presenters. This is followed by the second main reconstruction, which in turn precedes a brief feature on stolen property. Next comes 'Photocall', 'television's version of the wanted poster', presented by Ross and Cook, which makes use of videos shot by concealed cameras in banks and building societies and of still photographs. Finally, the third reconstruction is transmitted.

Each reconstruction is followed by an interview with the police officer leading the inquiry into the case in question. The public is given the relevant telephone numbers of the police forces concerned and as information comes into the studio this is relayed to the viewers. Behind the presenters sit police officers and BBC researchers manning a bank of telephones. *Crimewatch* is followed later in the evening by a ten-minute update, giving information about the public response; there is a further follow-up the morning after. The update is suffused by a sense of urgency as, at times, is the main programme itself.

Despite the varied programme menu, the 'reconstructions' occupy centre stage; they are the longest items by far, running for up to ten minutes each. The programme's 'founding father', Peter Chafer, has stressed that *Crimewatch* engages in 'documentary reconstruction' as opposed to 'drama-documentary': 'the word "drama" is considered to be rather a filthy word down in the *Crimewatch* office'. The directors were all initially recruited from within the documentary tradition, and it was only after the programme's format had become well established that Chafer 'allowed one or two guest people to come in who had done a bit of drama'. A firm line is therefore drawn between 'fact' and 'fiction'. In Peter Chafer's words: '*Crimewatch* is about a . . . rather unpleasant reality, and therefore I do everything I can to remind people that this is not cops and robbers *à la Dempsey and Makepeace, Cagney and Lacey, The Bill* [or] *The Sweeney*.'

This last remark underlines the realist ideology of documentary production, central to which is the notion of adequately capturing processes and occurrences in the real world. *Crimewatch* self-consciously fits into a realist model. Where documentary *reconstruction* is involved, the ability to convince an audience needs to be rooted in the detailed authentication of the events portrayed. Normal journalistic practice involves the production of accounts based upon the use of various forms of source material. *Crimewatch's* programme-makers have at their disposal a single, authoritative source, namely the police, who have themselves engaged in a prior process of reconstruction based on the taking of testimony from witnesses and the use of forensic evidence. *Crimewatch* makes televisual sense of accounts available to the police. In the realist documentary framework it is precisely the establishing of correct detail that counts in making a reconstruction, as is clear from the following account:

> the team ploughs through pages of detailed statements, meets witnesses, where necessary gathers photographs for casting actors, and tracks down props ... In *Crimewatch* we always use the originals when they are available from the scene of crime, but where something is missing we will go to great trouble to replicate it.
>
> (Ross and Cook, 1987, p. 32)

Not only does *Crimewatch* draw upon police research and by reconstructing it turn it into popular television, it has also developed other visual techniques as a means of engaging the audience. The computing skills of producer Ritchie Cogan have been used in developing simplified 'micromaps' to display movements by criminals and their vehicles in the area of a crime. His 'other innovation was more spectacular' and, it is proudly claimed, 'will one day be regarded as a standard tool of criminal investigation' (Ross and Cook, 1987, p. 88). Following the existing police technique of constructing photofits, Cogan developed the 'videofit', which used a powerful graphics computer program to produce a colour image of a suspect's face without the distracting jigsaw lines. Television's visual power has thereby been harnessed both to the needs of policing and to the journalistic value of offering verisimilitude to the audience.

The videofits are often used in the round-up 'Photocall'. As Ross and Cook (1987, p. 111) point out, these hi-tech reconstructive techniques are 'television's answer to the wanted poster. We discovered there was a rich fund of photographs of suspects, of escaped prisoners and of criminals caught in the act by security cameras. They made good television and television made good use of them.' The wanted poster is a staple both of the Western and of the gangster movie and derives from a tradition of representing criminality that precedes photography. Steve Chibnall (1980) has noted that the entire history of such representations, one in which fact and fiction substantially overlap, betrays a tension between the commercial imperative to entertain and the expectation that responsible crime news will act as a vehicle of social control.

Crimewatch is therefore part of a long journalistic tradition in which pictorial forms of representation have always been an audience-building technique. The visual representation of the criminal remains central to news reporting, with the mugshot arguably becoming 'a universal mythic sign – the face of all the "hard men" in history, the portrait of Everyman as a "dangerous wanted criminal"' (Hall, 1972, p. 85). It is within these parameters that *Crimewatch's* visualization of deviance should be understood.

SELECTION CRITERIA AND INVESTMENT OF RESOURCES

Crimewatch actively seeks out stories appropriate to its popular audience-holding goal, with researchers routinely calling each police force about 'major unsolved crimes'. In addition, press reports in both the national and the local press are used to select cases to be followed up. 'Moreover,' as the programme presenters observe, 'any crime that has hit the headlines is followed up, for though the motive may not be entirely virtuous, *we believe it is in the programme's interests to be seen at the centre of the crime detection business*' (Ross and Cook, 1987, p. 29, emphasis added). In other words, *Crimewatch* capitalizes on existing media attention as part of its audience-building strategy.

One major televisual criterion at work in *Crimewatch* is variety: 'We need a spread of different types of cases, not just murder, in different places, not just Liverpool or London, and we need different types of action, not just high-speed chases through city streets. Some cases are too trivial to contemplate, others have only a local interest or point of appeal' (Ross and Cook, 1987, p. 29). The reference to 'not just murder' is noteworthy, given the programme's tendency to select instances of murder, armed robbery with violence, and sexual crime as the main stories for reconstruction. The *Crimewatch* book, accordingly, selects the following as tales to be recounted in detail: a violent robbery in Essex, a murder in a Scottish village, a violent pub raid in Merseyside, a double murder in Wales, an armed building society robber's activities in Essex, the murder of two young boys in Essex, a series of antiques robberies, and the murder of a shopkeeper in Bristol. These crimes against the person and against property are typical of the popular news story.

A criterion of geographical spread also comes into play. Since *Crimewatch* prides itself on its *national* appeal, there is an attempt to find stories that represent different parts of the country. Nevertheless, there are practical limits on the national spread since Northern Ireland presents difficulties because of problems in disentangling the political from the criminal. However, a 'straight murder' in the Province can be covered, as in the Inge Hauser case broadcast in June 1988, which concerned a young West German student travelling throughout Britain who ended up murdered in Northern Ireland. Scotland has also been complicated to cover for the *Crimewatch* team because of the stringent application of the Lord Advocate's rules on reporting cases under investigation. Potential stories have usually been offered to the programme only when the crimes have been almost beyond solution.

The problems of reconstructing 'complex fraud' also affect what is selected. 'White-collar crime' is generally judged to have less visual appeal than violent crime (although *Crimewatch* has, for instance, successfully reconstructed the passing of phoney bank drafts). Action stories are regarded as more attractive for a programme conceived as popular television. Where *Crimewatch* holds itself apart from downmarket tabloid journalism is in the producer's concern to try to avoid prurient interest in sexual detail. There is also concern with how violence should be represented.

Finally, a further criterion involves the assessment of risk in committing resources, in particular whether the programme is going to strike a chord with the audience by running a particular reconstruction. A rule of thumb for judging impact is the number of telephone calls received from members of the public as a result of transmission.

MOBILIZING THE AUDIENCE

Crimewatch's high-audience formula derives from the selection criteria applied by the production team. Peter Grimsdale put it thus:

> *Crimewatch* has to be a piece of television that caters for people who may not have anything to offer just in order to attract that big audience. *So it has to be a piece of television in its own right which will engage the viewer* – I prefer to use that word rather than 'entertain' – and have pace, and have a sense of drama about it. (emphasis added)

For the programme to have its mobilizing effect on the casual viewer, *who may just turn out to know something relevant to a case*, it has to be compelling. Peter Grimsdale went on to describe how the programme team tries to produce the requisite effects:

> First and foremost, it's a television programme just like *Out of Court*, or *That's Life*, or *Tomorrow's World*, or *The Money Programme* ... therefore it needs to have a mixture and balance of items ... This month we did the sexual assault and murder of a woman in Tunbridge Wells ... and then we did a reconstruction-stroke-report on the investigation into the so-called Notting Hill Rapist. Now, you could say that perhaps there were similarities there ... we set out to separate them both in terms of where they were in the programme and how they were treated, so that they were actually quite different items ... What [the police] wanted to do was to try and encourage ... people to come forward. We said 'OK, in that case this is how we think you should do it.' For example, it was our choice to have the woman detective doing the [studio] interview because it just seemed apparent to us as programme-makers that if you're going to appeal to women to come forward who have felt uncomfortable about coming forward, that if the police claim that they can offer a sensitive interview in agreeable surroundings, then we should make something of that.

This tells how *Crimewatch* is constructed in televisual terms and how the medium might best be used for the purpose of evoking a public response. The above account also shows that considerable thought goes into projecting the most positive image possible of the police in the highly sensitive area of sexual crime. As noted earlier, providing such a service for the police has been part of a package deal that maintains the programme's singular credibility with them.

The production team's reluctance to make the unqualified statement that *Crimewatch* offers a form of entertainment is significant: they stress their contribution to the public good of helping to solve crimes, and are highly sensitive to the accusation made by some critics that they are simply using crime as an audience-pulling vehicle. The charge that gratuitous violence is shown, that the programme might glamorize crime, or that there might be alleged 'copy-cat' effects as a result of the reconstructions produced a concerned rebuttal in the *Crimewatch* book: 'any reporting of crime (or of open courts and open justice) shoulders all these dangers. There is no simple choice between taking and avoiding risks like these. In any case *Crimewatch* would add only a tiny fraction to the general outpouring on crime' (Ross and Cook, 1987, p. 155). There is a related concern to reassure the public at the end of each programme that fear of crime is greatly exaggerated: this is condensed in Nick Ross's customary signing-off: 'Don't have nightmares, do sleep well!' There is some evidence that such reassurances may misfire for sections of the audience, notably among women.

To hold the audience serves two sets of *organizational* aims – those of the police and those of the broadcasters – as is clear from Peter Chafer's account:

> Of course we need results, but for quite different reasons to policemen. Policemen want results because they know they're going to have to explain their clear-up rate or lack of it. We don't. But ... it would be pretty insufferable if we showed chapter and verse and produced no results, because critics could quite legitimately say that we were being merely exploitative for fun or for entertainment.

Crimewatch's own 'clear-up' rate therefore becomes a central justification for the choice of a popular television form and functions defensively to rebut potential or actual criticism (cf. the *Crimewatch UK Results* in Ross and Cook, 1987, p. 159). The broadcasters' concerns about being accused of producing an *entertaining* form of factual television do not appear to be shared by the police, who may see the programme as a straightforward entertainment vehicle that happens to be performing a useful function for them, both in helping to solve outstanding cases and in generally portraying a positive image of the service. For example, Detective Superintendent Roy Payne, investigating a murder reconstructed by *Crimewatch*, observed of the programme: 'If it wasn't entertainment and it wasn't watchable they just wouldn't run it. Or if they did run it, they'd run it at some obscure time in the middle of the afternoon when nobody's watching ... I think the public service element of it would take very, very much a back seat.' Thus, from a police perspective the facts that the programme is highly selective and that it is transmitted during peak viewing hours are seen as key ingredients to its success. So is the relative infrequency of the transmissions, currently running at ten programmes a season.

Concern about how the public might view the role of the police in the programme is typified by remarks made to us by Superintendent David Hatcher, who has been presenting 'Incident Desk' from the start:

> Editorial control should be retained – I'd argue wholeheartedly – by the BBC, not as happens in some other countries where the police try and dictate too much what is going to happen on the programme. I think then it ceases to be the kind of television that people want. I hesitate to use the word 'entertainment', but that, in essence, is what people are looking for, and you've got to be a realist: without the viewer you get no phone calls, without phone calls you don't get results, without results why would we want to become involved?

Superintendent Hatcher was selected for his presenter role after competitive auditions involving several forces. His advantage lay in past experience as a press officer in the Kent police, in which role he had made video appeals and half-hour-long monthly programmes. His original co-presenter, WPC Helen Phelps, was trained within this public relations framework. Given Superintendent Hatcher's experience, his views on editorial control offer an appreciation of the perspectives both of television production and of policing. So far as the police were concerned, he had noticed that some officers 'meet the programme staff no doubt with suspicion and potential hostility' but that 'somehow it's built a credibility with police officers that other programmes haven't done, shown by the fact that officers want to get their cases on'. It was Hatcher's acceptance of broadcasters' sensibilities that made him put 'entertainment' in quotation marks. Moreover, apart from solving crimes, the less immediate goal of improving the police's image is also a major concern. David Hatcher's conception of his role is this: 'I wanted it to be somebody who could represent a friendly image of the force and represent an ... open-minded image of a police officer.' This ties in with the police's increasingly sophisticated awareness of the need to use television for their own ends. Their concern about the public's frequent lack of response to appeals for information has also been thoroughly internalized by the production team (see Ross and Cook, 1987, p. 115).

The desire to mobilize the audience, hold it, and achieve quantifiable results, therefore, fundamentally informs the construction of the programme. The televisual imperative leads to frequent changes of pace coupled with the tension that comes from 'live' production, a variety of content in order to provide visual interest, and a stress upon presenter credibility.

[. . .] *Crimewatch* has a privileged relation with its source of information, the police, who have complete control over access to evidence and a determining voice over the possible uses to which this might be put. In recent years, the relations between sources of information and news media have become a growing focus of research, particularly for those taking what Richard Ericson (1991) has termed an 'institutional approach'. Such research has concerned itself with the strategies pursued by both sources and media in struggles to control the interpretation of meaning (cf. Ericson *et al.*, 1989; Schlesinger, 1990; Tiffen, 1989). In the present case, it is clear that the police as source broadly define the terms of reference within which *Crimewatch* may operate. Thus, although the production team exercise editorial judgement over how the cases that they reconstruct are to be presented in televisual terms, their decisions take place within a well-defined framework. The producers also exercise judgement as to which cases they wish to pursue. But it is within these limited professional spheres that 'editorial control' functions. The BBC team has a symbiotic relation of exchange with the various police forces. Each needs the other. But clearly, although the police would continue to pursue criminals without television, without the active co-operation of the police no programme such as *Crimewatch* could exist. In terms of a power relation, it is plain that control over access is decisive, and that is where power ultimately lies.

The benefits of this bargain for the BBC lie in the winning formula of socially useful popular television, uncriticized by the police and law and order lobbies, although occasionally reservations on grounds of good taste and possible adverse effects are expressed by some television critics and academic researchers. As for the police, apart from undoubtedly achieving some results (though obviously on a minuscule scale in terms of the total incidence of crime), the main benefit, at a time of mounting public concern about crime, lies in the widely diffused sense that something is being done about the problem. *Crimewatch* offers a generally useful public relations context in which the police are portrayed in an unambiguously positive and sympathetic light.

Crimewatch is close to popular journalism in terms of its selection of types of crime to handle, particularly its emphasis on murder, sexual crime, and robbery with violence, and the general absence of fraud and corporate crime (Schlesinger *et al.*, 1991). Given that the institution of television can be conceived of as distributing a range of spaces within which various forms of creative action may take place (cf. Schlesinger *et al.*, 1983, chs 3, 4), *Crimewatch*'s location on the main BBC channel locks it into high audience-seeking goals, particularly so given its prime-time location after the *Nine O'Clock News*. *Crimewatch* has successfully avoided current controversies over the dramatic 'reconstruction' of real events because its form has posed no threat to the law enforcement and criminal justice establishments. Aside from the Grade report [1989 Home Office report of working group chaired by Michael Grade,

Channel 4 Chief Executive], official concern about the role of media in increasing public fear of crime remains relatively low-key.

What will become of this form of 'responsible' tabloid journalism as market conditions change significantly? Some believe that it might follow the explicitly violent and graphic model of the Fox network's *America's Most Wanted* (cf. Hebert, 1988; Minogue, 1990). Although extrapolation from the very different system and circumstances of the USA is not to be undertaken without caution, the impact of the Broadcasting Act 1990 in changing the parameters of competition in British television is beginning to become clearer, with a general shift downmarket now under way. It is increasingly evident that crime pays in audience terms, in attracting large numbers for both fictional and factual programming. At the time of writing, *Crimewatch*, *Crimestoppers*, and *Crime Monthly* have been joined by *Crime Limited*, *Cops*, and *Michael Winner's True Crimes*, all dramatizing real-life incidents from robbery to rape, and increasingly important as popular television. With traditional public service goals in broadcasting being increasingly marginalized, the sensationalist temptation may prove impossible to resist.

REFERENCES

CHIBNALL, S. 1980: Chronicles of the gallows: the social history of crime reporting. In Christian, H. (ed.), *The sociology of journalism and the press*. Sociological Review Monograph 29. Keele: University of Keele, 179–217.

DIGGINS, T. 1986: The right combination. *Police Review* 24, January, 186–7.

ERICSON, R.V. 1991: Mass media, crime, law and justice: an institutional approach. *British Journal of Criminology* 31, 219–49.

ERICSON, R.V., BARANEK, P.M. and CHAN, J.B.L. 1989: *Negotiating control: a study of news sources*. Toronto: University of Toronto Press.

HALL, S. 1972. The determinants of news photographs. *Working Papers in Cultural Studies* 3, 53–87.

HEBERT, H. 1988: The nightmare of nark's corner. *Guardian*, 2 June.

MINOGUE, T. 1990: Putting real crime on prime time. *Guardian*, 3 Sept.

ROSS, N. and COOK, S. 1987: *Crimewatch UK*. London: Hodder & Stoughton.

SCHLESINGER, P. 1990: 'Rethinking the sociology of journalism: source strategies and the limits of media-centrism. In Ferguson, M. (ed.), *Public communication: the new imperatives. Future directions for media research*. London and Newbury Park: Sage, 61–83.

SCHLESINGER, P., MURDOCK, G. and ELLIOTT, P. 1983. *Televising 'terrorism': political violence in popular culture*. London: Comedia.

SCHLESINGER, P. and TUMBER, H. 1992. Crime and criminal justice in the media. In Downes, D. (ed.), *Unravelling criminal justice: nine British studies*. London: Macmillan.

SCHLESINGER, P., TUMBER, H. and MURDOCK, G. 1991: The media politics of crime and criminal justice. *British Journal of Sociology* 44, 397–420.

TIFFEN, R. 1989: *News and Power*. Sydney: Allen & Unwin.

TUNSTALL, J. 1971: *Journalists at work: specialist correspondents, their news organisations, news sources, and competitor-colleagues*. London: Constable.

ACKNOWLEDGEMENT

The authors of this article gratefully acknowledge the support of the Economic and Social Research Council (UK). They also wish to thank all those at *Crimewatch* who gave their time and help, in particular Peter Chafer and Peter Grimsdale. Finally, the assistance of the BBC and IBA broadcasting research departments in making available relevant reports is also appreciated.

8

MTV

Andrew Goodwin

From Goodwin, A. 1993: *Dancing in the distraction factory*. London: Routledge, 132–42, 149–55

Among the most significant developments in television entertainment has been the huge increase in programmes and then in channels built around popular music. The rise of the 'pop video' as a means of promotion and then as a new genre of visual expression, borrowing vigorously from other forms but subsequently influencing these, has been important here. The styles associated with pop video have been taken up and adapted variously by, for instance, sports coverage, documentaries, special-interest magazine programmes and advertising.

In this extract from his book, Andrew Goodwin looks at MTV, the world's first 24-hour all-music television channel and a huge international success. He puts the launch of the station in 1981 in the context of the music business and television at the time and identifies the phases of its development and the shifts in its musical emphases and overall styling. The 'look' of MTV is clearly dependent to a large extent on the range and kind of the clips it shows and Goodwin examines when and why stylistic changes occurred here. The local success of the clips and the music is organized into channel identity by the speech of the VJs (video jockeys). These are the personality 'anchors' of MTV, embedding its varied offerings in an ongoing programme address. In assessing the role they play, Goodwin draws on the developing area of enquiry into television talk.

Our extract also includes the opening of the final section of Goodwin's chapter, in which he assesses directly the critical discourse about 'post-modernism' which has surrounded the channel. Raising questions about the specific aesthetic combination which MTV represents and about how the channel 'works' communicatively, Goodwin should prove helpful in looking at the very wide range of music–image combinations in current television.

> Turn on the radio or the TV – you don't see anything that inspires you or makes you think about anything.
>
> (Sinead O'Connor[1])

Unlike the journalistic accounts of MTV, academic writing has usually described MTV as though it were an unchanging form, significant only for its differences from network television. The development of its schedule (which has been considerable indeed) has been almost universally neglected by media scholars. This is thoroughly unmaterialist, because changes in the MTV text result from institutional factors such as shifting personnel and changes in ownership patterns, each of which is intimately connected to the economic and social forces at work in the broadcasting, advertising, and music industries.

Furthermore, to miss the development of MTV's schedule is to miss a central Romantic imperative, for MTV, like pop music, needs to display its creativity, its ability to change, its refusal to stop moving. It is not just that MTV must be seen as hip and irreverent, but that it must seem always to be hip and irreverent in *new* ways. Former MTV president Robert Pittman has summed up the problem:

> One of the interesting things is that for all the 'issues' that have been raised about MTV, no one has ever touched on the real issue of MTV, which is: How do you keep the creativity going? How do you convince the creative people to give up a great idea and move on to a new idea? If there is one thing we worry about day after day, it is that issue.
> (quoted in Hilburn, 1986)

The imperative is not just to change, but to be seen to keep changing. It is an ideology drawn directly from rock culture that should encourage us to consider the historical development of MTV.

It is possible to identify three stages in MTV's history, each relating to its increasingly successful efforts to ally itself simultaneously with the major record companies and national advertisers. In the first phase (roughly 1981–1983), the need for visually evocative clips led to an emphasis on promotional videos made in Britain. The dominant pop form at that time was the 'New Pop' – music whose stress on style and artifice perfectly suited marketing through video, and whose production practices perfectly suited the promotional techniques of music video. As a consequence, MTV in this period was identified heavily with the so-called second British Invasion of synth-pop acts (such as Duran Duran, ABC, the Thompson Twins, Culture Club, Thomas Dolby, and the Human League).[2] Although more conventional forms of AOR (album-oriented rock) were in fact dominant in the playlist at this time,[3] it was the distinctive look of the New Pop that gave MTV its 'cutting edge' kudos and established its visuals as nonnarrative, or antirealist, in the eyes of many cultural critics.

Both AOR music and the New Pop were dominated by white musicians. During its first seventeen months MTV was accused, time and time again, of racism in its programming policy (see, for instance, Levy, 1983). Stories abound of its exclusionary attitude to black music,[4] but the explanation was quite logical, however unfortunate. MTV followed the music industry in defining 'rock' in essentially racist terms, as a form of music that excluded blacks. It based its playlist on the 'narrowcasting' principle of American radio that viewed rock and 'urban contemporary' (i.e. dance music, often produced by black artists) as incompatible. Consequently, blacks were largely excluded from its screens (with the exception of black VJ J.J. Jackson) on grounds of music policy. MTV denied racism, sincerely perhaps, but it nonetheless followed the rules of the rock business – which were the consequence of a long history of racism.[5]

In its early years MTV was concerned to mark itself out from conventional television. It needed to establish itself as a unique, new cultural service. In September 1981 Robert Pittman, then vice president of programming, put it like this:

We're now seeing the TV become a component of the stereo system. It's ridiculous to think that you have two forms of entertainment – your stereo and your TV – which have nothing to do with one another. What we're doing is marrying those two forms so that they work together in unison. We're the first channel on cable that pioneers this . . . I think that what we've been doing up to now in cable has been dealing with forms that have already had some success on TV. MTV is the first attempt to make TV a new form, other than video games and data channels. We're talking about creating a new form using existing technologies.

(quoted in *Videography*, September 1981)

MTV's only discrete programs at this time were 'concert specials' and other occasional special programming (such as interviews and music-related movies). MTV was, as Frith (1988a, 1988b) has noted, a form of visual radio, using the format of continuous flow associated with all-music radio stations. As Blaine Allan (1990) notes:

In music television, videos are analogously linked to the unfolding of programming; their beginnings often remain imprecise and they frequently do not quite end. As disc jockeys cross-fade music with similar beats to make a sound transition as nearly seamless as possible, so broadcasters use visual and sound techniques to bridge the end of one video into the start of the next.

(p. 6)

This initial phase represents the peak of the postmodern claim on MTV, for two reasons. First, it is the period when the MTV schedule most closely dovetailed with the arguments advanced by academics. There were only a few discrete programs during this phase of MTV history, and the relatively small number of video clips available led to a high degree of repetition. For that reason, incidentally, MTV was also postmodern in another sense, because the mixing up of clips in continuous 'flow' blurred the categories of art-rock and pop, thus contributing toward a conflation of popular and high-cultural discourses (see Goodwin, 1991).

Second, the video clips themselves, generated in large part by the British music industry, tended toward the abandonment of narrative, and the New Pop groups of this era eschewed the bland realism of performance videos (partly because many of them did not perform, in any traditional sense). Typical of the genre are clips such as ABC's POISON ARROW and THE LOOK OF LOVE, Duran Duran's GIRLS ON FILM, RIO, and HUNGRY LIKE THE WOLF, Visage's FADE TO GREY and THE MIND OF A TOY, Ultravox's VIENNA, the Human League's DON'T YOU WANT ME, and the very first MTV clip – Buggles' VIDEO KILLED THE RADIO STAR. Other key clips by older British acts who nonetheless played with nonnarrative form include David Bowie's ASHES TO ASHES, XTC's MAKING PLANS FOR NIGEL, Peter Gabriel's SHOCK THE MONKEY, and Elvis Costello's ACCIDENTS WILL HAPPEN. Post-1982 clips in a similar New Pop/nonrealist vein are Thomas Dolby's SHE BLINDED ME WITH SCIENCE, Culture Club's KARMA CHAMELEON, Cabaret Voltaire's SENSORIA, and Eurythmics' SWEET DREAMS (ARE MADE OF THIS) and LOVE IS A STRANGER.[6]

However, these points have to be qualified with three observations. In the first place, it needs to be said that even in this period, there were separate program slots (interview-based programming and concert specials) that demanded some acknowledgment – something that most scholars failed to provide. Second, while the visual aspect of the early videos was often nonnarrative and nonrealist, a full account of these texts involves a discussion of the lyrics and music. While narrative and realism might yet appear to be absent at these levels, there are certainly extraordinary degrees of repetition and stability at the aural level. No one has argued that these videos are as subversive aurally as they are visually. (Instead, it is either asserted or implied that the visual is dominant.) Furthermore, while the impact of British-based New Pop videos is important, MTV even in this innovative period devoted more airtime to the firmly established format of AOR, whose videos were often extremely conventional in being either minimal realist narratives or performance clips.

Third, it must be noted that this initial phase of MTV, which forms the basis of much scholarly writing about music television, was the least significant historically. MTV's impact on the audience and the industry during its opening seventeen months was negligible, and – as Denisoff (1988) reports – many MTV insiders see January 1983 as the true beginning of the new service, partly because this is the point when it became available in the crucial media gatekeeper markets of Manhattan and Los Angeles.

Following this 'second launch,' the next phase of MTV (1983–1985) saw a shift in both music and programming policy that severely undermines postmodern arguments. The New Pop had gone out of fashion and, in any case, as MTV expanded from the main urban centers of the United States on the coasts into midwestern cities and towns, it needed to reach out with music that appealed to the rockist tastes of its new demographics. Furthermore, the network was no longer dependent on a relatively small number of clips originating in Europe. These factors colluded to generate MTV's embrace of heavy metal music.

In this phase MTV programmed heavy metal with a vengeance, and in doing so keyed into one of the evergreen forms of American popular culture. This was a make-or-break phase for MTV, in which it fought off network and cable competitors (including Ted Turner's Cable Music Channel), an antitrust suit from the Discovery Music Network, and criticism from both liberals (charging sexism and racism) and conservatives (the National Coalition on Television Violence).[7] Most important, MTV counterattacked its rivals economically by signing exclusivity deals with six major record companies (Viera, 1987). Programming policy during this period saw the beginnings of a shift away from continuous 'flow' and toward the use of discrete program slots (such as *The Basement Tapes* and *MTV Countdown*, which programmed tapes from new, unsigned acts and the Top 20 clips, respectively).

The most significant developments here, for cultural studies theorists, are the increasing use of discrete program slots and the ascendancy of the 'performance' clip. The latter was a direct result of the need for heavy metal acts to establish an 'authentic' (i.e. documentary rather than fictional) set of images and to display musical competence. Thus, 'on the road' pseudodocumentaries and the use of close-ups to emphasize musical virtuosity became the main staples of the promotional clips. Unlike the New Pop artists, metal acts had no interest in playing with artifice or in displaying their ironic modernism. Between the edits of fingers buzzing up and down fret boards, denim-clad musicians getting on and off tour buses, and the fans sweating and swaying in the stadiums of North America, antinarratives and antirealism quickly faded into MTV history.

In August 1985, the Warner-Amex consortium, which created MTV, sold off its controlling interest in MTV Networks (MTVN) to Viacom International. This development is absolutely central for any materialist engagement with the MTV text. As Denisoff (1988) reports, chief executive Robert Pittman had attempted a leveraged buy-out of MTVN along with some colleagues, and when this effort lost out to Viacom, Pittman's ascendancy at MTV was bound to end. With it went two of MTV's conceptual building blocks: narrowcasting and flow.

MTV's third phase (since 1986) thus represents a widening musical scope and an accelerated movement toward a more traditional televisual schedule. In February 1985 MTV had announced a cutback in commitment to heavy metal clips, but this led to a period of falling ratings and crisis at the network, as MTV was viewed by insiders and critics alike as bland and outdated. For a service that was dependent on viewer perception that it was on the 'cutting edge' of pop culture, this was potentially disastrous. The ratings share fell from a peak of 1.2 in the fourth quarter of 1983 (during the screening of *The Making of Michael Jackson's 'Thriller'*) to a 0.6 share in that same period of 1985 (Dannen, 1987).[8]

The third phase was born out of this crisis; it involved a return to heavy metal (which became especially marked in 1987), the shift of some middle-of-the-road artists to VH-1 (a twenty-four-hour music video station aimed at twenty-five to fifty-four-year-olds launched by MTV Networks in January 1985), the departure of chief executive Robert Pittman in August 1986, and two trends associated with his absence: the decline of narrowcasting and the development of more discrete program slots, many of them abandoning the staple diet of promotional clips.

While heavy metal acts are still prevalent, MTV now screens a wider variety of rock and pop music than ever before. The question of racism has been resolved by two developments: the emergence of rap crossover music that combines black and white musical forms (the Beastie Boys, Run-DMC/Aerosmith's WALK THIS WAY, Public Enemy/Anthrax's BRING THA NOISE, Fat Boys/Beach Boys' WIPE OUT)[9] and the success of black heavy metal act Living Colour, who were featured heavily throughout 1989. (J.J. Jackson left MTV in 1986, but black Briton Julie Brown has been appearing as a VJ since then, coming to MTV from Europe's Music Box network.) Along with heavy metal, rap music was the success story in American music in the 1980s, and was afforded its own show on MTV – *Yo! MTV Raps*. Other kinds of music were also given distinct slots (*Club MTV*, *Headbanger's Ball*, and *120 Minutes*, programming dance music, hard rock, and 'alternative' music, respectively). MTV's new traditionalism was displayed in its use of broadcast television formats, such as its Beatles cartoons (first aired on the networks) and *The Tube* (which came from Tyne-Tees Television in Britain). And MTV increasingly came to rely on nonmusic programming (comedy, a game show, a phone-in show, a movie news/review magazine, interview programming), some of it derived directly from broadcast television (*Monty Python's Flying Circus*, *The Young Ones*).[10] A key development was the success of its reruns of *The Monkees*, first begun in February 1986.

The post-Pittman sea change was very successful for MTV – which is one reason (among many) that it is a mistake to conceptualize Robert Pittman as MTV's 'author'. Ratings began to pick up in mid-1986, and by the third quarter of 1988 Viacom was reporting a 44 percent gain in earnings from MTV Networks (as reported in *Billboard*, November 19, 1988), and its Nielsen ratings made it the second-highest-rated basic cable service in the United States.

By 1989 the progress was less dramatic, but MTV Networks was nonetheless in an extraordinary period of expansion. In the summer of 1987 it had launched MTV Europe (in association with British Telecom and Robert Maxwell's Mirror Group Newspapers – the latter partner subsequently dropped out) and was syndicating

MTV packages to broadcasting systems in Japan, Mexico, and Australia. It had established an MTV Record Club, selling music, videos, and merchandising items such as T-shirts. MTVN became extensively involved in concert sponsorship and scored a coup in 1989 when it contributed to the sponsorship of the long-awaited 1989–1990 Rolling Stones tour of North America. In September 1989 an MTV comedienne (star of *Just Say Julie!* and also, confusingly, named Julie Brown) debuted on network television with a CBS pilot program titled *Julie Brown: The Show* (she also starred in and co-scripted the Julien Temple movie *Earth Girls Are Easy*). That same year, a weekly version of the MTV game show *Remote Control* went into national syndication in the United States.

In its first decade MTV has thus moved from an almost exclusive focus upon the promotion of specific areas of pop music (New Pop, heavy metal) to a role as an all-encompassing mediator of rock culture – a televisual *Rolling Stone* (or *Q* magazine) that seeks to keep its viewers up to date with all current forms of music, with developments in popular culture generally (TV, cinema, sports, celebrity news), and occasional 'hard news' stories (abortion, the environment, political news). The network has used its involvement in concert sponsorship to gain exclusive rights to announce tour dates and screen brief television premieres of live 'in concert' footage. MTV News is reminding its viewers of the costs of *not* watching when it concludes with the portentous voice-over: 'MTV News – You hear it first.'

These developments render highly problematic statements such as this: 'Important tools of sense making like sequence and priority are constantly rejected on MTV ... MTV has no boundaries ... It delivers random, uniform flow at all times' (Tetzlaff, 1986, p. 82). This was not true when that analysis was written, since MTV already had a number of programs organized thematically and sequentially. Since then, the growth of genre-based slots and new features such as 'Rock Blocks' (four clips from one artist) have further eroded the credibility of such pronouncements. Furthermore, the use of these slots tends to compartmentalize the 'popular' (*Club MTV, MTV Top 20 Videos*) from rock's 'high-cultural' forms (*120 Minutes, Post Modern MTV*), thus preserving a distinction that music television was supposed to destroy. These trends are important in terms of both the *structure* of MTV's schedule and the *content* of the programming. It is to those questions that I now turn, beginning with some remarks on the role of the VJs who guide us through the MTV schedule and the sets and locations they inhabit.

TALK, TALK, TALK

One reason film theory remains inappropriate for the analysis of music television lies not in the specific musical properties of the videos, but in the more general importance of *sound* in *television*. The detailed account of broadcast television forms presented by John Ellis (1982) is instructive here:

> The broadcast images depend upon sound to a rather greater degree than cinema's images ... In psychoanalytic terms, when compared to cinema, TV demonstrates a displacement from the invocatory drive of scopophilia (looking) to the closest related of the invocatory drives, that of hearing.
>
> (pp. 112, 137)

The explanation for this lies in the conditions of exhibition that govern television viewing, where the set is left on for long periods of time while it is not necessarily being looked at. In an important essay on television sound, Rick Altman (1987) directs our attention to the central importance of this aspect in the consumption of television and develops Raymond Williams's concept of 'flow'. Altman suggests that the sound portion of the television text is designed primarily to interrupt the 'household flow' of everyday life and push our attention toward the television screen. This aspect of MTV remains neglected after nearly a decade on the air. Clearly, it would require an engagement with the music itself; here I am concerned with the other central aspect of MTV's sound track: the on-screen VJs and what they say.

The voices of the VJs offer a variety of appeals, from information and gossip concerning the video clips and their stars (VJ Adam Curry and news presenter Kurt Loder), through endorsement of particular acts (China Kantner and Julie Brown), to humorous and sometimes satirical comments on the world of rock culture (of the current MTV VJs, Kevin Seal is the nearest to the rock-critic-as-cynic).[11] Both visually and aurally, the VJs thus *anchor* the MTV text, using the familiar conventions of the radio DJ and the news presenter. Just as close-ups of rock stars' faces ground the visual component of video clips, so the VJs help to forge a path through the fast pace and sometimes oblique imagery of MTV, undertaking the role identified by Altman – that of linking televisual and household flow. Thus the VJs routinely trail upcoming segments, with comments such as 'coming up in the next hour, Madonna, Def Leppard, and the new video from the Jeff Healey Band'.

But the VJs do more than this. In Altman's (1987, pp. 578–9) terms, the VJ presents the 'sound advance', in which talk is used to redirect the viewer's attention toward the screen by previewing the images that are about to be screened – a vital function for a televisual form that is especially open to distracted, sporadic viewing. As Allan (1990) observes:

> Along with sports broadcasting, it [music television] is technically one of the most innovative and adventurous visual forms available on television. Yet it is also the one that permits you *not* to watch, but to listen continuously until, to put it paradoxically, you hear what you want to watch.
>
> (p. 9)

The VJs also offer a girl/boy-next-door point of identification for MTV viewers that is mirrored in the gossipy, humorous scripts, in the *mise-en-scène* of the MTV set (an adolescent's 'den', a dance club) and in the VJs' interactions with viewers during phone-ins, contests, and outside broadcasts (such as *Amuck in America* and MTV's Spring break and Super Bowl specials). The identification point established by the VJs is, unsurprisingly, a conscious MTV strategy:

> There were no specifics except that we wanted to create a human status for MTV. We wanted those individuals who would get up and wouldn't try to become stars, that wouldn't try to become entertainers . . . For that reason we didn't look for celebrities, we looked for those people who wouldn't be overbearing or overpowering.
>
> (John Sykes, MTV's vice president of programming, quoted in Denisoff, 1988, p. 47)

Or, as Robert Pittman put it, the VJs should be 'guides who could sublimate their egos, be *human faces you could relate to*' (quoted in Levy, 1983; emphasis added).

This anchoring identification point is one that has generally been missed in accounts of MTV as an unstable text. Importantly, during the long periods of time that the camera focuses exclusively on the VJs, it usually remains stationary, in a mid- to close-up shot that typifies the framing of television presenters and personalities. Often there will be distracting moving images in the background, but the VJ will usually remain motionless and, generally speaking, so does the camera. In contrast, then, to the aurally motivated camera movement in the video clips, the framing of the VJs gives us a single point of view from which to position ourselves, utilizing a direct mode of address that is a routine broadcast TV code. Thus MTV mobilizes televisual strategies of signification that are remarkable only for their traditional adherence to fifty years of television convention. Where the videos themselves draw on techniques established in television light entertainment (and in the pro-televisual presentation of rock concerts), the MTV text presents its VJs using the standard features of news and documentary programming.

My account of the VJs' function echoes John Langer's (1981) analysis of television 'personalities', and suggests the operation of a *hierarchy of identification* in MTV (and perhaps in television more generally). The VJs represent the ordinary, and the rock stars in the video clips represent the glamorous. The hierarchy of identification goes beyond this fairly obvious point, however, in ways that help to illustrate the stable nature of the MTV text. Langer's opposition of cinema and television works surprisingly well for rock music and television also. For instance, Langer notes that while cinema represents a world that is somehow 'out there', television remains intimate, domestic, and always available. This is exactly the relation between pop stars and the VJs. The VJs have little media life outside MTV. They are thus (like news anchors and talk-show hosts) conduits who give us, the television viewers, access to pop star celebrities who enjoy fame beyond the confines of the small screen.

This anchoring function of the VJs is partly achieved through the appearance of 'live' transmission. This occurs in two ways. First, the prerecorded VJ introductions are scripted and presented as though the VJs were (like radio DJs) playing the clips to us live from the television studio, in real time. (In fact, the taped VJ segments are being edited live into video clips and advertisements by an engineer).[12] Second, the VJs, unlike the pop stars, are actually speaking. Since most of the musicians who appear on MTV are lip-syncing, the VJs inevitably enjoy a more direct channel of communication. Again, this is an important part of the MTV text that has generally gone unnoticed. The contribution of the VJs can be understood better if MTV is compared with those music television services that have no mediating direct address (the Video Jukebox Network) or that use disembodied announcers on sound only (superstation WTBS's *Night Tracks*, for instance), where their absence blocks the possibility of constructing an ambience linked to a station identity, or with the use of celebrity guest VJs (on NBC's *Friday Night Videos*, for instance). In that respect, MTV is very much like *Top of the Pops*, where broadcast media 'personalities' contextualize individual segments of 'real' stardom.

Importantly, Robert Pittman was initially anxious about the stiffness of VJ presentation, and soon the VJs were encouraged to take a casual attitude to fluffed lines and on-air mistakes, which are often broadcast despite the fact that these segments are recorded and could thus be corrected before transmission. Here, the VJ portion of the MTV text is clearly drawing on rock and roll, rather than televisual, conventions, in which 'feel' is more important than accuracy. There are two correlations here between MTV and rock culture. First, MTV seeks to present itself as a 'rock' alternative to the prerock culture of network television, hence the emphasis on the construction of spontaneity, which has primacy over competence – a fundamental tenet of rock musicology. Second, the VJ presentation calls attention to itself (through the inclusion of 'mistakes', and through the VJ's references to other, off-camera, studio personnel) and thus echoes the nonnaturalistic nature of pop performance. Far from being anarchic, VJ talk is therefore absolutely conventional when read in the light of a rock aesthetic. Therefore, while it is true that music television's mode of representation breaks with the classic realist text of Hollywood cinema, it nonetheless continues to use processes of identification (the rock star and the TV personality) that are fundamental sources of textual stability, not to mention key elements in the aesthetics of pop music. [. . .]

MORE THAN ZERO

Postmodern writers have had a field day with the question of MTV's supposedly ahistorical, apolitical, asocial, amoral aesthetic: 'MTV denies the existence of all but the moment, and that moment exists only on the screen . . . There aren't any problems on MTV', writes David Tetzlaff (1986, p. 89). John Fiske (1986) concurs: 'The flashing crashing image-sounds *are* energy, speed, illusion, the hyperreal themselves: they simulate nothing, neither the reality nor the social machine' (p. 79). E. Ann Kaplan (1987) observes that 'MTV is part of a contemporary discourse that has written out history as a possible discourse' (p. 146). This is a vivid gloss on Baudrillard, but it is difficult to sustain empirically in relation to MTV.

In one of its most revealing sequences (initially developed by MTV Europe as 'One Planet–One Music'), an MTV station ID segment culminates in the legend: 'One World, One Image, One Channel.' But in fact, there are *two* MTVs. One MTV discourse is the nihilistic, pastiching, essentially pointless playfulness that is invoked in postmodernist accounts of MTV. The other is responsible, socially conscious, satire and parody based, vaguely liberal – and almost invisible in academic accounts of MTV.

The MTV logo itself exemplifies the devil-may-care discourse, which is constructed in part in explicit (and quite conscious) opposition to network television, in that the logo is both inconsistent and irreverent – it takes many different forms and is often presented through visual jokes. Many of its slogans clearly promote just the kind of discourse the postmodernists analyze: 'MTV: We're Making It Up as We Go Along' and 'MTV: Better Sorry than Safe' are two such examples. Something similar occurs when the slogan 'The Whole World Is Watching' is used in conjunction with images of cows chewing the cud in a field. (Given the roots of *that* slogan in the student demonstrations at the 1968 Democratic convention in Chicago, the Frankfurt school notion of 'incorporation' would be every bit as appropriate as postmodern theory here.) Many of the filmed minifictions inserted between clips also fall into this category. The sometimes pointless (but extremely funny) humor of Gilbert Godfrey, who performs stand-up comedic blips between videos from time to time, is a good example. Trailing MTV's *Half-Hour Comedy Hour*, Godfrey asks, 'If it's half ours, who does the other half belong to?'

However, there is another cluster of discourses at play within MTV programming and presentation material – a grouping of quasi-political, volunteerist, socially responsible, and sometimes countercultural appeals that the postmodernists have chosen to ignore. What, for instance, are we to make of this statement, from former MTVN president Robert Pittman? In an interview in *Channels* magazine, Pittman appears to return to a classic Romantic rock ideology when he says, 'You have to be careful that you stay this side of the line of being perceived by the consumer as a sellout' (quoted in Robins, 1989). MTV's sales pitch has to be seen in relation to this ideology of rock as well as postmodernism. The complicating factor here is the transformation, in the 1980s, of rock's countercultural ideology into a discourse that combines traditional notions of rebellion and Romantic rejection of everyday life with a new sense of social responsibility and philanthropic concern. Thus, at the same time that MTV has kept its tongue firmly in its cheek, it also had to come to terms with cause-rock events such as Live Aid, Amnesty International's Conspiracy of Hope tour, and the Smile Jamaica benefit concert. [. . .]

This brings me to the question of MTV's political stance. Analyzing one area of MTV's nonmusic programming (its brief, often humorous, fictional clips), Lawrence Grossberg (1988) presents a view of postmodernity that has become a standard interpretation:

> MTV offers us a series of ads promoting Randee (the imaginary leader of an imaginary rock group, Randee and the Redwoods), for president. His entire media campaign is composed of clichéd paradoxes: e.g. Randee at a press conference says that he was misunderstood when he said that 'First there is a mountain, then there is no mountain, then there is.' He points out that he did not mean to say that there is no mountain. 'There is one,' he says to thunderous applause. 'And after I'm elected there will be one.' Feeling something, anything, is better than feeling nothing.
>
> (p. 44)

Grossberg's analysis is worthwhile and suggestive, because he goes on to show that this postmodern structure of feeling is not merely nihilistic. Grossberg's category of 'ironic inauthenticity' is a useful addition to our understanding of the formations of readership that inform the reception of MTV and contemporary pop music. (But even this complex category is double-edged, for what is the slogan 'One World, One Image, One Channel' but an Orwellian effort to pursue MTV's global intentions and retain countercultural credibility by owning up to the intent? In other words, as with Isuzu's infamous 'Joe Isuzu' television commercials, it is the *incorporation* of ironic inauthenticity.)

However, we can also provide an alternative concluding sentence for this passage. I would like to rewrite Grossberg's gloss thus:

> MTV offers us a series of ads promoting Randee (the imaginary leader of an imaginary rock group, Randee and the Redwoods) for president. His entire media campaign is composed of clichéd paradoxes: e.g. Randee at a press conference says that he was misunderstood when he said that 'First there is a mountain, then there is no mountain, then there is.' He points out that he did not mean to say that there is no mountain. 'There is one,' he says to thunderous applause. 'And after I'm elected there will be one.' Thus parody is used to establish a critique of campaigning strategies in the US political system.

This, in my view, is the *other* MTV. It is the MTV that organized voter registration drives in 1984. And it is the MTV that is neglected in nearly all the published research on music television.

None of this is to deny MTV's innovations, or its potential for a postmodern reading. As Pfeil (1988) and Grossberg (1988) suggest, work on postmodernism as a condition of reception can be extremely fruitful. But in the analysis of music television as a postmodern *text*, scholars need to pay much greater heed to the empirical data and to the contradictions within MTV, which cannot be seamlessly reduced to a single aesthetic category. These contradictions are mutually supportive. The two MTVs depend upon each other. A music television station that was simply frivolous, playful, pleasure centered, and so forth would quickly be dismissed as corporate froth – not just by critics, but by music fans who expect more than 'entertainment' from rock, pop, and rap culture. On the other hand, an environment that is too serious, worthy, and socially commited would be equally inappropriate for a rock culture that must also embody hedonism, self-expression, and so on.

However, MTV (and services like it) are not determined solely by their relation to aesthetic forms and discourses. Music television services are also an advertising 'environment'. In the case of MTV, that environment will seem credible only if it seems to speak to (an increasingly fractured) youth culture – one that now includes people in their thirties and forties and that encompasses a generic 'breakup' in terms of musical styles. (This fracturing explains MTV's announcement, in the spring of 1991, that it will divide up into three separate services in 1993. If this happens, it will inaugurate a *fourth* phase in MTV's history.) It is a paradox, then, that in order to function as a successful service for the delivery of viewers to advertisers and record companies, MTV must promote countercultural and antiestablishment points of view. Therefore, MTV aligns itself with liberal causes, mounts a critique of everyday life that is at times almost situationist,[13] sets itself apart from 'mass culture' (especially network television),[14] and constantly emphasizes rock's roots in pantheism (see Pattison, 1987) through its strident pro-ecology spots, and in social concern (items and videos on the homeless, for instance).[15] This could be seen as the 'incorporation' of counterhegemonic discourses in the name of corporate profit. (Although, in Williams's terms, 'alternative', as opposed to dominant or oppositional, would be a better general summary of its politics; see Williams, 1973.) Yet this analysis reveals the inadequacy of such a reading, for one way of understanding MTV would be through an 'innocent' framework that takes rock myths at face value and that goes beyond cynicism (either through ignorance or choice) in discarding the issue of MTV's broader economic concerns. As with the debate about rock philanthropy (Live Aid and so on), one interpretation simply insists that the message is more important than the motive. MTV is thus simultaneously involved in the incorporation *and* the promotion of dissent [. . .]

NOTES

1. Quoted in an interview by David Wild in *Rolling Stone* (March 7, 1991, p. 36).
2. Phil Hardy (1983, pp. 19–20)/John Qualen (1985, pp. 14–16), who are actually the same person, argue that music video was consciously used by the British record industry as a cost-effective way into the US market.
3. Denisoff (1988) quotes Les Garland, then vice-president of programming, talking in August 1982, thus: 'About 30 to 40 percent of the music we play is not on the typical AOR radio station' (pp. 84–5). Note, therefore, how much of the playlist was AOR! In early 1983, Garland told a reporter: 'We can show REO Speedwagon and Duran Duran. We can show Kenny Loggins and Haircut One Hundred. We've been able to invent our own format, because we're the only ones doing it' (quoted in Jackson, 1983).

4. Denisoff (1988) and others have reported that CBS was able to persuade MTV to screen Michael Jackson's BEAT IT only by threatening to withdraw all CBS clips from the station. The problem of black airplay persisted beyond this early period. At a Gill Chair Seminar at San Jose State University (held November 6, 1986), Polygram Records president Dick Asher reported that his company experienced great difficulty in gaining MTV airplay for the 1986 WORD UP clip, by black dance act Cameo. By the late 1980s MTV's promotion of rap music (on *Yo! MTV Raps*) significantly changed attitudes toward its negotiation of race, leading many musicians and executives to credit the channel with playing a major role in the national success of that genre of black music. In that respect it is certainly true that MTV has been more adventurous in its programming than radio, including stations with formats focusing on 'black' and 'urban contemporary' music. MTV was also very visible in its promotion of the radical black hard rock group Living Colour, especially during 1989.

5. The history of white appropriations of black music is intrinsic to the development of rock, as Gillett (1983) and Harker (1980) have shown. More particular accounts of racism are delineated, for example, in Chuck Berry's (1987) autobiography, in Gerri Hirshey's (1984) account of soul, and in Dave Hill's (1989) analysis of Prince.

6. It is also important to note the contribution of American New Wave and punk acts, whose clips also tended to fall in the nonnarrative category (Devo's WHIP IT, SATISFACTION, and SECRET AGENT MAN, the Cars' YOU MIGHT THINK, Talking Heads' PSYCHO-KILLER and ONCE IN A LIFETIME) or to utilize a New Pop–like self-consciousness (see Blondie's long-form tape, *Eat to the Beat*, Chrysalis, 1983).

7. The liberal/feminist arguments against MTV were frequently articulated in the newsletter *Rock and Roll Confidential* (see, for example, Marsh, 1985, pp. 204–8).

8. MTV ratings are often miscited as the figure that derives from the number of basic cable-subscribing households on systems that offer the service. By December 1990, MTV was the seventh-largest cable service in the United States, with a potential audience of 52.9 million (*Channels*, December 3, 1990, p. 48). However, this figure has only a distant correlation with the number of viewers. MTV's actual audience has usually been less than 1 percent of this figure. For instance, in August 1990, MTV averaged a 0.6 percent share in prime time and a 0.7 percent share during the hours of 7 a.m. to 1 a.m. (see *Channels*, August 13, 1990). A 'share', in the US cable market, represents the percentage of potential viewers who watched.

9. Public Enemy, De La Soul, Ice-T, and Hammer subsequently emerged as black rap acts with mass appeal who sell in large quantities to white audiences.

10. In the spring of 1991 MTV began broadcasting a coproduced show titled *Liquid Television* (an episodic cartoon series), made in association with the BBC, for *DEF II*.

11. For instance, introducing a clip from the group Bad English (formed by two veteran members of Journey and the Babies), Seal refers dryly to their ambitions to emulate Blind Faith – the 1970s 'supergroup' featuring Ginger Baker, Eric Clapton, Steve Winwood, and Rick Gretch, whose music notoriously failed to add up to the sum of its parts.

12. The VJs' linking segments are recorded in blocks ahead of time and then edited in, live, with the videos, commercials, station IDs, and so on.

13. In addition to the 'Words' art-break cited below, MTV runs many station identification sequences that critique everyday life and attempt to expose the society of the spectacle. (This was once incorporated into an 'I Hate My Miserable Life' contest.) Many such art-breaks satirize television, advertising, and mass culture. In one sequence the words EAT, WORK, and SLEEP are repeated with increasing speed (and appropriate imagery) until the whole segment blurs into indistinguishable montage and stops only with the arrival (of course) of the legend 'MTV'.

14. The apotheosis of this address is MTV's 'Words' art-break, which is mainly silent and consists entirely of the following white-on-black captions: WORDS / THESE ARE WORDS / BLIND PEOPLE CAN'T [blank space] THEM / FOREIGNERS DON'T UNDERSTAND THEM / BUT YOU CAN / NOWADAYS PEOPLE WHO MAKE TV / COMMERCIALS /

USE WORDS JUST LIKE THESE / TO COMMUNICATE / A / MESSAGE / SO THOSE PEOPLE WHO DO NOT / LISTEN / UNDERSTAND / THIS PRACTICE IS SUPPOSED TO BE / SIMPLE / AND / EFFECTIVE / THESE WORDS CAN'T REALLY SAY ANYTHING / THEY COULD BUT THEY'RE NOT / THEY WANT TO BUT THEY CAN'T / SO, THEY WILL HANG OUT FOR FIFTEEN SECONDS / UNTIL IT'S TIME / FOR / ANOTHER / COMMERCIAL / THESE ARE WORDS / THAT COULD BE SAYING SOMETHING / FUNNY OR COOL OR INTERESTING / BUT THEY'RE NOT / THEY'RE JUST SITTING THERE / LIKE YOU / mtv.

15. Homelessness figures prominently in videos such as DAY IN, DAY OUT (David Bowie), BORN IN THE USA (Bruce Springsteen), MAN IN THE MIRROR (Michael Jackson), ANOTHER DAY IN PARADISE (Phil Collins), and SOMETHING TO BELIEVE IN (Poison).

REFERENCES

ALLAN, B. 1990: Musical cinema, music video, music television. *Film Quarterly* 43(3).

ALTMAN, R. 1987: Television sound. In Newcomb, H. (ed.), *Television: the critical view*, 4th edn. London: Oxford University Press.

BERRY, C. 1987: *Chuck Berry: the autobiography*. New York: Harmony.

DANNEN, F. 1987: MTV's great leap backwards. *Channels* (July/August).

DENISOFF, S. 1988: *Inside MTV*. New Brunswick, NJ: Transaction.

ELLIS, J. 1982: *Visible fictions: cinema, television, video*. London: Routledge & Kegan Paul.

FISKE, J. 1986: MTV: post structural post modern. *Journal of Communication Inquiry* 10(1).

FRITH, S. 1988a: *Music for pleasure*. London: Methuen.

FRITH, S. 1988b: Video pop. In Frith, S. (ed.), *Facing the music*. New York: Pantheon.

GILLETT, C. 1983: *The sound of the city: the rise of rock and roll*, 2nd edn. New York: Pantheon.

GOODWIN, A. 1991: Popular music and postmodern theory. *Cultural Studies* 5(2).

GROSSBERG, L. (with FRY, A., CURTHOYS, A. and PATTON, P.). 1988: *It's a sin: postmodernism, politics and culture*. Sydney: Power.

HARDY, P. 1983: *The record industry*. Economic Policy Group Strategy Document 16. London: GLC.

HARKER, D. 1980: *One for the money: politics and popular song*. London: Hutchinson.

HILBURN, R. 1986: MTV's creator tackles new goals. *Los Angeles Times*, 5 September.

HILL, D. 1989: *Prince: a pop life*. New York: Harmony.

HIRSHEY, G. 1984: *Nowhere to run: the story of soul music*. London: Pan/Macmillan.

JACKSON, B. 1983: America gets its MTV! (Interview with Les Garland, MTV). Bay Area Music Magazine, Feb. 11.

KAPLAN, E.A. 1987: *Rocking around the clock: Music Television*. London: Methuen.

LANGER, J. 1981: Television's 'personality system'. *Media, Culture and Society* 3(4).

LEVY, S. 1983: Ad nauseam: how MTV sells out rock and roll. *Rolling Stone*, 8 December.

MARSH, D. (ed.). 1985: *The first rock and roll confidential report*. New York: Pantheon.

PATTISON, R. 1987: *The triumph of vulgarity: rock music in the mirror of romanticism*. Oxford: Oxford University Press.

PFEIL, F. 1985: Making flippy-floppy: postmodernism and the baby-boom PMC. In Davis, M. (ed.), *The year left*. London: Verso.

PFEIL, F. 1988: Postmodernism as a 'structure of feeling'. In Nelson, C. and Grossberg, L. (eds.), *Marxism and the interpretation of culture*. London: Hutchinson.

QUALEN, J. 1985: *The music industry: the end of vinyl?* London: Comedia.

ROBINS, J. 1989: Into the groove. *Channels* (May).

TETZLAFF, D. 1986: MTV and the politics of postmodern pop. *Journal of Communication Inquiry* 10(1).

VIERA, M. 1987: The institutionalization of music video. *ONETWOTHREEFOUR: A Rock 'n' Roll Quarterly* 5 (Spring).

WILLIAMS, R. 1973: Base and superstructure in Marxist cultural theory. *New Left Review* 82 (November–December).

9

The aesthetic experience: soap opera

Christine Geraghty

From Geraghty, C. 1991: *Women and soap opera: a study of prime time soaps.* Cambridge: Polity Press, 25–38

Since its origins in the daytime radio drama attractive to the 'housewife', soap opera has posed something of a challenge for both critics and audiences. This form of long-running and open-ended drama, normally structured around strong female protagonists, derived its title and presumed low cultural status from its funding in America by soap manufacturers intent on constructing and addressing a female market. In the relatively young world of television studies the form has become something of a litmus test for gauging both degrees of interest in the popular and levels of sensitivity to the historical reality and experience of women. In Britain in the early 1990s the two programmes which constantly vied for the number one place in the ratings were both soaps: *Coronation Street* and *EastEnders*, though these – in their carefully chosen prime-time slots – were by no means exclusively viewed by women.

As Christine Geraghty points out, in her introduction to the book from which this extract is taken, the new feminist approaches of the 1970s had established within film studies a critical context for the re-evaluation of melodrama; this work had 'rescued a despised genre and turned it into a legitimate object for study'. Taken together with Richard Dyer's work on light entertainment and his influential and positive account of the utopian impulses of popular Hollywood drama, these developments created a new and fertile context for the critical recovery and re-evaluation of soap opera within American and British television studies. The form acquired a new interest for those concerned with the ways in which television might provide interpretative categories for lived experience, explore the tensions between the worlds of home and work – the presumed public culture of men and the private, domestic culture of women – and contribute in the process to a revived project of emotional literacy.

Geraghty's address to the issue of aesthetics in soap opera tackles head-on some of the tensions and anxieties which contemporary cultural studies has brought to older traditions of Western art and literary criticism. Within the great tradition of studying high and serious art the task of aesthetics has, by definition, involved the appreciation of beauty and the application of good taste. Cultural studies has offered a dangerous challenge to this task, proposing at once a more democratic but also a more relativistic approach to questions of beauty, taste and quality. The fertile contradiction at the heart of soap may become apparent if we see it as the epic of the banal; the arguably epic treatment of the everyday lives of ordinary people may help to explain the disputed cultural status of the genre.

This extract from Geraghty's work offers some useful methodological tools for analysing the aesthetic strategies of soap opera, suggesting that the form draws on the different and sometimes competing aesthetic traditions of light entertainment, melodrama and realism. She argues that this 'generic knot' needs to be untangled if the distinctive aesthetic experience offered by the soaps is to be recognized. The complexity of the form is such that we are both invited to 'sit back and relish the spectacle' and drawn in to identify with characters as our emotional representatives. A recognition of the diversity of the aesthetic devices that characterize soap should, Geraghty proposes, allow us to avoid both blanket condemnation and uncritical celebration.

'I see you've taken my advice on dressing for success; red is a very good colour.'

Alexis to Lesley, *Dynasty*

'It's not just you that finds marriage difficult. It's everybody.'

Rita to Brian Tilsley, *Coronation Street*

'She's a real Cockney.'

Dagmar yuppies to Angie, *EastEnders*

'Aesthetic' is not a word which readily springs to mind when thinking about soaps, nor is it much used in recent critical work on film and television. Hesitation about its use perhaps stems from an understandable desire to get away from the value judgements which have so blocked understanding of cultural works and have dismissed much popular culture as unworthy of sustained analysis. The notion that aesthetic qualities provide a source of pleasure in soap operas may seem unlikely but much of the criticism of soaps in this respect is based on a misunderstanding of the mixed nature of the soap genre. Just as the narrative organisation of soaps serves simultaneously to engage and distance the soap audience so the aesthetics of soaps work both to draw us into the programme and to permit us to stand back and comment on the effects. This chapter argues that soaps are not dominated by one aesthetic tradition but offer a range of experiences based on the different and sometimes competing values of light entertainment, melodrama and realism. It is only when the implications of this generic knot are untangled that it becomes possible to understand the nature of the aesthetic experience which soaps offer. [. . .]

LIGHT ENTERTAINMENT

Richard Dyer, in his book *Light entertainment*, looks at the pleasures and values of a particular kind of television programme – the variety show programmes 'akin to show-business, cabaret and musical comedy'.[1] Clearly, the light entertainment programmes he analyses, with their use of a host performer and guest artists, a series of acts and frequently a live audience, are very different from soaps, and their traditions in music hall and variety led to a mode of direct audience address which is not used in the narrative framework which constrains soaps. Nevertheless, part of the appeal of soaps is the way in which they use the values of light entertainment, sometimes so excessively that they challenge the dominance of the narrative. [. . .]

The pleasure in lavishness and extravagance leads to an emphasis on glamour which underpins the use of locations and the presentation of the stars. *Dynasty*, for instance, makes use of exotic locations such as Hong Kong and while the spectacle is limited by the constraints of a TV budget, the shots of scenery and the city, together with the use of luxurious hotel rooms, enormous offices and expensive shops, offer the audience a deliberately artificial world. Great emphasis is placed on the Carrington mansion with its imposing staircase, elaborately furnished rooms and luxuriant grounds. The milieu appears to be a parody of the myth of English country living with its servants, its cholesterol-laden breakfasts, its riding stables and formal gardens. *Dallas*, although deliberately more down-market, still rates a swimming pool, servants, candlesticks on the table and extensive land, and, significantly, when its ratings were falling it looked to more spectacular locations in Europe and the USSR to redeem its position.

In both cases, the settings provide an exotic backdrop for the characters themselves who are the main source of the spectacle of conspicuous consumption. It is on the women, in particular, that this spectacle is focused. They provide that slightly out-of-date glamour which is the hallmark of the programmes which Dyer described. There is always a sense of excess about their clothes because the decorative emphasis is so strong that their functional purpose is dangerously neglected. Their dresses are deliberately stylised and uncomfortable, the colours garish, the glitter out of place. They teeter on their high heels, the hair falling over the eyes as their walk is restricted by tight skirts. Tears do not affect the eye shadow, the lip gloss gleams through a passionate denunciation, a true flush never ruins the effect of the carefully applied blusher. This is particularly true of Alexis in *Dynasty*. The dress in which she conducts an emotional scene is almost as important as the dramatic implications of the scene for the narrative. [. . .]

If light entertainment aesthetics can be most clearly demonstrated in the US prime time soaps, British soaps also have their elements of spectacle. Setting is not so important here and glamour is even more closely associated in the British programmes with certain women characters. This element can be seen most strongly in *Coronation Street*, which has had a strong tradition of glamorous middle-aged women exemplified in the characters of Elsie Tanner, Rita Fairclough and Bet Lynch. Elsie began as a rather run-down and harassed mother but developed over the years her own style which aspired to a glamorous ideal well beyond *Coronation Street*. Unlike her US counterparts, Elsie's mascara did run but her bouffant hair-dos, stylish dresses and curvaceous figure referred back to a pre-sixties notion of glamour associated with stars such as Diana Dors. Other characters, such as Rita Fairclough, who, appropriately in terms of the light entertainment analogy, was once a night club singer, followed this model, while the barmaid, Bet Lynch, took it to extremes of parody, with the excesses of her hairstyles, earrings and tightly belted waist being subject to the same kind of comments as Alexis's ballgowns. Certain women in other British soaps carry the same kind of glamorous connotations: Angie, the publican's wife in *EastEnders*, was almost theatrically made up, while Nicola in *Crossroads* was specifically presented as the British version of the US female stars with her impeccable make-up and clothes which purport to be businesslike but which verge on the extravagant.

MELODRAMA

The values of light entertainment do not, however, go unchallenged in the soap aesthetic. While the glamour of light entertainment encourages the audience to sit back and relish the spectacle, the emotional drama of soaps also demands an aesthetic which will draw the audience in and establish the characters not only as objects of spectacle but as our emotional representatives. In understanding this phenomenon, we need to look at the way in which the elements of *mise en scène*, decor and performance operate in a melodramatic mode to engage the audience.

Critical theory on the aesthetics of TV melodrama is still not as developed as that on film melodrama and it is not possible simply to transpose debates within film study into the TV arena. Work on Hollywood melodramas of the 1950s, for instance, argued that the aesthetic forms of expression stood in for, or marked through formal excesses, explosive emotional issues which could not be directly addressed in the narrative. Thomas Elsaesser comments on 'a sublimation of dramatic conflict into decor, colour, gesture and composition of frame, which in the best melodramas is perfectly thematised in terms of the characters' emotional and psychological predicaments'.[2] Picking up this notion of sublimation and using the analogy of Freud's definition of conversion hysteria, Geoffrey Nowell-Smith states that 'in the melodrama, where there is always material which cannot be expressed in discourse or in the actions of the characters furthering the designs of the plot, a conversion can take place into the body of the text', into the *mise en scène* and performances.[3] Such analogies allowed fifties family melodramas to be read (and enjoyed) as critiques of US society and the bourgeois family, although it is unclear, as Christine Gledhill has commented, how far such 'radical readings' belonged only to the seventies critics rather than the fifties audiences.[4]

Looking at television melodrama, on the other hand, Jane Feuer has argued that this relationship in film melodramas between visual excess and the potentially subversive expression through visual signs of what is taboo in the narrative is much less evident on television. She goes on to describe how the melodramatic aesthetic in programmes like *Dallas* and *Dynasty* works *with* the narrative, rather than offering a critique of it, commenting that 'for *Dallas* and *Dynasty*, *mise en scène* would appear to function for the most part expressively'.[5] Far from undermining the logic of the narrative, various aesthetic devices underline and clarify it. Feuer thus points to the way that 'acting, editing, musical underscoring and the use of the zoom lens frequently conspire to create scenes of high (melo)drama'.[6] In this description, we can begin to see how the visual characteristics of US and British soaps – the close-ups of faces, of important objects, the deliberate movement of a character across a room, the lingering of the camera on a face at the end of a scene, the exchange of meaningful glances – work to make every gesture and action seem highly coded and significant, marking out emotional relationships and enabling the audience to understand the significance of every action. This is particularly important given the complicated nature of the stories being told. Soap narratives, like those of film melodramas, are marked by what Steve Neale has described as 'chance happenings, coincidences, missed meetings, sudden conversions, last-minute rescues and revelations, *deus ex machina* endings'.[7] These kinds of story can be seen in the whole range of TV soaps, *EastEnders* as well as *Dallas*, but Neale takes us further by commenting on the effect of such dramatic organisation. The 'course of events', he argues, 'is unmotivated (or undermotivated) from a realist point of view; such preparation and motivation as does exist is always "insufficient". There is an *excess* of effect over cause, of the extraordinary over the ordinary.'[8]

It is this excess of meaning over motivation which lies at the heart of soaps' adoption of the melodramatic aesthetic as a way of drawing the audience into the programmes. On first examination, it would seem that TV soaps leave the audience too little work to do. They lack the satisfying sense of achievement of working out the ramifications of *Tinker Tailor Soldier Spy* or even *Miami Vice*. If the *mise en scène* is over-expressive, if the acting gives us signposts to the meaning and if (in the US prime time soaps at least) music underlines it even for the slowest viewer, what is there left for members of the audience to do? It is this sense that soaps are too easy to understand, predictable and facile, which is the source of many a critic's dissatisfaction. And yet Neale's analysis indicates that there is a space for the reader at key moments to provide an explanation for the excesses of the melodramatic aesthetics which are inadequately explained by the cause and effect process of the narrative. What is the reason for the welling up of music, the exchange of glances, the slamming of a door? Such spaces are most characteristically signalled by a close-up on a character after a dramatic confrontation – on Sue Ellen, drunkenly starting at JR [*Dallas*], on Angie Watts looking unblinkingly into the camera as Den stalks away [*EastEnders*], on Sheila Grant, hunched in the corner of the sofa as her son Barry leaves once more [*Brookside*]. All these moments have narrative explanations but their intensity is more than the events of a particular episode warrant. They have to be filled in by the audience, those blank faces given a reason through the viewer's knowledge of the programme's past and a re-creation of the feelings which the character must therefore be experiencing. It is this identification with heightened emotion through the filling of the space created by the excessive expressiveness of the *mise en scène* and performance which is the most important element in TV soap opera's melodramatic aesthetic. It enables the most unlikely characters to take on a representative role for the viewer – 'It's everybody' – and dramatically engages those who only a moment before may have been detachedly commenting on Joan Collins's latest dress.

REALISM

If light entertainment and melodrama are important components in TV soaps, the British programmes are strongly marked by another element – that of realism. There is not space for a detailed discussion of this troubled term, which has a host of definitions and has generated a specific history of its own in debates central to the history of film theory. And yet some discussion of realism is essential if only because it crops up so regularly as a criterion for British soaps and as a reason for their popularity. As Julia Smith, the original producer of *EastEnders*, remarked on a TV phone-in celebrating its second anniversary, 'We don't make life, we reflect it', and a number of the viewers ringing in congratulated her on the programme's accuracy.[9] It is this notion of realism as a plausible picture of everyday experience and its use as a justification in itself for what happens in the soap which requires some examination here.

The seemingly straightforward comment that *EastEnders* reflects life is actually somewhat disingenuous given that it was made in the context of complaints about excessive violence and sexual frankness in the programme. It avoids the question of whose reality is being invoked in justification, whose life is being reflected. It hides also complex relations between what is understood to be reality and its representation and the nature of the choices made by the producer as to what is appropriate to take on in a programme which is very popular with a young audience.[10] The comment similarly refuses to acknowledge the importance of conventions in forming our understanding of what constitutes realism and the way in which, as John Hill puts it,

> No work can ever simply reveal reality. Realism, no less than any other type of art, depends on conventions, conventions which have successfully achieved the status of being accepted as 'realistic'. It is this 'conventionality' of realism which also makes its usage so vulnerable to change, for as the conventions change (either in reaction to previously established conventions or in accordance with new perceptions of what constitutes reality) so too does our sense of what then constitutes realism.[11]

The realist-documentary approach to film-making has long been recognized as crucial to British cinema, going back to the late twenties and thirties. The fact that such an interpretation of British cinema underestimated or repressed the existence of less respectable work (such as the romantic/gothic strains of the Gainsborough and Hammer studios) illustrates the hold that the realist tradition has had and the way in which its values came to be an apparently natural mark of quality and seriousness in British cinema. Realism, in this context, meant not only an attention to verisimilitude and plausible motivation but also a value placed on the representation of working-class life and an exploration of the problems caused by social change. The strong aesthetic hold of realism in British cinema transferred to television and as Andrew Higson has commented, 'each successive realist movement in British cinema and television has been celebrated both for its commitment to the exploration of contemporary social problems, and for its working out of those problems in relation to "realistic" landscapes and characters'.[12] In television, a climate developed in which the most praised and the most controversial programmes were firmly in this realist tradition: the series of single 'Plays for Today', drama-documentaries like *Law and Order*, fly-on-the-wall series such as Roger Graef's *Police* – powerful material and controversial precisely because of arguments about how accurately they did represent reality. If such programmes have got fewer in recent years, in a political and social climate that has changed considerably, the value placed on 'things as they really are'[13] still remains a strong strand in British critical perceptions.

British soap operas offer a particularly good example of the reworking of the realist aesthetic and of the way in which conventions change and develop in reaction to what has gone before. The first episode of *Coronation Street* was shown in 1960 and Richard Dyer has pointed to its emergence at a particular moment in British cultural history which is exemplified by the publication and popularity of Richard Hoggart's *The uses of literacy*. Dyer comments on Hoggart's emphasis on the specificity of working-class culture and the importance he attaches to notions of home and community and women's role in maintaining them; within that culture and community, particular attention is paid in *The uses of literary* to ' "the common sense" of "everyday life" for the working class'.[14] Dyer suggests that *Coronation Street* also 'takes as its mode the interactions of everyday life as realized in common-sense speech and philosophy'.[15] But we should in addition bear in mind that this was also the time of the 'New Wave' in British cinema exemplified by films such as *Room at the Top*, *A Kind of Loving* and *Look Back in Anger* (in turn of course calling on work being done in the theatre and the novel). 1960 was the year of *Saturday Night and Sunday Morning* as well as *Coronation Street* and the serial's concentration on a working-class community, its black and white images of northern streets, its rebellious and outspoken characters, and its insistent sense of place are examples of the particular conventions of realism which it shared with the British films of the period.

Coronation Street's appeal to realism (however mediated and changed by other pressures on it) was never really challenged by other British soaps such as *Crossroads*, and it took *Brookside*, over 20 years later, to stake its claim to a realism which it was argued *Coronation Street* had abandoned in a nostalgic appeal to the past. *Brookside* was first shown on Britain's new Channel 4 in 1982 and, in publicity interviews before it began, the producer, Phil Redmond, specifically attacked *Coronation Street*'s commitment to realism and in particular its emphasis on a working-class community. In an article published in *Woman* magazine, for instance, he criticized other serials for being 'soft and bland' in their approach to 'realistic issues and everyday problems'. Using a typical realist strategy, he calls on the audience to compare their own experience to that offered by *Coronation Street* – 'Did you ever live in a place where the whole street congregates in the same pub every night? It just doesn't happen.' Instead, Redmond argues that 'people will accept and actually want programmes that tell the truth and show society as it really is'.[16] One can feel the conventions of realism in British soap opera shifting as Redmond speaks.

The pre-echo in Redmond's statements of Julia Smith's words quoted earlier – 'We don't make life, we reflect it' – is no accident, for *EastEnders* too, first shown in February 1985, was launched on similar promises and with similar attacks on *Coronation Street* and, this time, on *Brookside* also. According to *Broadcast*, the trade magazine for British television, *EastEnders* 'promises to portray the everyday life of an East End community "warts and all" '. [. . .]

The pursuit of realism has been an impetus for change in British soaps but the bedrock of the appeal to realism has remained the same – a value placed on a specific setting, an 'authentic' regional experience and a particular class representation. [. . .]

The assumption, in British film history, that realism must take as its subject the working class can be traced back to the documentary movement of the 1920s and 1930s, and that patronising approach can still be discerned in some of the British soaps, but the commitment to bring to the screen working-class accents, mores, problems and pleasures – still largely absent from much of British television – is an important element in the soaps' claim to realism.

THE AESTHETIC INTERPLAY

By now it will be clear that soaps do not offer a coherent aesthetic experience and in particular that they do not work entirely in the realist tradition which is so valued in Britain. Instead, soaps deploy a range of aesthetic elements and offer a mix of generic conventions which confuses or makes them an object of scorn to those who seek to confine them to a particular format. Within a single episode, soaps can move from one set of conventions to another and back again, and within an evening's viewing the soaps offer a surprisingly wide range of aesthetic experiences within a common narrative organisation. This shifting between the different traditions contributes to the experience of engagement and distance which is so characteristic of soap viewing.

But the values of light entertainment, melodrama and realism do not always fit smoothly together, for while the melodramatic mode might work to pull the audience into the drama, the conventions of light entertainment demand a more detached approach. I will close this chapter, therefore, by demonstrating how an analysis of this shifting between light entertainment, realism and melodrama helps us to understand particular aspects of the aesthetic experience of watching soaps.

Acting style and performance are frequently the subject of critical condemnation or amusement. The classic complaint about soaps is that of bad acting. Thus, commenting on the cliffhanger episode in which Kristen shot JR, Clive James wrote:

> With the possible exception of JR himself, everybody in the cast is working flat out to convey the full range of his or her, usually her, emotional commitment. Sue Ellen, in particular, was a study in passionate outrage. Her mouth practically took off . . . It is even possible that Miss Ellie shot him, since she has been showing increasing signs of madness, singing her dialogue instead of saying it.[17]

What is not understood in this kind of criticism, however, is that acting in soaps is required to register in three different ways which are almost inevitably at odds with each other. First of all, in light entertainment terms, the performance is required to be that of a star. Light entertainment looks for an identity between star and character, and in that sense what is valued is not acting but being the character. Larry Hagman *is* JR and his appearances outside *Dallas* on chat shows, for instance, are used to reinforce that claim to identity. [. . .]

For the purposes of melodrama, acting is required to be both expressive and mysterious. It needs to express clearly the significance of key words and gestures and to leave sufficient space for the audience to make its own deductions. The emphasis on eyes and mouth, the number of meaningful looks and thoughtful nods, can be explained by these requirements. But the aesthetics of realism demand that acting be 'in character' so that the particularities of each fictional individual are drawn on to give weight to the performance. This mode values an acting style which depends on a distance between performer and character. Unlike the star persona valued by the light entertainment aesthetic, the realist approach demands a fictional character very different in looks and speech from the actor. Thus the actress, Jean Alexander, spruce, smartly dressed and middle class in speech, is in magazine articles set against the character of Hilda Ogden whom she played in *Coronation Street* as nagging, gossipy and down at heel, though capable of moments of dignified pathos. This space between actress and character can be understood as a guarantee of a realist performance but the detailed gestures required by such a style may be at odds with the melodramatic mode in which every gesture has a meaning in terms of the narrative and not just character. A major soap actor may be called on to work in three different modes: that of a star (light entertainment), an emotional representative (melodrama) and a character actor (realism). It is hardly surprising that soap opera acting is sometimes incoherent, although the critics who complain of inconsistency are usually unaware of the shifting significance of performance in these programmes.

As this chapter has indicated, a similar tripartite analysis could be made of other aesthetic elements, among them costume, setting, decor and lighting, but it might be useful to consider an apparently 'technical' element which is given less attention in television analysis than in film theory. Camera movement and position in soaps are clearly limited by the exigencies of time and money but the three aesthetic elements play their part here as well. Light entertainment, as we have seen, emphasizes both spectacle and stars and so camera positioning frequently alternates between long shots establishing the glamorous settings and close-ups of the stars. This is quite clear in *Dallas and Dynasty*, where the pattern of shots (outside establishing shot, interior long shot to take in setting and clothes, close-up(s) of speaker) is predictable. But the use of a long shot to establish and even explore the setting is not unusual in British soaps. The spectacle of the Liverpool setting is regularly invoked in *Brookside*, and *EastEnders* uses camera-work to draw attention to its sets – in a 1987 Christmas episode, the camera in a single shot moved through the Square, nudging the shoppers, emphasising the Christmas lights on the market stalls and dwelling on the group of carol singers. In its own way, such a shot is as spectacular, as pleasing to the eye, as any view of Hong Kong which *Dynasty* offers, but in British soaps such shots also have a realist function, serving to underline the specificities of the regional setting and the soap's function of representing one area of Britain to the rest of the country. The long shot can therefore work with both light entertainment and realist values. The close-up has the further advantage of fitting in with the melodramatic mode as well and I would argue that it is the fact that the close-up coincides with the aesthetic demands of all three modes which gives it a dominant role compared with other camera positions in the programmes. The close-up allows, as we have seen, appropriate emphasis on the star but it also offers the audience access to the significant object or gesture, giving them time to draw their own conclusions and fill in meaning. In addition, the close-up can be used to draw attention to realist detail – the photographs on Hilda's mantelpiece or the unwashed dishes in the Corkhill kitchen after Doreen has left both the family home and *Brookside*. Such shots do not progress the narrative but they help to fill in our understanding of the context of what is being presented. Camera-work, when looked at in this tripartite way, becomes not merely a matter of economics or convenience; it can be recognized as integral to the soap aesthetic.

The two examples given here show that the different aesthetic modes at work in soap operas may sometimes be in conflict, as they often are when we analyse acting and performance, and sometimes work together, as they do in terms of camera movement and position. What is important is to move away from the blanket condemnation of the aesthetic experience offered by soaps and the defensive response which refuses to acknowledge the justification of any criticism. The tripartite framework outlined here should enable us to begin to analyse why soaps look as they do and to understand the sometimes contradictory aesthetic pleasures they offer.

NOTES

1. Richard Dyer, *Light entertainment* (London, British Film Institute, 1973), p. 7.
2. Thomas Elsaesser, 'Tales of sound and fury', in Christine Gledhill (ed.), *Home is where the heart is* (London, British Film Institute, 1987), p. 52.
3. Geoffrey Nowell-Smith, 'Minnelli and melodrama', in Gledhill (ed.), *Home is where the heart is*, pp. 73–4.
4. Christine Gledhill, 'The melodramatic field: an investigation', in Gledhill (ed.), *Home is where the heart is*, p. 11.

5. Jane Feuer, 'Melodrama, serial form and television today', *Screen*, 25(1) (January–February 1984), p. 9.
6. Feuer, 'Melodrama, serial form and television today', p. 10.
7. Steve Neale, 'Melodrama and tears', *Screen*, 27(6) (November–December 1986), p. 6.
8. Neale, 'Melodrama and tears', p. 7.
9. Julia Smith was appearing on BBC Television's *Open Air*, 19 February 1987.
10. For an account of young people's response to *EastEnders*, see Chapter 4 of David Buckingham, *Public secrets: EastEnders and its audience* (London, British Film Institute, 1987).
11. John Hill, *Sex, class and realism: British cinema 1956–1963* (London, British Film Institute, 1986), p. 57.
12. Andrew Higson, '"Britain's outstanding contribution to the film": the documentary-realist tradition', in Charles Barr (ed.), *All our yesterdays* (London, British Film Institute, 1986), p. 95.
13. Raymond Williams, *Keywords* (London, Fontana, 1976), p. 218.
14. Richard Dyer (ed.), *Coronation Street* (London, British Film Institute, 1981), p. 2.
15. Dyer (ed.), *Coronation Street*, p. 4.
16. 'Where *Coronation Street* has failed', *Woman*, 4 December 1982. Redmond repeated his comment in his introduction to *Phil Redmond's Brookside: the official companion* (London, Weidenfeld & Nicolson, 1987): 'People in modern Britain tend not to go into the pub and announce all their private and personal business to all concerned', p. 6.
17. Clive James, *Glued to the box* (London, Picador, 1983), p. 92.

10

Oranges Are Not the Only Fruit: reaching audiences other lesbian texts cannot reach

Hilary Hinds

From Wilton, T. (ed.) 1995: *Immortal invisible: lesbians and the moving image*. London: Routledge, 52–69. First published in Munt, S. (ed.) 1992: *New lesbian criticism: literary and cultural readings*. Hemel Hempstead: Harvester Wheatsheaf

The 'new social movements' of the 1960s and 1970s developed in the West in the context of generally rising incomes and improvements in educational provision, but also drew upon an earlier vocabulary and set of principles derived from national liberation movements against colonial domination. A new language of rights and of liberation – for black people, for women, for gay and lesbian people – was developed and counterposed to a dominating and oppressive reality consisting of innumerable acts of systematic and individual discrimination. These movements constituted a great and confident upsurge of contestation as millions claimed, invented and celebrated a more positive sense of self and identified and attacked those economic, social and cultural practices which contributed to their subordination.

Changes in both mainstream and independent media provided, over time, a voice for those who had – in the field of culture – been so systematically silenced; though many taboos, prohibitions and prejudices remained in place. In Britain, in 1990, the BBC broke one of those taboos in the area of the explicit representation of lesbian sex, in a much-written-about and much-praised serialisation of Jeanette Winterson's first novel: *Oranges Are Not the Only Fruit*, broadcast in prime time on BBC2. Winterson's prize-winning novel, first published in 1985, had already achieved the kind of high-art cultural 'cachet' which inevitably became a factor in its adaptation for television, and may – as Hilary Hinds suggests – have eased its reception by normally conservative critics.

In the extract that is given here, Hinds offers an assessment of the broader cultural significance of the series with a detailed and subtle account of the ways in which it was prefigured and then commented upon in both the mainstream and alternative press. In so doing she gives us a precise example of the work of that 'public sphere' in which the meanings of a cultural text are, to some extent, produced and 'fixed'. Her own evaluation of the series is generally positive, on the grounds that it 'made lesbianism a visible presence on television', that the lesbian protagonist was never transformed into either a villain or a victim, that it attracted considerable praise from reviewers and that it provided much pleasure for a lesbian audience.

Hinds traces the 'pre-broadcast nervousness' of the BBC, its institutional anxiety (some three years after conservative political pressure had forced the resignation of its Director-

General) about the likely audience response to 'the uncompromising lesbianism of the text'. In the phase of pre-broadcast publicity the tabloid press focused on the threat and promise of 'explicit nude lesbianism' but this seems to have been followed, after the screening, by an unexpected and generally positive response. Hinds attributes this not only to its status as art, but also to the way in which the critique of Christian religious fundamentalism in *Oranges* may have struck a welcome chord with journalists. An anti-fundamentalist discourse had become common in the press since the 1989 death threat against Salman Rushdie, following the publication of his novel *The satanic verses*. In re-evaluating these discourses, Hinds offers an extremely useful case study of the mediation and representation of a minority culture and its values by the institutions of both broadcasting and the press, at a particular moment in time.

'FIRST FRUIT': *ORANGES* THE NOVEL[1]

Jeanette Winterson's *Oranges are not the only fruit* was published on 21 March 1985 by Pandora Press, the feminist imprint of Routledge & Kegan Paul. Usually described by reviewers as a 'semi-autobiographical novel', it focusses on the childhood and adolescence of 'Jeanette', and her relationship with her evangelical-Christian mother. Her mother's plans for Jeanette to become a missionary are thwarted when she discovers that she is having a sexual relationship with her best friend, Melanie; the rest of the narrative is concerned with Jeanette's resolution of the divergent pulls of church and sexuality on her life. Interspersing this narrative are short fables or fairy tales, commenting on the principal action, and direct interventions by an authorial voice. [...]

'THE YEAR OF THE FRUIT': THE TELEVISION ADAPTATION IN CONTEXT

At the end of December 1989, the television and newspapers were suddenly full of a forthcoming television serial, Winterson's adaptation of her novel *Oranges are not the only fruit*, to be shown in January 1990. A good deal of media publicity and excitement, in the form of extracts, previews and interviews with Winterson herself, heralded the first episode. However, the screening of *Oranges* was also subject to a degree of pre-broadcast nervousness: what would a television audience make of the uncompromising lesbianism of the text? The BBC took precautions, many of the previews making clear that there could be scenes of an 'explicitly' lesbian nature. Despite the producer, director and writer predicting that controversy 'was as likely to result from the satirical treatment of evangelical religion as the sexual content' (*Guardian*, 3 January 1990), the newspapers focussed unerringly on the 'explicit nude lesbianism' (*Today*, 10 January 1990) in their build-up to the screening. Its lesbianism was seen to be the text's defining characteristic, and was the prime focus of the pre-broadcast press excitement.

Elsewhere, however, Winterson also suggested that the lesbianism would indeed be the focus for any controversy generated amongst viewers, because of the way that the protagonist, Jess (Jeanette in the novel), was represented:

> What will make people most angry is a feeling that they have been manipulated because
> it is very difficult *not* to be sympathetic with Jess. You want her to win out and it is very
> difficult to sympathize with the other side which is where most people would normally
> place themselves … Finding themselves in complete sympathy with Jess (rather than
> family or church) is what some will find most difficult.
>
> (*Lancashire Evening Telegraph*, 9 January 1990)

Being 'manipulated' into identifying with a lesbian character, she predicts, will be the source of this hostility. But it did not work out this way; instead, reviewers in tabloids and broadsheets alike applauded long and loud.

What happened, then, to this expected rumpus, the outrage at 'explicit' lesbian sex scenes? In order to investigate this question, two factors contributing to the context in which the text was produced are worth exploring further, before turning to the press responses: first, the specifically historical and political context of the production, and second, the context formed by the history of television drama itself.

Particularly significant for the reception of *Oranges* were the repercussions from the arguments that had circulated in relation to two events of 1988 and 1989 respectively: the passing of Section 28 of the Local Government Act, which aimed to ban the 'promotion of homosexuality' by any bodies funded by local authorities, and the death threat made against Salman Rushdie on the publication of his novel *The satanic verses*. These two events had elements in common, most significantly in the responses and opposition that they elicited: the liberal arts establishment saw each as undermining the principle of free speech. One of the most successful counter-arguments made in opposition to Section 28 was that posed by the arts lobby, who saw 'great works', either by lesbian and gay writers or concerning lesbian and gay issues, as being under threat from this legislation.[2] This argument carried the implication that lesbianism and homosexuality were to be understood differently in this context: they necessitated a response in keeping with their status as art, rather than in relation to their sexual/political status. Concerning Rushdie, the arguments were similar: the novel may be offensive to Islam, nevertheless the artist should not be silenced but allowed to function free from outside political or religious constraints. In both instances, then, the issue of 'art' was seen to be paramount: a text's status as art should protect it from the crudities of political critique. Thus *Oranges* was read in a cultural context where high-cultural 'art' had been established as having a meaning separable from questions of politics, sexual or otherwise.

Significant, too, in relation to Rushdie and to *Oranges*, is the way that religious fundamentalism was represented in the media: freedom of speech was being threatened by religious extremists, who were characterized as repressive, violent and alien to the liberal traditions of their 'host' country. Although this related specifically to the Muslim faith, it fed into and fortified a pre-existing climate of opinion regarding so-called fundamentalism fuelled by news stories from the USA exposing financial corruption and sexual intrigues within the ranks of high-profile evangelical groups. 'Fundamentalism', then, came to be characterized as both a violent threat (viz. Rushdie) and an object for our superior laughter, as its essential hypocrisy was exposed (viz. US groups).[3] Both these elements can be seen to have played their part in the TV representation and media reception of the evangelical group so central to Jess's childhood in *Oranges*.

Also important for the reception of *Oranges* was the specifically television context: the traditions of drama and literary adaptations which have formed such a significant part of (particularly) the BBC's output. One line of the heritage can be traced from the *Wednesday Play* in the 1960s, through *Play for Today* to the current Wednesday night positioning, dubbed by the press the 'controversy slot'; these all have a reputation of presenting high quality work, although the subjects they treat and their modes of visual representation have also earned them the reputation of being 'difficult' or controversial. The other line of the heritage is traceable through the long tradition of literary adaptations on television, initially of nineteenth-century 'classics' by Dickens, Austen, Trollope and so on; and latterly of more contemporary novels such as *Brideshead revisited* and *The jewel in the crown*, until, as with the instances of David Lodge's *Nice work* and Winterson herself, adaptations followed very swiftly on the publication of the novel. *Oranges* was able to draw on these two traditions, the drama and the literary adaptation, for it occupied a drama slot, associated with such prestigious writers as Dennis Potter whose *The Singing Detective* is still used as a benchmark of 'quality' television drama, and yet it was also a literary adaptation and thus took advantage of the pre-existing status of the novel and the author.[4] *Oranges*, then, was able to benefit from the institutional significance of the television drama and the literary adaptation even before the first episode was screened.

'HIGH-QUALITY DRAMA TO SILENCE THE PRUDES': LESBIANISM AND ART TELEVISION

The traditions of television drama and the literary adaptation, then, have strong associations of 'quality' and 'high culture', and are traditions on which, by virtue of its scheduling and publicity, *Oranges* was able to draw. 'Quality' was a watchword from the start, both for author – 'whatever else *Oranges* is, it is very high quality television' (Winterson in *Spare Rib*, February 1990) – and for the previewers and reviewers: 'We *are* discussing art in the case of *Oranges Are Not the Only Fruit*' (*Sunday Times*, 21 January 1990). One of the ways it was identified as 'art' was to mark it out as different from the everyday output of television: 'This series may not be the "safe" kind which automatically delivers huge audiences, but it undeniably provides some of the most moving and humorous scenes seen on television for a long time' (*Television Today*, 18 January 1990).

The programme's quality was widely expected to result in formal recognition through TV awards: many joined with Tom Bussmann in predicting that 'there's a whiff of BAFTA in the air' (*Guardian*, 11 January 1990), and suggested that this was the natural sequel to the novel having won the Whitbread. Only Louise Chunn, writing in the *Guardian*, wondered if Winterson was not straying away from the pinnacles of high culture in adapting her work for the small screen: 'But this is the woman Gore Vidal called "the most interesting young writer I have read in 20 years", she's a Whitbread prize winner, a *serious* writer. Surely she's a novelist above all else?' (*Guardian*, 3 January 1990).

Although Chunn wondered if Winterson's literary credentials were not being compromised by this dallying with a mass medium, and thus with popular culture, other reviewers were more confident that she was simply translating her talents from one area of high culture into another: from 'literature' into a television equivalent of 'art cinema': namely, 'art television'.[5] *Oranges*, placed as it was in the 'serious' Wednesday night slot, can be seen to share a number of characteristics with what film critics have identified as 'art cinema'. With its high-cultural overtones of European seriousness and the avant-garde, 'art cinema' has come to hold an almost revered place in some circles, in contrast to other more popular cultural forms such as Hollywood cinema or television. Thus *Oranges* was able to retain its high-cultural status despite its translation into television, usually ascribed as a low-cultural form. However, the question remains as to how a *lesbian* text was able to occupy this high-cultural space so successfully.

Mandy Merck, in her article '*Lianna* and the lesbians of art cinema' (1986), has suggested that there is a particular relationship between art cinema and the representation of lesbianism: as she aphoristically puts it, 'if lesbianism hadn't existed, art cinema might have invented it' (ibid., p. 166). By this, she means that the representation of lesbianism in art cinema is sufficiently 'different' from dominant (more popular) cinematic representations of sex and sexuality to be seen as courageous and challenging, and yet at the same time it simply offers more of the same: that is, it works with the familiar equation 'woman = sexuality' (ibid.). Merck concludes that 'it is the legitimisation of the female spectacle which makes lesbianism such a gift to art cinema' (ibid., p. 173). Thus what is at stake is not only *what* is represented, but *where* it is represented: the underlying equation of women with sexuality may be the same in all kinds of representation, but none the less lesbianism is read as 'meaning' something different in art cinema than in other contexts; similarly, it was read as meaning something different in 'art television', the context in which *Oranges* was read, than it would have done elsewhere on television.

The 'controversy slot'

As with other 'quality' dramas, the controversy of *Oranges* was seen to arise primarily from the explicit representation of sex. Certain of these productions acted as sexual reference-points for *Oranges*:

> A lesbian love scene between two adolescent girls on BBC2 next week could mark a new stage in the passage of television from the kitchen sink to the boudoir.
> This new challenge to viewers comes after the explicit straight sex of David Lodge's *Nice Work* and Dennis Potter's *Blackeyes*.
>
> (*Sunday Times*, 7 January 1990)

The representation of sex in *Oranges*, then, was seen as an advance on the work of Potter and Lodge in two ways: first, it showed lesbian rather than 'straight' sex, which of necessity represented something more challenging, risky and 'adult'. This seems to confirm that for 'art television', as for art cinema, there is a strong association with and expectation of 'adult' and 'realistic' representations of sex. The sexualized context of this position in the schedule was of significance for the serial's reception: the representation of sex in *Oranges* could be seen as risky and challenging, rather than merely titillating. Secondly, the 'quality' of Winterson's drama was better: *Blackeyes* was repeatedly berated as 'that over-publicized, overrated Dennis Potter effort' (*Lancashire Evening Telegraph*, 9 January 1990) or as 'exploitative nonsense' (*Today*, 10 January 1990). Its 'quality' was a guard against 'those dreary public outbursts of British prudishness' (*Birmingham Post*, 18 January 1990). Together, then, these two elements worked to produce a context in which lesbianism could be read as something positive.

Decentring lesbianism

A second possible reason for the acceptability of the lesbianism in *Oranges* follows from Merck's claim that another of the features of art cinema is that it 'characteristically solicits essential humanist readings' (1986, p. 170). If this were also the case in relation to *Oranges*, then, it would imply that the adaptation's success rested on the critics' ability to read it as being *really* about something other than its lesbianism. If this was so, then it would confound Winterson's own stated hopes, for she asserted quite clearly that she framed the whole text as a challenge:

> I know that *Oranges* challenges the virtues of the home, the power of the church and the supposed normality of heterosexuality. I was always clear that it would do. I would rather not have embarked on the project than see it toned down in any way. That all this should be the case and that it should still have been so overwhelmingly well received cheers me up.
>
> (Winterson, 1990, p. xvii)

The critics, in the mainstream press at least, signally failed to pick up the gauntlet that Winterson had thrown down. As with the novel, the lesbianism is decentred and the critics present us with a drama 'about' all sorts of other things. The three-part series, we are told, 'is fundamentally about a young person looking for love' (*Today*, 10 January 1990); it is 'a wonderfully witty, bitter-sweet celebration of the miracle that more children do not murder their parents' (*Observer*, 14 January 1990); it 'follows Jess in a voyage of self-discovery from her intense religious background, via a friendship with another girl' (*Todmorden News*, 18 August 1989); it is 'a vengeful satire on Protestant fundamentalism' (*Listener*, 18 January 1990). Although *Time Out* complains about 'the author's own use of that hoary liberal cop-out about *Oranges* being about "two people in love" – who wants to see that tedious story again?' (*Time Out*, 18 January 1990), most critics welcomed the opportunity to read *Oranges* as essentially about *all* human relationships, rather than specifically about lesbianism.

As with the novel, the decentring of the lesbianism does not involve its denial: in most accounts of the storyline it is mentioned, but nearly always in relation to something else, generally the ensuing rejection and exorcism of Jess by members of the evangelical group. In this context, lesbianism is seen either as comic comeuppance for her mother's repressive childrearing methods – 'Warned off boys by this hell-fire freak, Jess turns instead to girls' (*Financial Times*, 10 January 1990) – or as a source of pathos: 'a bitter-sweet tragedy, the tale of how a young woman tries and fails to reconcile her religion with her lesbianism' (?1, 11 January 1990).[6] Lesbianism, then, is always seen in relation to other issues, be they religion, the family or simply 'growing up'.

'Unsafe sects'

However, this humanist perspective on the text is only one element in this decentring of lesbianism; another is the emphasis that is placed on the representation of religion. This is important not only as an example of this decentring, but also because, contrary to what most previewers predicted, it was this that became the focus for viewers' and reviewers' anger, rather than the representation of lesbianism itself. So, as well as the evangelical group being seen as one of the main sources of the humour of the series, its members are also written about as ridiculous ('prattling, eye-rolling, God-fearing women', *Daily Express*, 11 January 1990), and as a potentially violent threat ('each and every one ... looked as though she could kill with a blow of her nose', *The Times*, 11 January 1990). Class stereotypes of small-minded working-class women here reinforce the ridiculousness of the evangelicals. Furthermore, their Christian fundamentalism is explicitly linked to Muslim fundamentalism, by now associated with repression and violence in the press reviews: Jess is brought up 'in a provincial family whose fundamentalist religious beliefs make the Ayatollah Khomeini, by contrast, seem a model of polite tolerance' (*Evening Standard*, 22 January 1990). This association of the two fundamentalisms, Christian and Muslim, with repression is further strengthened when *Television Today* expresses the hope that the 'small, if vocal, number of objectors' to the serial will not 'turn writer Jeanette Winterson into the nineties Salman Rushdie' (*Television Today*, 18 January 1990).

Subject to the most anger, however, was the exorcism of Jess carried out by the pastor and assorted members of the congregation when her sexual relationship with Melanie is discovered. Critics commented on the 'brutal' nature of this scene, noted that it is 'sexually charged', and Steve Clarke suggested that: 'if anybody was disturbed by the scene in which the pastor – armed with rope, gag and pulsating neck – straddled the young Jess to exorcise the demon of illicit love, then so they should have been' (*Sunday Times*, 21 January 1990). Hilary Kingsley in the *Mirror* concurred: the headline announced that the scene was 'Brutal, Shocking, Horrifying. But You Mustn't Miss It' (*Daily Mirror*, 15 January 1990). Anger and disgust were not only legitimate – they were to be actively sought as the 'correct' response; thus emotions that many expected to be directed towards the lesbian scenes were actually located instead with the representation of this repressive religious group. Perhaps it was possible for so much sympathy to be shown to the plight of Jess and Melanie not only because of the way their relationship was interpreted, but also because of the brutality of the punishment that they underwent. Their persecutors had already been established as outmoded, repressive and anti-sex, and it was a small step to add violence to this list by drawing on pre-existing connotations of fundamentalism: 'Jess ... is promptly subjected by her mother's fundamentalist sect to the sort of persecution and torture so dear to the hearts of religious fanatics throughout the ages' (*Financial Times*, 10 January 1990).

This clearly suggests that the punishment tells us more about religious fundamentalists than it does about the status of lesbianism in our society. The liberal viewer can feel distanced from the punishment meted out to Jess because these people, after all, are not 'normal' members of our society. This sympathy, then, can be seen to rest on two mutually reinforcing bases: first, it is a response to the punitive, anti-sex attitudes of the evangelical group – and even gay and lesbian sexual rights had increasingly become the objects of liberal championing since the passing of Section 28; and second, it is responding to the representation of fundamentalism, which had become a prominent liberal target in the wake of the Rushdie affair. Thus it appears that the yoking of the lesbianism with the fundamentalism was itself crucial for the favourable mainstream liberal response: lesbianism became an otherness preferable to the unacceptable otherness of fundamentalism.

'Unnatural passions': the role of the sex scene

If the representation of the evangelical group is a crucial factor in determining critical response to the series, this raises the question of what place *was* ascribed to lesbian sexuality by the reviewers. In relation to art cinema, Merck suggests that the lesbian love scene carries a particularly heavy burden of meaning: because of the tendency to allegorize these films, to read them as essentially about something other than the overt narrative, these scenes have taken on a particular symbolic function, namely 'the ability to represent "lesbian experience"' (1986, p. 169), to encapsulate the entire range of meanings of lesbianism, whether sexual, social or political. What meanings, then, were ascribed to *Oranges'* long-awaited sex scene, 'arguably the most explicit female love scene yet broadcast on British television' (*Sunday Times*, 7 January 1990)?

The makers of the series declared that their intention with this scene was 'to avoid the kind of romantic idealism with which lesbian scenes were portrayed in the 1988 BBC production of D.H. Lawrence's *The Rainbow*' (*Sunday Times*, 7 January 1990). The producer, Philippa Giles, told the *Daily Mirror*: 'We decided to make it obvious that the girls were having a sexual relationship, not a wishy-washy thing . . . We wanted to face the question everyone asks – *What do lesbians DO?*' (*Daily Mirror*, 15 January 1990). Most reviewers, however, read it with the kind of romantic idealism the makers were trying to eschew. It is 'romantic, innocent and beautiful', wrote Christopher Dunkley (*Financial Times*, 10 January 1990); the erotic relationship is portrayed in a way 'which maintains its essential innocence' (*7 Days*, 11 January 1990). Steve Clarke, in the *Sunday Times*, surpassed the others in his breathless enthusiasm for the scene: 'the two girls' tentative exploration of each other's bodies was almost Disneyesque in its innocent wonderment' (*Sunday Times*, 21 January 1990); anybody who objected to these scenes would simply be 'dreary' (*Today*, 10 January 1990). There is scant evidence, then, that these reviewers were shocked by this representation of lesbianism. Not only did the manifest youth of Jess and Melanie allow them to define and praise the relationship in terms of its tenderness and innocence, it also implicitly allowed the lesbianism to be understood as an adolescent phase, a naive exploration that would be outgrown. Moreover, the fact that the critics ignored any other scenes that might modify, or even contradict, this reading of tenderness and innocence meant that this characterization of the sex scene alone was allowed to represent the text's 'lesbianism', avoiding any broader or more challenging meaning of lesbianism.

Significantly few of the mainstream reviewers commented on *Oranges* as in any way erotic. Whilst most talked only of Jess's first relationship, with Melanie, in the 'quality' press only Mark Steyn allowed Jess's relationship with Katy, her second lover, to contribute to his assessment of the text:

> More shocking than any nudity was the parallel between religious salvation and sexual discovery, subtly drawn in scenes which were nevertheless masterpieces of suppressed eroticism. 'You were going to tell me about Jesus,' said Katy. 'Well, what is it you wanted to *know*?' asked Jess. 'Why don't you tell me,' Katy replied, lolling against the caravan, '*gradually*'.
>
> (*Independent*, 25 January 1990)

Steyn alone showed a willingness to go beyond the feeling that for lesbianism to be acceptable it had to be tender, innocent, essentially asexual.

Critics elsewhere, however, were more willing to contemplate an active erotic reading of the text. In the alternative publications, on the one hand, and in some of the tabloids, on the other, there is a marked contrast to this predominantly liberal mainstream interpretation of the sexuality in *Oranges*. Some of the tabloids, for example, made a concerted effort to construct a pornographic reading of the text.

They anticipated the 'fruitiest lesbian love scenes ever on British TV' (?2, 11 January 1990), employing words like 'steamy' or 'torrid', and concentrated on the actresses' feelings about the sex scene to try to enhance this sense of the illicit and risky. Most notable of these attempts was one that appeared in *Today*:

> According to a male friend, the lesbian love scenes in this drama are not nearly fruity enough. In order to fully fulfil the 'ultimate male fantasy' he says the actresses should have had bigger breasts.
>
> What we need, he adds, is a lot more tits. Samantha Fox and Maria Whitaker would be ideal.
>
> Had this transpired, I would have had to suggest a slightly different title for this excellent serial: Melons Are Not the Only Fruit . . .
>
> *(Today, 25 January 1990)*

By referring to perhaps the two most famous 'Page 3' models as potential participants in this drama, there is a clear – perhaps even rather desperate – attempt to recruit what had looked as if it was going to be 'the ultimate male fantasy' for that function. The serial had evidently fallen short of what might be expected of something that included 'explicit nude lesbianism'. Since it was not close enough to the ethos of 'Page 3', it was necessary both to force this reading on to the text by means of such epithets as 'torrid' and 'steamy', and to reconstruct it as a tabloid ideal by recasting and renaming it, both of which would emphasize more strongly its pornographic possibilities. Whilst, then, the 'eroticism' of the text was acknowledged as central here, this review makes clear that the text did not lend itself easily to the expected and desired pornographic understanding of lesbianism: it was seen as having a meaning independent of, or separate from, dominant male fantasy, and was thus in need of reworking in line with such conventions.

In the alternative presses, by contrast, this separateness both from male fantasy and from 'Disneyesque' tenderness was seen as one of the serial's strengths: Jonathan Sanders in *Gay Times* noted that 'Jess and Melanie's fireside coupling steered a fine course between eroticism and the straight male prurience consideration' (*Gay Times*, March 1990). Cherry Smyth's assessment of the sex scene, in *Spare Rib*, identified it as 'radical' and different from more usual representations of lesbianism on TV:

> Although a little pre-Raphaelite in style, the scene is uncomplicated and unapologetic. Their refreshing lack of embarrassment and shame is a breakthrough for a mainstream TV drama slot. Is BBC2 stealing the radical remit from Channel 4? Jess is too knowing and sure of her desire for the scene to collapse into pre-pubescent coyness and 'innocent' caressing.
>
> *(Spare Rib, February 1990)*

The very quality of innocence which the mainstream reviewers identified is denied here, and is instead replaced by its opposite: the assertion that Jess is 'knowing' and 'sure of her desire'. Sanders, similarly, had found 'heartening' the 'uniform moral ease and technical skill with which the teenage lesbians expressed their desires' (*Gay Times*, March 1990). Although Rosalind Brunt identified one of the main themes of *Oranges* as 'passionate erotic friendship between young women' (*New Statesman and Society*, 12 January 1990), it was only the lesbian and gay critics who situated the text firmly within a discourse of desire. Not only was 'innocence' countered in these reviews, but also, in *Spare Rib* in particular, there was an emphasis on the subtlety of the sexual references employed: 'Jess introduces Melanie to church and leads the congregation in "When I was sleeping, somebody touched me", a delightful innuendo that prefigures the scene where the young women make love' (*Spare Rib*, February 1990). This interpretation and emphasis from Smyth suggests that perhaps the text operated rather differently for lesbian and gay audiences: used to relying on the subtleties of innuendo and veiled meanings, they read the text through a specific set of codes apparently undiscerned by other audiences.[7]

The politics of the lesbian text

As well as discussing the sex scene, Smyth also broadened out the political focus of her review by stressing the radical possibilities of the representation of lesbianism in *Oranges*: 'At the point where the fate of many a dramatic lesbian character is firmly sealed, Jess continues to convert young women to her way of loving' (*Spare Rib*, February 1990); Jess thus retains her position as agent and heroine throughout. This review is notable, too, for referring outside the series, to a 'lived experience' of lesbianism, in order to measure the 'quality' of the drama: 'The awkward milkshakes and doorways she shares with Katy, her young Asian lover, convey the desperately unhappy courtship of adolescents who haven't "somewhere proper to go"' (ibid.).

It was not only the alternative publications that hinted at the political significance of the drama. Kate Battersby, in *Today*, hinted at a feminist reading of the text when she suggested that 'many women will identify with the adolescent Jess's bid for freedom and self-expression' (*Today*, 10 January 1990). Another very favourable piece, also by a woman, Hilary Kingsley, says that *Oranges* is:

> an important milestone for women.
>
> Male homosexuality has been represented in television drama frequently over the years.
>
> But to television, as to Queen Victoria, lesbians do not exist – except in an Australian jail.
>
> No wonder the late night soap *Prisoner: Cell Block H* has a high following among gay women.
>
> (*Daily Mirror*, 15 January 1990)

Despite historical inaccuracies (lesbianism clearly *had* been represented on television before),[8] Kingsley was identifying something important by suggesting that *Oranges* was an exceptional text in making lesbianism its central concern.

Lesbian viewers seemed to agree that *Oranges* was a milestone, staying at home in droves on Wednesday nights to watch it. This enthusiasm was in part, no doubt, because it made lesbianism a visible presence on television where, with the exceptions of *Prisoner*, *Out on Tuesday* and some documentaries and films, it was usually invisible. Moreover, it became visible in a mainstream slot, rather than in the furtive late-night positions of most representations of lesbian and gay issues on television. The way that the lesbianism was represented was also unusual: rather than becoming either villain or victim, the lesbian protagonist remained a heroine throughout. The screening of *Oranges* on BBC2 also represented the infiltration of that bastion of television high-cultural respectability by a programme directed and produced by women, scripted by a lesbian, and one whose main theme was lesbianism; this, too, added a certain edge to the pleasure of *Oranges* for a lesbian audience. Furthermore, whatever debates may rage about the dangers or desirability of being accepted by dominant culture, here, at last, was a programme about lesbianism that, far from being run down or ignored by the reviewers, was praised to the skies. From many perspectives, then, *Oranges* signified something pleasurable and exceptional for lesbian viewers.

CONCLUSION: *ORANGES* TO EVERYONE'S TASTE

BBC's *Oranges Are Not the Only Fruit* . . . had the capacity to make us laugh and cry, to shock us with its brutal exorcism scene, to move us with its compassion for youthful lesbian love and to leave us – as at the end of a good book – silently grieving the loss of a friend.

   Oranges is a book, of course. And how delighted author Jeanette Winterson must have been. Seldom can a fine novel have been transported with such skill and with such little disruption to the small screen.

(*Daily Express*, 25 January 1990)

In many ways Peter Tory's review summarizes some of the complexities of what *Oranges* represented for viewers, as well as suggesting some of the reasons why it met with the success that it did. To begin with, it confirms the text as an example of high-status 'art': the prestige lent to the whole enterprise by the presence of the original novel; the 'faithfulness' of the adaptation, avoiding what Mark Steyn had called 'the coarsening effects' of translation into a mass medium (*Independent*, 25 January 1990); the text's capacity to appeal to our common humanity and provoke the great and enduring human emotions and responses of joy, sadness, anger and compassion – all these confirm the text's relationship to high culture.

   And yet this review did not appear in a 'quality' newspaper, where we might expect to find support for such a cultural product, but in the popular press, endorsing a serial whose precursors, such as Potter's *Blackeyes*, had often been roundly condemned as pretentious nonsense. Moreover, it appeared in the *Daily Express*, a newspaper not usually noted for its sympathy for 'do-gooding' liberal causes. Tory's 'compassion for youthful lesbian love' may not be the response which many lesbians would seek, but it is none the less an unequivocally and uncharacteristically welcoming reading of the production's representation of lesbianism.

   These complexities and ambiguities demonstrate the need to consider the validity of the terms of the high/popular culture divide, for *Oranges*, as a complete cultural product – author, novel, television drama – seems consistently to elude and collapse these categories. Central to this elusiveness seems to be the text's lesbianism. Although it may be true to say that the lesbianism is defused by the text's associations with high culture and its consequent openness to a liberal interpretation, it is also true that *Oranges* has retained, and increased, its lesbian audience and its subcultural consumption, and has also been praised by a tabloid press usually hostile to lesbian and gay issues.

   Not all lesbian texts, of course, operate as *Oranges* does. However, the remarkable, if rather confusing, popularity of this text highlights some of the general complexities that emerge when one introduces the category of the 'lesbian text' into cultural analysis. Whilst it is possible to think of several lesbian texts that come within the category of high culture, such as those of Gertrude Stein or Radclyffe Hall, and others, such as those by Sarah Dreher and Anne Bannon, that would be considered lesbian pulp fiction, many lesbian texts defy such categorizations. Indeed, even the examples mentioned above pose problems: some critics happily claim *The well of loneliness* for the canon whilst still conceding that it is 'bad writing'. Moreover, the readership of much recent lesbian pulp fiction is arguably more diverse than its heterosexual equivalent. Precisely because of the lack of representations of lesbianism within mainstream culture, lesbian texts which are available take on a particular significance. Lesbian readers and viewers do not divide neatly into consumers of high or popular culture, since their prime interest here is often the representation of a lifestyle, an identity or a sexuality which is marked by its absence elsewhere within the media or literature. This, then, raises the question of whether the introduction of the question of lesbianism confounds many of the assumptions about texts and readers which have informed debates about high and popular culture in much criticism in recent years.

And what, finally, of *Oranges* itself? Its fluidity, its ability to cut across so many critical and cultural categories and positions, its refusal to be pigeonholed as one sort of text or another, its appeal for a diversity of audiences all having been asserted, it is impossible to arrive at a conclusive statement about it. Perhaps it is enough to suggest that any text that can transgress so many barriers deserves all the critical attention – from whatever source and from whatever perspective – that it can get.[9]

ACKNOWLEDGEMENTS

I would like to thank the following people for their help, and for their perceptive and encouraging comments on earlier drafts of this article: Richard Dyer, Lynne Pearce, Martin Pumphrey, Margaret Reynolds, Fiona Terry and, especially, Jackie Stacey.

NOTES

1. Subtitles appearing in inverted commas are borrowed from newspaper reviews of *Oranges*.
2. For further exploration of the terms of the challenges presented to Section 28, *see* Jackie Stacey (1991).
3. For a discussion of Western characterizations of Islam, *see* Edward Said (1978). For a discussion of the impact of the Gulf War on such notions, *see* Kevin Robins (1991, pp. 42–4).
4. For discussions of the notion of 'quality' television, *see* Paul Kerr (1982) and Charlotte Brunsdon (1990).
5. 'Art television' remains a rather tentative concept within critical work; John Caughie, however, provides a useful discussion of it (1981).
6. Extracts that are referenced ?1 and ?2 are from uncredited reviews kindly sent to me by Pandora Press.
7. For examples of studies which have moved away from textual analysis and investigated audiences and readers of popular texts, *see* Ien Ang (1985) and Janice A. Radway (1984).
8. Previous representations of lesbianism on television are few and far between. They include isolated episodes in serials and soap operas such as *Brookside, EastEnders, St Elsewhere, The Golden Girls*, and the 1988 dramatization of D.H. Lawrence's *The Rainbow*; or, more unusually, TV movies such as *The Ice Palace* and *A Question of Love*, which dealt more centrally with lesbianism.

9. In relation to the author's n. 7 (above) it is worth mentioning a study which valuably connects this drama's structure with particular readings of it made by sample viewers. See J. Hallam and M. Marshment, 'Framing experience: case studies in the reception of *Oranges Are Not the Only Fruit*', *Screen* 36(1) (1995). (Eds.)

REFERENCES

ANG, I. 1985: *Watching Dallas: soap opera and the melodramatic imagination*. London: Methuen.

BRUNSDON, C. 1990: Problems with quality. *Screen* 31(1), 67–90.

CAUGHIE, J. 1981: Rhetoric, pleasure and 'art television' – dreams of leaving. *Screen* 22(4), 9–31.

KERR, P. 1982: Classic serials – to be continued. *Screen* 23(1), 6–19.

MERCK, M. 1986: *Lianna* and the lesbians of art cinema. In Brunsdon, C. (ed.), *Films for Women*. London: BFI Publishing.

RADWAY, J.A. 1984: *Reading the romance: women, patriarchy and popular literature*. Chapel Hill: University of North Carolina Press.

ROBINS, K. 1991: The mirror of unreason. *Marxism Today*, March.

SAID, E. 1978: *Orientalism*. London: Routledge & Kegan Paul.

STACEY, J. 1991: Promoting normality: Section 28 and the regulation of sexuality. In Franklin, S., Lury, C. and Stacey, J. (eds.), *Off centre: feminism and cultural studies*. London: HarperCollins Academic.

WINTERSON, J. 1985: *Oranges are not the only fruit*. London: Pandora.

WINTERSON, J. 1990: *Oranges Are Not the Only Fruit: the script*. London: Pandora.

11

Situation comedy and stereotyping

Andy Medhurst and Lucy Tuck

From Cook, J. (ed.) 1982: *Television situation comedy*. London: British Film Institute, 43–5, 49–52

'Stereotype' is a much-used word in public discussion of the media as well as in media studies. However, a number of problems surround it. Initially a metaphor drawn from printing – the use of preset metal type-blocks for certain kinds of routine use – the word now carries with it a strong sense of distorted portrayal, of prejudice and unfairness. Criticism of 'stereotyping' has been applied to the full range of media output, but comedy programmes are a particularly sensitive area. First of all, they routinely draw on 'social types' in order to proceed with sufficient colour of character and pace of narrative. Second, they routinely project certain social characteristics as derisory, trading to a large extent on pre-existent audience disposition here and quite possibly thereby reinforcing it.

Medhurst and Tuck explore stereotyping in relation to situation comedy, a form distinctive to television and one in which 'typing' is conventional. We include here two extracts from their early 1980s article. In the first of these, the authors have valuable things to say both about the nature of situation comedy – its social relations, the kind of sense of community which it attempts to generate – and about stereotyping too. In the second extract, they look specifically at the way in which gays and gay culture have been presented in sitcoms. They are interested in documenting not only the predictable connotations of 'deviance' which surround many sitcom depictions of gay people but also the variety of ways in which these are articulated and in the presence, too, of less negative approaches, where gay characters are closer to being integrated within the terms of the main narrative.

Since Medhurst and Tuck wrote their piece, there have been many changes in television's depiction of sexuality (for instance, see item 10), but much of their commentary remains insightful and of continuing relevance. In making their points, they refer to a number of British television programmes of the period which will not be known to students today. However, since the points about individual programmes are brief, helpful to the development of their argument and clear in implication, we have included them in the extract.

Sitcom cannot function without stereotypes. In a space as brief as a thirty-minute sitcom, immediacy is imperative, and for a character to be immediately funny that character must be a recognisable type, a representative embodiment of a set of ideas or a manifestation of a cliché. Dependence on stereotyping was always a reason for the dismissal of popular television as unimaginative masses-fodder, but the primary alternative tradition of character depiction, the 'well-rounded individual' as found in the nineteenth-century novel, simply would not work in sitcom. Over a period of years and series we have come to know more 'facts' about George and Mildred, come to see them more and more as fleshed-out individuals, but we would not have laughed at them in the first place, never wanted to see more of them (leading to their elevation from supporting roles in *Man about the House* to stars of their own series), if they had not been immediately recognisable types that fitted in with our cultural notions of the comic: nagging, sexually demanding wife with delusions of bourgeois grandeur, and threatened, likeably devious husband.

Sitcom situations are usually just as stereotyped (predictable, ritualistic) as the characters: in fact, they are often one and the same thing. Nothing outside the central personal battle need actually happen in *George and Mildred* – he and she *are* the plot; any other elements or characters in an episode become nothing more than framing devices around what viewers really want to see – this week's variation on the theme of the warring couple. George and Mildred are at one end of the spectrum of couples present in sitcom: they are the recognisably stereotyped, intrinsically funny couple; the other extreme is a bland pair like Oliver and Sandy in *Rings on Their Fingers*, not in any way strong stereotypes, not even funny in themselves, but humour is generated by placing them in intrinsically funny situations. Of course we are not using terms like 'intrinsically funny' at face value, and we shall be returning to the ideological assumptions behind standard sitcom notions of what is or is not funny later in this essay.

Another device prevalent in sitcoms is the tendency to resolve conflicts, reduce problems, by resorting to folk wisdom and proverbialism. Their constant reaffirmation of 'common sense' attitudes is a way of defusing crises that at times border on melodrama (*George and Mildred*'s recurrent themes of class conflict, marital strife, childlessness and impotence all seem more suitable for agonising over than laughing about) and a way of resigning oneself to things with the sigh of 'well, life's like that'. Given a basic, non-judgmental description of sitcom as stereotypically funny characters going through the mechanisms of predictable situations, the continual recourse to cliché and proverb comes as no surprise. Class must be mentioned here since as sitcoms seem to assume that working-class audiences have a greater familiarity with proverbial solutions, this might account for bourgeois criticisms of sitcom as 'unoriginal', which is in itself a position deriving from the middle-class dread of cliché.

The association of sitcom with working-class audiences is best examined via the notion of sitcom as collective experience. Cultural historians[1] have stressed that a vital factor of such working-class cultural experiences as Victorian melodrama and music hall (before these became patronised, in both senses of the word, by more middle-class visitors) was the sense of community, of solidarity, felt by the audience. Such entertainments were deliberately escapist, in that they allowed audiences to briefly recapture the sense of community destroyed by industrialisation and urban expansion. The earliest years of cinema were similarly enjoyed as collective experience, and the last genuine survivors of this tradition were Northern music halls of the 1920s and 1930s. Jeff Nuttall and Rodick Carmichael, in their bafflingly neglected book on Northern working-class culture, illustrate the collective nature of this tradition in humour:

> Two Rochdale millworkers are stuck in a corner of the Co-op Hall. Gracie Fields . . . is giving a concert for her own folk. In this corner nothing can be seen or heard because of the density of the crowd between them and the stage.
> 'We shan't see owt from 'ere,' says the old chap.
> 'Ne'er need,' says his wife. 'We shall 'ave to laugh when t'others laugh.'[2]

Television sitcom is an attempt, in the face of changing historical realities, to recreate precisely that tradition – implicitly by its outdated view of society, explicitly by its use of an audible laugh track, the vestigial reminder of the music hall audience, the electronic substitute for collective experience. Sitcom invites the viewer to feel at one with the few dozen people s/he can hear laughing, and by extension with millions of others across the country. To perpetuate this myth of a unified population, laughing with one voice at *On the Buses*, sitcom must ignore the fragmentary nature of modern society and instead posit an idealised organic nation. This can be done either by deliberately re-creating a (suitably sanitised) past era, as in *Dad's Army* or *Backs to the Land*, or by removing all disturbing contemporary issues from series ostensibly set in the 1980s. *Terry and June* probably epitomises this second tendency, set as it is in what has been aptly called 'the timeless nowness of television situations'.[3] Such conservatism is nowhere more clearly revealed than in attitudes to sex and gender, which in most sitcoms seem to be stuck in the early 1950s: pre-'permissiveness', pre-feminism.

Certain recent sitcoms have attempted to dispense with such conservatism, even with stereotype and cliché, and we will be looking at *Agony* and *Shelley* in this context, but another example is instructive here. The 'quality' press only takes seriously those sitcoms which proclaim their intention to break the mould, and so Peter Fiddick welcomed *Roger Doesn't Live Here Anymore* in October 1981. Yet the most cursory glance shows that *Roger* is just as reliant on the old stereotypes as Fiddick's least favourite ITV schedule-filler, whatever that might currently be, containing as it does the shrill unforgiving wife, the likeably feckless husband and the generous, sexy girlfriend. [. . .]

GAYS IN SITCOM

We have already argued that one major function of comedy is to reassure its audience, via laughter, of the existence of a community of which the individual viewer or viewing group is an unproblematically integrated member. This illusion of community is strengthened by literally making fun of any behaviour deemed to be unacceptable to that community; in other words: deviance. In the area of sex and gender, this leads to the rendering as comic of any form of marginalised and/or oppositional sexual self-expression, notably homosexuality. Sitcom deals almost exclusively with male homosexuality, lesbianism being an intriguing absence, perhaps explained by its implicit disregard of male heterosexual ego and the fact that the overwhelming majority of sitcoms are produced by heterosexual men. It is briefly mentioned in the last episode of the first series of *Solo* (written by a woman). Gemma's mother expresses her relief that Gemma and Danny are living together again by saying 'she's normal, my daughter's normal', a remark she has prefaced by admitting her worry that Gemma was 'turning butch'. Given such remarks, perhaps we should be grateful that lesbianism is so rarely mentioned.

To understand sitcom's treatment of male homosexuality, we shall have to return, with greater specificity, to the question of stereotyping. The sitcom queen, all wrists and sibilants, is surely, many would argue, where discussions of the positive possibilities of stereotypes must break down. The instinctive reaction to such an offensive caricature is to reject it entirely, yet, as Richard Dyer has written:

> Righteous dismissal does not make the stereotypes go away, and tends to prevent us from understanding just what the stereotypes are, how they function, ideologically and aesthetically . . . In addition, there is a real problem as to just what we would put in their place.[4]

Dyer's excellent essay is part of the critical tendency which attempts a re-evaluation of stereotyping. Dyer contrasts stereotypical portrayals of gays in cinema with other, more traditionally three-dimensional characterisations to be found in films like *Sunday Bloody Sunday*, and argues that a politically committed analysis must find the latter inadequate, since they,

> by their focus on uniqueness and inner growth, tend to prevent people from seeing themselves in terms of class, sex, group or race . . . make it very difficult to think of there being solidarity, sisterhood or brotherhood, collective identity and action . . . tend to stress gayness as a personality issue, a problem to which there are only individual solutions . . .[5]

These remarks should be enough to convince most people of the value of typing in theory, if not every stereotype in practice.

In a sense it is not male homosexuality *per se* that is the butt of so many sneering jokes, but male femininity (we prefer not to use the value-laden word 'effeminacy', which is itself a product of the narrow conception of gender we are attacking). The stereotype of the mincing, lisping man is all that the mass heterosexual audience has seen as identifiably homosexual (until recently), being present in music hall jokes, silent film comedy (Chaplin's *Behind the Screen*, from 1916, is the earliest example we know of) and popular song (a dance band tune called 'Masculine Women and Feminine Men' dates from the late 1920s) long before its incarnation in television sitcom. The merciless ridicule that the idea of feminine men has been subjected to shows how threatening such an idea has been to the prevailing sexual ideology and must make us wary of dismissing those types out of hand. As Dyer points out, this is as hasty and defensive as the self-righteous tendency of some gay men to disown their more flamboyantly nonconformist brothers, and must be resisted. Some sitcom stereotypes, however, make such judiciousness difficult to maintain.

As a test case for these ideas, consider Gloria in *It Ain't Half Hot Mum*. It would be possible, should one feel in a generous mood, to make a fairly positive appraisal of this character. Sexuality aside, he is a funny sitcom type because of his ludicrous over-ambition to re-create MGM musicals in the middle of the jungle, and ambition is always mocked and frustrated in sitcom – think of Mildred or of Harold Steptoe. The problem is that we just cannot say 'sexuality aside', since the immediate reaction of any mass 'family' audience is to see him as homosexual, and funny for that reason alone. His ambitiousness may be a secondary source of humour, but Gloria is coded as funny primarily because of his 'unnatural' behaviour, his visible difference, his campness, which has long been the only instantly recognisable signifier of homosexuality in popular culture. To read homosexuality as intrinsically funny is aided, indeed directed, in *It Ain't Half Hot Mum* by the figure of the Sergeant Major, with his insulting, Alf Garnett-like shouts of 'poofs!'. Unlike Garnett, however, there is no suggestion in the text that the Sergeant Major is an intentionally ridiculous figurehead of prejudice. The main joke against him, the fact that those he labels 'poofs' are, with the undeclared exception of Gloria, in fact heterosexual, serves to reinforce the idea of homosexuality as an insult.

This is a common link in sitcom. In a 1980 episode of *Robin's Nest*, two non-gay men are forced to share a bed (this situation deserves an essay in itself; as an indication of the growth of public awareness of gayness as a sexual practice and not just a set of mannerisms, we have seen the shift from Morecambe and Wise unproblematically sharing a bed to Cannon and Ball's paranoid dread of even touching each other). One warns the other against any 'funny business', to which the reply is 'oh come on, that's insulting'. The statement is as simple and direct as that. There is no audience laughter. This episode was transmitted on Christmas Eve, at peak time. Family viewing indeed.

It is against such a background that we must set Rob and Michael in *Agony*. It could be argued that in their middle-class monogamous niceness they are unlikely to overthrow patriarchy, but such a response is not only nit-picking, it also reveals a lack of awareness of the institutional (which is to say ideological) structures within which sitcom is situated. Perhaps the most positive factor in *Agony* is not the presence of Rob and Michael, but the crucial absence of any character mouthing anti-gay prejudices. It would have been only too easy to slip in a few homophobic jibes, but instead it is the gay couple who can smile at heterosexual men's inadequacies. Len Richmond's comment that his great hope was that 'some little gay boy in Scotland on a farm somewhere will see the show and realize that everyone who is gay isn't a neurotic weirdo'[6] might at first seem rather glib and earnest and naive in its assumptions about the 'effect' of television, but Rob and Michael are unquestionably an improvement on the indelibly inscribed homophobia of *It Ain't Half Hot Mum* (a programme which, one of us can testify from personal experience, was hardly conducive to the growth of a positive self-image for at least one gay schoolboy, even if not on a Highland croft).

Even the most positive reading of, say, Gloria would be necessarily undermined by the fact that the character is conceived by and for heterosexuals. Gays have the right to present themselves as camp, since campness is a part of gay culture – but for heterosexuals to reduce gayness to a handful of ridiculed gesticulations is another matter entirely. Melvyn Hayes' otherwise excellent portrayal of the star-struck queen Gloria is repeatedly betrayed by his assertions to the press that he's a real man after all, proof of which he flourishes in the number of children he's fathered (the actor who played Rob in *Agony* was guilty of a similar needless muscle-flexing). Dyer has extended this point:

> What is wrong with these stereotypes is not that they are inaccurate ... What we should
> be attacking ... is the attempt of heterosexual society to define us for ourselves, in terms
> that inevitably fall short of the 'ideal' of heterosexuality ... the task is to develop our own
> alternative and challenging definitions of ourselves.[7]

A possible way of doing this, which would circumvent the rather anaemic 'positive images' of Rob and Michael, would be to take the raw material of the Gloria stereotype, the uncompromisingly non-masculine man, and shape a new type out of this. The only achievement that has come close was in radio comedy: Julian and Sandy in *Round the Horne*. These characters worked on two levels. While the mass audience was laughing at their difference, their absurdly theatricalised male femininity, gay audiences picked up on their use of gay slang, a genuine subtext. A favourite example (which must stand as a triumph over censorship): Julian, remarking on Sandy's piano-playing abilities, says, 'And you should see him perform on a cottage upright', 'cottage' being gay slang for public toilets. If this is rather exclusive (though it does show how in comedy language *is* power), *Round the Horne* was progressive in two more general ways which still leave almost all television sitcoms standing: it acknowledged that a proportion of its audience was not part of the dominant social group (i.e. was not heterosexual) and it often made non-gay characters the stooges of gay characters' jokes.

Radio comedy, however, is less institutionally constrained than television sitcom. Given sitcom's absolutely central position within the mass cultural production of television (with mass equalling heterosexual), can we expect to see 'alternative and challenging definitions', or is such a hope unattainable idealism? The latter is quite possibly true, and political purists would in any case argue that a minority's first duty is to strengthen its own culture; but a ghetto culture, though essential in many respects to any marginalised group, is not going to counter the ignorance-based myths of the mass audience, let alone make contact with Len Richmond's hypothetical young gay Scot. Interventions must be made.

Having said that, we are still waiting for a sitcom with an uncomplicatedly positive depiction of gayness. *Agony* has come closest, and the character of Lukewarm in *Porridge* is pleasurably integrated into the narrative of that series. Then again, comedy does not deal with the uncomplicatedly positive in any sphere, but with manageable quantities of upheaval and disruption. Is it, then, too much to hope for a treatment of gayness analogous to the distinction we have identified in sitcom's approaches to the heterosexual couple – a spectrum ranging from the deliberately stereotypical funny gay to the ordinary gay who is placed in deliberately stereotypical funny situations?

NOTES

1. *See*, for example, Douglas A. Reid, 'Popular theatre in Victorian Birmingham', in Bradby, D. *et al.* (eds.), *Performance and politics in popular drama* (Cambridge, 1980).
2. Jeff Nuttall and Rodick Carmichael, *Common Factors/Vulgar Factions* (London, Routledge & Kegan Paul, 1977).
3. Mick Eaton, 'Television situation comedy', *Screen* (Winter 1978/9), p. 70.
4. Richard Dyer, 'Stereotyping', in Dyer, R. (ed.), *Gays and Film* (London, British Film Institute, 1980), p. 27.
5. Dyer, 'Stereotyping', p. 36.
6. Quoted in Brayfield, *Evening Standard*, 9 March 1979.
7. Dyer, 'Stereotyping', p. 31.

12

History with holes: Channel 4 films of the 1980s

Paul Giles

From Friedman, L. (ed.) 1993: *Fires were started: British cinema and Thatcherism.*
London: UCL Press, 70–91

Britain acquired its fourth national television channel in 1982. The new entrant was advertiser-funded but set up as a non-profit-making institution, with a parliamentary remit to foster experiment and innovation and to cater to audience needs not met by other channels. Cinema attendances had been declining since the 1950s, under the impact of the increasing popularity of virtually 'no cost' television, and were to reach an all-time low in 1984, shortly after the new channel's inception.

Channel 4 was innovative in many different ways: in providing an hour-long news programme in peak time, an audience 'Right to Reply' slot, a late-night experimental programme, *The Eleventh Hour*, and a host of special screenings and seasons as well as a sharp and sometimes provocative new 'soap', the Liverpool-based *Brookside*. However, arguably one of its greatest structural innovations was its deliberate policy of helping to sustain the ailing British film industry. Under the direction of its Chief Executive, Jeremy Isaacs, and Head of Drama, David Rose, a national television company embarked on the radical project of positively developing cinema as an institution, and not just peacefully coexisting with it. Between 1982 and 1990 under the 'Film on Four' label Channel 4 partially funded around 170 feature films. And while it is easy, with the wisdom of hindsight, to celebrate the success of this initiative it was, at the beginning, a bold and risky undertaking.

Paul Giles offers not only a general account of this innovative development but also an aesthetic and ideological analysis of selected examples of the 'Film on Four' output during the 1980s. He distinguishes a particular cluster of films which, he argues, offered both a critical and a self-reflexive account of British history, while positively recognizing and working within the aesthetic limitations of the television medium. The extracts offered here proceed from an account of the significance of the initiative for the British film industry to an argument about the cultural quality of the work, suggesting that, by contrast with the conventional character of the American 'B' movie made for television, these Channel 4 films offer a self-consciously innovative representation of Britain's past.

Giles suggests that a complex aesthetic is at work in these films, arguing that they offer a dialectic of the familiar with the unfamiliar, exposing in the process the 'fissures and ambiguities' within the national television audience's understanding of history. As a kind of magical realism replaces any kind of 'simplified nostalgia', and as films like *The*

Ploughman's Lunch explore the politicized repackaging of recent British history (Suez, the Falklands), these stories refuse to accept history as received wisdom. Rather they present a 'history with holes, perforated history' (here Giles draws on a terminology developed by Fredric Jameson) offering an audience the space and opportunity to re-evaluate the national past.

This essay examines how Channel 4 contributed to British filmmaking in the 1980s and how involvement with television affected the aesthetic shape of many British films during this era. The writer and director Mike Leigh, interviewed in *American Film* (1989), claimed that during the 1970s and 1980s in Britain 'all serious filmmaking was done for television' (Fitch, 1989, p. 12). Leigh exaggerated here, of course; still, media critics in the United States usually fail to appreciate how extensively British cinema remains institutionally and artistically bound with the London stage and television companies. In America, the typical television movie appears as an inexpensive B-movie program negotiating some current social problem and containing the most conventional narrative forms of romance and melodrama.[1] British television broadcasts this kind of material, too, but during the 1980s the medium also offered space to many of the country's best writers and directors, whose films for the small screen surpassed most 'British cinema' during this period. [...]

Thus British television offered considerable inducements to filmmakers: substantial financial rewards, a highly visible medium, a captive audience. The viewing figures, as David Hare said, are 'crazy'. Anywhere from three million to twelve million people watch a single work on a single evening (Hare, 1982, p. 49). A conservative figure of eight million roughly equates to filling an average-sized theater in London every night for six years. Americans accustomed to flicking past fifty television channels may find it difficult to appreciate the power each individual broadcasting station wields when only four of them exist, as in Britain during most of the 1980s. In this sense, the situation seems more like American television in the network-dominated 1950s than in the cable market of the 1980s. Accordingly, British television filmmakers felt, as Alan Bennett put it, that they were 'addressing the nation' (Bennett *et al.*, 1984, p. 121). Stephen Frears similarly remarked that he made *My Beautiful Laundrette* (1985) for Channel 4 because he wanted a large number of people to see and talk about the film (Howkins, 1985, p. 239). The statistics reinforce this shift toward television as the focal point of social narratives and popular memory. For instance, 74 percent of the British population never visit a cinema (Lane, 1986, p. 36), but every British adult in 1988 watched on average over twenty-five hours of television each week (Harvey, 1989, p. 61). As a consequence of these structures of public broadcasting, British television has traditionally generated what John Caughie calls 'a collectively shared experience' (Caughie, 1986, p. 168), a discourse predicated upon the compulsive pleasures of familiarity and communal recognition. The most successful British television films internalize these communal aspects of television, allowing audience members to witness these easily identifiable aspects of popular memory; yet such films also interrogate those comfortable assumptions, inducing the audience to reconceive its perspectives upon past and present in new and unsettling ways. [...]

Between 1981 and 1990 Channel 4 partially funded the production of some 170 films by independent companies, and it quickly became a major player in the impecunious arena of the British film industry. By Hollywood standards, of course, the resources available to Channel 4 were miserly: David Rose, the first commissioning editor for fiction, made twenty films in his first year for a total of $9.6 million, the average budget of one Hollywood feature (Park, 1982–3, p. 8). Usually production companies released these films first in the cinema theaters, thereby gaining enough critical notice and reputation to make their subsequent appearance on television something of a special event. A few films arrived in theaters after their television appearance, usually with unhappy financial results. Toward the middle of the decade, after several failures on the commercial cinema circuit, Channel 4 supported fewer films entirely from its own finances, instead collaborating on the funding with organizations such as the Goldcrest Company, the National Film Finance Corporation, and others. Still, the general prominence of Channel 4 cannot be denied: ten out of the twenty-eight British features made in 1984 had Channel 4 investment (Ellis, 1990, p. 376), and the company gradually developed a strong presence at film festivals. At Cannes in 1987, for example, David Rose accepted the Rossellini Award for the contributions made by Channel 4 to filmmaking, while in the same year the British journal *Sight and Sound* congratulated Channel 4 for providing 'film-makers with a continuity of financial support not seen since the heyday of Michael Balcon's Ealing Studios' back in the 1940s (Kent, 1987, p. 260). By the end of the 1980s, other British television companies started to emulate their example, with both Granada and the BBC coproducing more and more feature films.

As with the Ealing cinema, we can identify a particular kind of aesthetic style as characteristic of the Channel 4 movie. John Ellis describes Ealing comedies as negotiating a series of 'aspirations and utopian desires', wherein the petty bourgeoisie express their resentment against an increasingly bureaucratized postwar world (Ellis, 1975, p. 115). Channel 4 films work with something similar, insofar as they often juxtapose what is foreign, strange, or sinister with the safe haven of the drably domestic. Although 'Film on Four' offerings addressed many potentially disturbing themes, they usually framed and contained them by structures of reassuring normalcy. For instance, in *Another Time, Another Place* (1983), director Michael Radford visually represents the Italian prisoners of war billeted upon an isolated farm in Scotland from the crofters' point of view, so that the Italians come to seem devils dressed in black, satanic figures who carry pitchforks over their heads as if wearing diabolic horns. The sexual knowingness of these Italians tantalizes Jane (Phyllis Logan), her marital misery reinforced by a sense of geographical isolation. Jane's laconic husband, Finlay (Tom Watson), responds less sympathetically to the glamour of foreignness: he will, he says, be 'thankful to be rid of them lot' now that the war is ending. Jane, left to gaze longingly out of the window, tells herself, 'There's other days, and other places.' Yet, as the heavy weight of familiarity associated with the BBC radio programs that waft over this bleak Scottish landscape implies, for Jane, other times and places will exist only in her fantasies. Recognition of these old BBC favorites binds the viewer into complicity with that sense of repressive familiarity that the film disseminates, and hence engenders an air of fatalism. Such styles of fatalism or inertia are characteristic of many different types of television production. As theorists of television situation comedy show how its narratives traditionally rotate upon an axis of transgression and restitution, with 'order' reestablished after the mild allure of the forbidden, so Channel 4 films in the 1980s often follow a similarly conservative pattern, albeit in a more sophisticated way.[2]

The form of this threat varies, of course: homosexuality in *Another Country* (1984), *Maurice* (1987), *Prick Up Your Ears* (1987); West Indians and the drug culture in *Playing Away* (1986); Jewishness in *Sacred Hearts* (1984); Americans in *Stormy Monday* (1987) and in *The Dressmaker* (1988); the Soviet Union in *A Letter to Brezhnev* (1985). The latter movie features a Liverpudlian girl (Alexandra Pigg) who defies her family and British consular advice by flying to Russia to pursue a Soviet sailor she met during a night on the town. Scripted by Frank Clarke and directed by Chris Bernard, this film features a creative team that also worked on the Channel 4 soap opera *Brookside*, again set in Liverpool. This authorial link with *Brookside* helps explain the film's sensitivity to Elaine's domestic plight, shut up in her parents' deadly suburban house where the continuous noise of the television only partially drowns out the perpetual family quarrels. To put it another way, *A Letter to Brezhnev* deals more convincingly with containment than with escape. As Martin Auty has written, the public mind associates television with 'naturalism' and cinema with 'the realm of fantasy' (Auty, 1985, p. 63), and, in the terms of this hypothesis, *A Letter to Brezhnev* fits more comfortably with its televisual than with its cinematic characteristics.

It would not, then, be difficult to argue that Channel 4 films implicitly reinforce dominant conservative national ideologies, however much they explicitly seem to challenge such concepts. Jeremy Isaacs's contention that these films should reflect 'our preoccupations here in Britain' rather than be geared for 'a bland international market' (Bennett *et al.*, 1984, p. 118) uneasily overlaps those 'national concerns' articulated by William Whitelaw, patriarchal Home Secretary at the time of Channel 4's inception. Whitelaw, a loyal member of Thatcher's government for many years, wanted a channel that would provide space for 'minority interests', a television station 'somewhat different, but not too different' (Docherty and Morrison, 1987–8, p. 11). Clearly Whitelaw's views of 'national concerns' were not synonymous with the 'preoccupations' of Isaacs. The former, concerned frankly with repressive tolerance, remarked that 'if they don't get some outlet for their activities, you are going to run yourself into more trouble' (ibid.). Isaacs, on the other hand, had no obvious vested interest in television as a means of social control. But for many radical filmmakers, these positions stood too close to each other for artistic comfort. Directors such as Chris Petit, Derek Jarman, Alan Parker, and Lindsay Anderson, all outspoken in denouncing the general timidity of British cinema, found such pusillanimity reinforced by the unwelcome restrictions imposed by television production codes. Jarman openly associated Channel 4's small-screen cinema with the Thatcherite 'little England' of the 1980s, complaining that the 'TV men' only wanted films to 'complement the ads' (Jarman, 1987, p. 86) and accusing fellow directors such as Frears and Peter Greenaway of conformity to the demands of the television medium. Petit similarly scorned British cinema as being merely 'television hardback' (Walters, 1987, p. 62), while Alan Parker described Channel 4 as a cage within which the trapped filmmaker beats frantically against the bars (Houston, 1986, p. 153). More thoughtfully, Anderson addressed what he saw as the restrictions of the Channel 4 medium in a 1989 interview: 'I think the real difference is the kind of subject liable to be financed by Channel Four, which leads to some of the new British films being a bit lacking in the ambition one associates with a cinema film. There is a certain restriction of imagination or idea, rather than the feeling that if you make a film financed by television you have to restrict it in terms of technique or style' (Pratley, 1989, p. 95).

What I want to argue, however, is that the whole issue of television aesthetics should be seen as more complex than Anderson suggests here. Despite those confining parameters and the structural containment observed in many Channel 4 movies, the best of these make skillful and sometimes experimental use of their small-screen medium, creatively exploring the whole idea of limits. Here aesthetic complexity becomes a crucial critical factor: while most television films simply reflect the dominant ideology, the most illuminating reflect back actively upon it. In Mike Leigh's *High Hopes*, to take one example, the thematic as well as formal emphasis rests on physical claustrophobia and psychological immobility. The central characters find themselves locked into a round of urban poverty and obligations to cantankerous relatives, the grotesque scenario peppered with frequent cups of tea and trips to the lavatory. This theater of embarrassment challenges its onlookers by bathetically subverting the expectations of cinematic narrative and engendering a sense of queasy familiarity, a recognition of the film's disconcerting proximity to the trials of daily living. This is not, said Leigh, a form of naturalism, but rather 'heightened realism' (Fitch, 1989, p. 12): Leigh draws the viewer into uncomfortable empathy with his landscapes, exploiting the medium of television as a repository of the banal and the everyday to valorize that empathy. Despite its abjuring of the transparent window of naturalism, *High Hopes*, as Gilbert Adair says, produces 'an *effet du réel*' (Adair, 1988–9, p. 65), an illusion of verisimilitude inextricably interwoven with the structures of television and predicated upon a mimetic relay of ordinary domestic life. Leigh made most of his films in the 1970s and 1980s exclusively for television, and, though *High Hopes* played in cinema theaters, it remains a film crucially informed by a televisual perspective.

From this point of view, we can recognize the automatic preference for cinema over television as little more than nostalgia for a more traditionalist aesthetic ideology. In 1984 Mamoun Hassan, then managing director of the National Film Finance Corporation, inveighed against what he took to be Channel 4's 'hybrid' form of cinema by claiming television as more akin to 'journalism', and cinema to 'literature':

> Television films and programmes have to be topical; cinema films have to be more universal than timely ... Television is at its best dealing with concepts, explaining and describing (it is no accident that the drama documentary is the preferred form of television drama); cinema is at its best when it concerns itself with the ineffable, with that which cannot be expressed.
>
> (Bennett *et al.*, 1984, p. 116)

One hears this kind of reactive idealism – 'universal', 'the ineffable' – repeatedly in critiques of Channel 4 films; but, as Fredric Jameson remarks, such fetishizing of cinema over television is reminiscent of quests for that original 'aura' of a unique work of art that Walter Benjamin famously claimed had been undone by the twentieth-century age of mechanical reproduction (Jameson, 1990, p. 217) [. . .]

The conjunction of two distinct modes of production fosters [the] illusion of realism in television films. On the one hand, television gives the spectator an impression that what he or she is watching happens 'live': this, says Jane Feuer, binds the viewer into an imaginary presence, 'a sense of immediacy and wholeness' (Feuer, 1983, p. 16). On the other hand, film engenders an impression of historicity: the idea that these events once took place in the material world. David Hare writes about his great preference for film over videotaped television productions precisely because video lacks that 'visual finesse' and 'stylistic density or texture' (Hare, 1982, p. 48) that enable film to imply a complex historical world, the very stuff of Hare's fiction. Margaret Morse theorizes this difference in terms of film's assimilation of the Renaissance rationalization of perspective, designed to represent the truth of an object in space, rather than a television studio's two-dimensional surfaces, which eliminate all such spatial depth (Morse, 1985, p. 6). Consequently, television drama shot in a studio on videotape has a more atemporal feel, as though everything takes place in a vacuum. Back in 1977, when he was producing *Licking Hitler* for television, Hare spurned the use of video and declared himself willing to wait a whole year until one of the film slots became available at BBC Birmingham. Hare was supported on this occasion by his producer, David Rose, then head of drama at BBC Birmingham, later to become commissioning editor for fiction at Channel 4; Hare remarked gratefully that Rose's 'allegiance to the film system is absolute' (Hare, 1982, p. 47). Crucially, this televisual ontology of the live event, when crossed with the historicity of film, produces an illusion of the past unfolding as if in the present, as if happening 'live'. A great many of the Channel 4 films made in the 1980s portray the past, not so much in a simple 'nostalgia-deco' way (Jameson, 1990, p. 225) but rather in a manner that maintains a complex, bifurcated perspective shifting between past and present. These films foreground the difficulties of a contemporary representation and reclamation of the past, and highlight the elaborate apparatus locking Britain into its historical destiny. But their force also derives from how they translate history into a feigned simultaneity with the here and now, drawing upon television's fictive authorization of its discourse as a current event.

The frequent announcement after the opening title sequences of 'another time, another place' can be seen as one of the clearest distinguishing characteristics of these Channel 4 movies: 'Spring 1954, London' in *Dance with a Stranger* (1984); 'Michaelmas Term 1909, Cambridge' in *Maurice*; 'The North of Scotland, Fall 1944' in *Another Time, Another Place*. Other films immediately seek to establish a specific historical time and place by easily identifiable signs: a bus headed for the Welsh town of Pwllheli together with Helen Shapiro singing 'Walking Back to Happiness' in *Experience Preferred but Not Essential* (1982); newsreels of the 1948 England–Australia cricket internationals in *P'Tang Yang Kipperbang* (1982); icons from the Festival of Britain and Queen Elizabeth II's coronation in *Prick Up Your Ears*; BBC shipping forecasts and the 'Billy Cotton Band Show' on the radio in *Distant Voices, Still Lives* (1988). Such icons spark off communal memories to establish a bond of identity between the text and its viewers. Yet the best of these films engage in a complex dialectic of familiarity and defamiliarization, a dialectic probing and problematizing the hallucinatory images of the past evoked. Hare's 1985 film *Wetherby*, for instance, juxtaposes two different time periods, the 1950s and the 1980s, and elucidates seemingly inexplicable events of the present in terms of that deterministic historical continuity established by the film's images of the repressive 1950s, when ubiquitous family tea parties mask gaping sexual insecurity. The opening sequence of this film – mostly financed by Channel 4 – features a discussion about Richard Nixon: 'Do you remember?' 'It wasn't so long ago.' 'Only ten years.' 'It's funny how people forget.' This conversation anticipates the general tone of Hare's film, concerning the burdens of time, the vagaries of memory, and the perplexities of decoding and reordering the past. John Caughie suggests that the cinema elicits audience identification with its protagonists by the classic point-of-view shot, but that television fiction relies more upon the reaction shot, the audience witnessing knowledge dispersed to a wider group of characters

(Caughie, 1990, p. 54). This style of reaction shot permeates *Wetherby* and Hare's other television fiction, his emphasis falling upon groups of people responding to forces of history and events not of their own making. [. . .]

In the Channel 4 film *Wish You Were Here* (1987), written and directed by David Leland, different perspectives begin to emerge. Though this story concerns a rebellious girl growing up in East Anglia during the 1950s, the iconography of nostalgia remains rigorously framed by narrative structures weaving in and out of time. Leland shifts from the end of the war in 1945 to the picture palace movies of the 1950s to account for the claustrophobic climate of postwar Britain. The film self-consciously reconstitutes past time: the inhabitants of this seaside town loom out from the screen in statuesque fashion, as though caught in a series of still photographs; a plethora of shots heightens the style of projection and displacement that refracts objects through doorways and windows, as if to signify how this film is peering back on the 1950s from the distant vantage point of the 1980s. Moreover, Leland replicates the ways in which Lynda (Emily Lloyd) remains inextricably bound up with her dreary heritage by allowing the film's audience to empathize with the cultural icons represented here. The fish-and-chips stands, the Gracie Fields photographs, the sentimental war movies – all of these serve to lock the viewers, like Lynda herself, within the contours of collectively shared experience and popular memory. In this sense, Leland's film – whose very title implies nostalgia – crystallizes that urge toward identification and recognition that, as John Caughie suggests, the discourse of television customarily trades upon, promoting a sense of transference that allows the audience to witness these fictional scenes as if they were real. *Wish You Were Here* amalgamates its aesthetic self-consciousness with these more choric aspects of television, harnessing the medium's ability to involve its mass audience in a series of binding recognitions, yet also keeping the audience slightly off balance so that these recognitions are not transmitted merely in an unproblematic manner.

We can understand this dialectic of familiarity and defamiliarization in television fiction's reconstitution of the past as a mode not of realism but of magic realism. Refusing the glossy fetishes of simplified nostalgia, magic realism introduces 'history with holes, perforated history' (Jameson, 1990, p. 130): it insists on the structural disjunction between past and present that exists simultaneously with any attempt to reconstitute the lost objects of other eras. Many of the most effective Channel 4 films of the 1980s did not simply fictionalize history; they also implicitly commented on how history itself becomes fictionalized. Thus magic realism's disjunction between event and memory, between the object and its name, expanded into a broader investigation of how national mythologies are created, how history is reinvented and rewritten, sometimes unscrupulously. Richard Eyre's Channel 4 film *The Ploughman's Lunch* (1983) remains the most obvious example of this, with its suggestion that the Suez crisis and the Falklands war were both repackaged for the history books like commodities in the advertising market. The film's theme of manufactured appearances is underscored by its scenes shot at the Conservative Party conference in Brighton, an event notoriously staged with great care for the national television cameras. As if to reemphasize the interdependence of film and television in this production, Eyre's team received permission to shoot footage at this conference only through Channel 4's contacts with Independent Television News (Forbes and Pulleine, 1983, p. 235).

The distorting mirrors of the television medium again function self-reflexively in the Channel 4 serial *A Very British Coup* (1988), which features a beleaguered Labour Party prime minister (Ray McAnally) eventually going on television to complain about the media conspiracies undermining his administration. A more international reworking of this theme, the deflection of history into Machiavellian fictions, can be found in Tom Stoppard's treatment of the Polish Solidarity crisis, *Squaring the Circle* (directed by Mike Hodges), screened by the 'Film on Four' series in May 1984. Described by Stoppard as 'an imaginative history', this film was shot entirely in the studio with an assortment of gimmicky, alienating devices to reinforce the narrator's assertion: 'Everything that follows is true, except the words and the pictures' (Woolley, 1984, p. 33). The film depicts Lech Wałęsa (Bernard Hill) playing elaborate mind games with the old Russian bureaucrats as he tries to establish freedom in Eastern Europe. As with *The Ploughman's Lunch*, Stoppard's work represents politics as a series of elaborate intrigues, a deadly playing field where the disjunction between the rhetoric of the image and the more intangible processes of history is always teasingly apparent.[3]

Such displacement of history into fiction takes on a kind of ontological status in television films of the 1980s. Television films train their glance back on television itself, exploring the contradictions inherent in this medium's own recycled vision of the world. In this way, the fictional dialectic of familiarity and defamiliarization exposes those fissures and ambiguities latent within the nation's domesticated understanding of history. *A Letter to Brezhnev* undermines the stereotypes of 'evil' Russians regurgitated by the news media back in the pre-*glasnost* days; *Prick Up Your Ears* provides a more hard-edged, sexualized angle on the cutesy commodification of Brian Epstein and the Beatles in the 1960s; *Saigon: Year of the Cat* painfully undercuts official American rhetoric about the Vietnam War by portraying the evacuation from this lost city as undignified and frightening. A memorable moment occurs in *Saigon* when the American ambassador (E.G. Marshall), who sets himself up to launch into a grand speech about his country's contribution to the Vietnam cause, suddenly finds himself brusquely hustled away by his troops because there simply is not time. This bifurcated perspective, where rhetoric and image fail to confirm the validity of each other, also appears in several of the most effective BBC serials of the 1980s: in Alan Bleasdale's *The Monocled Mutineer* (1986), which plays off the military and political machine of the First World War against a startling sense of the ragged resistance to that organization among ordinary soldiers; in Troy Kennedy Martin's *Edge of Darkness* (1985), which concerns itself with the ruthless cover-ups perpetrated by British intelligence in order to protect the state's illegal experiments with nuclear energy [. . .]

The Channel 4 films of the 1980s, then, increasingly mark an implicit acknowledgement of the specific terrain of their aesthetic medium and of the ways in which this medium worked with the discourses of social convention, popular history, and communal memory. A hard-edged negotiation with such discourses helped to produce that dialectic between familiarity and defamiliarization characteristic of the best television films of this decade. As David Hare observes, the idea of eight million invisible people simultaneously watching a television production is so disorienting, so hard to conceptualize, that authors and critics sometimes contain this bewilderment by imagining that viewers cannot distinguish between superior works of fiction and 'dog-food commercials' (Hare, 1982, p. 49). But, suggests Hare, the truth of the matter is very different: in late twentieth-century Britain, the television film functions as a uniquely democratic art form, unique in bridging general accessibility with the power to reshape people's perceptions and so, potentially, to change their lives.

NOTES

1. For a recent analysis of American television movies, *see* Schulze, L.J. 1986: Getting physical: text/context/reading and the made for television movie. *Cinema Journal* 25(2), 35–50.
2. On situation comedy, *see*, for instance, Eaton (1978–9).
3. *Squaring the Circle* is a classic example of a major work by a major writer that is, at the present time, almost invisible because of the lack of accessible television libraries. Many films that addressed issues of representation were shown in Channel 4's 'Eleventh Hour' series, a showcase for more obviously avant-garde works that were screened for smaller audiences late at night. In this essay, however, I have chosen to concentrate upon the more well-known and widely seen Channel 4 productions.

REFERENCES

ADAIR, G. 1988–9: Classtrophobia: *High Hopes. Sight and Sound* 58(1), 64–5.

AUTY, M. 1985: But is it cinema? In Auty, M. and Roddick, N. (eds.), *British cinema now*. London: British Film Institute, 57–70.

BENNETT, A., HASSAN, M., ISAACS, J. and MILLAR, G. 1984: British cinema: life before death on television. *Sight and Sound* 53(2), 115–22.

CAUGHIE, J. 1986: Popular culture: notes and revisions. In MacCabe, C. (ed. *High theory/low culture: analysing popular television and film*. Manchester: Manchester University Press, 156–71.

CAUGHIE, J. 1990: Playing at being American: games and tactics. In Mellencamp, P. (ed.), *Logics of television: essays in cultural criticism*. Bloomington: Indiana University Press, 44–58.

DOCHERTY, D. and MORRISON, D. 1987–8: . . . Somewhat different, but not too different. *Sight and Sound* 57(1), 10–13.

EATON, M. 1978–9: Television situation comedy. *Screen* 19(4), 61–89.

ELLIS, J.C. 1990: *A history of film*, 3rd edn. Englewood Cliffs, NJ: Prentice-Hall.

ELLIS, J. 1975: Made in Ealing. *Screen* 16(1), 78–127.

FEUER, J. 1983: The concept of live television: ontology as ideology. In Kaplan, E.A. (ed.), *Regarding television: critical approaches – an anthology*. Frederick, MD: University Publications of America–American Film Institute, 12–22.

FITCH, J. 1989: High hopes. *American Film*, March, 12.

FORBES, J. and PULLEINE, T. 1983: Crossover: McEwan and Eyre. *Sight and Sound* 52(4), 232–7.

HARE, D. 1982: Ah! Mischief: the role of public broadcasting. In Pike, F. (ed.), *Ah! Mischief: the writer and television*. London: Faber, 41–50.

HARVEY, S. 1989: Deregulation, innovation and Channel 4. *Screen* 30(1–2), 60–79.

HOUSTON, P. 1986: Parker, Attenborough, Anderson. *Sight and Sound* 55(3), 152–4.

HOWKINS, J. 1985: Edinburgh television. *Sight and Sound* 54(4), 238–9.

JAMESON, F. 1990: *Signatures of the visible*. New York: Routledge.

JARMAN, D. 1987: *The last of England*, ed. David L. Hirst. London: Constable.

KENT, N. 1987: Commissioning editor: David Rose interviewed. *Sight and Sound* 56(4), 260–3.

LANE, S. 1986: Out dated. *Listener*, 24 April, 36.

MORSE, M. 1985: Talk, talk, talk – the space of discourse in television. *Screen* 26(2), 2–15.

PARK, J. 1982–3: Four films for 4. *Sight and Sound* 52(1), 8–12.

PRATLEY, G. 1989: 35 days in Toronto. *Sight and Sound* 58(2), 94–6.

WALTERS, M. 1987: Safe British cinema. *Listener*, 17–24 December, 62.

WOOLLEY, B. 1984: Being Poles apart. *Listener*, 24 May, 33.

13

Discriminating or duped? Young people as consumers of advertising/art

Mica Nava and Orson Nava

From *Magazine of Cultural Studies* 1 (1990), 15–21

Since the birth of the mass media – newspapers, magazines, radio and then television – advertising has been a crucial component both of finance and of the debate about influence and manipulation. Moreover, the idea of the power of advertising to manipulate consumer behaviour has been linked to the wider issue of the social consequences of commodity culture within consumer capitalism, where market value (the price tag hovering over the commodity) in some way conceals the specific value that human labour brings to the transformation of raw materials.

The notion that advertising has the power to influence, that it is a 'hidden persuader' (to use the term developed by the American social critic Vance Packard), has sometimes been seen within the Marxist tradition as a prime example of ideology-as-false-consciousness. The inauthentic advertisement hides reality behind a glitter of false appearances directing the consumer-sleepwalker to the act of purchase, of commodity consumption. Not all critiques of advertising have seen the form in such a negative light, and many have seen it as a realm of rich and sophisticated meaning production. It is no accident that the French cultural critic Roland Barthes, in his search for an adequate method of analysis for the language of images, took advertising as his example.

The Navas' initial research involved a critical investigation of arts and cultural provision for young people. Here, they develop this earlier work into argument about the actual mode of consumption of contemporary advertising by young people. They have thereby succeeded in making a fresh contribution to a long-standing debate. They argue that young people are highly visually and televisually literate and that they should be seen as active and critical readers, not as passive victims, of advertising. Young people are not especially vulnerable or gullible, they do not 'mindlessly imbibe'; rather they appreciate the complexity and sophistication of modern advertising with its characteristic use of pastiche and parody. They are the discriminating and demanding consumers of commercials who do not necessarily buy the product advertised.

The article suggests that the many well-established criticisms of the role and function of advertising in consumer society have resulted in an unacceptable denigration of advertising as a cultural form. This observation leads to their second argument, namely that the distinction between art and advertising must now be questioned both because it fails to recognize the aesthetic complexity of advertising (and the involvement of many creative people in this field) and because it reinforces the mistaken notion that 'art' is somehow above and beyond the realm of commodities.

The article proposes an alternative to the view of the audience as the dupes of a process of malign mass deception, and offers an account of the textual complexity of contemporary commercials. In attempting a redefinition of art in order to include advertising within this category of cultural production, it makes provocative and sometimes questionable, claims about the nature and status of various types of cultural expression.

An interesting TV commercial made by the agency Ogilvy & Mather was shown on Channel 4 each Sunday during the spring of 1988. Entitled 'Chair', its object was to promote the agency's own advertising services to potential 'marketing decision makers'. The advert opens with a shot of a modern young man in a stylish flat watching television. At the commercial break he gets up and goes to make a cup of tea. For a moment the camera focuses on the empty chair and the abandoned TV set. Then it cuts to the kitchen but we can still hear the noise of the ads coming from the unwatched television. The young man returns to his chair with his cup of tea just as the commercial break ends. Over the final frame a voiceover informs us that there are 600 commercials on TV every day; 'what's so special about yours?', it inquires of the potential advertisers among us.

As the press release for Ogilvy & Mather states, 'The film confronts the viewer with the question of whether or not people pay attention to commercial breaks.' At the same time it conveys another message. It represents young people as discriminating and hard to reach and suggests that they are likely to ignore all but the most challenging and entertaining commercials. This view of young people is one which is increasingly prevalent among advertisers and their clients and was frequently expressed to us in interview. Articles in trade magazines like *Campaign*, research conducted by advertising agencies like the McCann-Erickson Youth Study, advertisements themselves, and a spate of recent conferences organised for marketeers about the difficulties of targeting and persuading contemporary youth are further evidence of this growing preoccupation (Nava, 1988). Thus within the world of advertising today, concern is regularly expressed about how to reach young people (since they watch less TV than any other age group, even the under-fours) and how to persuade and gratify them, given what is referred to in the trade (and illustrated in the Ogilvy & Mather ad) as their high level of 'televisual literacy'. Bartle Bogle Hegarty, the agency responsible for the Levi ads, put it thus: 'Young consumers are sophisticated, video literate and acutely sensitive to being patronised. They pick up clues and covert messages quicker than you would believe.'

This image of young people and advertising is not, however, the one that circulates most frequently. The way in which advertising and consumerism are generally viewed today (although challenged by, for example, Myers, 1986; Nava, 1987) remains deeply influenced by the work of cultural theorists of the fifties and sixties such as Vance Packard, who argues in his seminal book *The hidden persuaders* (1981) that people are 'influenced and manipulated [by advertisers] far more than we realize ... Large scale efforts are being made, often with impressive success, to channel our ... habits, our purchasing decisions and our thought processes'.

For Herbert Marcuse (1964), one of the most influential thinkers of the left in this sphere, advertising – as an inherent aspect of consumer capitalism and its pursuit of profit – is capable not only of convincing us to buy, but of creating false needs, of indoctrinating us into social conformity and thus ultimately of suppressing political opposition. More recently, commentators of both the left and right who have been preoccupied by what they consider to be a decline in moral standards (see for example the work of Jeremy Seabrook on the one hand and statements issued by Mary Whitehouse on the other) as well as more academic analysts of advertising (Dyer, 1982) have been concerned to establish the effects of a constant diet of television programmes and commercials, particularly on young viewers, who are considered to be those most at risk of being corrupted and duped by entreaties to buy.

Given the pervasiveness of these debates, it is not surprising that certain ideas have now become part of received wisdom, a commonsense way of viewing the world. Thus we have a context in which the question of television advertising and youth is likely to conjure up images of undereducated, undiscriminating and undisciplined young people who are addicted to TV and who mindlessly imbibe the advertisers' message along with the materialist values of the consumer society. Characteristic of this view is the notion that there exists a simple cause and effect relationship between advertising and the purchasing of commodities. It is assumed not only that advertisements work but that the young are more likely than any other sector of the population to be taken in by the psychologically informed scheming of the marketeers. Youth are considered to be more vulnerable, more gullible and more inclined to be persuaded to buy totally useless things.

Significantly and interestingly, this is a far more demeaning view of youth than that held by the advertisers themselves. As has already been indicated, the British advertising industry is highly respectful of the critical skills and visual literacy of young people. Indeed, as emerges clearly from our research, no other age group is considered as discriminating, cynical and resistant to the 'hard sell'. Furthermore, no other group is as astute at decoding the complex messages, cross-references and visual jokes of current advertising (except perhaps the industry itself). These critical skills are untutored and seem to arise out of an unprecedented intimacy with the cultural form of the television commercial. No other generation has been so imbued with the meanings produced by quick edits, long shots, zooms, by particular lighting codes and combinations of sound. The young have a unique mastery of the grammar of the commercial; one might say that they have an intuitive grasp of the visual equivalent of the semicolon. This is the case even where, as one bemused advertiser put it, 'they are not very intellectually clever'.

Advertisers work hard to capture this discerning audience and to win its esteem. Indeed, many ads appear to utilise the codes that are most likely to appeal to that sector of the population with the most developed analytical skills – that is to say the young. [. . .]

It is not only 'youth' (14–24-year-olds) who watch and enjoy TV ads. Research carried out by the Association of Market Survey Organisations indicates that commercials also come high on the list of younger children's preferred television viewing. Favourite ads among those in the 6–14-year-old category include Carling Black Label, Anchor Butter's dancing cows and Mates condoms. Thus they too like advertisements promoting items which they are unlikely to buy.

What emerges quite clearly from this picture then is that young people consume commercials independently of the product which is being marketed. Commercials are cultural products in themselves and are consumed for themselves. Thus the success of any particular commercial is, in this respect, completely divorced from its effectivity in promoting sales. Evaluations are made on the basis of criteria which are indistinguishable from those employed in the appreciation of other cultural forms. Our argument therefore is twofold: an analysis of the mode in which the commercial is consumed not only gives us insight into the cultural skills of young people, it also radically interrogates conventional divisions between art and advertising.

The dominant view of 'art' today, despite current debates about postmodernism, is still permeated by nineteenth-century romantic notions of a process abstracted from social relations and untainted by material considerations. The artist in this scenario is an individual possessed of talent and blessed with inspiration. Expressivity and then technique are the privileged categories; modes of consumption are considered largely irrelevant to the creative process. Practitioners and arbiters of such established 'high art' forms have tended to resist the demand for aesthetic recognition and entry to the elite ranks made by others using new techniques and different relations of production. Nevertheless, the range of forms within which 'art' is considered to reside has gradually been extended so that today it encompasses, for example, photography, film, electronic music and more recently video and video scratch.

Advertising, however, has generally been denied this accolade. Although grudging recognition has been awarded to the occasional outstanding example of 'commercial art', on the whole positive aesthetic evaluations of this field have been unable to compete with the trenchant cultural critiques in which the focus tends to be on how advertisers produce particular meanings which exploit personal insecurities and convince consumers that their identities derive from what they buy (Marcuse, 1964; Williamson, 1978; Dyer, 1982). Artists, critics and even advertisers themselves rank advertising extremely low in the hierarchy of cultural forms – if indeed at all. This might be because advertisers – of all cultural practitioners – are the ones least able to deny the cultural and economic context of their work and the significance of audience. Yet, the very fact of excluding advertising from the sphere of 'art' forms and identifying it as 'other', as defined predominantly by its material concerns, not only serves to differentiate and cleanse other forms, but also obscures the material determinants which operate across all of them. Studies which examine art and advertising in isolation, or which focus on difference, serve then to perpetuate both difference and associated hierarchies.

In contrast, our intention in this article is to reveal the interconnections and overlap between commercial and other forms of art, in order to expand our understanding of the ways in which young people exercise critical abilities as audience. The indivisibility of these (apparently) different forms manifests itself at a number of stages. Thus at the level of conceptualisation and production, crossovers can be discerned in the utilisation of technologies and forms, ideas, and personnel.

Among the technologies and forms which have been requisitioned by the makers of advertisements since the turn of the century are painting, photography, cinema, graphics, animation, pop music, video promos and video scratch. Examples are numerous: Dada and surrealism have been used in cigarette advertising; Michelangelo's drawings have been used by Parker pens. As John Berger pointed out in *Ways of seeing* (1972), publicity regularly quotes from works of art. Of the popular cultural forms, hip hop and rapping have most recently been in vogue. More critical avant-garde form like video scratch are also increasingly drawn on, though not always with much understanding. On the whole, however, what is interesting is that these techniques are not only appropriated and 'quoted', but also developed (this is particularly so for photography, graphics and animation) in the innovative and generously funded climate of advertising today.

At the level of ideas we see that advertisements not only draw specific narratives and images from the other forms, and parody them, but increasingly cross-reference each other. In this sense they constitute the classic postmodernist form (if such a thing exists) wherein boundaries between forms and between their high and popular versions are effaced (Jameson, 1985). Works of art, despite ideologies to the contrary, have of course always been derivative; in so far as they make use of existing technologies, artistic conventions and archetypal themes, they are collaborative projects. In advertising, however, this process of the appropriation and reworking of ideas and motifs already in the public domain is not only not concealed, it is celebrated. Pastiche is increasingly becoming an integral part of the form.

Thus references are made to different genres of cinema. The Pirelli Tyre ad is a miniature *film noir*, complete with murder plot, *femme fatale* and moody lighting. Carling Black Label has made an ad which references the cinematic preoccupation with Vietnam yet also appears to be a critique of war films and traditional masculinity: the hero is an intellectual and a refusenik – an inversion of the archetypal Rambo figure. Barclays Bank has made use of the style and images of *Bladerunner* as well as its director, Ridley Scott. The Holsten Pils advertisements are famous for taking quotations from old movies and incorporating them into their own narratives; thus we witness an unlikely encounter in the ladies' wash-room between Griff Rhys Jones and Marilyn Monroe.

Cross-referencing between ads occurs frequently, particularly where an ad has been successful. In its recent campaigns Carling Black Label has made parodic references of this kind its trademark, hence its detailed and witty re-enactment – even the same extras are used – of the famous Levi's laundrette ad, which itself draws on images from fifties youth movies. In the same vein Carling Black Label references an Old Spice commercial in its ad about a surfer riding a wave into a pub. Another example of an obscure and in this case more laboured reference occurs in a Wrangler ad where the hero puts on a pair of jeans and drives a double-decker bus across a row of parked motor bikes. This is a very coded allusion to Eddie Kidd, star of a 1987 ad for black Levi 501s, who as a real-life stunt man in the seventies held the world record for jumping his motor bike across parked double-decker buses. [. . .]

At the level of behind-the-camera personnel there has in recent years been an escalating rate of crossover between commercials and cinema and TV. For some time now directors have been cutting their teeth on ads and progressing thereafter – where possible – to bigger things, even to Hollywood. Alan Parker, Ridley Scott and Tony Scott are examples of these. More recently, however, the movement has been in the other direction and already established cinema and television directors from a range of political and stylistic backgrounds have been recruited to direct commercials. Thus Ken Russell, director of *Crimes of Passion*, made an ad for Shredded Wheat; Peter Greenaway (*Draughtsman's Contract*) and Stephen Frears (*My Beautiful Laundrette*) have both directed commercials in the last few years. Ken Loach (*Kes*) made the award-winning ad for the *Guardian* in which the skinhead saves a passerby from falling scaffolding, and John Amiel (*The Singing Detective*) and Nic Roeg (*Bad Timing*) made two of the Government AIDS warnings. Amiel has described the condensed quintessential dramas currently being made for British advertisers by himself and other established directors as 'little haikus' (Rusbridger, 1988). They exist and are recognized as autonomous creations.

So far we have argued that it is extremely difficult to separate ads conceptually from cultural forms conventionally designated as belonging to the sphere of art because of the consistent pattern of intertextuality and cross-referencing which operates between them. This observation, however, does not address the fundamental objective of the ad, which is to sell. As we have seen, what an ad sets out to sell varies enormously, and includes itself, services, generic products, brands, life styles, ideas and information. The fact, however, that it has selling (or persuading) as its central purpose is what above all else is supposed to distinguish it from art forms like song, fiction, film, drama and fine art.

Yet our argument is that even this characteristic does not make it tenable to situate the ad in an analytically distinct sphere. All of the cultural forms referred to above are also in the business of selling. This happens in a range of ways; perhaps most familiarly, art objects are themselves constituted as commodities and are bought and sold as investments as well as symbolic markers of wealth. Thus the possession of a Matisse painting denotes the status of its owner in exactly the same way as the possession of a pair of Levis does, through referencing a commonly acknowledged chain of associations about ownership and style. [. . .]

Responsibility for the persistent marginalisation of advertising as cultural form must in part be attributed to the dominance of a kind of left-humanist-realist perspective – descendant from Marcuse and the Frankfurt School – within this intellectual field. This has effectively inhibited any understanding of advertising as other than 'ideological' and inextricably bound up with consumerism, the market and the pursuit of profit under capitalism. In this sense, though perhaps unintentionally, cultural analysts have joined forces with the traditionalist defenders of high cultural forms who have resisted the incorporation of the commercial into the exalted ranks of 'art', who have insisted on keeping advertising in its place.

The upstart is not, however, acquiescent. Assaults on the historic fortifications of artistic status are escalating and emanate from a number of sectors, not least from young people themselves whose impact on the form will be returned to later. To some extent the criteria used to measure the success or failure of a commercial are negotiated and established within the profession itself. *Campaign*, the weekly of the advertising industry, has its own reviews of the latest commercials which are evaluated for originality, style, humour, technical innovation and, yes, even misogyny. These criteria are of course indistinguishable from those employed by any newspaper critic to review a movie. In fact *City Limits* also has an occasional TV commercial review section which operates with these criteria and is listed alongside the other review sections. Prizes awarded to the best ads by the industry itself mobilize distinctions, not between ads and other forms, but between 'good' ads and 'bad' ads. Good ads, the ones that win awards or acclaim, do so on the basis of the 'quality' of the ad as a product in itself, and not on the basis of marketing success. [. . .]

Here we must return to young people. How do youth fit into this analysis of the commercial as (at its best) an increasingly innovative and sophisticated cultural form – as 'art'? What has the relationship of young people been to this redefinition? Is it possible to argue that, as audience, they have in fact contributed to the complexity, elegance and wit of some contemporary television commercials?

In order to unravel and respond to these questions it is necessary to investigate in a little more detail the current state of advertising and marketing theory and practice. What has emerged quite clearly in recent years, concurrently with the refinements in form, is that advertisers no longer have confidence in the old theories about how ads promote sales. This view was frequently confirmed in the interviews we conducted with members of the industry and was reiterated in the papers delivered at the New Wave Young conference (Nava, 1988). Beliefs in the power of subliminal messages to penetrate and manipulate the mass psyche no longer have currency. Advertisers are now as aware as other cultural producers that there is no formula or scientific method which can guarantee success. Market research has not come up with the answers. Marketing managers cannot precisely identify the components of a successful campaign; they are unable to anticipate what will spark the public imagination; they do not know exactly who their target audience is, nor how to reach it; and, at a more pedestrian level, they do not even know whether an ad is more effective if placed before or after a particular programme. Some go so far as to insist that advertising is hardly effective at all, that what is required is consistent media coverage in order to shift a product. So what we see is that marketing is a far more haphazard process than the intellectual orthodoxies would have us believe. There are no rules. There is no consensus.

These uncertainties do not mean, however, that the classic objectives of the industry have been abandoned. Advertisers of course still aim to increase sales for their clients, and in order to do so they need to take into account the culture and preferences of young people, who constitute a significant proportion of the market both in terms of their own disposable income and their influence on friends and family. They must be recruited, their cynicism must be overcome. Yet in the absence of the confident and clear guidelines of earlier times, how is this to be achieved?

Although the industry continues to be enormously productive, the undermining of old convictions and the growing anxiety about public (youth) cynicism combine to reveal a picture of the advertising process itself in a state of crisis. Indeed the paradox is that the industry's productivity appears to be both a symptom and a cause of its malaise. More numerous and more subtle and sophisticated advertisements have generated more discriminating audiences. As we have already argued, at the forefront of these are the young themselves whose scepticism and powers of analysis are, in this respect, a great deal more developed than those of older generations. It is through the exercise of these refined critical skills and through the consumption of the ad rather than the product that the young have contributed to the spiralling crisis.

Given the current climate of uncertainty and the lack of clarity about what might be an appropriate response to the crisis, the solution of the marketeers has been to turn to the creative departments within their agencies, to hand over responsibility to individuals largely trained in art schools, who rely not on research and surveys, for which they have little respect, but on imagination, inventiveness and intuition. [. . .]

Alternatively they have hired film makers from outside the industry with already established 'artistic' credibility. There is no doubt that the experimental forms produced in this way have had unprecedented success in recruiting and retaining viewers. Above all, they have been able to satisfy the gourmet appetites of the discerning young. What emerges quite clearly then from this account is that young people, in their capacity as active consumers, have, as Willis (1988) suggests, 'shaped the contours of the commercial culture' which they inhabit. Unlike the young man in the Ogilvy & Mather commercial which we described at the beginning of this article, they do watch the ads. But they do not necessarily buy.

CONCLUSION

In this article we have developed an argument about young people and their relation to contemporary advertising. In order to do this we have used a very undifferentiated model of youth: we have not investigated – or even postulated – distinctions based on class, race or gender because our argument does not require these refinements. Not all youth – and certainly not only youth – read advertisements in the ways in which we (and indeed the advertisers themselves) have argued, though sufficient numbers do to justify our thesis. Our central preoccupation in this article has been with the consumption of advertising and the skills brought to bear in this process. This has included examining not only transformations in the production of advertisements but also the ways in which historically advertising has been defined. Thus our argument has been that although ads have in the past been primarily concerned to promote sales, they increasingly offer moments of intellectual stimulation, entertainment and pleasure – of 'art'. To focus in on this phenomenon is not to exonerate advertisers and their clients from responsibility in the formation and perpetuation of consumer capitalism. Nor is it to deny totally the influence of advertising in purchasing decisions. Our intention has been to bypass these debates. Instead we recognize the relative autonomy of the ad as product and view it as no more or less inherently implicated in the economic organization of life than any other cultural form. (Advertisements can after all also promote progressive products and causes, like Nicaraguan coffee and the Greater London Council; Myers, 1986). More importantly, however, we have emphasised in this article the very considerable though untutored skills which young people bring to bear in their appreciation of advertisements and which they exercise individually and collectively, not in museums and public galleries, but in millions of front rooms throughout the country – and indeed the world.

The critical question arising from this is whether or not the possession of such decoding skill by young people, and the revolution in the advertising process itself, can be interpreted as progressive. Debates of this kind have always surrounded new stages in the dissemination of knowledge. Reading the written word was considered a contentious activity in the nineteenth century: some people thought it would serve to discipline and pacify the population while others feared (or hoped) it would prove subversive. Earlier in this century Walter Benjamin (1970) claimed that the new technology of film would help to develop in spectators a more acute and critical perception. Film as cultural form was not only more popular and democratic, it was potentially revolutionary. Arguing against this position, Adorno and Horkheimer (1973) condemned the culture industry for what they alleged was its taming both of critical art and the minds of the people. More recently Fredric Jameson (1985) has asked similar questions about the advent of 'postmodernism'. To what extent can postmodern forms be considered oppositional or progressive? Is there a way in which they can resist and contest the logic of consumer capitalism? Our answer must be that the forms alone cannot be subversive, but that the critical tools as well as the pleasures they have generated, and from which they are in any case inseparable, may indeed subvert and fragment existing networks of power-knowledge.

NOTE

This argument is developed further in Nava, Mica 1992: *Changing cultures: feminism, youth and consumerism*. London: Sage.

REFERENCES

ADORNO, T. and HORKHEIMER, M. 1973: *Dialectics of enlightenment*. London: Allen Lane. (Originally published in 1947.)
BENJAMIN, W. 1970: The work of art in the age of mechanical reproduction. In *Illuminations*. London: Fontana. (Originally published in 1936.)
BERGER, J. 1972: *Ways of seeing*. Harmondsworth: Penguin.
DYER, G. 1982: *Advertising as communication*. London: Methuen.
JAMESON, F. 1985: Postmodernism and consumer society. In Foster, H. (ed.), *Postmodern culture*. London: Pluto Press.
MARCUSE, H. 1964: *One-dimensional man*. London: Routledge & Kegan Paul.
MYERS, K. 1986: *Understains*. London: Comedia.
NAVA, M. 1987: Consumerism and its contradictions. *Cultural Studies* 1(2).
NAVA, M. 1988: Targeting the young: what do the marketeers think? for the Gulbenkian Enquiry into Young People and the Arts.
PACKARD, V. 1981: *The hidden persuaders*. Harmondsworth: Penguin. (Originally published in 1957.)
RUSBRIDGER, A. Ad men discover a fatal attraction. *Guardian*, 3 March 1988.
WILLIAMSON, J. 1978: *Decoding advertisements*. London: Marion Boyars.
WILLIS, P. 1988: Position Paper for the Gulbenkian Enquiry into Young People and the Arts.

Section III

CONTEXTS

14

Television in the family circle

Lynn Spigel

From Mellencamp, P. (ed.) 1990: *Logics of television*. London: British Film Institute, 80–9

The domestic character of television has been discussed by a number of critics and researchers. The fact that television is conventionally received in the 'home' has had a considerable influence upon its development and has further distanced its relationship to cinema. The particular time patterns, work and leisure routines, interests and anxieties that have variously been seen to characterize family life (nationally various and always changing) have fed back into the scheduling of television, its modes of address to viewers and its generic system. Only more recently, with the dispersal of television across a wider range of channels and the availability of more television sets in the average home, is this connection being loosened or, at least, quite radically changed.

Entering households as a supplement to, or a substitute for, the family hearth, television was initially projected as consolidating family life, becoming, in one resonant phrase, 'the shining centre of the home'. However, it was not long before exactly the opposite tendency was being discussed: television's capacity to increase tension between husband and wife and to drive a wedge between parents and children.

More specific concerns which have followed from TV's domesticity are fears about breaches of taste (in respect of language, sexuality, violence), the exposure of children to time-wasting and possibly even educationally impairing material, and the effect (largely presumed to be on women and children) of advertising.

Looking at contemporary magazines, Lynn Spigel reviews some of the issues raised by television during its first decade in US homes. She finds that response to the new medium drew on a number of sources, including familiarity with the precedent of radio but also new and developing tensions around 'technology'. The way in which television was seen to impact upon parenting is discussed and, throughout, the gendered character of what were seen to be 'television problems' (it was regarded by some as threatening the very idea of manhood!) is brought out for analysis.

Historical work on television has until quite recently been a neglected area of research. By partially reconstructing the context in which television entered and then radically reorganized domestic life, Spigel makes a useful contribution to the terms of contemporary analysis. Current work on household technology is having to engage not only with a 'dispersed' television but with the other information technologies, notably computers, which are restructuring the meanings and relationships of 'home'.

[. . .]

While television rapidly came to signify domestic values, the attempts to domesticate the machine belied a set of grave anxieties. Even if TV was often said to bring the family together in the home, popular media also expressed tensions about its role in domestic affairs. Television's inclusion in the home was dependent upon its ability to rid itself of what *House Beautiful* called its 'unfamiliar aspect'.[1]

At a time when household modernization was a key concern, women's magazines continually examined the relationship between the family and the machine. The magazines were undecided on this subject, at times accepting, at times rejecting the effects of mechanization. On the one hand, they offered their female readers technological fantasy worlds which promised to reduce the time and energy devoted to household chores. Dream kitchens, which had been displayed by women's magazines since the 1920s, resembled Technicolor spectacles found on the cinema screen, only here the bold primary colors depicted a woman's Shangri-la of electric gadgets and sleek linoleum surfaces.

Just in case this pictorial display of technological commodity fetishism was not enough, the magazines didactically reminded their readers of the need to be 'up to date'. In 1951 *House Beautiful* included a quiz entitled 'How Contemporary Is Your Life?' Most of the fifty-eight questions had to do with the degree to which the home was equipped with 'modern' appliances, and the magazine warned that if 'you score less than forty . . . you are depriving yourself of too many contemporary advantages'. Owning a television set was a must, according to this modernity exam.[2]

Whereas in the prewar and war years a fully mechanized household would have been presented in the popular press as a futuristic fantasy, in the postwar years it appeared that tomorrow had arrived. Living without an array of machines meant that you were anachronistic, unable to keep up with the more progressive Joneses. Still, this rampant consumerism and its attendant 'machine aesthetic' had a dark underside from which the new household technologies and mechanized lifestyles appeared in a much less flattering light.

By the postwar years, ambivalence toward technology was well established in US culture. As other cultural historians have shown, by the second half of the nineteenth century, US thinkers embraced the new industrial order, but they also feared the devastating consequences of economic depression, urban crime, and labor strikes. The ambivalent response to technology grew stronger in the twentieth century. By the time of the World's Fairs of the 1930s, Americans represented technology in highly hyperbolic and contradictory ways. As Warren Susman has argued, at the same time that Americans were celebrating the technological future in the 'Land of Tomorrow' at the New York World's Fair, Gallup polls revealed that most people believed technological development caused the unemployment of the Great Depression.[3]

The home magazines of the postwar era adopted this ambivalence toward machines, scrutinizing each step forward in household technology for its possible side effects. *House Beautiful*, the same magazine which tested its readers on their modernity quotients, just as often warned of the dismal future in store for the residents of the mechanized household. In 1951, the magazine asked if the 'houses we live in . . . accustom us . . . to feel more at home in surroundings where everything suggests only machines . . . that do as they are told and could never have known either joy or desire'. And if so, there is an overwhelming threat that 'man is nothing but a machine . . . [who] can be "conditioned" to do and to want whatever his masters decide'.⁴ This threat of the 'machine man', couched in the rhetoric of behavioralism, gave rise to a host of statements on the relationship between television and the family. Would the television set become the master and the family its willing subject? The adage of the day became 'Don't let the television set dominate you!'

The idea of 'technology out of control' was constantly repeated as the language of horror and science fiction invaded discussions of everyday life. The television set was often likened to a new breed of man-made monster which, like Frankenstein's monster before it, threatened to wreak havoc on the family. *American Mercury* called television the 'giant in the living room', describing it as a kind of supernatural child, a bad seed, whose actions might turn against its master at any moment. The essay proclaimed,

> the giant ... has arrived. He was a mere pip-squeak yesterday, and didn't even exist the day before, but like a genie released from a magic bottle in *The Arabian Nights*, he now looms big as life over our heads. Let us therefore try and circle round him and see if he will step on us, or make us sick and happy, or just what.⁵

As such statements suggest, television posed the intimidating possibility that private citizens in their own homes might be rendered powerless in the face of a new and curious machine.

The threatening aspects of television technology might have been related to TV's use during World War II. Television, like radio before it, was a valued technology during wartime, serving as both a surveillance and a reconnaissance weapon. To some degree, the public was aware of this because television's aircraft and military applications were discussed in literature of the thirties and during wartime.⁶ TV's function as a powerful weapon continued to engage the public's imagination in the postwar years and was often discussed in such men's magazines as *Popular Science*.⁷

Television's associations with World War II and its apocalyptic aftermath sharply contradicted the images of TV and domestic bliss that were put forward after the war. It seems plausible that television's military applications created doubts about its ability to enter the home.⁸ In fact, television's effect on culture was sometimes discussed in the context of warfare and atomic weaponry. Words such as 'invasion' and 'battle' were often employed in criticisms of the new medium. A popular assumption was that television would cause cancer by transmitting waves of radiation. Later, in 1961, when FCC Commissioner Newton Minow chided the TV industry in his famous 'vast wasteland' speech, he used the imagery of atomic warfare to suggest the powerful effects that TV might have on the public. He claimed:

> Ours has been called the jet age, the atomic age, the space age. It is also, I submit, the television age. And just as history will decide whether the leaders of today's world employed the atom to destroy the world or to rebuild it for mankind's benefit, so will history decide whether today's broadcasters employed their powerful voice to enrich the people or debase them.⁹

Although popular discourses suggested that TV technology was out of control, they also provided soothing antidotes to this fear of machines. In 1953, the Zenith Corporation found a way to master the beast, promising consumers, 'We keep them [TV sets] in a cage until they're right for you.' A large photograph at the top of the page showed a zoo cage which contained a Zenith scientist testing the inner components of the receiver. On the bottom of the page was the finely constructed

Kensington console model, artfully integrated into a living room setting. As this ad so well suggests, the unfamiliar technology could be domesticated by turning the set into glamorous furniture.[10]

Another popular strategy was anthropomorphism. In 1951 *House Beautiful* declared, 'Television has become a family member.' The magazine[11] variously described TV as a 'newborn baby', a 'family friend', a 'nurse', a 'teacher', and a 'family pet'. Advertisers particularly drew on the image of the faithful dog – a symbol which had proven particularly useful since the turn of the century when RCA/Victrola used the picture of a fox terrier, with ears perked up, listening to 'his master's voice'. As the domesticated animal, TV obeyed its owner and became a benevolent playmate for children. A 1952 ad for Emerson shows a typical scenario. The immanent petlike quality of the television set emanates from the screen where a child and her poodle are pictured.[12]

Even if anthropomorphism helped to relieve the tensions about television technology, the media continued to express doubts. The idea of 'technology out of control' was turned around and reformulated. Now it was viewers who had lost control of themselves. Considering television's negative effects on the family, Bogart claimed that 'the bulk of the disadvantages listed by the TV owners reflect their inability to control themselves once the set has been installed in the house'.[13] At least at the level of popular discourse, Bogart's suggestions are particularly accurate.

More than any other group, this discourse on human control was aimed at children. Here, TV was no longer simply a source of domestic unity and benevolent socialization. Instead, it had potent effects which needed to be understood and properly managed.[14] Most typically, television was said to cause passive and addictive behavior which in turn would disrupt good habits of nutrition, hygiene, social behavior, and education. A cartoon in a 1950 issue of *Ladies' Home Journal* suggests a typical scenario. The magazine showed a little girl slumped on an ottoman and suffering from a new disease called 'telebugeye'. The caption describes the child as a 'pale, weak, stupid looking creature' who grew 'bugeyed' from watching television for too long.[15]

As the popular wisdom often suggested, the child's passive addiction to television might itself lead to the opposite effect of increased aggression. These discussions followed in the wake of critical and social scientific theories of the 1930s and 1940s which suggested that mass media injected ideas and behavior into passive individuals. Adopting this 'hypodermic model' of media effects, the magazines circulated horror stories about youngsters who imitated TV violence. In 1955, *Newsweek* reported on young Frank Stretch, an eleven-year-old who had become so entranced by a TV Western that 'with one shot of his trusty BB gun [he] demolished both villain and picture tube'.[16] In reaction to the popular furor, as early as 1950 the Television Broadcasters' Association hired a public-relations firm to write pro-television press releases which suggested the more positive types of programming that TV had to offer.[17]

While scholarship has centered around the reform movements concerning children's television, little has been said about the popular media's advice to parents on how to control TV's effect on their children. What I find particularly interesting is the degree to which such discussions engaged questions concerning parental authority. In a time when juvenile delinquency and problem children were a central concern, television opened up a whole array of disciplinary measures that parents might exert over their youngsters.

Indeed, the bulk of discussions about children and television were offered in the context of mastery. If the machine could control the child, then so could the parent. Here the language of common sense provided some reassurance by reminding parents that it was they, after all, who were in command. As TV critic Jack Gould wrote in 1949, 'It takes a human hand to turn on a television set.'[18] But for parents who needed a bit more than just the soothing words of a popular sage, the media ushered in specialists from a wide range of fields: child psychologists, educators, psychiatrists, and broadcasters recommended ways to keep the problem child in line.

In 1950 *Better Homes and Gardens* wrote, 'Because he had seen the results of . . . viewing – facial tics, overstimulation, neglect of practicing, outdoor play . . . homework – Van R. Brokhane, who produces education FM programs for New York City schools, decided to establish a system of control.' Brokhane's control system was typical; it took the form of a careful management of time and space. 'The Brokhanes put their receiver in the downstairs playroom where it could not entice their teen-age daughter away from her homework.' And 'then they outlined a schedule – their daughter could watch TV before dinner, but not afterward, on school nights.'[19]

The publication of B.F. Skinner's *Walden two* in 1948 precipitated a popular embrace of behaviorist psychology in the fifties. The women's home magazines discussed ways to control children's behavior through positive reinforcement, and television found its way into the behaviorist technique. In 1955, *Better Homes and Gardens* reported: 'After performing the routine of dressing, [and] tidying up his room . . . Steve knows he can . . . joy of joys – watch his favorite morning TV show. His attitude is now so good he has even volunteered . . . to set the table for breakfast and help his little sister dress.'[20] Thus discipline was conceived not only in the negative sense but also in the positive, 'prosocial' terms suggested by behavior modification.

Expert advice also borrowed principles from psychoanalysis and typically engaged in a kind of therapeutic interrogation of family dynamics. Here television was not so much the cause of aberrant deeds as it was a symptom of deep-rooted problems in the home. As *Better Homes and Gardens* advised in 1950, 'If your boy or girl throws a tantrum when you call him away from the set, don't blame television. Tantrums are a sign that tension already exists in a family.'[21]

The paradox of this expert advice on television and children was that the experts – rather than the parents – took on the authoritative role. To borrow Jacques Donzelot's phrase, this expert advice amounted to a 'policing of families' by public institutions.[22] By the turn of the century in the US, doctors, lawyers, clergymen, educators, industrialists, architects, and feminists had all claimed a stake in the management of domestic affairs. One of the central conduits for disciplined domesticity was the new mass-circulation women's magazines which functioned in part as a site for reform discourses on the family. During the Progressive Era and especially in the 1920s, the public control of domestic life was regularized and refined as public agencies began to 'administer' private life. In the 1920s, the secretary of commerce, Herbert Hoover, became a housing crusader. His policies encouraged a proliferation of government administrations as well as civic centers which disseminated advice on subjects ranging from building to child rearing. Hoover, in conjunction with private industry and civic groups, thought that the public agencies would help stabilize social and economic turmoil by ensuring a proper home life for all Americans. Women's magazines were closely linked to Hoover's campaigns, most obviously when Mrs William Brown Meloney, editor of the *Delineator*, asked him to serve as president of Better Homes in America, a voluntary organization which by 1930 had 7,279 branches across the nation.[23] More generally, women's magazines were inundated with advice from professionals and industrialists who saw themselves as the custodians of everyday life.

Television appears to have been an ideal vehicle through which to regulate the family. As in the above example, TV was typically figured as a sign of larger family problems which needed to be explored by outside authorities. In this sense, it served to support the social regulation of family life. It made parents more dependent upon knowledge produced by public institutions and thus placed parents in a weakened position. In 1951, an article in *House Beautiful* complained about this loss of parental dominion, claiming:

> It seems that raising a child correctly these days is infinitely more difficult than it was 30 years ago when no one had ever heard of Drs Kinsey and Gessell, and a man named Freud was discussed only in women's beauty parlors ... 20 or 30 years ago when there weren't so many authorities on everything in America, the papas and mamas of the nation had a whole lot easier going with Junior than we have today with the authorities.

The author connected his loss of parental power directly to television, recalling the time when his little boy began to strike the TV with a large stick. Unable to decide for himself how to punish his son, the author opted for the lenient approach suggested by the expert, Dr Spock. Unfortunately, the author recounted, 'the next day Derek rammed his shovel through the TV screen [and] the set promptly blew up'.[24]

In part, anxieties about parental control had to do with the fact that television was heavily promoted to families with children. During the fifties, manufacturers and retailers discovered that children were a lucrative consumer market for the sale of household commodities, including television. Numerous surveys indicated that families with children tended to buy TV sets more than childless couples did. Basing their appeals on the data, manufacturers and retailers formulated strategies by which to pull parents' purse strings. In 1950, the American Television Dealers and Manufacturers ran nationwide newspaper ads that played on parental guilt. The headline read, 'Your daughter won't ever tell you the humiliation she's felt in begging those precious hours of television from a neighbor.' Forlorn children were pictured on top of the layout, and parents were shown how television could raise their youngsters' spirits. This particular case is especially interesting because it shows that there are limits to which advertisers can go before a certain amount of sales resistance takes place. Outraged by the ad, parents, educators, and clergymen complained to their newspapers about its manipulative tone. In addition, the Family Service Association of America called it a 'cruel pressure to apply against millions of parents' who could not afford TV sets.[25]

Just as TV advertisements bestowed a new kind of power onto child consumers, TV programs seemed to disrupt conventional power dynamics between child and adult. Popular media complained that the television image had usurped the authority previously held by parents. As TV critic John Crosby complained, 'You tell little Oscar to trot off to bed, and you will probably find yourself embroiled in argument. But if Milton Berle tells him to go to bed, off he goes.'[26] Here as elsewhere, television particularly threatened to depose the father. TV was depicted as the new patriarch, a machine which had robbed men of their dominion in the home.

TV critics (most of whom were male) lashed out at the appearance of bumbling fathers on the new family sit-coms. The forum for such criticism was not the women's magazines but more typically the general weeklies and news magazines which were popular with male as well as female readers. In 1944, *Time* magazine claimed, 'In television's stable of 35 home-life comedies, it is a rare show that treats Father as anything more than the mouse of the house – a bumbling, well-meaning idiot who is putty in the hands of his wife and family.'[27]

The kind of criticism directed at television and its bumbling fathers had its roots in a well-established tradition of mass-culture criticism based on categories of sexual difference. As film and literary scholars have observed, culture critics have often paired mass media with patriarchal assumptions about femininity. Mass amusements are typically thought to encourage passivity and are represented in terms of penetration, consumption, and escape. As Andreas Huyssen has argued, this link between women and mass culture has served since the nineteenth century to valorize the dichotomy between 'low' and 'high' art (or modernism). Mass culture, Huyssen claims, 'is somehow associated with women while real, authentic culture remains the prerogative of men'.[28] The case of broadcasting is especially interesting in this regard because the threat of feminization was particularly aimed at men. Broadcasting quite literally was shown to disrupt the normative structures of patriarchal (high) culture and to turn 'real men' into passive homebodies.

The 'feminizing' aspects of broadcast technology were a central concern during radio's installation in the twenties. Radio hams of the early 1900s were popularized in the press and in fiction as virile heroes who saved damsels in distress with the aid of wireless technology (a popular example was the 'Radio Boys', Bob and Joe, who used wireless to track down criminals and save the innocent).[29] But as Catherine Covert has argued, once radio became a domestic medium, men lost their place as active agents. Now they were shown to sit passively, listening to a one-way communication system.[30]

In the early 1940s, the connection between radio technology and emasculation came to a dramatic pitch when Philip Wylie wrote his bitter attack on US women, *Generation of vipers*. In this widely read book, Wylie maintained that American society was suffering from an ailment he called 'momism'. US women, according to Wylie, had become overbearing, domineering mothers who turned their sons and husbands into weak-kneed fools. The book was replete with imagery of apocalypse through technology, imagery which Wylie tied to the figure of the woman. As he saw it, an unholy alliance between women and big business had turned the world into an industrial nightmare. Corporations such as Alcoa and General Electric had created a new female 'sloth' by supplying women with machines which deprived them of their 'social usefulness'. Meanwhile, claimed Wylie, women had become 'Cinderellas' – greedy consumers who 'raped the men, not sexually, but morally . . .'[31]

In his most bitter chapter, entitled 'Common women', Wylie argued that women had somehow gained control of the airwaves. He suggested that they had made radio listening into a passive activity which threatened manhood and, in fact, civilization. As Wylie wrote,

> The radio is mom's final tool, for it stamps everyone who listens to it with the matriarchal brand . . . Just as Goebbels has revealed what can be done with such a mass stamping of the public psyche in his nation, so our land is a living representation of the same fact worked out in matriarchal sentimentality, goo, slop, hidden cruelty, and the foreshadow of national death.[32]

In the 1955 annotated edition, Wylie updated these fears, claiming that television would soon take the place of radio and turn men into female-dominated dupes. Women, he wrote,

> will not rest until every electronic moment has been bought to sell suds and every bought program censored to the last decibel and syllable according to her self-adulation – along with that (to the degree the mom-indoctrinated pops are permitted access to the dials) of her desexed, de-souled, de-cerebrated mate.[33]

The mixture of misogyny and 'telephobia' which ran through this passage was clearly hyperbolic; still, the basic idea was repeated in more sober representations of everyday life during the postwar period.

Indeed, the paranoid connections which Wylie drew between corporate technocracies, women, and broadcasting would continue to be drawn in the 1950s when large bureaucracies increasingly controlled the lives of middle-class men. Television was often shown to rob men of their powers, making them into passive, helpless women, or even children. Unlike the male spectator of the classical cinema, who has been represented in terms of mastery and control over the scene, television in these popular accounts was shown to take away authority over the image. It threatened to make men into female spectators.

Here, one popular theme had to do with Dad's inability to control TV technology. In a 1952 episode of *I Love Lucy* entitled 'The Courtroom', Ricky Ricardo shows his friends, Fred and Ethel Mertz, how to operate their brand-new TV set. Bragging of his technical know-how, Ricky takes two wires from the back of the TV set. But when the wires connect, the set goes up in smoke along with Ricky's masculine pride. Enraged by the destruction of their new console, the Mertzes march upstairs to the Ricardo apartment where Fred retaliates by kicking in the picture tube of Lucy and Ricky's TV set.

Finally, the Mertzes take the Ricardos to court, where we are given yet another example of male incompetence. This time the bumbling man turns out to be the judge – the ultimate patriarchal authority – who is also emasculated by TV technology. Attempting to reenact the crime, the judge brings his TV out from his chambers. Convinced that he's an authority on television technology, he believes that he can connect the wires without causing the disastrous results that Ricky did. The last laugh, of course, is on the judge who winds up destroying his own TV set.

A related theme was that of the man's inability to control his passion for mindless TV entertainment. Against his better judgment, the father would succumb to television and become childlike. The first episode of *The Honeymooners*, entitled 'TV or Not TV' (1955), revolved around this dilemma. In the opening scene, Alice Kramden begs her husband, Ralph, for a TV set. After buying it, Ralph and his friend Ed Norton are turned into passive viewers. Ralph sits before the set with a smorgasbord of snacks which he deliberately places within his reach so that he needn't move a muscle while watching his program. Norton's regressive state becomes the center of the comedic situation as he is turned into a child viewer addicted to a sci-fi serial. Wearing a club-member space helmet, Norton tunes into his favorite TV host, Captain Video.

In an episode of *The Adventures of Ozzie and Harriet* ('An Evening with Hamlet', c. 1953), this form of technological emasculation was tied directly to the father's parental authority, and by extension to the traditions of patriarchal culture. The episode opens at the breakfast table as the young son, Ricky, sadly announces that the television set is broken. As was the case in many postwar households, the father in this home is unable to fix the complicated technology himself. Instead, the family is dependent upon a new cultural hero, the TV repairman. Ozzie uses this occasion to assert his parental authority by finding family amusements which compete with television for the boys' attention. His idea of family fun recalls Victorian modes of domestic recreation – specifically, dramatic reading. But his sons are less than pleased. As Ricky says in a subsequent scene, 'Hey Mom, that television man didn't get here yet . . . now we're stuck with that darn Shakespeare.'

This episode goes on to highlight the competition for cultural authority between fathers and television by objectifying the problem in the form of two supporting characters. While the Nelsons recite *Hamlet*, two men visit the family home. The first is a wandering bard who mysteriously appears at the Nelson door and joins the family recital. The bard, who looks as though he is part of an Elizabethan theater troupe, evokes associations of high art and cultural refinement. The second visitor, a TV repairman, represents the new electronic mass-produced culture. He is presented as an unrefined blue-collar worker who is good with machines but otherwise inept. A conversation between Ozzie and the repairman succinctly suggests this point:

REPAIRMAN: Oh, a play, huh, I used to be interested in dramatics myself.
OZZIE: Oh, an actor.
REPAIRMAN: No, a wrestler.

As this scene so clearly demonstrates, television not only competes with the father at home but also disturbs the central values of patriarchal culture by replacing the old authorities with a new and degraded form of art. [. . .]

NOTES

1. 'Television has become a member of the family', *House Beautiful*, 93 (September 1951), p. 118.
2. *House Beautiful*, 97 (January 1955), pp. 39–43, 84.
3. Warren I. Susman, 'Culture and communications', in *Culture as history: the transformation of American society in the twentieth century* (1973; New York, Pantheon, 1984), p. 268.
4. Joseph Wood Krutch, 'Have you caught on yet . . .', *House Beautiful*, 93 (November 1951), p. 221.
5. Calder Willingham, 'Television giant in the living room', *American Mercury*, 74 (February 1952), p. 117.
6. For discussions of this, *see* Jeanne Allen, 'The social matrix of television: invention in the United States', in E. Ann Kaplan (ed.), *Regarding television* (Los Angeles, University Publications of America, 1983), p. 113; and Robert Davis, 'Response to innovation: a study of popular argument about new mass media', dissertation, University of Iowa, 1965, pp. 100–1.
7. *See*, for example, Bill Reiche, 'Television is the navy's school teacher', *Popular Mechanics*, 90 (November 1948), pp. 125–7, 270, 272; Devon Francis, 'TV takes over test pilot's job', *Popular Science*, 158 (March, 1951), pp. 144–8; 'Dismantling bombs by TV', *Science Digest*, 35 (January 1954), inside cover.
8. Elsewhere I discuss this military association with reference to popular fears about television's status as a surveillance mechanism. *See* my article 'Installing the television set: popular discourses on television and domestic space, 1948–55', *Camera Obscura*, 16 (August 1988), pp. 11–47.
9. Newton Minow, 'The vast wasteland', Address to the 39th Annual Convention of the National Broadcasters, Washington, 9 May 1961.

10. *Look*, 21 April 1953, p. 18.

11. 'Television has become a member of the family', *House Beautiful*, 93.

12. *Better Homes and Gardens*, 30 (December 1952), p. 133.

13. Leo Bogart, *The age of television: a study of viewing habits and the impact of television on American life* (New York, Ungar, 1958), p. 97.

14. This concern with media effects on children was part of a larger history. For example, controversies about these influences were launched by middle-class reformers during the Progressive Era. By the 1930s reform arguments had gained particular strength, with film and radio as prime targets of public scrutiny. In the 1950s, this concern with broadcasting was transferred to television – most strikingly in 1955 when the Kefauver investigation held special hearings on television's effect on children. For more on this, *see* Davis, 'Response to innovation', especially pp. 163–71, 209–16, and 233–53.

15. *Ladies' Home Journal*, 67 (April 1950), p. 237. For a similar cartoon *see Ladies' Home Journal*, 72 (December 1955), p. 164.

16. 'Bang! You're dead', *Newsweek*, 21 March 1955, p. 35.

17. Edward M. Brecher, 'TV, your children, and your grandchildren', *Consumer Reports*, 15 (May 1950), p. 231.

18. Jack Gould, 'What is television doing to us?', *New York Times Magazine*, 12 June 1949, p. 7.

19. Dorothy Diamond and Frances Tenenbaum, 'Should you tear 'em away from TV?', *Better Homes and Gardens*, 29 (September 1950), p. 56.

20. *Better Homes and Gardens*, 33 (March 1955), p. 173.

21. Diamond and Tenenbaum, 'Should you tear 'em away?', p. 239.

22. Jacques Donzelot, *The policing of families* (New York, Pantheon, 1979). Donzelot discusses the history of the public regulation of the family in France.

23. For a detailed discussion *see* Gwendolyn Wright, *Building the dream: a social history of housing in America* (New York, Pantheon, 1981), p. 197.

24. Lloyd Shearer, 'The parental dilemma', *House Beautiful*, 93 (October 1951), pp. 220, 222.

25. 'Television tempest', *Newsweek*, 27 November 1950, p. 62.

26. John Crosby, 'Parents arise! You have nothing to lose but your sanity', in *Out of the blue! A book about radio and television* (New York, Simon, 1952), p. 115.

27. 'Daddy with a difference', *Time*, 17 May 1954, p. 83. For additional examples *see* Eleanor Harris, 'They always get their man', *Colliers*, 25 November 1950, p. 34; 'The great competitor', *Time*, 14 December 1953, p. 62; 'Perpetual honeymoon', *Time*, 22 March 1954, p. 82.

28. Andreas Huyssen, 'Mass culture as woman: modernism's other', in Tania Modleski (ed.), *Studies in entertainment: critical approaches to mass culture* (Bloomington, Indiana University Press, 1986), p. 191.

29. Susan J. Douglas discusses this in 'Amateur operators and American broadcasting: shaping the future of radio', in Joseph J. Corn (ed.), *Imagining tomorrow: history, technology, and the American future* (Cambridge, Mass, MIT Press, 1986), pp. 46–7.

30. Catherine L. Covert, '"We may hear too much": American sensibility and the response to radio 1919–1924', in C.L. Covert, and J.D. Stevens (eds.), *Mass media between the wars: perceptions of cultural tension 1914–41* (Syracuse, Syracuse University Press, 1984), pp. 199–220.

31. Philip Wylie, *Generation of vipers* (1942; New York, Holt, 1955), pp. 199–200.

32. Wylie, *Generation of vipers*, pp. 214–15.

33. Wylie, *Generation of vipers*, pp. 213–14.

15

Gender and generation: the case of *thirtysomething*

Margaret J. Heide

From Heide, M.J. 1995: *Television culture and women's lives:* thirtysomething *and the contradictions of gender*. Philadelphia: University of Pennsylvania Press, 2–9

The study of television has its roots in earlier studies of mass communication and, as the use of the term 'mass' suggests, these studies tended to assume that the same message or messages reached and impacted upon very large numbers of people with similar effects. A focus on the one-way nature of these communication systems and some considerable concern about their widespread and supposed 'hypodermic' effects also fuelled the fears of a new, homogenized, 'one-dimensional' society. And, indeed, the commercial film and broadcasting industries from the early part of this century saw their strategies for maximum profitability as being intimately linked to the creation of the largest possible and least differentiated markets. In American cinema, for example (unlike the situation in Europe), a classification system for films aimed at different audiences was introduced only in 1968. From a marketing point of view it was highly desirable to bring into being, even to 'construct', a homogenized audience for a largely homogenized product.

However, the radically different life experiences of different members of the mass audience, combined with improvements in education and more liberal social views, together with the proliferation of new cable and satellite channels, has made it increasingly difficult for either the big producers of commodity culture or the communications scholars to continue to assume a mass audience united by the similarity of its needs and responses.

Margaret Heide's book, from which this extract is taken, offers a historically grounded account of the new media environment of the 1980s with particular reference to the ways in which television drama seeks to recognize and represent the changing position of women (and men) and changing patterns of childcare, work and family life. In an era marked by a major expansion in the numbers of women in paid employment and by the consequent strains and stresses created for traditional gender and parenting roles, she is particularly interested in the use which women make of television fiction. She selects for detailed study the dramatic series *thirtysomething* which was aired on the American ABC network from 1987 to 1991, and subsequently on Channel 4 in Britain. In the United States the series was both a critical and a commercial hit. It attracted a loyal and enthusiastic audience and evoked widespread media comment on its unprecedented success in reaching its marketing target: the affluent and white portion of the post-Second World War baby-boom generation.

Heide's research on the responses of the women viewers in her predominantly middle-class sample contributes to the growing body of knowledge developed by feminist scholars on the 'gendered' character of viewing, offering the basis for a fairly systematic critique of earlier theories of mass communication. Moreover, although she concentrates predominantly on middle-class responses, she also records the views of lower-middle-class and working-class women who identified with many of the dilemmas represented in the series yet criticized its privileged 'yuppie' protagonists. Finally, and perhaps paradoxically, she notes that ABC – faced with increasing competition for audiences from other media – cancelled the series, turning to more conventional and less demographically targeted programmes.

To look at television today is to enter a world that is at once fantastic and eerily familiar. One way television makes claim to the familiar is to draw on existing conflicts in American society, commenting on them in comfortable and well-known forms (Gitlin, 1985, p. 12; Taylor, 1989, p. 3; Newcomb and Hirsch, 1984, p. 63). Television not only is able to draw on social crises and anxieties, but has become one of the primary resources that individuals rely on to help them make sense of the world and of their actions in the world (Jensen, 1984, p. 108).

Observing this capacity of network television to serve as a kind of cultural forum that organizes and shapes our understanding of our social selves, I became interested in exploring how television frames ideas about gender and the family for the post–World War II so-called 'baby-boom' generation. For this generation is the first in history to have lived not only through a large-scale movement for women's liberation but at the same time through the historically unprecedented entry of great numbers of women into the paid labor force (Silberstein, 1992; Gerstel and Gross, 1987). These two factors have created a tremendous upheaval in the lives of women, which television in turn tries to represent (Silberstein, 1992, p. ix). Shows from *That Girl* in the 1960s to *The Mary Tyler Moore Show* in the 1970s to *One Day at a Time* in the 1980s have provided public images, for example, of white middle-class women's entry into the labor force.

These images on television, furthermore, are not neutral but often reflect competing interests as to how social life should be organized. A conservative vision of work and family life affirms the traditional division of men and women into separate 'spheres', where women primarily occupy the private sphere of the home and men the public sphere of the paid labor force. A more liberal vision, on the other hand, entertains a variety of flexible social arrangements to be negotiated between partners, with both men and women participating fully in home life as well as the paid labor force.[1]

The media feud over out-of-wedlock births that broke out between Dan Quayle and the producers of *Murphy Brown* during the 1992 presidential campaign is just one example of how competing ideologies about women's place in the family and work confront each other on TV screens. In such disparate television formats as celebrity talk shows, the evening news, situation comedies, and dramas the battle over competing visions of gender is waged. Television thus serves as a site of contestation, reflecting contemporary struggles over gender and family (Barrett, 1980, p. 112).

One of the most ambitious efforts to represent the family in the last decade is the network television series *thirtysomething*, now in rerun on the Lifetime cable channel. An hour-long dramatic series, *thirtysomething* aired from 1987 to 1991, in the twilight of a decade in which the post-war generations came of age. Set in an area somewhere outside Philadelphia, *thirtysomething* revolves around the personal lives of seven friends in their thirties: Michael Steadman and his wife, Hope, the primary characters; Elliot Weston, Michael's business partner and close friend, and his wife, Nancy; Melissa Steadman, Michael's cousin; Gary Shepherd, Michael's oldest friend; and Ellyn Warren, Hope's oldest friend. Of the main characters, five are married and have children; two are single women. All of them are white, well-educated, middle and upper middle class; all have had or are currently pursuing careers.

The plots of *thirtysomething* usually center on personal crises or events that the characters are facing in their work or family life, and the main 'action' consists of discussions between the characters about these events. This primary focus on the characters' work and family lives is in keeping with what the producers, Edward Zwick and Marshall Herskovitz, wanted to explore in their effort to capture the 'small moments' of people's lives as a means of creating a bond between the characters and the viewing audience.[2]

In terms of the problem of gender, some of the day-to-day or 'real life' conflicts the married female characters Hope and Nancy go through revolve around wanting to go back into the paid labor force versus wanting to stay home with their children full time; wanting to be taken seriously as autonomous individuals versus wanting to be immersed in the mothering role; wanting equality with their mates versus wanting to be 'taken care of'; and more generally, trying to communicate and establish sexual intimacy with their spouses, relating to their single women friends, and dealing with the conflicting burdens of home, family, and their desire to find meaningful outside employment.

The single women characters Melissa Steadman and Ellyn Warren, for their part, experience conflicts over pursuing their careers while at the same time finding men and getting married; over dealing with the social pressure of *not* being married; over wanting to have freedom versus wanting to be in a relationship; and, finally, over wanting to have children before their biological clock runs out or coming to terms with their recognition that they do not want children. The men on the show also experience a variety of conflicts relating to what kind of role they should play in their marriage, family, and work lives, and the show deals with men's ambivalent feelings toward fulfilling traditional roles as well (Hanke, 1990). Through exploring these conflicts, the makers of *thirtysomething* hoped to reach a large and affluent, primarily white audience who were themselves grappling with a whole new set of confusing and bewildering choices as to how to negotiate their work and family lives (O'Connor, 1989). A key premise behind the great bulk of episodes is that the characters' life choices involve mutually exclusive goals that their parents did not have to face. At the root of this lies a changing sexual division of labor: being a good mother and wife might now conflict with being a successful professional; being a good provider economically might now be insufficient to be counted as a good husband and father (Zwick and Herskovitz, 1991, p. 3).

While confronting many of the same problems that their parents faced, then, this new generation also find themselves in the position of having to choose what kind of life and what gender roles they want to adopt. Far from being a liberating experience, this ability to choose is experienced as a psychic and emotional burden attended by a great deal of pain and confusion. Ultimately, Zwick and Herskovitz perceive their stories as revealing an important truth about the moral and political choices facing their generation, choices that involve fundamental conflicts over the self-conscious creation of social and gender identities. This is the source of the pervasive sense of anxiety, self-doubt, and complaint that the main characters, despite their affluence, typically feel.

As it turns out, this emphasis on capturing the 'stuff of real life' by exploring contemporary gender conflicts struck a deep chord not only in the viewing audience it was targeted toward, the baby boomers, but in the larger culture as well. *Thirtysomething* was a critical and commercial success, being nominated for and winning numerous Emmy awards including, in its first broadcast year, 'Outstanding Dramatic Series'. The program attracted an enormous amount of attention from the mainstream media as well as from the television industry and entertainment press. Much of this attention centered on its uncanny ability to reach the baby-boom generation to which it was marketed.[3] One commentary, for example, highlighted the characters' 'recognizable inner lives' (Hoban, 1988, p. 49). Another reviewer remarked on *thirtysomething*'s ability to arouse its viewers, to 'force' their engagement by mirroring aspects of their lives that television had not presented before (Anon, 1990). Writing for the Jewish literary magazine *Tikkun*, Jay Rosen claimed that *thirtysomething* functioned as a kind of 'consciousness raising' for its audience by showing how personal problems are rooted in larger social conditions (Rosen, 1989, p. 30).

Compared to television programs put out in the early 1980s, such as *Dallas* and *Dynasty*, with their fantasies of money, power, and glamor, *thirtysomething* was also viewed by many commentators as the quintessential television show for the late 1980s, in its ability to take the 'pulse of society' and mirror the temperament of a generation grappling with a profound sense of ambivalence and confusion in relation to the values of the past. Articles sometimes included interviews with stars of the show, who talked about the way that the stories emerged and fed back into their off-screen lives. Such commentary became a kind of secondary narrative, reinforcing the themes of the show.

THIRTYSOMETHING AND THE BUSINESS OF TELEVISION

Thirtysomething's emphasis on exploring the ambivalence of the post–World War II generation can be seen as part of a larger trend in the television industry that occurred in the late 1980s to market programs to specific audiences, particularly the baby-boomer audience, who are generally more up-scale and consumer oriented than other demographic groups with less disposable income and who, having been weaned, in fact, on television, form a large, media-savvy blip in the demographics of post–World War II America. 'Demographics', the process of breaking down a mass audience by a series of social characteristics, including age, sex, and income, is used by networks in the rating games to select the most profitable audiences for their advertisers. The most profitable demographic group was considered to be urban viewers between the ages of 18 and 49, primarily women, who were most likely to be the chief consumers for their families (Taylor, 1989, p. 45).

The first signs of these attempts by the networks to target the post-war generation could be seen in television shows earlier in the 1980s such as *St. Elsewhere*, *Hill Street Blues*, *Cagney and Lacey*, *Cheers*, and *Moonlighting*. These programs were characterized by a kind of hip sensibility and skepticism that was thought to play well with the up-scale, baby-boomer audiences they were targeted to.[4] From this original parry toward the 'new generation', programs such as *Baby Boom, Murphy Brown, China Beach, L.A. Law, The Days and Nights of Molly Dodd* and *thirtysomething* came into being, signaling a move from programs simply marketed toward this post-war generation to shows explicitly about them.

The strategy of targeting specific audiences was an attempt to counteract the networks' loss of viewers to the burgeoning cable industry. All three networks lost 5 percent of their prime-time audience share in the 1989 season, for example, at which time their overall share of viewers had dropped to 62 percent of the viewing public (Auletta, 1991, p. 20). So, in part as an attempt to staunch the flow of viewers to cable, as well as to market their television 'product' selectively to a specific niche rather than cast a wide net, programs like *thirtysomething* were given the go-ahead as a lure to the baby-boomers (Carter, 1991b).[5]

Ultimately, although the networks' marketing strategy was intent on creating programs for certain niches of the market, they could not guarantee that the programs would be watched. For, with competition from cable and home video continuing to whittle away at network audiences, network television knew it would be increasingly difficult to get their audiences to stay with them for an entire evening. One strategy the networks began to pursue was to capture younger viewers who were not the privileged yuppies of the *thirtysomething* genre. Such programs as *Roseanne* on ABC, as well as a grittier, working-class version of *thirtysomething* produced by Zwick and Herskovitz called *Dream Street* (jokingly referred to in the industry as *dirtysomething*), represented just such an attempt to attract a larger group of baby-boomers (Gerard, 1988, p. 28).

In general, however, the networks have been playing a losing game, despite their different marketing strategies, as audiences shift and age and move around to different media (cable and video) to get their entertainment. In fact, some people have argued that marketing programs to younger viewers does not make sense any more because that historical age group is now part of the 35 to 54 age bracket (Carter, 1991b). In other words, the aging of the 'boomers', who had been the primary market for ABC, means that these viewers have now been bumped into an older demographic grouping.

Despite the fact, then, that ABC had been pursuing a specific target marketing strategy for four years, by the summer of 1991 it had reversed its position and decided to cancel *thirtysomething*. Whereas the earlier strategy was on innovative shows addressed to specific demographic markets, the three networks, faced with shrinking advertising dollars and smaller budgets, reversed themselves and decided to produce much more conventional programs in the hopes of once again going for the mass market of earlier eras (Carter, 1991a). Citing the fact that it was difficult to bear the burden of producing programs that were unprofitable, ABC canceled not only *thirtysomething* but two other shows that also appealed to the now aging boomers, *China Beach* and *Twin Peaks* (Carter, 1991a). Because *thirtysomething*'s ratings fell that year from 12.3 to 10.6, and its audience now consisted primarily of younger women, its narrow demographics made it increasingly unattractive to a network seeking to boost ratings and increase viewers (Carter, 1991a).

Instead of unconventional dramas, ABC added a number of new comedies.[6] *Thirtysomething* itself was replaced not by a comedy, but by a show called *Home Front*, a drama about Americans in the years just following World War II. Though also a drama, the program was much more conventional in its storyline, about a historical period that gave birth, ironically enough, to the demographic group depicted on *thirtysomething*.

TELEVISION, FEMINISM, AND THE CULTURAL BACKLASH AGAINST WOMEN

While *thirtysomething*'s stories emerged from the artistic vision of its creators, Herskovitz and Zwick, the show may also be seen as arising within a televisual landscape that had closed off many of the more explicitly feminist concerns aired during the active phases of the women's movement in the 1970s. These concerns included questioning traditional roles for men and women, fighting for equal rights and relief for working mothers, and encouraging women to strike out on their own and develop themselves. As television scholar Ella Taylor has pointed out, many of the prime time shows of the 1970s, from *The Mary Tyler Moore Show* to *One Day at a Time* to *Maude* and even *All in the Family*, addressed themselves to women's new lives as a result of the women's movement, and as such arguably constituted a kind of 'prime-time feminism' (Taylor, 1989). This 'feminism' was not without contradictions, of course. For example, the feminist impetus behind having Mary Tyler Moore shown as a single woman 'making it on her own' was offset by her relationship with her male boss, played paternalistically by Ed Asner. But considering the prior silence of television on such issues, their representation did achieve a certain breakthrough.

In the 1980s, this prime-time feminism had been altered in the wake of a general re-questioning of many of the goals of the women's movement. Taylor notes that in such shows as *Cagney and Lacey*, *The Cosby Show*, and *thirtysomething* women's roles were being seriously re-evaluated, with attention now being paid to the unintended costs of the women's movement. Looking specifically at *thirtysomething*, Taylor observes how the married female character Hope goes through tortured deliberations about whether to return to work after having her child, while the single characters are made out to be miserably unhappy because they do not have a husband or children. Taylor ultimately questions the feminist potential of programs such as *thirtysomething*, seeing in them only a kind of backlash against the women's movement (Taylor, 1989, p. 159).

In entering into contemporary discussions about gender and family through their portrayal of 'real life', the creators of *thirtysomething* indirectly took up a position in the debate. This position, most scholars have agreed, is conservative in that it portrays more traditional roles for men and women as the most viable ones, even though most men and women cannot in fact reproduce these roles as they had in earlier eras (Loeb, 1990; Taylor, 1989; Hanke, 1990; Torres, 1989). Yet this may not be the whole story. While the text of *thirtysomething* can reasonably be described as part of a cultural backlash toward women, female viewers may not see themselves as part of this backlash. In fact, many of the viewers saw themselves as feminists, or at least as holding views long associated with feminism. Thus there is a gap between the critical interpretations of the show put forth by scholars and the experience of many women who were faithful viewers of the show.

This tension between viewpoints, between the ideas of critical media scholars and those of the female viewing audience, prompted me to explore this terrain in more detail. What did *thirtysomething* mean to its viewing audience? What themes about gender emerged and did they relate to conflicts in viewers' lives? How did women think and talk about fictional characters on a television show? And why did these characters feel so real to women?

Writing about female audiences and their use of popular romance novels, Janice Radway has pointed out that, in order to understand why romance novels sell so well, it is first important to know what a romance *is* for women who buy and read them (Radway, 1984).[7] Following this lead, I interviewed female viewers of *thirtysomething* to try to understand what place the program had in their lives, why they watched it, and what meanings about gender, if any, they generated through the experience of viewing, thinking, and talking about it. During the 1990–91 television season, I conducted interviews with twenty female viewers in the New York metropolitan area and handed out written questionnaires to another thirty women for a total of fifty respondents. I deliberately chose female viewers who belonged to the demographic group that the programmers of *thirtysomething* most wanted to reach: primarily white, middle-class Americans between the ages of 25 and 45. I wanted to see how it was true that a certain cultural text was able to 'speak' to its intended audience in such a way as to elicit strong identifications on the part of the viewer.

The interviewed women lived in Brooklyn, Manhattan, and Staten Island, New York, and Princeton, New Jersey, and ranged in age from approximately 20 to 45. Slightly more than half were in their thirties. The majority of the women had attended some amount of college, and over a third were currently in school. Approximately half were married, and half were single, either never married or divorced. In addition, at least a third of the women had children and over three-quarters were planning to have them.

FEMALE VIEWERS AND SOCIAL CLASS

A number of scholars have tried to come to terms with the complex nature of assigning a class status to an individual. Some have utilized Marxist approaches, which locate class primarily in relation to the means of production, and look at the job the individual occupies in a capitalist society (Bottomore *et al.*, 1983; Parkin, 1979). Feminist scholars, too, have entered the debate. Writers such as Mary Ryan (1979) and Ann Oakley (1974) argue that women's specific work under capitalism casts doubt on the notion that women simply belong to their husbands' class. These writers instead view women in a capitalist society as potentially having more in common with one another than with the class of their husbands. Other feminists, including Kate Millett (1971), argue that women perhaps themselves make up a separate class altogether in our society, and challenge the very notion of class based on economics, status, or prestige as ignoring the fundamental division in society between men and women.

Given the as yet unresolved debate about how to determine an individual's class background, the most reasonable strategy for my study seemed to lie in combining a number of traditional sociological variables for a comprehensive portrait of an individual woman's class affiliation. Thus I began my investigation by looking at the occupations of the women (and their husbands if they were married) as well as those of their parents. I also included the women's income level, whether they were professionals or skilled or non-skilled workers, how much disposable income they had, how much property they owned, their educational status and aspirations, where they lived and how much money, if any, they had saved.

The responses yielded some interesting differences in terms of individuals' sense of whether they had the same life options as the female characters on *thirtysomething*. Lower-middle-class women felt that they did not have the same opportunities to make the kinds of decisions that the female characters often did. In addition, lower-middle-class women tended not to identify so much with the female characters as with the *situations* these characters found themselves in. Often, they were annoyed with the female characters themselves, seeing them as a bunch of whining 'yuppies'. At the same time, however, they found that the situations these yuppies were in were similar to situations they were facing in their own lives: the division of labor at home, trying to meet men, spending enough time with their children, and so on. For this reason, while lower-middle-class women tended to judge the female characters more harshly than did their upper-middle-class counterparts, they nevertheless 'bonded' to these characters in terms of the situations that were depicted. More provocatively, they often used these characters to define their own class limits and horizons, by saying what they would do if they had the same privileges as the upper-middle-class female characters. In this way, class may be understood as a lived category for the lower- and upper-middle-class women; in a sense they constituted and reaffirmed themselves as class subjects in part through their interaction with the program.

Upper-middle-class women too used *thirtysomething* as a springboard for articulating not only their gender conflicts but also their lives as upper-middle-class women. That is, they tended to use the program to affirm some of the life choices they had made as women who were privileged and had the option, say, to leave their job if it conflicted with the demands of home. In addition, they tended to identify with and draw on the language (or 'whining') that the female characters used to describe their conflicts, and were much less put off by the class privileges that this verbalizing seemed to imply to the lower-middle-class women. Upper-middle-class women felt entitled, in other words, to complain about their lives, even when those lives seemed privileged to someone looking at them from the outside. In addition, they also felt comfortable with the therapeutic aspects of verbalizing discontent, while the lower-middle-class women tended to resent women who seemingly had it all but nevertheless felt the need to complain. [. . .]

NOTES

1. Included in the liberal vision is the idea that more than one type of family exists, with extended generations, same-sex partners, single parents, and divorced partners all viewed as having the potential to be loving caregivers. It also recognizes that both men and women have to work in today's economy, for financial and personal reasons, and that gender roles should be open enough to reflect these economic realities.
2. Marshall Herskovitz and Edward Zwick, the co-creators of *thirtysomething*, make reference to their desire to create a program about the 'real life' of the thirtysomething generation. For a good discussion of this goal, which characterizes a number of programs in this genre, *see* their Introduction in *Thirtysomething stories* (Zwick and Herskovitz, 1991, pp. 3–9).

3. Eleanor Blau, for example, reporting for the *New York Times*, found that the viewers identified with the characters and that the characters' lives seemed to mirror the lives of many in the baby boom generation. She also found that the viewers were women between 18 and 34 years old, followed closely by men of the same age and women 35 to 49 (Blau, 1990).

4. For an interesting discussion of the marketing aspects of shows such as *thirtysomething*, *see* Gerard (1988).

5. Perhaps because of this marketing strategy on the part of ABC, it had not led the household ratings race for more than ten years, as Bill Carter goes on to point out. However, it had been the leader in attracting young adult viewers, which meant that while it lost the so-called 'ratings game' it actually *won* in terms of the overall category of profits generated from advertisers, who wanted to go after this group. ABC earned about $220 million in 1991 with this demographic strategy, while NBC brought in only about $50 million (Carter, 1991b). As executives such as Brandon Tartikoff, formerly of NBC, have conceded, the biggest catch remains the approximately 75 million baby-boomer viewers. To develop shows that would appeal to this group, furthermore, he believed was in some sense an easier task, because the majority of the staff working in television at that time were precisely in this age group (Gerard, 1988).

6. For example, listing the new shows, ABC offered such fare in place of shows like *thirtysomething* as *Home Improvements*, a comedy about a home repairs expert; *Grown-ups*, a comedy starring Marsha Mason; *Good and Evil*, a satire about twins with opposite natures; *Bird and Katt*, the previous year's *Gabriel's Fire* reworked as an action comedy; *Step by Step*, a comedy about newlyweds, with Suzanne Somers and Patrick Duffy; *FBI: The Untold Stories*, a 'reality' series with stories from the files; and *The Commish*, a drama about a tough police commissioner (Carter, 1991a).

7. As she continues, 'To know that, we must know what romance readers make of the words they find on the page; we must know, in short, how they construct the plot and interpret the characters' intentions' (Radway, 1987, p. 11).

REFERENCES

ANON, 1990: Why we're *still* watching and arguing about *thirtysomething*. *Entertainment Weekly*, 4 May, 78.

AULETTA, K. 1991: The network takeovers: why ABC survived best. *New York Times*, Sunday 28 July, 20.

BARRETT, M. 1980. *Women's oppression today: problems in Marxist feminist analysis*. London: Verso.

BLAU, E. 1990: Can *thirtysomething* fans accept a bout with cancer? *New York Times*, 22 January, C14.

BOTTOMORE, T. *et al.* (eds.) 1983: *A dictionary of Marxist thought.* Cambridge, MA: Harvard University Press.

CARTER, B. 1991a: Reporter's notebook: despite the praise, these shows won't be back. *New York Times*, 23 July, C13.

CARTER, B. 1991b: The media business: for networks, is no. 1 a winner? *New York Times*, 16 September, D1.

GERARD, J. 1988: TV mirrors a new generation. *New York Times*, Sunday, 30 October, Arts and Leisure Section 2, 28.

GERSTEL, N. and GROSS, H.E. 1987: *Families and work: towards reconceptualization*. Philadelphia: Temple University Press.

GITLIN, T. 1985: *Inside prime-time*. New York: Pantheon.

HANKE, R. 1990: Hegemonic masculinity in *thirtysomething*. *Critical Studies in Mass Communication* 7, 231–48.

HOBAN, P. 1988: All in the family. *New York Magazine* 29 (29 February), 48 (5).

JENSEN, J. 1984: An interpretive approach to culture production. In Rowland, W.D., Jr and Watkins, B. (eds.), *Interpreting television: current research perspectives*. Beverly Hills, CA: Sage.

LOEB, J. 1990: Rhetorical and ideological conservatism in *thirtysomething*. *Critical Studies in Mass Communication* 7, 249–60.

MILLETT, K. 1971: *Sexual politics*. New York: Avon.

NEWCOMB, H. and HIRSCH, P.M. 1984: Television as a cultural forum: implications for research. In Rowland, W.D., Jr and Watkins, B. (eds.), *Interpreting television: current research perspectives*. Beverly Hills, CA: Sage.

OAKLEY, A. 1974: *The sociology of housework*. New York: Vintage.

O'CONNOR, J. 1989: The series for these ambiguous times. *New York Times*, 30 May, C20.

PARKIN, F. 1979: *Marxism and class theory: a bourgeois critique*. New York: Columbia University Press.

RADWAY, J. 1987: *Reading the romance: women, patriarchy and popular literature*. London: Verso (first published 1984; Chapel Hill, NC: University of North Carolina Press).

ROSEN, J. 1989: *Thirtysomething*. *Tikkun* 4(4) (July/August).

RYAN, M. 1979: Femininity and captialism in antebellum America. In Eisenstein, Z.R. (ed.), *Capitalist patriarchy and the case for socialist feminism*. New York: Monthly Review Press.

SILBERSTEIN, L. 1992: *Dual career marriage: a system in transition*. New Jersey: Lawrence Erlbaum Assoc.

TAYLOR, E. 1989: *Prime-time families: television culture in post-war America*. Berkeley: University of California Press.

TORRES, S. 1989: Melodrama, masculinity and the family: *thirtysomething* as therapy. *Camera Obscura* 19, 87–106.

ZWICK, E. and HERSKOVITZ, M. (eds.) 1991: *Thirtysomething stories*. New York: Pocket Books.

16

Radical shopping in Los Angeles

John Fiske

From Fiske, J. 1994: Radical shopping in Los Angeles: race, media and the sphere of consumption. *Media, Culture and Society* 16(3), 469–86

This extract is taken from an article in which John Fiske looks at different mediations of the 1992 disturbances in South Central Los Angeles. Fiske places these disturbances in the context both of long-term racial inequality in the United States and of the relationship between the spheres of production and of consumption. He starts by examining the way in which 'public' and 'private' are related in the sphere of consumption and then moves on to examine how the classification of what happened drew on terms ('riots', 'uprising', 'looting') which immediately served to frame the incidents in different ways. Focusing on the 'looting', he explores how this framing did not square with the way in which things were perceived by most of the inhabitants of South Central themselves. He contrasts perceptions 'on the ground' with a variety of framings and explanatory models used by television, including Oprah Winfrey and the star presenter/reporters of ABC and CNN. Much of the value of his account is due to the way in which he regularly cites the voices of other people trying, in their own socially specific terms, to make sense of what happened. Although his discussion is concise, he is able to show how, in temporary conditions of crisis, some of the deeper and lasting inequalities of the economic system 'surface' in the language of media descriptions and attributed causality.

In a second section abstracted from the article, Fiske presents a general argument about hierarchies of mediated knowledge. He remarks on the way in which what is often considered 'low' TV nevertheless offers the space for voices to be heard which are frequently marginalized altogether in the genres of conventionally 'serious' coverage. The specific kinds of populism of these outlets, often the subject of critical scorn, really do make connections with popular politics.

John Fiske is very much identified with an emphasis on popular media and the way in which cultural consumption is now a primary ground for political expression. This emphasis has been criticized by those who feel that, among other things, it may detract too much both from the need to pay attention to the way in which the production side of the media is organized and from the need for the media to sustain, albeit in a revised form, the project of serious journalism. Here, however, the points around which he constructs his commentary are important enough to deserve consideration in any politically aware media analysis.

The places of consumption adjoin both the public and the private: people and goods move constantly between the shop, the street and the home in an intricate web of everyday, intimate connectedness between public life, private life and the sphere of consumption. This is not the case in that of production with its clear boundary and singular pathway between home and work. Public places, with their close links to the market place and to the home, are also places of visibility and are thus where the behavior of private people or consumers can be seen by TV, can be made into news and can thus gain national and international attention. Public places are readily accessible to TV and in the image-saturated world of late capitalism political protest that is not covered by TV has had most of its teeth pulled.

A position of privilege allows the powerful to speak publicly, almost at will: for the powerless, however, public space is the only position for public speech. Intentionally disruptive behavior in public is, therefore, one of the most readily available, if not the only, means of access to the media for the most deprived and repressed segments of our society. Of course, any such access will always be on the media's own terms, but even that may seem preferable to invisibility and silence. The discourse into which the media put events is inevitably one that promotes the interests of the power bloc to which they are, on most occasions, closely allied. But, despite their best efforts, discursive frames can never contain and control *all* the meanings of events, particularly ones as disruptive and polysemic as an urban uprising.

The mainstream media consistently tried to frame the events of LA in a discourse characterized by the vocabulary of 'riots', 'arson', 'murder' and 'looting'. White Republican politicians used the same discourse, and the same words peppered the speeches made by George Bush, Dan Quayle and Pat Buchanan, to mention only those who were most vigorously electioneering at the time. Very few African Americans, however, used the word 'riot'; for them the words of choice were 'insurgency' or 'rebellion', while left-leaning Whites preferred 'uprising' (which is why I use it in this article). A change of word is always significant, for it indicates a change of discourse, and by discourse I refer to a socially located and politically interested way of making and circulating a particular sense of social experience.

The word 'looting' set the strugglers-over-discourse a harder task than that of 'riot'. The mainstream media and members of the power bloc used it freely, but alternative words were hard to find. Property rights appear to be as deeply ingrained in capitalism's discursive system as in its legal and economic ones, so that the only words available that refer to the transfer of property from the strong to the weak without payment are ones that put this transaction into the discourse of crime. A word such as 'confiscation' refers to the non-economic transfer of property to the strong from the weak, and not vice versa, and, as another disqualification, it lacks any sense of the opportunism that characterizes the tactics of the weak. Nobody tried to coin terms like 'radical shopping', for such neologisms have no social currency and would thus be semiotically unexchangeable: a pity, for 'looting' needs the semiotic shock of a term like 'radical shopping' to deliver the discursive blow that 'rebellion' or 'insurgency' did to 'riot'.

'Looting' was one of the key words by which the media attempted to confine the dominant understanding of the uprising to the discourse of law and order ('arson' and 'murder' were others), and in using it, I set it within quotation marks in an attempt to disarticulate it from its normal discursive, and therefore social, relations. The power over discourse is a material power, for the power to call the activity 'looting' was also the power to put those who engaged in it into prison and to know that prison was the solution to the problem.

Of course, one sense of 'looting' must be the dominant legal one: 'looters' knowingly break the laws that underpin property rights and organize the economic relations between buyers and sellers. 'Looting' does involve grabbing goods illegally, it does involve seizing the opportunities afforded by a breakdown of law and order, and in *some* cases this may have been all that it involved – there were reports, for instance, of 'yuppies in BMWs' (Davis, 1993, p. 144) joining in, but limiting its meaning to its legal dimension is a strategy of the power bloc that represses others. The White media, like the White politicians, put 'looting' into the discourse of law and order in a way that colored that order indelibly White and the disorder Black or Brown. Images of Whites engaged in this 'blackened' disorder were repressed from both the airwaves and mainstream common sense. At WITI-TV, the CBS affiliate in Milwaukee, Wisconsin, for example, two reporters were compiling a round-up of the second day's events for the late-night news. In an attempt to achieve a degree of balance they included footage of a White woman loading designer dresses into her Mercedes who explained her behavior with a casual 'Because everyone else is doing it.' The producer cut the footage. The producer was White, the reporters Black.[1]

To those engaged in it, 'looting' was multidimensional: it could be, for example, both a form of public speech and a statement of self-assertion. 'Looting' enabled the silenced to be heard and the overlooked to be seen. For those who are normally denied an identity and refused a social presence, 'looting' could bring self-satisfaction and could give them an opportunity to remind the nation of Frederick Douglass's words, 'We *are* here. We *are* here.' The uprisings caused Oprah Winfrey to move her show from Chicago to LA and thus to give the Black residents an opportunity for media access that is normally denied them, and one young Black woman, among many others, took it:

> The looting? OK, I'm not saying that attacking the Koreans solved the problem, but when this Rodney King verdict came down, people were angry, and I'm still angry, I get angrier daily, how are we supposed to get it? We're not allowed to rally, we were going to meet Saturday, but that was cancelled – I'm not saying attacking the Koreans was the way, but it did get national attention. We *are* here, we *are* here.[2]

Commodities are goods that speak as well as goods to use, and unequal access to commodities is part of the same system that makes access to public discourse unequal. 'Looting' can temporarily correct both inequalities in one guerrilla action. Baby Saye, a South Central resident who has spent her life on welfare, understood this clearly as she 'looted' eighteen rolls of two-ply Charmin toilet paper. 'I know what you're thinking but basically fuck you', she said, 'I've been wiping my ass and my children's asses with that scratchy shit all my life because I can't afford the good shit. Now I got Charmin, just like those white jurors. So there!' (Institute for Alternative Journalism, 1992, p. 36).

Calling looting 'theft' and 'senseless', as the White media so often did, involved seeing each 'looter' as an individual thief. But when 'looting' is a form of public speech, it not only makes sense, but that sense may be communal: 'looters' then become not individual criminals but popular spokespeople whose actions give voice to a communal sentiment: radical shopping is communal, not individual. One study of the 1965 Watts uprisings emphasized their popular nature by pointing out that some 50,000 to 60,000 people lined the streets cheering on the 22,000 who actually 'looted' (much, we might think, as a chorus supports a folk singer) (cited in Davis, 1993, 144). Mike Davis saw the same pattern in South Central, but estimated that the numbers were probably double though the ratio remained about the same.

But 'looting' was not just speech; much of it was occasioned by simple survival needs: with stores closed, power off and refrigerators not working for an unknowable period, many 'looted' as their only means of providing for their families. As a Chicana mother said, 'No, this has nothing to do with Rodney King. This is about trying to get something to eat for the kids. Who knows where they're going to get food, now that everything has been destroyed? We have no choice' (*LA Times*, 1992, p. 68).

Looting makes sense only in the intertwining of class and race. Even the comparatively conservative *LA Times* (1992, p. 59) recognized that 'the protest over police abuse had become a poverty riot' and others referred to them as 'bread riots'. Omi and Winant (1993) consider that, for the urban poor of all races, the riots exhibited class alliances rather than racial ones, but for middle-class Blacks who identified with the rioters, the racial alliances overcame class difference. Many of this group made their way to South Central later in the uprisings, not only to check on the safety of friends and relatives, but also to express solidarity (Omi and Winant, 1993, pp. 105–6). In general, this would seem a convincing account, but it needs complicating even more: middle-class Blacks whose businesses were attacked tended to align themselves with Koreans and Whites, and Oprah Winfrey tried (without complete success) to stop herself joining the same alliance and thus distancing herself from the economically deprived Blacks of South Central. She wobbled on a discursive tightrope as she gave 'looters' a rare chance to put their case on national television, but still equated looting with stealing and saw no sense in it. The contradictions were clear in one image on her show: a Black man passionately pointed out the differences in the African American community between the haves and have-nots, and as his words put him and Oprah into opposite economic alliances, she put her arm around his shoulder to draw them into the same racial one:

> OPRAH WINFREY: Don't we all live in this world together, don't we all live in this world together?
>
> BLACK YOUTH NO. 4: Miss Oprah, when you leave this show, you go home to a lavish place, lots of us don't go home to lavish things, we go home to empty refrigerators, you know, crying kids, no diapers, no jobs, you know what I'm saying. (She puts her arm around him.) Everybody ain't got it like everybody – the people who didn't want to loot didn't want to loot because you have something to live for, you had a job to go to, lots of people haven't got a job to go to, I had a job, I had a job to go to, that's why I didn't loot.[3]

In a similar attempt to negotiate the same contradiction, a Black business owner accused those who looted his store of not understanding how difficult and expensive it is for a Black business to get insurance. The power of the White economy to deny middle-class African Americans equal access to insurance, mortgages and venture capital is the same power that denies underclass African Americans equal access to jobs and commodities: the power is directed to a different class of African Americans so the place and method of its application is different. Consequently it can remain unseen and unrecognized by those who do not experience it directly. In both these cases, however, we must recognize that the divisiveness of class differences was overlooked by the successful, but loomed large in the eyes of the deprived.

For the mainstream White media, however, the complications of race and class were largely repressed. For them, 'looting' was a matter of criminality and ethics in which racial difference could be criminalized. ABC's *Nightline*, for example, in summarizing the first 24 hours of the uprisings used three main image clusters: one of attacks on White drivers (including Reginald Denny), one of burning buildings and one of looting. Against these images of disorder, it showed the order of the National Guard being mobilized. Ted Koppel's introduction conforms to the standard, if simple, journalistic definition of objectivity as giving both sides of the issue (as though an issue like this had only two!):

> It has already begun turning into another dialogue of the deaf. On the one hand those for whom the verdict in the Rodney King case confirmed yet again the insensitivity, the callousness, the downright racism of The System, capital T, and capital S. And then, on the other hand those who view the violence spreading throughout Los Angeles as an expression of sheer lawlessness, unwarranted, unjustified and unrelated to the King verdict except in so far as it is being used as an excuse. Most tragically of all, the country seems to have run out of honest brokers, anyone genuinely capable of bridging the gap between the two sides. There is a reservoir of hostility on both sides of the line.[4]

But even here the intentionality of his language (it is White journalese) betrays his professional intention: the modifier 'yet' before 'again', and the tone of 'capital T, capital S' are discursive alienations in his account of 'their' position that have no equivalent in his description of 'ours'.

This gesture towards objectivity is as empty as it is professionally necessary; from this point on, the story is told entirely in the language of those who saw the uprisings as 'sheer lawlessness, unwarranted, unjustified and unrelated to the King verdict':

> Most of the trouble is taking place within a one hundred and five square mile area of South Central LA, but there are reports now of looting in Hollywood, Beverly Hills and several locations in the San Fernando Valley. In South Central the looting has become brazen. There seems little connection to outrage over the King verdict. Most of the looters, like these seen breaking into a Sears store, seemed to be making the most of the chaotic situation to grab some goods. In fact, one looter arrived at this location in a yellow cab.[5]

The situation may have been chaotic, but ABC's reporter on the spot was able to read the motives of the 'looters' with certainty, and could apparently differentiate looting that was merely 'grabbing some goods' from looting that expressed 'outrage over the King verdict'. Her understanding of the cab arriving at a 'looting' scene was indelibly White and middle class: she gave no pause to consider that it may have carried the driver (who was almost certainly Black or Latino) to the scene of the action, but was content with the class- and race-based assumption that cabs function only for their passengers.

CNN's Greg LaMotte walked the same path:

> The fact is there are too many looters, too many arsonists, and too few police officers to do anything about it. Police stand helplessly by as hundreds of looters bash their way into stores and take, seemingly, whatever they want. The looting is sporadic, but it is citywide; Hollywood and Beverly Hills are affected. Three major banks have been closed down out of fear of robbery; most stores have closed in the downtown area but the looters just crashed through the glass and gates with no fear of being caught. In fact, the police, when

they do see it, only try to scare them away. Given the level of crime here, only a handful
of people have been arrested, because police are too busy trying to contain certain areas,
not make arrests. At stores that are looted, it's almost like a feeding frenzy, they pour in,
grab what they want and run out. There is thick black smoke everywhere from the
hundreds of fires that have been set. The National Guard is now on the streets, but it
seems as each hour passes, the strength of the masses grows – people realize that they can
get away with something, so they do, and nobody seems to know when it will end.[6]

Greg LaMotte talks of a 'feeding frenzy' and of how 'senseless' it all is; he calls the
people 'the masses' and so denies the uprisings any purpose because to do so would
be to admit that such a purpose is directed against the White position from which
LaMotte speaks. The discourse of 'masses', 'senselessness' and 'lawlessness' absolves
White society from any responsibility for the uprisings. By using this as their
dominant discourse, the mainstream media were able to submerge both the broader
social situation in which their role is so formative and the history of dominations of
which they are themselves a product. The mainstream media's refusal to see anything
from a point of view other than their own represses any alternative knowledge that
there was an order and a sense to the uprisings.

Black Liberation Radio, however, an illegal micro-radio station in Springfield,
Illinois, is far from mainstream, and on it Mbanna Kantako repeatedly reminded his
listeners that the burning and 'looting' was systematic, not random. Starting 4000
fires in less than 24 hours and confining them to businesses was, for him, clear
evidence of organization and purpose.[7] In South Central almost no private residences
were burned or 'looted': as one gang leader put it, 'We didn't burn our community,
just their stores.' A piece of graffiti made the same point: 'Day one, burn them out.
Day two, we rebuild.' Sister Adwba, reporting on Black Liberation Radio by phone
from LA, saw order, purpose and mutual respect or politeness in the 'looting':

SISTER ADWBA: ... and these are the very kids that were so orchestrated and organized
that nobody could stop them. And it was so organized – if you could have seen
it happen, them moving around, doing businesses and stuff ...

MBANNA KANTAKO: Just like we saw it, right here, last night.

SISTER ADWBA: It was something, it was really something, because with me, I had a sense
of pride in me, I could see the city falling all around me, and some black people
were complaining, and they were saying 'We're destroying our community.' We
have to understand the definition of a community, it's not just because you live
in it, do you own it, do you control it, and do you run it? And so it wasn't our
community that we destroyed, anyway.

MBANNA KANTAKO: Yes, sister, it was strategic. In fact they were more precise than those
'smart bombs' that Bush dropped on Baghdad.

SISTER ADWBA: Exactly, but then they said 'Well, our property value's going down,' and
my response was, 'Good, maybe now we'll get a chance to own it.' We ought to
be glad the property value's going down. So that's right, we ought to turn this
around and butt out all the markets and stuff. I was very pleased, you know, I
was really pleased, I was really pleased to my soul, because I told the people, I
said, 'Now you'll maybe see the Black-owned grocery in our neighborhood' ...
It makes a Black woman like me, I was so proud, these were our children, and
we had raised them correctly. The people talk about them looting and whatever,
I think that five hundred years of free labor is supposed to be paid for by any
means necessary, and they were taking Pampers and stuff, who can blame them
for looting for their babies?

MBANNA KANTAKO: Who can blame them for taking food?

SISTER ADWBA: Yes, they were so organized, brother. You've never seen so much respect and harmony and co-operation in a looting situation, half the stuff that people didn't know, they were helping each other, saying 'Excuse me' – it was beautiful, it was just beautiful.[8]

[. . .] In times of crisis the media may be forced to carry a wider range of voices than in normal times, but they do structure these voices in a hierarchy of legitimation that is a product of the dominant value system. In this hierarchy of legitimation talk shows are not only seen as lower-brow and less 'good' than the network news, but their core audience is 'lower' in the social hierarchy. Entertainment news is lower than 'real' news and MTV is 'lower' even than talk shows. Many of those who criticize the media's coverage of political issues have a structure of taste that leads them to watch the network news rather than talk shows, *Nightline* rather than *Oprah Winfrey*, and to walk the dog rather than watch MTV. The print media, from the mainstream dailies to the alternative weeklies, do cover a broader spectrum than television, but they still reproduce a similar hierarchy of legitimation. Unlike television, however, the US radical or alternative press rarely uses discourse that appeals to the structures of taste of those lower in the social hierarchy: they lack the populist tone of an Oprah Winfrey, and rarely, as do MTV and the music press, allow rappers to speak directly of their material conditions. Communal voices of the oppressed, such as those of Mbanna Kantako, are rarely quoted on their pages, whose space is more likely to be reserved for middle-class White dissidents.

The populism of tabloid TV, of MTV and the talk shows carries a wide variety of topics and points of view, only some of which would be applauded by progressive critics. But when these same critics dismiss 'low' TV or ignore it completely they are participating in the same hierarchy of legitimation as the media they criticize. Our media resources are limited, and will always be so, particularly when they are commercial or reliant on corporate sponsorship, so it is doubly important to take advantage of the range that they do offer. Even when a crisis produced from below (such as the LA uprisings) gives the oppressed opportunities for media access (such as that taken by the 'looters') we need actively to search for and listen to those rarely heard voices. Urgent speakers require engaged and motivated listeners, and the sphere of consumption is often where this communication can best occur. Late capitalist societies in particular are centered around consumption, but the commonality, the everydayness and the necessity of the market place have always made it a site of cultural as well as economic exchange. When the economically oppressed disrupt the normal economic processes of the market, the culturally silenced simultaneously disrupt its cultural processes, for the economic and the cultural are two sides of the same coin. 'Looting' gives the oppressed access to both commodities and public speech.

There can be no guarantee that bringing the dirt out from under the carpet will encourage the occupiers to clean up the room, but it is a first step. More importantly, we liberal Whites who wish to mitigate the worst effects of racial discrimination and economic deprivation cannot formulate adequate programs of action from our good intentions alone: to have any chance of success such programs must be produced by inter-racial alliances, preferably Black-led ones, and for such alliances to hold, we Whites have to listen to the voices of the racially oppressed and learn from their experiences. The mainstream media prevent this, and part of our political effort must involve searching the media margins for otherwise silenced voices. On a minor scale we can thus pick up in the sphere of media consumption some of what the 'looters' are trying to say in their disruption of the public market place.

NOTES

1. Personal interview with one of the reporters, Darryl Newton.
2. The *Oprah Winfrey Show*, 5 May 1992.
3. The *Oprah Winfrey Show*, 5 May 1992.
4. *Nightline*, 30 April 1992.
5. *Nightline*, 30 April 1992.
6. *CNN Newsnight*, 30 April 1992.
7. Black Liberation Radio, 2 May 1992.
8. Black Liberation Radio, 2 May 1992.

REFERENCES

DAVIS, M. 1993: Uprising and repression in LA. In Gooding-Williams, R. (ed.), *Reading Rodney King/Reading urban uprising*. New York: Routledge.
INSTITUTE FOR ALTERNATIVE JOURNALISM 1992: *Inside the LA Riots*. New York: IAJ Press.
LA TIMES 1992: Understanding the riots. Los Angeles: *LA Times*.
OMI, M. and WINANT, H. 1993: The LA race riot and US politics. In Gooding-Williams, R. (ed.), *Reading Rodney King/Reading urban uprising*. New York: Routledge.

17

Mediating the ordinary: the 'access' idea and television form

John Corner

From Aldridge, M. and Hewitt, N. (eds.) 1994: *Controlling broadcasting*. Manchester: Manchester University Press, 20–33

The idea of 'access' television is historically rooted in a belief that certain voices and views, certain experiences and values, have been excluded from the world of television. The term thus involves a campaigning polemic at least as much as a generic description, and generally reflects the view that inequality in the field of communication is but one instance of a more general political and social inequality. From an access perspective, television is thought of as an institution with the potential to construct a public space, fostering the social dialogue required by a participatory democracy and reflecting all shades of opinion and the full range of social experience. Underpinned by the values of public service and social responsibility, this idea of access is virtually incompatible with an exclusively market view of television as one more entertainment or information commodity.

John Corner's article offers a working definition of access, a detailed and persuasive account of its historical emergence as a form of television and an argument in favour of its distinctive contribution to political life. The access project is seen to involve a critique and to offer a corrective to what is believed to be a 'systematic imbalance in social and cultural power'. It thus entails a directly political project, responding to perceived social inequality and recognizing the importance of social *groups*. The access project is thus, Corner argues, quite distinct from the 'Right of Reply' project which, by contrast, is rooted in a belief in the rights of *individuals* to respond to misrepresentation or inaccuracy. His emphasis on the broadly social character and function of broadcasting leads him also to express some reservations about the 'localism' of some community media access work, fearing the inadequacy of 'a local remedy for a national ill'. However, the campaigning for access slots is, in itself, seen as an indication of a relative failure on the part of broadcasting professionals to draw sufficiently on ordinary (not élite or specialist) sources for mainstream factual programming.

The establishment of a regular access slot, *Open Door*, at the BBC in the early 1970s and the work of its Community Programmes Unit is recognized as a landmark, though preceded in the United States by a nightly half-hour programme, *Catch 44*. This latter series was regarded by one British critic of the time as 'the nearest thing yet to genuine citizens' television'. In Britain the pre-history of such work can be traced in the 'social documentary' cinema of the 1930s with its commitment to representing ordinary life and what John Grierson had called the 'drama of the doorstep', bringing the voices of working-class people, their lives and concerns, into the realm of cinema. Noting these developments, Corner goes on, in the extract given here, to explore two examples of the early history of access in mainstream television documentary: the 1955 series *Look In on London* and a BBC series of the early 1980s, *Brass Tacks*.

In conclusion, and looking to the future of access television, Corner notes the transformative potential of the new domestic camcorder technologies (notably in the BBC's *Video Diaries* series), but also a concern that the new market-driven forms of television may produce more sensational, more entertaining and more objectifying work in this field, thereby discounting the broader, political purposes of the access project.

A small puncture in the rotating machinery of television, through which fairly ordinary people can catch glimpses of fairly ordinary other people without the interposition of a mind exterior to either.

The notion of 'access' is an important one in respect of many different aspects of broadcasting. In this chapter, it is the use of the term to indicate a particular kind of project – the giving to ordinary people of a chance to 'have their say' – with which I will be most concerned. And within this project, broadly conceived as an attempt to increase the democratic character of broadcast services, it is questions of communicative form which provide my primary topic. For it is *how* 'ordinary people' appear and speak on television, within particular programme formats, which determines both the character and the success of 'access' socially and politically. This has a pre-history in the ways in which social documentaries have represented ordinary people through a variety of visual and verbal devices, some of which have been projected as providing 'direct' renderings of ordinary views and ordinary life. It also has a future in which, at least in Britain and probably in the United States too, the development of new genres of non-fiction television, including formats extensively drawing on home-shot camcorder material, will increasingly change the terms on which the ordinary is perceived by television audiences. [. . .]

TELEVISION AND THE ACCESS IDEA

'Access is the newest word in the onward march of broadcasting.' So commented broadcaster/writer Frank Gillard in *The Listener's* lead article of 6 July 1972. Although Gillard might well have known that plans were under way for a regular BBC 'access' slot to start the following year, his article was principally concerned with the American model of public access television. In particular, he discussed the success of the Boston nightly half-hour programme *Catch 44*, which he considered 'the nearest thing yet to genuine citizens' television'. His citation of the *Boston Globe's* own comments on the innovatory series, as 'a small puncture', provides my epigraph above. This campaigning sense of access, precisely as 'citizens' television', was grounded in a feeling by the *Catch 44* workers that the broadcasting industry was increasingly getting out of touch with 'views, life-styles and community backgrounds different from those of the broadcasting professionals themselves'. In Britain at roughly the same time, the people behind the planning of the BBC's pioneering national access programme, *Open Door*, had come to a similar conclusion. One of them, Mike Fentiman, subsequently to become a key member of the BBC's access team (the Community Programmes Unit), tells of a decisive moment in the development of the idea:

> I was involved in the conspiracy that created public access. And it was a conspiracy, it had to be a conspiracy otherwise it probably wouldn't have happened. On the evening discussion programme *Late Night Line Up* in 1972 we did a few things that were started by an interview done by Tony Bilbow with some workers from the Guinness factory. These workers, when asked questions by a very sympathetic interviewer, said they were being manipulated and 'that's the trouble with television, television manipulates us. You know how to do it. We work with our hands, you work with words and you'll take this film back and you'll edit it to what you want, and you'll shorten this and change that and you can make it do what you want it to'. So we brought it back to look at it and because we'd shot it on two cameras, other than tidying it up, the whole thing went out. Every single word, including the clapperboard shots, went out unedited. So what we had was workers saying 'you're going to take this back and edit it' and it all went out unedited.

The Community Programmes Unit went on to produce an often controversial strand of BBC programming which, however marginal in budget and in audiences (when judged by the national ratings lists), succeeded in accessing to the screen groups, individuals and issues of a kind then heavily under-represented on television (see Oakley, 1990 for a brief historical account). The main method, first of all limited to live, studio broadcasting but subsequently extended to location shooting and recorded material, was the provision of directorial and technical aid to 'accessees' who had been judged as having something interesting and/or important to say on national television. The accessees had editorial control over the content and form of the programme within the limits of the regulations affecting broadcast output. In the topic areas which were selected for treatment, the programmes often contributed substantially to wider debate. A decade later, the launch of Channel 4, with a specific commitment to minorities and to the correcting of imbalances of representation across the other three channels, put the access project a little more firmly on the institutional agenda of British broadcasting.

I shall return to some aspects of the social history of access later; as we can see, it is a history of expressed dissatisfaction with conventional practice, with the exclusive sweep of institutionalised 'professionalism', and with the relegation of ordinary people to being simply the raw material of 'human interest' stories. But the access idea is one which raises (and sometimes begs) fundamental issues about public representation and it is these issues which I now want to explore further.

PRINCIPLES OF 'ACCESS'

First of all, it might be useful to attempt a working definition of the access idea in broadcasting. Among other things, this has the merit of suggesting immediately how politically and socially contentious – and how difficult to *implement* – it may be. Without aspiring to categoric perfection, we can say that access is the avoiding or the correcting of imbalances in broadcasting's representation of politics and society by the articulation of a diversity of 'directly' stated views from different sections of the public and by the reflection, again 'directly', of the real diversity of cultural, social and economic circumstances, particularly those which require attention and action.

Such a definition connects access ideas to the political principle of equality. And it is worth pointing out that, given the way in which national broadcasting services have developed, it is nearly always the case that access projects have emerged as partial remedies for perceived *in*equality. Access is in this respect most often a *corrective* idea, a point I shall return to. My definition also suggests that access is a broader, more socialised notion than that of 'Right of Reply', itself a campaigning slogan for media reform. Whereas the latter idea has, as its core, the citizen's individual opportunity to respond to misrepresentation, the former concept works more with the idea of the accessee as speaking for a misrepresented or under-represented *group*. Moreover, and relatedly, whereas in 'Right of Reply' the 'Reply' is generally understood to be a quite specific act of correction or response, access projects have sought to offer a *general* corrective to what is seen as being a systematic imbalance in social and cultural power. Within the terms of access therefore, specific items have had the freedom to take on a socially pro-active rather than reactive character; they have not needed to be framed as 'replies'.

The 'socialised' nature of the access idea means, as I have indicated, that access is also a quite directly political project, implying theories about the nature of the political system and about the extent and scale of social inequality of which communicational inequalities are but one aspect. In placing its corrective emphasis on the disadvantaged and the marginalised, the access project has politicised both itself and its versions of 'ordinary people' in a way which has sometimes proved controversial in its degree of explicitness and in the strategic imbalance of its own representations. Again, 'Right of Reply' has available to it a defence of the rights of the individual citizen which is nowhere near as politically contentious. Indeed, 'Right of Reply' is a project quite compatible with a political viewpoint in which generalised and systematic inequalities are not admitted to exist at all.

Within these general terms of conceptualisation, we can see access initiatives as being put forward principally on one or other of *three* different levels within the broadcasting system.

1. As a mainstream principle of broadcasting policy and programming, institutional-ised into practice. According to such a principle, news, current affairs, documentary and special interest programmes would draw on a diversity of 'ordinary' sources as a routine part of their production and structure. McQuail (1992) discusses how access is a fundamental concept in the formulation of a democratic broadcasting system.
2. As an ongoing alternative to mainstream networking and the major broadcast and narrowcast options. This manifests itself most obviously in the idea of the 'public access' channel, in Britain an idea related to the the development of cable systems. The 'localism' of most projects at this level (clearly indicated in the philosophy of the Community Media movement, but often technologically unavoidable given available means of distribution) often raises the question of the adequacy of a local remedy for a national ill. The British Channel 4 model has provided a distinctive precedent for alternative programming at national level, but this is essentially grounded in a pluralism of independent professional production and of audience-interest groups, not in access programming as such.
3. As a regularly scheduled opportunity on a channel mostly devoted to other kinds of output. This is 'access as slot' or, in the terms of my epigraph, as 'small

puncture'. However, as I shall discuss later, both its identity as a marginal genre of television and the scope it offers for self-representation have been transformed recently as a result of the use of camcorder technology.

I have suggested that it is at levels 2 (e.g. the fight for 'community cable') and 3 (the developing genre of 'access slots') that access projects have been most active. Of course, much of this activity would not have been necessary had provision at level 1 been anything like satisfactory.

ACCESS AND DOCUMENTARY FORM

It is within the documentary tradition of broadcasting, whose practices refer back to the longer history of documentary cinema, that what I have earlier called the 'pre-history' of access can be traced. This 'pre-history' has had implications for discussion about access at all three levels outlined above. It has also provided influential precedents for ideas about the kinds of communicative 'directness' which can be achieved by public access communication and about the methods for producing it.

In documentary, a level of the accessed ordinary is an integral part of the project of critical social revelation and social inquiry. This is particularly so in the British tradition of the 'social documentary', within whose visual and aural discourses it is, routinely, aspects of the 'ordinary' which are brought into 'official' public view, with the intention either of affirming the integrities of work, trust and community which they exemplify or of exposing inequality and hardship, or perhaps both. A key communicative component of this investigative and representational practice has been the *interview*.

The interview has a 'dual' character not only insofar as it is devised as communication with an audience (devised, that is, as *public* communication) whilst being usually set up in terms of communication between two people (that is, as a form of *conversation*). It is also 'dual' in its accessing function. Through the interview, audiences are accessed to particular themes and problems, whilst particular interviewees are accessed to the public, and have their views, feelings and experiences widely disseminated. However, the terms of this double accessing cannot but be unbalanced. For no matter how minimal a role the film or programme-makers wish to give themselves in the project, it is impossible for the accessees of documentary inquiry to be placed other than in a position of relative objectification before the initiating activities of the researchers, reporters and crew members whose job it is to make public communication happen. If this is true in the planning and shooting stages of documentary practice, it is even more true at the post-production stages. Here, decisions about the editing of interview sequences and their deployment within the finished text according to different strategies of visual and aural combination and in relation to other materials inevitably have the effect of further 'objectivising' the accessed speakers. Paradoxically, some of the changes introduced at this stage (for instance, the editing out of interviewers from the visuals and perhaps of their questions from the soundtrack too; the 'lifting' of interviewee speech from the shot interview and its placing over other visual material) may have the effect of 're-subjectivising' the speakers, giving their speech the appearance of unsolicited testimony, of 'direct', self-initiated utterance.

I want to take two examples from what I termed earlier the 'pre-history' of access in order to explore in more detail questions concerning the televisual representation of the ordinary. The examples are from documentaries in which a key part of the overall communicative design is an accessing of 'ordinary people', an accessing which is self-consciously foregrounded in the film or programme's structure as an element of its formal or thematic originality. Such documentaries are thus different in their mediation of the ordinary from those many others that display a more routine use of interviewees to pursue their inquiries, a use more conventionalised than innovative and therefore not as marked or self-conscious. [. . .]

When, in 1955, the commercially financed ITV system began broadcasting in Britain, a re-thinking of the terms for depicting the ordinary in current affairs and documentary programming was the result of the imperative to be popular. This often meant an attempt to distinguish programme formats from what was regarded as the 'stuffy, middle-class' attitudes dominant in the BBC schedules, at levels ranging from the social perspectives informing programme ideas through to the particular styles of behaviour and speech of those who were most often invited to appear. A number of ITV programmes tried to achieve a more popular (and, some might say, populist) appeal by working hard at 'meet the people' formulas, in which a television presenter would go out on location and encounter ordinary people in the business of their everyday work. These people would then be interviewed, often in lengthy sequences of question-and-answer shot in a workplace setting. [. . .]

The newer formats both socialised and dramatised the very terms of access as a *meeting* between the 'television world' (represented by the reporter) and the 'ordinary world' (represented by the interviewees). Access was organised as a narrative episode, often one appearing to have the openendedness of happenstance. One of the most interesting features of this type of programme is the way in which any ostensible *topic* quite often becomes secondary to the interest which the interviewees hold for the programme as 'ordinary people'. So, for instance, whilst an interview might start with inquiries about the details of a particular trade, the novelty of this kind of casually accessed ordinariness is seen to be such as to permit the interviewer to extend questioning to a whole range of other issues, including housing conditions, preferences in food and recreational choices.

I have discussed elsewhere (Corner, 1991) a series from this period of development, *Look In on London* (Rediffusion 1955). In one of the programmes in the series, 'Streetcleaners', a streetcleaner is 'encountered' on the streets of Maida Vale and is interviewed about his job and the people he meets. Although other, more conventional reportage is edited in, the programme's main narrative development quickly becomes centred around this single streetcleaner, whose 'significance' as a television accessee is no longer related to his specific job but, more generally, to his social position and housing conditions. Indeed, at mid-point, the reporter takes the programme off on an entirely new course by accompanying the man back to his home to meet his wife and to 'see how they live'. At the conclusion, over a shot of the streetcleaner now returned to his duties, the terms of extended social communication and social knowledge become transformed into the more affective terms of an extended *sociability*. The last words of the reporter include not only the accessee but also the audience in this broadened set of relations: 'This time we shall know who it is we are passing the time of day with.' Not only has access been dramatised, but the programme itself has, in part, turned into an *enactment* of a 'possible' social democratic community.

Such Mayhew-like adventures on the part of the television institution in its discovery of working-class Britain represent a significant stage in the development of the 'televised ordinary'. Though they often seem, by current conventions, to be heavily and clumsily mediated, they represent real moments of uncertainty and expansion in the social relations of the medium. And in the very awkwardness and transparency of their interfacing activity they establish both new televisual iconographies and forms of talk. The developing impulse towards access has to define its own aims and its own communicative terms in relation to these.

My second example of the access mode within documentary television is much more recent and is therefore concurrent with the modern 'access' movement rather than an element of its pre-history. 'A Fair Day's Fiddle?' (BBC 1982) was broadcast in the *Brass Tacks* series of investigative reports. Its topic is the extent of the various 'fiddles' (including undeclared part-time work) engaged in by people on state benefit. In exploring the nature and scope of the 'black economy' in areas of high unemployment, it chose one housing estate in Liverpool upon which to focus selective and personalised attention. Looking at how people manage in circumstances of unemployment, it examines not only 'fiddles' but self-help schemes like locally organised credit unions, which work to provide low-interest loans. In its opening sequence of commentary-over-film, the programme clearly indicates its access designs: 'In this programme, local people speak for themselves.' The rest of the programme is almost entirely without commentary, working largely through a mix of '*vérité*' sequences of everyday life on the estate and interviews. Perhaps the most important of the interviews is with an unemployed man involved in community organisations. As well as speaking about his own problems as a husband and parent, he sets these in a broader social and political context. Over shots which variously show him alone – leaving his house to buy tobacco, rolling a cigarette, walking on estate paths, moving around his flat, peering out through lifted venetian blinds in his front room, sitting on the couch watching television – his interview speech is placed as reflective, voiced-over commentary and as *argument*. For instance: 'Our fiddles have been forced on us. Our fiddles are not done for gain, or for profits. Our fiddles are done because it is necessary, it's necessary for us to exist.' He also talks of class division, of the political motivation behind the label 'scroungers' and of the manipulative effect of TV advertising.

Research on the reception of the programme (Corner and Richardson, 1986) showed that the problem with this sequence as access communication was certainly not that the speaker was unprepared for his interview opportunity. In fact, some viewers considered him to be *too* well-prepared, and also to have exceeded his qualifications to speak by talking of other things than his own experience. The key problem, however, was the mode of his 'objectification' by the visuals, an objectification which placed him in his wider environment and in his home as well as (by sustained close shots) paying attention to his physical personhood. Although there is no evidence of any intention by the programme-makers to 'set him up', many of the viewers in the research sample perceived a mismatch between his claims to poverty and the furnishing and possessions seen in his house (including a video recorder). Even his ability to buy cigarettes (emphasised in a number of close-up shots of him smoking) was seen by some to be evidence of exaggeration in his self-account of deprivation. What *might* have seemed like a visualisation perfectly suited to reinforce his comments became for many viewers a separate and often conflicting strand of meaning in the sequence. For those who were unsympathetic to him, these objectifying visuals (mediating a 'problem' first personified and then observed) were naturalised as the truth which falsified his talk. For those who judged him more positively, the possibility of a conscious directorial attempt to 'damage' him was often entertained. [...]

ACCESS FORM AND 1990s TELEVISION

What implications do these examples carry for 'access' as a communicational enterprise in the nineties? First of all, they show how representation (including self-representation) of the ordinary on television is always in active relation to the existing professional conventions for producing immediacy and continuity and for telling a 'human story'. These conventions are, in part, derived from tested recipes for producing 'watchable' television. But they are not fixed conventions, they are subject to the social and cultural change which affects the 'social optics' of the medium as a whole, perhaps extending the range of broadcast forms which have access functions (if only in part) and requiring that the modalities of accessed speech and imagery be updated in their relation to practice elsewhere in the schedules (even if this relation is finally a consciously oppositional one). The shifts in the history of 'access slot' broadcasting from simple, studio presentations to camera through to professionally assisted documentary productions, contrasting filmed reports run back-to-back and the range of other formats involving co-operation between independent production units and various interest groups are a response to this.

In recent British broadcasting, the tendency has perhaps been for access to be increasingly 'professionalised' as it has been partly subsumed within the movement towards minority programming, supplied to the networks by small 'independents' as part of the reorganisation of the industry away from the established practice of in-house production. This has gone along with what might be seen as a dispersal of the access idea across a number of different programme genres, including children's shows, youth television, national and regional chat shows and audience participation programmes. Mediations of 'ordinary' people and of 'ordinary' views have become key ingredients in the strongly inter-generic developments which have occurred around these forms.

However, it seems to me that the most significant element of the new context for access is the emergence of D-i-Y camcorder material as a source of popular and *cheap* television. With the exception of the phenomenally successful 'funny clips' shows (e.g. ITV's *You've Been Framed*; the BBC's *Caught in the Act*), the most important development to date has been the series *Video Diaries*, shown on BBC2 and produced by the BBC's Community Programmes Unit (see Fraser, 1992 for a critical appraisal by a Channel 4 access editor). The format of the series is simple. A member of the public judged to have an interesting idea for a programme is given the go-ahead to shoot material on a VHS camcorder. The tapes which result (usually a very large number) are sent through to the BBC and edited by a member of the unit in consultation with the 'director'.

Video Diaries was launched in 1991 with 'A Fan's Diary' of the 1990 football World Cup. With its mix of *vérité* action (including scenes of violence at the British supporters' campsite), its rendering of detailed, personal experience and its highly 'non-official' reportage, it proved very popular with viewers. Subsequent programmes have varied widely in subject matter and degree of seriousness, whilst always keeping a focus on a 'personal' and 'ordinary' perspective and on the projection of an account which both in theme and (necessarily, given the mode of shooting) in form is distinctive from the mainstream. If much recent non-fictional output has inclined towards the more stylistically ambitious, involving a new symbolic density and an overall textual self-consciousness, then *Video Diaries* might be seen as an attractively 'raw' alternative to elaborate varieties of the 'cooked'. But although the method gives accessees a far freer hand in determining how they shall be represented than any previous format was able to do, it nevertheless raises questions both of intent and of viewing relations which may have a bearing on whatever new generic codes emerge in this area. Even within the unit itself some of these questions are being posed. Hugo Irwin, unit researcher and editorial assistant, comments:

> I think that because of *Video Diaries* the Community Programme Unit is smelling of roses.
> It has been a huge success. I'm not sure that anyone realised that it was going to be quite
> such a success. It does of course bring up the problem of multi-skilling, doing people out
> of jobs. It's extraordinary, *Video Diaries*. The secret of it is that it's immediate and it does
> give you one hundred per cent access to somebody's life and that's what its charm is.
> Also, it has to be said the diarists are chosen fairly carefully.

Mike Fentiman, no longer involved directly in the work of the unit, and able to reflect on current developments from the standpoint of an access pioneer, goes further:

> I have to say there's an editorial drift towards the sensational, towards those programmes
> that say 'Hey, you know we've got a man looking for a Loch Ness monster.' Atypical
> people. Now obviously people don't want to sit down and just watch their neighbour, but
> I think sometimes the balance goes wrong ... So they become very much more
> personality-based than issue-based. In creating a seeming opportunity for the public to
> be on television, which they do, what they are actually doing is separating the idea of
> broadcasting from being a social tool.

So the emergence of domestic video technology, whilst it radically alters the production potential for access, is still dependent on the institutional system of broadcast television for its public status. The system also regulates the relationship with a potential audience, organising the way in which material is likely to be watched. Fentiman's comments suggest the possibility of a growing tension between the modality of access as social dialogue and that of access as a new, generic commodity. The first model works along the axis 'accessee–public', the second along the axis 'programme–consumers'. This has implications for how access ideas are formulated – for intentions as well as for mode of address and discursive organisation.

As television becomes increasingly open to market-driven channel choice in Britain, the survival of the very public space in which access has always had its difficult, marginalised existence is threatened. Within the new programme formulas, there will inevitably be a tendency for the accessed ordinary to be made *productive* within the terms of market competition. This will undoubtedly mean a move towards the entertaining and towards those modes of objectification (including self-objectification) which are a precondition of social voyeurism. Yet as the layers of professional mediation in public life increase in number and degree of subtlety, as the dynamics by which society is imaged and described grow in scale, intensity and velocity, the particular energies, sheer *awkwardness*, of communication by 'fairly ordinary people' have never been more necessary to political health.

ACKNOWLEDGEMENTS

Interview comment transcribed in this article is from interviews with Mike Fentiman and Hugo Irwin, recorded at the BBC Community Programmes Unit, London, on 19 August 1992. I am grateful for their co-operation.

NOTE

Episodes from *Look In on London* are available in the United Kingdom from the British Film Institute Distribution Library.

REFERENCES

CORNER, J. 1991: The interview as social encounter. In Scannell, P. (ed.), *Broadcast Talk*. London: Sage.
CORNER, J. and RICHARDSON, K. 1986: Documentary meanings and the discourse of interpretation. In Corner, J. (ed.), *Documentary and the mass media*. London: Edward Arnold; reprinted in CORNER, J. and HAWTHORN, J. (eds.) (1993): *Communication studies: an introductory reader*, 4th edn. London: Edward Arnold.
FRASER, N. 1992: The frames people play. *Sunday Times*, 20 September.
McQUAIL, D. 1992: *Media performance*. London: Sage.

FURTHER READING

CORNER, J. 1991a: Documentary voices. In Corner, J. (ed.), *Popular television in Britain: studies in cultural history*. London: British Film Institute.
OAKLEY, G. 1990: Opening up the box. In Willis, J. and Wollen, T. (eds.), *The neglected audience*. London: British Film Institute.

18

Programmes for black audiences

Thérèse Daniels

From Hood, S. (ed.) 1994: *Behind the screens: the structure of British television in the nineties*. London: Lawrence & Wishart, 65–81

In the United States the legacy of the civil rights movement, and in Britain the radicalism of a new generation born of immigrant parents from the West Indies, Africa and the Indian subcontinent, has provided the basis for a challenge to the representational and employment practices of television, drawing attention to the routine reproduction of white privilege and to the continuing failure to recognize widespread and racially based discrimination. In the course of the 1970s and 1980s some effective changes were made in order to establish equal opportunities in employment practice, and to facilitate the production of a richer and more representative range of images on television screens. However, the last decade of the twentieth century, though continuing to see some inroads made against systematic and institutionalized racism, has also been marked by a conservative backlash against these changes and in favour of the consolidation of a traditional and white-dominated culture.

Thérèse Daniels offers an account of the emergence of black programmes on British television since the 1980s and situates this account in the context of broader debates about race, culture and integration. She notes that television programmes in the 1950s did address issues of black immigration, the history of British imperialism and contemporary racism, but that black creative voices in drama had only sporadic opportunities to be heard and that, in general, the 'address' of programmes tended to assume a white viewer.

However, from the 1970s various pieces of campaigning research were developed to investigate what were believed to be some of the inadequacies and misrepresentations of current television practice. Critics argued that black people appeared seldom and were offered an extremely limited range of roles, appearing as the 'problems' in race relations drama and, in sitcoms, in roles that were consistent with commonly held racist stereotypes.

The advent of Channel 4 in 1982, with its parliamentary remit to experiment and innovate and to complement the services offered on the other channels, along with the considerable public policy changes which flowed in the wake of urban violence in the black communities of Brixton and Toxteth in 1981, created a more positive climate for the creation of new and more varied images. The catch-all address of 'black' programming was replaced by more specialized programmes directed variously at Afro-Caribbean and at Asian audiences. Moreover, as Channel 4's practice became more sophisticated, producers were encouraged to make programmes from a black perspective but aimed at a general (including white) audience.

Daniels explores the advantages and disadvantages of specifically black programming on television, weighing the benefit of a 'platform' against the limitation of a 'ghetto', and noting also the increasingly problematic notion of a homogeneous black culture, since black communities are divided by gender, sexuality, religion and class. Her examination of these issues concludes with an observation that, historically, black programming has been facilitated and encouraged by the public service ideal in British broadcasting. As the principles of public service and the language of rights and duties give way increasingly to the imperatives of the market-place she expresses concern about future opportunities for developing a pluralistic television culture.

The history of programmes for black audiences on British television shows that the demands of black viewers, media workers and campaigning groups often conflict with those of channel controllers, the broadcasting authorities and Parliament. I would argue that this position is hardly likely to improve, and is indeed more likely to deteriorate in the de-regulated television world of the future. However, any discussion of the future should consider the lessons of the past. In this chapter I will look at the evolution of black programmes since their earliest appearance on British television in the 1960s. In doing so, I want to locate the emergence of institutional provision for black audiences in the wider context of the race relations policies of the past thirty years, in an attempt to clarify the concepts of race, culture and integration on which the provision of black programmes has been based. I will, however, concentrate the discussion on the 1980s, since it was during this decade that the conflict between lobbyists and institutions was at its height.

BLACK REPRESENTATION: THE FIRST THIRTY YEARS

British television's initial response to post-war black settlement was slow and uncoordinated. From 1946, when BBC television resumed transmission after closing down for the war, until the mid-1950s, there was little representation of black settlers on British television. The majority of programmes featuring black people showed American entertainers, had an anthropological theme, or were about the colonies.[1] The limited range and quality of programming was a reflection of the infancy of the medium; the television service lacked the technology and finance needed to make, for example, weekly domestic current affairs programmes or drama serials. It also lacked a clear commitment from BBC management, whose main interest was still with radio.[2]

From 1951, when the television service was re-organized, the range and quality of programmes improved. As the decade wore on, and black immigration became an increasingly contentious political issue, the black British population began to be explored on television. Studio discussions, documentaries and dramatic productions examined the troubled state of race relations. Black entertainers from the Caribbean and Africa were seen alongside the Americans. Human interest series and slots in daytime women's programmes gave people from various settler communities the opportunity to explain their way of life to (white) British viewers. There were sporadic opportunities for black voices to be heard in drama, with the production of plays by writers such as Errol John, Sylvia Winters, Horace James and Jan Carew. Educational strands dealt with issues such as the history of British imperialism, contemporary racism and cultural difference.[3]

However, although programme-makers were beginning to include black people in the content of television output, they had not yet begun to address black people as viewers. These early programmes were very much an attempt to represent or explain black communities to a white audience. It was not until the 1960s that television first began to provide programmes specifically for black audiences. These programmes were not so much concerned with giving black people a voice, as with providing them with a service. Asian settlers were considered to be most in need and the needs that were identified were for tuition in the English language, and general information on settling into British society. *Apna Hi Ghar Samajhiye*, which began on 10 October 1965, was designed to teach the English language, and was transmitted both on BBC1 and on radio on Sunday mornings. *Nai Zindage Naya Jeevan* began, also on Sunday mornings, on 24 November 1968, with *Apna Hi Ghar Samajhiye* moving to Wednesdays. *Nai Zindage Naya Jeevan* continued broadcasting until 1982.

Early 'ethnic minority' programmes were very different in concept from those that were to appear in the late 1970s. They were shaped by the prevailing politics of race, and the liberal consensus under which many institutions then operated. Liberal discourse did not speak in terms of black people having the rights of access to, or control over, institutions. Rather, it argued that cultural differences were often the source of intolerance and conflict on both sides of the racial divide.[4] The programmes for Asian settlers – the group which, among the 'Commonwealth immigrants', was felt to be most different – were an attempt to ease their transition into British society.

CAMPAIGNS AGAINST RACISM IN THE MEDIA

Increasingly in the post-war years, and especially during the 1970s, a number of arguments were raised by black viewers, media workers, academics and campaigning groups expressing dissatisfaction with media representations of black people.[5] These complaints, and the political events of the 1970s and early 1980s, led eventually to the provision of a different kind of black programming. The media came to be seen as a source of oppression and site of conflict, along with other state institutions, in black struggles.

There were complaints about many aspects of the portrayal of black people. In television, infrequent but stereotypical representation was said to be the norm. Monitoring of television output showed that, excluding the coverage of foreign affairs and American programmes, there was very little representation of black people on British television. Where they did appear they were seldom in leading, or even speaking parts. If they were in leading roles they were often in problem-centred race relations dramas, or in situation comedies such as *Love Thy Neighbour*, which, though very popular, was criticized for its potentially damaging effect on race relations. It was felt that black people often appeared in a limited number of roles which were consistent with commonly held racist stereotypes. They would be seen doing menial jobs, such as those of bus conductor, hospital ancillary worker, street cleaner or factory hand, they would feature in light entertainment or sports programmes, or they would be criminals involved in illegal immigration, prostitution or robbery.[6]

In terms of drama, black actors often voiced their frustration at the narrow roles available to them in television and the theatre. They were rarely cast in classical or historical plays. Leading parts were usually only in the context of problematic race relations. They were routinely denied parts which were not specifically written as black characters.[7] One solution was to set up black theatre companies, but this did not solve the problems of representation on television.

A third source of dissatisfaction with the industry was raised by the black people who sought to work within it. Very little of television's output before the late 1970s was produced, directed or presented by black people. Reporters and presenters such as Barbara Blake and Trevor MacDonald, scriptwriters such as Michael Abbensetts, Mustafa Matura and Dilip Hiro, and directors such as Horace Ove were exceptions. Away from the television industry, in the economically precarious black independent film sector and in print journalism, black practitioners had to struggle to develop their careers or even to work at all. Many of these people wanted access to television. Mainstream programming was difficult to penetrate for anybody not of the middle-class, university-educated prototype. For those black practitioners who saw working in the media as an extension of political activism, who wanted to make programmes that would address their own and black people's political concerns, and who were not interested in working in existing formats, access was virtually non-existent.

A potential opportunity for black practitioners to gain a steady foothold in the industry was recognized when proposals were aired for a fourth television channel. The Annan Report of 1977 suggested that the new channel be wholly different in character from existing BBC and IBA channels. There were two proposals in particular which offered some hope that the new channel would provide a space for black voices and satisfy the demands of black audiences. First, it was proposed that the channel's output should emphasise diversity and new ideas. A new authority, which the report termed the Open Broadcasting Authority (OBA), would control the channel. Second, this new authority would not itself make programmes but would commission them from existing ITV companies and, most importantly, from other independent producers. The role of independent producers was stressed as a means of ensuring diversity.[8]

The intense lobbying of government that followed these proposals included efforts by the Campaign Against Racism in the Media, the Commission for Racial Equality[9] and others to ensure that the interests of black audiences were adequately addressed. The structure which eventually emerged as a result of the Broadcasting Act 1980 placed the fourth channel under the authority of the Independent Broadcasting Authority (IBA). This was a disappointment to the campaigning groups that had lobbied for the OBA. On the whole, however, those groups with a primary interest in race were more concerned with content than with structure, and here, at least, although there was room for scepticism, hopes had not been dashed. The new channel had a duty to appeal to 'tastes and interests not generally catered for by ITV' and 'to encourage innovation and experiment in the form and content of programmes'.[10] It was these two clauses which gave campaigners grounds on which to argue that black programmes should figure strongly in the schedules, and that they should be made by black independent production companies.

Meanwhile, in the interim before Channel 4 began broadcasting, the opportunities within the existing industry for black media workers were marginally improved. This resulted from the independent ITV companies revamping their schedules in anticipation of the franchise reallocations due in 1980. Among other things, these regional companies decided to use off-peak slots to improve their community programmes. For the London area, London Weekend Television (LWT), whose Head of Factual Programmes was John Birt, produced a short series aimed at young black people entitled *Babylon* (1979). Birt then set up the London Minorities Unit, which produced a number of series aimed at different minority audiences, including black people, gays and the elderly. *Skin* was a 30-minute documentary series which concentrated on the political concerns of both Afro-Caribbean and Asian communities. Executive producer Jane Hewland described LWT's minority programmes as having two equally important tasks:

> One was to satisfy the *minority groups* themselves that their concerns were being fairly reported, the other was to inform the *majority* audience and to dispel the ignorance and prejudice against them. Our programmes about blacks had also to interest and concern the white audience. Our programmes about gays had to do the same for straight viewers, and so on.[11]

These were not, therefore, programmes intended to be accountable primarily to their respective minority audiences. However, there was at least some awareness of the issue of accountability which had not previously been institutionalized in programming.

Skin's overriding concern with racism, and its treatment of the common concerns of both the Afro-Caribbean and Asian communities, was a reflection of racial politics of the late 1970s. The heyday of multiculturalism was yet to come. These were years in which the National Front was a significant political force, both on the streets and in electoral politics. In the latter case, their strength was in galvanizing the Conservative Party into playing the race card yet again, with the debate which culminated in the British Nationality Act 1981. Racism in policing, housing, education, employment and other areas united many Afro-Caribbean and Asian people.[12]

Channel 4 was due to begin broadcasting in the autumn of 1982. The Channel Four Company came into operation on 1 January 1981, and its Board of Directors began the appointment of Commissioning Editors. The fact that black programming was built into the structure was a victory; there would be a Commissioning Editor for Multicultural Programmes. Under this generic title, black representation would be assured. This would not preclude commissions from other editors.

However, the many disappointments that followed this initial gain highlighted the fact that Channel 4, for all its seemingly radical potential, was, in one respect, just like the other channels: it was answerable to a broadcasting authority which in turn was accountable to Parliament. While viewers were the rationale for its existence, it was not *ultimately* accountable to them. Certain campaigners clearly felt that it should have been subject to much greater community control, but that was neither promised nor implied in either the Broadcasting Act 1980 or in Channel 4's terms of reference. Quite apart from the technical problems of how community control and accountability could democratically operate, the history of public service television in Britain suggests that *relative autonomy* is the only condition under which a state-licensed broadcasting authority is likely to exist.[13]

That the black 'community' would not be given control was underlined during 1982 when Sue Woodford, formerly a producer/director with Granada's *World in Action*, was appointed Commissioning Editor for Multicultural Programmes. There was fury when, after considering a number of bids for black current affairs programmes, Woodford commissioned LWT to fill the slot. The regular current affairs series would be the channel's black flagship, taking up the bulk of the multicultural programmes budget. The award of the commission to a major ITV company was hardly likely to provide the black perspective that campaigners had sought. Even less would it provide the foothold within the industry that some black independent producers, such as the newly formed Black Media Workers' Group, felt was their right. Woodford's justification for commissioning LWT was that there were very few experienced television producers and directors among the black population in this country.[14] A major series such as this required a company capable of delivering the work on time, to budget and to the standards required. LWT was an established ITV company, capable of meeting professional requirements, and had proved that it could address black interests. *Skin* had allowed talented but inexperienced black people to learn from the experience of white programme-makers, thereby creating for the future a pool of skilled black practitioners. Woodford's argument did not succeed in persuading her most vocal critics, who kept up their attack on her commissions for the remainder of her tenure.

Thus, from the very start, Channel 4's black programming was marked by bitter feuding and controversy. Although the volume of black criticism diminished during the 1980s, the underlying dissatisfaction with the institution never did. Because of the particular circumstances in which expectations were raised, it was mainly 'black', as opposed to Asian, activists who loudly and consistently expressed their grievances. Significantly, this controversy never affected black programming on other channels. Channel 4's main rival, BBC2, never faced such attacks, principally because the BBC was never expected to deliver its programming to the black independent sector, or to bypass the Board of Governors and suddenly become accountable to and controlled by the communities. Channel 4 became the subject of false expectations.

Two presenters on *Skin*, Trevor Phillips and Samir Shah, were chosen as producers of the new series, with Jane Hewland as Executive Producer. By now they had come to regard *Skin*'s attempt to address both Afro-Caribbean and Asian communities in one programme as problematic, as was its task of having to take account of a white audience. Their approach was in keeping with the philosophy behind multicultural policies that were being developed elsewhere, particularly in local government, as a response to the urban violence of 1981. In these policies the ideals of cultural diversity in conditions of enlightenment, education and celebration, which were actually proposed in the 1960s, were coming to fruition. Central government was concentrating on crisis management in the form of increased spending on the Urban Programme and increased police training in riot control and community relations. Local authorities were struggling to improve their own employment practices and service delivery, and also to educate their white communities about the effects of racism. In the spirit of the Scarman report,[15] their conceptualization of the needs of the black communities became ethnically specific. Each ethnic minority had particular needs based on its language, religions, customs and so on.

The LWT producers of Channel 4's black programmes felt that the common experiences of racism were not enough to justify the two groups being lumped together for all purposes; to do so was to suggest that the groups had no history or identity of their own but existed only in relation to white people. Also, to continue this common treatment would limit the new programmes to the exploration of racism and would preclude coverage of other areas of black life, such as arts and entertainment.[16] Thus it was decided to alternate the weekly hour-long slot which Channel 4 was allocating to black audiences between Afro-Caribbean (or, as they were now being termed, 'black') and Asian viewers. It was decided to adopt a studio-based magazine format with a studio audience in both cases. The programmes were entitled *Black on Black* and *Eastern Eye*.

Shortly before *Black on Black* was due to be transmitted, the BBC launched a pre-emptive strike with *Ebony*. Earlier in 1982, soon after the announcement of Channel 4's programmes, the BBC had revamped and restructured the long-running *Nai Zindage Naya Jeevan*. Retitled *Asian Magazine*, the new format was designed to match the proposed structure of *Eastern Eye*. The BBC thereby signalled that it was not going to let Channel 4 walk away with all the prizes for innovation and racial awareness.

Like *Black on Black*, *Ebony* was a studio-based magazine but without the former's studio audience. It was shown weekly, rather than fortnightly, although programmes were only thirty minutes long, and it was limited to two eight-week runs per year. This gave it a lower profile than *Black on Black*, despite its peak-time showing. With hindsight it may be argued that this was probably something of a blessing. The series lacked the sense of anti-climax which heralded Channel 4's programmes. Perhaps this was why it did not at any time suffer the furore that dogged *Black on Black*. Indeed, rather than invite such a possibility, the producers and presenters went out of their way to stress that the series was not being targeted at black viewers:

> Our target audience is as large as we can get on BBC2 in the early evening. The subject matter is black and there to attract as many black viewers as it can, but we're not excluding whites. They should get from it what they want to.[17]

Black audiences generally expressed greater satisfaction with *Black on Black* than with *Ebony*. *Black on Black*, with its studio audience, was able to involve its audience in the production. The monologues by Victor Romero Evans playing the character Moves were much enjoyed. Conversely *Ebony* was often described as being remote and too concerned with professionalism. However, both series were criticized for the shallowness which derived from their magazine formats, and the lack of depth in their treatment of important issues.[18]

Farrukh Dhondy was appointed Channel 4's new Multicultural Commissioning Editor in 1984. His background as a playwright, journalist, member of the Black Theatre Co-operative, former political activist and member of the *Race Today* collective gave him much of the legitimacy which his predecessor never gained. It seemed likely that he would be able to work more effectively with black media workers than had Sue Woodford.

Dhondy announced that *Black on Black* and *Eastern Eye* would be commissioned for the last time during 1985. Despite all the attacks which had been made since they were first commissioned, there was some consternation at their being axed. Giving his reasons for the change, Dhondy cited the need to develop the current affairs output and the desire to place the responsibility for production in the hands of a black independent production company.[19] Once again the hopes of black producers were raised.

They were dashed when the commission for a weekly, hour-long series, which again would hold flagship status and require much of the multicultural programmes budget, was given to Bandung Productions. The directors of this company were Darcus Howe, one of Dhondy's former colleagues at *Race Today*, and political activist and writer Tariq Ali. Once again the black independent producers who had fought for the commission were furious. They argued that Dhondy was helping his friends and choosing a company which had no track record in the film or television industries.

However, the criticisms that were made of the LWT programmes – that their magazine format was shallow and haphazard, that they divided the black communities, and that they were produced by a mainstream independent – were dealt with at a stroke by *Bandung File*. The series adopted a documentary format, with fewer issues covered during the sixty minutes of airtime. Issues of relevance to the different ethnic groups which made up 'the black communities' were covered under a single umbrella. And Bandung Productions was an independent, black-led company.

Bandung File won praise in the quality national press.[20] However, it did not please those viewers who, whatever the critics said, had enjoyed the LWT programmes, or at least felt that they spoke to ordinary people. For them *Bandung File* was too highbrow. In fact, the series attracted a largely white, middle-class audience. Since its last appearance in 1989 Channel 4's black current affairs slot has been filled by different companies under the strand title *The Black Bag*.

THE ADVANTAGES AND DISADVANTAGES OF BLACK PROGRAMMING

The arguments for and against the provision of separate black programmes have by now been well rehearsed.

The arguments in favour of provision are that they provide an opportunity for the positive portrayal of black people, they guarantee funds and airtime for black voices to be heard, they provide a market for black independent producers, and they are a point of entry for black people to the major broadcasting institutions.

However, there is no guarantee that these favourable outcomes will result. First, by no means all black practitioners are interested in producing 'positive images'. Television dramas from writers like Mike Phillips, Hanif Kureishi and Farrukh Dhondy have produced an angry critical response from some sections of the black community. Speaking about the reception of his BBC drama serial *King of the Ghetto* (1986), Farrukh Dhondy has said that, as a writer, he is not interested in 'protecting the image of the community':

> [it] is, in a sense, an absurd enterprise. However, it has developed into a pseudo-science nowadays, with people saying things like 'Let's have positive images.' When Mrs Thatcher wanted a positive image of her government, she didn't ask a novelist or a television writer to do it, she hired Saatchi & Saatchi. But now we have people who are posing as writers and protectors of the community's image and they are no better than public relations salespersons. There's no harm in that as such. If indeed there is a need for such a function, they ought to be paid handsomely for it. But, in my view, it is not the function of creative writing or film-making to indulge in that sort of activity.[21]

Positive images aside, the content and angle of some programmes have laid them open to charges of scandalous, and even racist, portrayal that is no better than that of the mainstream:

Examples include *Panorama's* 'Underclass in Purdah' which informed us that British Muslims were largely pimps and drug dealers. The BBC's *All Black* and Channel 4's *Black Bag* series have overwhelmingly concentrated on stories about black pimps, rent boys, drug dealers and thugs.[22]

Clearly, there are no guarantees that the content of black programmes will be any different from that which is offered by the mainstream. An unfavourable response attracts charges that certain black people wish to censor the discussion of unpleasant truths, which implies that black people as a whole are unable to develop a mature response to art.

Second, there are those who argue that the guarantee of a voice and funding also has its disadvantages; black programming can be seen as a ghetto. This view is based on the belief that programmes targeted at black audiences will not necessarily have any effect on the rest of television. Only black audiences will take any notice of them. Mainstream programmes will not draw on them or be affected by their existence to any significant degree. The people who produce and present them will find it difficult to develop their careers and gain wider expertise, because their experience will not be taken seriously by the mainstream media.

In fact, history provides little evidence that black programmes have become ghettos, in terms of their effects either on other programmes or on the careers of the people who work on them. Trevor Phillips and Samir Shah have reached executive positions within LWT and the BBC respectively. Others too have gone on to work in the mainstream. There is also now a black presence in many non-black programmes. Black programmes as a whole have evolved to the point where they are not spoken of principally in terms of black audiences. Programmes are, rather, described as being *about* black issues, or as representing 'black perspectives'. The audience is seen as being anybody who is interested in the issues.

The third reservation about black programming is that, while it does provide a market for black independent producers, there is no guarantee that black programmes will be produced by black-led companies. The arguments over commissions which dominated Sue Woodford's tenure have continued under Farrukh Dhondy, who has spiritedly defended his decisions and dismissed his critics. He appears unruffled by the arguments of members of the black independent lobby. He argues that he has commissioned a large number of independent producers.

This is true; under both Sue Woodford and Farrukh Dhondy other black independent producers have won commissions. Since 1990 these producers have also been able to offer their work to the BBC, which is now required to commission at least 25 per cent of its original television programmes from independent companies. At Channel 4 they have secured contracts from, in the main, the Arts, Drama and Independent Film editors. Indeed, this last department provides some of the funding which has maintained the subsidised independence of black workshops such as the Black Audio Film Collective, Sankofa, Retake, Ceddo and others. However, for those independent production companies outside the workshop movement, which have not received large commissions, economic survival has been precarious. The independent sector has provided steady employment for relatively few groups. The process of more secure white-led companies employing black professionals to work on their commissions has continued, and even increased since *Bandung File* ended its run in 1988.

Finally, it is true that there is now greater access to television institutions than ever before. There are a number of training schemes, bursaries and fellowships which support the training of black people for various jobs. These go some way towards mitigating the past racism of the industry, but once again there is no guarantee of the effect this will have on output. While it is unlikely that black media workers will help to produce the stereotypes of yesteryear, there is no certainty that they will want to make committed, interventionist programmes. Indeed, they might want to work on breakfast television. It is also likely that the institutions will favour university-educated, career-minded blacks over community activists.

However, individuals and campaigning groups have often argued that black people must gain entry to the boardrooms of society's institutions. It is counterproductive to attack black media workers who wish to work in the mainstream. Their right to do so must be defended at the same time as seeking access for radical and committed work.

Nevertheless, there will still be limits to the potential for such work. Public service broadcasting channels are answerable to their governing bodies, which are in turn accountable to Parliament. They must necessarily apply control over their programmes. Channel 4 is intended to be more innovative than the others, but it still has to satisfy the ITC's interpretation of its duties. To hope that state-licensed television will provide black control and accountability, and programmes that are uncompromisingly critical of our political system, is simply not realistic.

PUBLIC SERVICE VERSUS THE MARKETPLACE

The audience for black current affairs programmes since their inception has been about half a million viewers. Such an audience size might not be enough to interest advertisers should the market be called upon to play a greater part.

The Broadcasting Act 1990 makes provision for the further development of local television services. Local delivery licences will be awarded by competitive tender. As with 'community interest' radio stations, services could be aimed at black audiences. Since income would be dependent on advertising, the size of the communities would affect the viability of such enterprises. Even if such a development occurred, large, established companies would again have advantages over small black independents in winning a licence. Similar commercial considerations govern cable television, where multinational companies would have greater economic power than British black independents.

So far it has been the public service ideal which has allowed black programming to develop, whether on Channel 4 or on BBC2. The argument that broadcasters have a *duty* to cater to minority interests has given black audiences the grounds on which to talk in terms of rights. Both BBC2 and Channel 4 programmes have thus far operated under conditions of subsidy, either from the BBC licence fee or from ITV revenues. Channel 4 is now having to raise its own advertising revenue, and the BBC has for several years faced threats to its future. If the BBC survives after 1996 it will probably have to look to its audience figures and deliver more 'popular' programmes. If public service, as practised so far, has disappointed black audiences and media workers in the past, the market-led philosophy of the 1990s will not make things any better.

The discussion about the future of black programming has involved groups such as the Commission for Racial Equality, black media workers, channel controllers, academics and viewers. The demands which they make often do not deal with what is possible given unpleasant economic realities.

It is not possible to predict whether, in future, local or national television, cable and satellite will be able to deliver enough black programmes to satisfy the interests of a diverse population. If there ever was a homogeneous black community, there is no longer such a thing. Differences of gender, sexuality, religion and social class are rendering the concept of 'the black community' increasingly problematic.[23] The mixed reception given to black programmes so far, and to films such as *My Beautiful Laundrette*, *Handsworth Songs*, *The Passion of Remembrance*, *Young Soul Rebels* and others, shows this. All the independent films mentioned were criticized for not being 'representative' enough. It was argued that they, in their various ways, did not reflect the 'reality' of the lives of most black people.[24]

It is almost impossible accurately to reflect the lives of an increasingly diverse population within a single production. In addition, there are increasing numbers of black artists who do not want to do so. They wish to explore other avenues. Their innovative work will inevitably create offence in some quarters, but it is not in the interests of the development of black art to suppress such work. It seems unlikely that there will be room for everybody in the marketplace, but this is what we must strive for.

NOTES

1. The history of black representation in the early years of television is discussed in the BBC documentary *Black and White in Colour: Television, Memory, Race*, part 1, director Isaac Julien, first broadcast in June 1992. The publications which accompany the broadcast are Jim Pines (ed.), *Black and white in colour: black people in British television since 1936* (London, British Film Institute, 1992) and T. Daniels, *Black and white in colour* (London, BBC Education, 1992).
2. Asa Briggs, *The BBC: the first 50 years* (Oxford, Oxford University Press, 1985).
3. *See* references under note 1 above.
4. In the then Home Secretary Roy Jenkins's oft-quoted phrase, government policy should encourage 'equal opportunity, accompanied by cultural diversity, in an atmosphere of mutual tolerance'. Quoted in J. Solomos, *Race and racism in Britain* (London, Macmillan, 1993), p. 86.
5. *See* the history of the Campaign Against Racism in the Media in P. Cohen and C. Gardner, *It ain't half racist mum: fighting racism in the media* (London, Comedia, 1982).
6. P. Hartmann and C. Husband, *Racism and the mass media* (London, Davis Poynter, 1974); Commission for Racial Equality, *Television in a multi-racial society* (London, Commission for Racial Equality, 1982).
7. Thomas Baptiste, 'The case for integrated casting in the British theatre', unpublished paper, British Actors' Equity Association, February 1978, quoted in Commission for Racial Equality, *Television in a multi-racial society*.
8. Lord Annan, *Report of the Committee on the Future of Broadcasting* (London, HMSO, March 1977), Cmnd 6753; Simon Blanchard, 'Where do new channels come from?', in S. Blanchard (ed.), *What's this Channel Four?* (London, Comedia, 1982).

9. Commission for Racial Equality, *Broadcasting in a multi-racial society* (London, Commission for Racial Equality, 1979).

10. Blanchard, 'Where do new channels come from?'

11. Jane Hewland, 'Not divisive in context but a necessary filling of gaps', *The Stage and Television Today*, 2 December 1982, p. 18.

12. A. Sivanandan, 'From resistance to rebellion', in *A different hunger: writings on black resistance* (London, Pluto Press, 1982).

13. J. Curran and J. Seaton, *Power without responsibility: the press and broadcasting in Britain* (London, Methuen, 1991).

14. Sue Woodford, 'Replies', *Caribbean Times*, 7 January 1983, p. 17.

15. Lord Scarman, *The British Disorders 10–12 April 1981: Report of an Inquiry by the Rt Hon. the Lord Scarman OBE* (London, HMSO, November 1981), Cmnd 8427.

16. *See* the interviews with Trevor Phillips and Samir Shah in J. Pines (ed.), *Black and white in colour*.

17. C. Spencer, 'Black opinion', *Stills* 18, 1993.

18. P. Gilroy, 'C4: bridgehead or bantustan?', *Screen* 24(4–5), (1983).

19. Jane Hewland, 'Is Channel Four poking itself in the Eastern Eye?', *Guardian*, 7 January 1985; Farrukh Dhondy, 'Karma after the storm', *Guardian*, 14 January 1985.

20. Nicholas Fraser, 'Racing away from the bland centre', *Observer*, 17 December 1989, p. 63.

21. *See* the interview with Farrukh Dhondy in Pines (ed.), *Black and white in colour*.

22. Yasmin Alibhai-Brown, 'Sold out by media wallahs', *New Statesman and Society*, 28 January 1994.

23. The importance of this heterogeneity to black arts in Britain is discussed in P. Gilroy, *Small acts: thoughts on the politics of black cultures* (London, Serpent's Tail, 1993).

24. The mixed responses to some of these films are discussed in ICA Documents 7, *Black film, British cinema* (London, Institute of Contemporary Arts, 1988).

19

Reception as flow

Klaus Bruhn Jensen

From Jensen, K.B. 1995: *The social semiotics of mass communication*. London: Sage, 108–17

Television research needs to pay attention to individual programmes but, at the same time, to recognize the way in which programmes are part of a channel schedule. Schedule-building, with its use of 'pre-echo' and 'carry over' to catch viewers' attention and sustain it across programme changes, has been an important part of the television industry and has exerted a significant influence over the way television programmes look and sound. Raymond Williams used the word 'flow' to indicate the larger durational and culturally significant context within which specific programmes worked. There has been much debate about the use of this term in television analysis, together with the negative judgement it implies, but it serves as a warning against regarding television as being made up of clearly discrete 'texts' in the way that, for instance, literary studies has regarded books and newspapers. Williams's idea of flow also suggests the larger entity of, for instance, an 'evening's viewing', which may move across a number of channels. More recently, research has had to pay further attention to the way in which programmes are part of a multi-channel viewing environment involving various channel schedules competing for viewers.

Klaus Bruhn Jensen addresses these issues with a useful directness. In the course of a sustained examination of the idea of flow, he identifies a 'super-flow' comprising other flow variables. His account then cites extensively from a pilot empirical study, as he examines the actual shifts made by a number of respondents on a particular night. How often did viewers shift, and how often was a change of programme the reason for shifting? Jensen moves back to theoretical considerations to ask how the pattern of flows might bear on the pattern both of generic preferences and of certain over-arching themes linking viewers' world to televised world. Far from seeing multi-channel availability and the practices of 'zapping', 'grazing' and 'surfing' as self-evidently reducing the importance of questions of 'influence', Jensen wants to hold on to the idea of television in its new multiplicity and optionality as a major agency of cultural reproduction.

As television becomes a more 'dispersed' medium in many countries, the kind of inquiry Jensen undertakes here, plotting variability yet still attempting to engage with general tendencies, will become an increasingly necessary dimension of research. It will be complementary to those other studies, some of which are represented in this book, which engage with television's textuality at the more local level of generic specificity and particular instance. Jensen's particular approach is open both to accusations of 'reductionism' (from those wanting more attention to cultural expression) and of statistical inadequacy (from those wanting a firmer social scientific basis), but the agenda he develops is one which indicates a convergence point of issues (in theory and method) for television research.

This chapter reexamines a neglected condition of mass media reception, namely, the structured flow of media discourses. Both 'administrative' and 'critical' studies, particularly of television, have suggested that viewers autonomously select, interpret, and apply programming within their everyday context. Research in the industry has referred to increasingly selective viewers who zip, zap, and graze their way through an expanding TV universe (for example, Ainslie, 1988). Critical cultural studies have interpreted the documentation of oppositional decodings of whatever material is shown as evidence of viewer control over the medium.[1] The present study of television reception as flow in a sample of American households entails a critical assessment of the common notion of a 'new television viewer'.

Having shifted the theoretical emphasis from text to audience, current research may be losing sight analytically of the textual aspect of the reception interface, in effect implying that there is no text in this living-room (Fish, 1979). Like the institutional frameworks of mass communication, however, the discursive structures of media could be conceived as determinations in the first instance (Hall, 1983). If, in methodological terms, meaning flows from the media to the audience and into the wider social context, this makes media discourses a necessary, constitutive element of empirical designs. Whereas it is especially apparent in the case of radio and television that audiences are confronted not with 'works', but with sequences of discourse, and with complex discursive relations between segments, newspapers and other print media also offer the experience of a sequence of more or less related segments. In each case, moreover, the segment refers back to a long history of earlier segments as received and processed by audiences. In a sense, the flow never stops.

The empirical study examined both the actual flow segments that were watched in the households and the potential meaning of the discursive relations between segments. Starting from a redevelopment of Williams' (1974) concept of flow, I first report on the 'viewer flows' that households constructed for themselves out of the available programming, asking to what extent viewers can be said to select their flow autonomously. Next, I analyze and interpret the viewer flows with reference to their discursive form and thematic universe. Thus, whereas the study emphasized the media constituent of *flow*, it addressed the context constituents of actual *consumption* and potential *decoding* with reference to a range of *demographic* categories of the audience constituents; the objects of analysis were the videotaped *records* of the viewer flows that were examined, first, through a *coding* of channel changes and, second and primarily, through *discourse analysis*. Finally, I discuss the implications of research on media flows, both as a new, complementary source of data about the reception process and as a contribution to theory development.

FROM ONE TO THREE FLOWS OF TELEVISION

Raymond Williams first introduced the concept of flow into communication theory. His definition is worth quoting in full:

In all developed broadcasting systems the characteristic organization, and therefore the characteristic experience, is one of sequence or flow. This phenomenon, of planned flow, is then perhaps the defining characteristic of broadcasting, simultaneously as a technology and as a cultural form. In all communications systems before broadcasting the essential items were discrete. A book or pamphlet was taken and read as a specific item. A meeting occurred at a particular date and place. A play was performed in a particular theatre at a set hour. The difference in broadcasting is not only that these events, or events resembling them, are available inside the home, by the operation of a switch. It is that the real programme that is offered is a *sequence* or set of alternative sequences of these and other similar events, which are then available in a single dimension and in a single operation.

(Williams, 1974, pp. 86–7)

While this classic definition captures a distinctive feature particularly of commercial television, Raymond Williams appears to imply that broadcasting leads, as a matter of course, to a specific audience experience. John Ellis has taken that implication one step further by suggesting that it may be in the nature of television to structure communication in a sequence of very short segments, each about the length of a commercial break (Ellis, 1982, ch. 7).

In order to capture the specificity both of the historical form of American commercial television and of its reception, I propose an analytical distinction between three aspects of TV flow (Fig. 19.1). First, a *channel flow* is the sequence of program segments, commercials, and preannouncements that is designed by the individual station to engage as many viewers as possible for as long as possible. The assumption is that an appropriate form and mixture of segments may retain the viewers who are already in the flow, and that it may further recruit new viewers who are grazing the spectrum. It is this strategy which results in the characteristic narrative structure that climaxes, with increasing intensity, before each commercial break, a *bricolage* in which the boundaries of the sequence are blurred.

Second, viewers create their own customized *viewer flow* from the available channels. Whereas viewers are likely to stay with a given channel, carrying over or flowing from one program to the next (Barwise and Ehrenberg, 1988, p. 34), they are

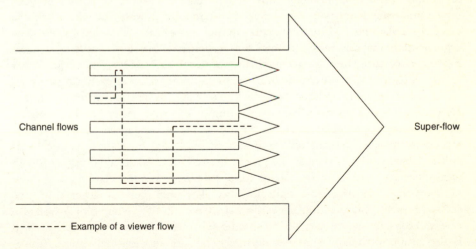

Channel flows — Super-flow

------- Example of a viewer flow

Figure 19.1   The three flows of television

free, in principle, to make any type and number of changes at any point. It is not well understood how the process of selection comes about, or what kind of experience arises from viewing as flow.

Third, the sum total of possible sequences represents a *super-flow*. Stations must establish a profile, or house style (Ellis, 1982, p. 219), that is recognizable within the super-flow of competing stations. Viewers equally must be able to orient themselves in the super-flow in order to make an informed selection. The super-flow of competing channel flows, rather than flow as such, should be seen as the defining characteristic of American commercial television in its present stage of development.[2]

The interrelations between the three flows, while bearing on the relative power of medium and audience, have not been analyzed in previous empirical reception studies.[3] Research in the area follows the familiar tendency for social science to focus on audiences, while humanistic studies focus on texts. The issues relating to the audience selection and use of program sequences have primarily been examined through quantitative measures of audience behavior, such as the ratings (Nielsen, 1989) and the overlap between audiences for different programs (Barwise and Ehrenberg, 1988). Because of their commercial purposes, however, these studies emphasize aggregated measures of the audience for particular segments of the flow, while giving less attention to the combination of segments in individual or household viewing. And because no record is produced, for example on videotape, of actual viewing, it is normally not possible to explore the relationship between viewers' channel selection and the discursive structures of the content. Some recent research has examined the flow of individual viewers across broadcast and other television channels (Heeter and Greenberg, 1988; Pingree *et al.*, 1991), again without examining the discursive structures of the selected programming in any detail. Cultivation studies (Gerbner and Gross, 1976), while offering one relevant, if contested, conception of audience-cum-content analysis, have not approached television as a structured flow.

In the humanistic tradition, a couple of studies have analyzed television flow as a text. Nick Browne (1987), first, has argued that the American networks' historical strategy of aiming for a common denominator that would appeal to as many of the available viewers as possible has resulted in the relative homogeneity of TVs 'super-text' (in the present terminology, super-flow). There is a political economy at work which limits the diversity of the super-flow at any given time, and which helps to explain the placement of different genres in the course of the television day. Browne argues further that this homogeneity is self-perpetuating because, over time, viewers have been socialized through the 'mega-text' of television history to expect particular (super-)texts. The 'mega-text' lives on, then, in the audience's interpretive repertoires.

A second, culturally optimistic perspective on flow has been advanced by Horace Newcomb (1988). Through a thematic reading of a 'strip' (viewer flow) of network programs on a particular evening, he develops the argument that television represents an open forum (Newcomb and Hirsch, 1984) for diverse political and cultural issues and viewpoints. The programs are said to enter into dialogue – with each other and with viewers – about social problems, gender relations, and other issues of public debate. Surprisingly, however, Newcomb's reading does not include the commercials and preannouncements that are constitutive elements of flow; it also does not consider selections made by specific audiences. Instead, the analysis, which is also an appreciation by a fan who normally watches the series in question, focuses on possible combinations of the program segments as such. Television flow thus highlights the need for several forms of data about the reception process and for comparative analysis of audience and media discourses.

METHODOLOGY

The empirical study, first of all, produced a 'reverse video' – a record of the viewer flow in specific households on a particular night – by asking the respondents to make all channel changes with their VCR running and attached to their main TV set.[4] The videos document what was shown (but not necessarily watched) on the set. The recordings were made on a Wednesday evening (February 1, 1989), an 'average' night of regular programming when the scheduled programming was not disrupted by specials replacing regular shows or by major news events. It was also a night in the middle of the TV season when neither specific program choices nor extensive grazing would more likely be due to new program offers. Respondents were asked to watch some TV between 7 and 9 p.m., but not necessarily for the entire period. The early evening was chosen because this is a time when members of a household are likely to be selecting and viewing programs together as a group. In addition, respondents filled in basic questionnaires about demographics and television use as well as a diary concerning their channel selections and changes. The additional information provided by viewers, for example on motivations for channel changes or disagreements in the viewing group, had few details, but helped to identify programs and in some cases served to explain the combination of programs in the recordings, which were examined as the primary objects of analysis. The local *TV Guide* (January 28–February 3, 1989) documents the availability of network, independent, and public TV stations in the super-flow, as well as additional cable channels, to which a majority of the households in the study had access.

A sample of twelve video households from the Los Angeles metropolitan area was selected by a local market research firm. The aim was to explore a range of household types in terms of household size and socioeconomic status; the actual sample was predominantly white and middle class, but included both young and elderly viewers (in their twenties to sixties) as well as households with/without children and with one/two parents.

Before reporting two sets of findings, I note that, while relying on a small sample, the study identified several types and structures of viewer flow. These structures lend themselves to further research on a representative scale, possibly in combination with TV meter data; they also complement previous interview and observation studies on the decoding and social uses of specific texts and genres. Although the design entailed an intervention into daily routines, the households were familiar with the video technology, and they were not required to watch for the entire two-hour period. The recordings document some actual instances of reception as flow that bear on the notion of a new and powerful television viewer.

A POWER INDEX OF TELEVISION?

The first form of analysis examined the number of channel changes made by the respondents, compared to the content changes resulting from a channel's introduction of a commercial, a preannouncement, or a program segment. The ratio between these two kinds of changes may be interpreted as an index of the relative power of TV and its viewers, in the sense that each change controls which flow segment is subsequently shown on the screen. The capacity to control which texts and genres one is to receive can be defined as a minimal form of cultural self-determination. This is in spite of the fact that the variety of segments in itself may also be part of the attraction for viewers. The basic implication of the 'new television viewer' is that the selection of a *specific* variety of contents is left to the discretion and free choice of viewers.

This first form of analysis accepts, for the sake of the argument, the premise of the industry position, namely that, increasingly, viewers select the segments they prefer to watch while avoiding not least the commercials. Simultaneously, the analysis prepares the ground for an immanent critique (Bernstein, 1991, p. 315) of the logic behind the argument. Even if one pursues the industry argument on its own terms, an alternative conclusion suggests itself.[5]

Table 19.1 reports the number of viewer-initiated and channel-initiated changes. The channel-initiated content changes include only changes between commercials, preannouncements, and program segments, *not* between scenes of fictional series, news stories, or music videos, and only simultaneous changes of image and sound. The viewer-initiated channel changes include the initial switching on of the set. Channel changes were made both at the transition between programs and in the middle of a program segment or a commercial break.

The average ratio of 1:13.93 suggests a relative, but notable, degree of control by the medium in these terms, at least in this sample of viewers and given the super-flow at this time of day; the findings call for replication on a representative sample and during other time periods. The highest ratio (1:87) occurred in the viewing of a live sports

Table 19.1   A power index of television

Household no.	Viewer-initiated channel changes	Channel-initiated content changes
1	30	71
2	3	77
3	1	48
4	2	88
5	4	49
6	1	87
7	3	110
8	2	34
9	5	48
10	2	64
11	2	54
12	4	92
Mean	4.92	68.50

The ratio of viewer-initiated to channel-initiated changes:
   Mean: 1:13.93   High: 1:87.00   Low: 1:2.37

program on commercial broadcast television. To exemplify how the lowest ratio (1:2.37) came about, an intensive sequence of viewer-initiated channel changes occurred in this household when the credits at the end of a news program began to roll, and the household, in making the eighth change, managed to return to the same channel before the news credits had been completed. Even this form of viewer activity, while standing out in the sample as a whole, still does not put the viewer in control.

To anticipate a few counterarguments, I recognize that viewers have been socialized to the super-flow and thus have a sense of how long an ongoing segment will last. The point is that no information with sufficient detail is available, on television or in the listings in print media that list only 'real programs', for it to be possible to make an informed choice of particular segments on a particular channel. In effect, viewers can only make a negative choice, knowing what they are changing *from* (a specific program segment, commercial, or preannouncement), but not what they are changing *to*. Viewers do not in fact control the specific variety of their own flow. Even the conceivable devotees of commercials, watching advertising as either shopping information or a cultural form in its own right, will find it most difficult of all to orient themselves in the flow, since 'their' genre is defined negatively as an unlisted absence within other programming.

Rather than concluding in quantitative terms that, hence, viewers are powerless, or that more frequent channel changes as such would make them more powerful, my purpose has been a preliminary critique of the widespread conception of a 'new television viewer' in industry rhetoric as well as some academic research and public debate. The super-flow establishes particular conditions of reception, which are not eliminated through even a great measure of zapping or, as I go on to argue, an oppositional decoding of particular segments. The next step is to ask which specific range of meanings are available in the viewer flows that audiences construct for themselves from the super-flow. An answer is suggested by a second form of analysis examining two types of discursive structures – intertextuality and super-themes – across the different genres of flow.

FLOWS, GENRES, AND SUPER-THEMES

The *genres* which predominate in American television on weekdays between 7 and 9 p.m. present an opportunity for viewers to negotiate the relationship between private and public areas of life, and between everyday life and major social institutions. The three predominant genres are situation comedies, tabloid journalism (for example, *A Current Affair*, *Entertainment Tonight*), and tabloid science (for example, *Unsolved Mysteries*). In social-structural terms, the genres of this period serve to mediate between the public life of work or school during the day and the private life of evening (Scannell, 1988, p. 26). On the one hand, situation comedy is a fictional genre which, though focusing on the home, raises social issues pertaining to families and individuals; on the other hand, the tabloid programs present facts about the world that affect families and individuals in fundamental respects. Despite other options, including cable programming, the households themselves also emphasize these three genres in their actual viewer flows. It is interesting to note that some of the subscribers to pay movie channels would only watch part of a movie before selecting another channel, thus apparently treating a pay channel as any other element of the super-flow. Similar findings in a study of a larger sample (Heeter and Greenberg, 1988, pp. 167–76) suggest that, from the viewers' perspective, commercial-free movie and other pay channels may not in fact be conceived as a distinctive alternative to broadcast television, even if this conception is commonly taken to explain, in part, the development of cable television.

Information from the diaries suggests how the specific combination of genres was negotiated in the households between parents and children, and between male and female viewers. The information is in keeping with earlier research finding that male viewers may be especially oriented toward news and other factual programming, whereas female viewers may prefer sitcoms, soaps, and other fictional genres (Hobson, 1980; Morley, 1986), even if some women in the sample indicate a preference for news. Children specifically report liking (or actively disliking) particular sitcoms. The sample includes examples of both news and fiction genres prevailing as well as family compromises involving the selection of first a news program and later a sitcom. Moreover, the negotiation of program selection bears witness to gender and other family roles and conflicts. In one case, a father labels *The A Team* (an action series featuring Vietnam veterans as its main characters) one of the worst programs on television, while his twelve-year-old son labels it one of the best. The series can be said to place gender identities on a cultural agenda, offering an occasion to explore definitions of masculinity. In another case, *Charles in Charge* (a sitcom with a male teenager as the central character) is labeled as one of the best programs by a twelve-year-old boy, and as one of the worst by his fourteen-year-old sister.

The viewer flows, as recorded on videotapes, were analyzed in detail with reference to the category of *super-themes*, defined as specific, highly generalized concepts that serve to establish meaningful relations between the discursive realities of programs and the everyday social realities of viewers. Previous research in the United States, Denmark, and Italy has identified such super-themes as principles structuring the reception of television news as well as the everyday conceptualization of politics (Crigler and Jensen, 1991; Jensen, 1988; Mancini, 1990). The present study identified a set of super-themes across the different genres of the super-flow. Although the study did not observe or interview viewers apart from analyzing the questionnaires and diaries, the actual viewer flows are examined as potential structures of meaning, as constructed by the respondents, and the flow sequences are interpreted with reference to the theoretical categories of discourse and reception analysis. The configuration of super-themes in the present sample of viewer flows is summarized in Fig. 19.2, and discussed below.

	Private sphere	**Public sphere**
Central or legitimated areas	The family	The nation
Peripheral or delegitimated areas	The body, insanity	Other cultures, the supernatural

Figure 19.2   Super-themes of television flow

FLOW AS DISCOURSE

The super-themes were inferred from a detailed analysis of three categories of television discourse: actors, coherence, and presuppositions or implicit premises. First of all, the verbal and visual representation of *actors* and their actions carry a range of positive and negative connotations (Barthes, 1964/1984, pp. 89–94). Further, such representations cumulatively imply the appropriate public and private roles of actors. To exemplify, the viewer flow of one household (Household 2) featured *Charles in Charge*, *A Current Affair*, and *Unsolved Mysteries*, in which actors relating to all four super-themes appeared. *A Current Affair* reported, for example, on a doctor's sexual abuse of a patient, a Congress politician allegedly having sex with teenagers, and an update of a story on marriage fraud. Articulating a discursive boundary between the family and a deviant private or sexual life, and employing a terminology of insanity, the reports on these cases establish a contrast with the 'normal' family life of *Charles in Charge*. Similarly, a contrast is established between the nation and supernatural dangers. *Unsolved Mysteries* included coverage of the exploration of Mars, where traces of ancient civilizations may be found. In the reference to 'America's romance with Mars', it is significant that 'America', not humanity or Earth, engages with other forms of life. Supernatural powers in the form of UFOs also appear briefly in *Charles in Charge* as a threat to family security.

Second, the discursive *coherence* of the flow contributes to developing the super-themes. Coherence is carried not just by the explicit verbal and visual structures of television, but as importantly by the functional relations between shots and verbal segments, which indicate, for example, a causal or temporal relationship or a conclusion (van Dijk, 1977). Crucially, such relations obtain both within and between the three types of flow segment. Exemplifying coherence within a segment, Household 2 selected *Unsolved Mysteries*, which included a classic narrative comparable to folk tales (Todorov, 1968). This was the story of a little girl who, when living with her parents in Austria as a refugee following World War II, was taken to a Christmas party by an American soldier. Now, through the intervention of this program, the two have been reunited in the United States. The story of their lives, then, can be interpreted through categories such as The First Encounter, Separation, Quest, and Reunion.

Most important, coherence is established between segments, not least through the intervention of commercials. In the course of the video from Household 2, several commercials represent other cultures with an implied contrast to the American nation. A soldier wearing a Nazi uniform and speaking with a heavy German accent drives his tank up to a fast-food stand, and, discovering the low prices, he decides to 'fill up the tank'. The immediately following item advertises a new book with reference to an ominous atmosphere in a Japanese context. And several later commercials featuring a cream cheese depict a band of dancing cucumbers singing a Latino tune and wearing Mexican hats. Another commercial in Household 2's flow is a parody of a United Nations assembly debating heatedly where to have dinner, leading up to the solution: a local hamburger chain.

Finally, *presuppositions* carry the fundamental assumptions of discourse (Culler, 1981; Leech, 1974). Although they may be explicit, presuppositions are often the implicit premises of an argument or narrative, constituting the conditions of possibility for interpretation. One commercial for a traditional steak dinner that presents a singing cowboy, while behind him what is evidently a movie set is being dismantled, may mobilize the viewers' interpretive repertoire (Potter and Wetherell, 1987) for the Western genre. At the same time, the ambiguity regarding the status of the myth of the West, and by implication the American nation, suggests the more general point that the super-themes, in articulating a common conception of social reality, can also bear witness to specific contradictions within that conception. This conclusion is substantiated by a further analysis of the configuration of super-themes in the entire sample. [...] [The author develops a more detailed analysis of the themes. *Eds.*]

NOTES

1. John Fiske's *Television culture* (1987) remains the most significant statement of this position. For a timely and well-argued critique of what is termed 'the new revisionism' of reception studies, *see* Curran (1990). Responding to the critique, Morley (1992) has noted that while it remains important not to overstate the social power of audiences, the new reception studies represented a necessary step in the history of research, transcending the dominant text-centrism of much work during the 1960s and 1970s as well as differentiating the understanding of reception processes.
2. The flow feature of television increasingly is found in other cultural contexts as well, particularly the semi-commercial television systems of Western Europe. The design of the present study has later been used to examine Danish television audiences, this time including household interviews about the flow experience as well as a quantitative component examining different viewer types. (*See* the findings in Jensen *et al.*, 1994.)
3. In his theoretical analysis of the reception of film and television, Ellis (1982) has suggested that whereas the cinema context mobilizes the concentrated 'gaze' of the spectator, television typically attracts only the intermittent 'glance' of the viewer. Such a distracted mode of reception may lead to a relatively selective decoding and to the interpretation of several discrete segments as belonging to the 'same' message.
4. A majority of the households in the sample had two or more television sets. However, the diaries and questionnaire responses suggested that joint viewing of programs remained common. The recordings, together with the diaries, offer insight into the viewer flows that were available for viewing in the households. Survey evidence also supports the conclusion that joint viewing, while decreasing as the number of household sets increases, still accounts for a large proportion of all television viewing (Bower, 1985, p. 111).
5. Since the ratio of changes was taken, following the 'new viewer' argument, as the measure of relative control, the duration of each segment in the viewer flow was not singled out for analysis.

REFERENCES

AINSLIE, P. (ed.) 1988: The new TV viewer. *Channels of Communication*, September, 53–62.
BARTHES, R. 1984: *Elements of semiology*. New York: Hill & Wang. (Originally published 1964.)
BARWISE, P. and EHRENBERG, A. 1988: *Television and its audience*. London: Sage.
BERNSTEIN, R. 1991: *The new constellation*. Cambridge: Polity Press.
BOWER, R.T. 1985: *The changing television audience in America*. New York: Columbia University Press.
BROWNE, N. 1987: The political economy of the television (super)text. In Newcomb, H. (ed.), *Television: the critical view*, 4th edn. New York: Oxford University Press.

CRIGLER, A. and JENSEN, K.B. 1991: Discourses of politics: talking about public issues in the United States and Denmark. In Dahlgren, P. and Sparks, C. (eds.), *Communication and citizenship*. London: Routledge.

CULLER, J. 1981: *The pursuit of signs*. Ithaca, NY: Cornell University Press.

CURRAN, J. 1990: The 'new revisionism' in mass communication research: a reappraisal. *European Journal of Communication* 5(2–3), 135–64.

ELLIS, J. 1982: *Visible fictions*. London: Routledge & Kegan Paul.

FISH, S. 1979: *Is there a text in this class? The authority of interpretive communities*. Cambridge, MA: Harvard University Press.

FISKE, J. 1987: *Television culture*. London: Methuen.

GERBNER, G. and GROSS, L. 1976: Living with television: the violence profile. *Journal of Communication* 26(3), 173–99.

HALL, S. 1983: The problem of ideology: Marxism without guarantees. In Matthews, B. (ed.), *Marx: a hundred years on*. London: Lawrence & Wishart.

HEETER, C. and GREENBERG, B. 1988: *Cableviewing*. Norwood, NJ: Ablex.

HOBSON, D. 1980: Housewives and the mass media. In Hall, S., Hobson, D., Lowe, A. and Willis, P. (eds.), *Culture, media, language*. London: Hutchinson.

JENSEN, K.B. 1988: News as social resource. *European Journal of Communication* 3(3), 275–301.

JENSEN, K.B., SCHRODER, K., STAMPE, T., SONDERGAARD, H. and TOPSOE-JENSEN, J. 1994: Super flow, channel flows, and audience flows: A study of viewers' reception of television as flow. *The Nordicom Review* 2, 1–13.

LEECH, G. 1974: *Semantics*. Harmondsworth: Penguin.

MANCINI, P. 1990: Selective reception and super-themes in decoding television news. Paper presented to the conference of the International Communication Association, Dublin, Ireland, 24–29 June 1990.

MORLEY, D. 1986: *Family television*. London: Comedia.

MORLEY, D. 1992: *Television audiences and cultural studies*. London: Routledge.

NEWCOMB, H. 1988: One night of prime time: an analysis of television's multiple voices. In Carey, J. (ed.), *Media, myths and narratives*. Beverly Hills, CA: Sage.

NEWCOMB, H. and HIRSCH, P. 1984: Television as a cultural forum: implications for research. In Rowland, W. and Watkins, B. (eds.), *Interpreting television*. Beverly Hills, CA: Sage.

NIELSEN, A.C. 1989: *Nielsen report on television*. Northbrook, IL: Nielsen Media Research.

PINGREE, S., HAWKINS, R., JOHNSSON-SMARAGDI, U., ROSENGREN, K., and REYNOLDS, N. 1991: Television structures and adolescent viewing patterns: a Swedish–American comparison. *European Journal of Communication* 6, 417–40.

POTTER, J. and WETHERELL, M. 1987: *Discourse and social psychology*. London: Sage.

SCANNELL, P. 1988: Radio times: the temporal arrangements of broadcasting in the modern world. In Drummond, P. and Paterson, R. (eds.), *Television and its audience*. London: British Film Institute.

TODOROV, T. 1968: Le grammaire du récit (The grammar of narrative). *Languages* 12, 94–102.

VAN DIJK, T.A. 1977: *Text and context: explorations in the semantics and pragmatics of discourse*. London: Longman.

WILLIAMS, R. 1974: *Television: technology and cultural form*. London: Fontana.

Section IV

POLICY

20

Channel 4 television: from Annan to Grade

Sylvia Harvey

From Hood, S. (ed.) 1994: *Behind the screens: the structure of British television in the nineties*. London: Lawrence & Wishart, 102–29

The range and kind of television programmes which get on to the screen, and therefore the way in which television works as a political and social agency, are of course partly determined by the nature of the *institutions* which produce television – the corporations, the stations, the channels. It is, in turn, the funding of these institutions, and then their regulation, which are powerful factors in influencing their functions and commitments. Internationally, the relationship between 'public' principles and 'market' structures is a varying one, with different kinds of hybrid system – some showing more tension and contradiction than others – as well as examples of almost 'pure' extremes. 'Public service' approaches often rely on a good measure of public subsidy and attempt to provide a television service which reflects and supports the needs of political democracy and a public, if also plural, culture. The variations of 'free market' provision, whatever the adjudged quality of their output, necessarily relate primarily to viewers as consumers and have, in the end, to regard profitability as of more importance than public function.

Sylvia Harvey provides a case-study in interplay and tension in her account of the setting up and first decade of Britain's Channel 4. This channel, with its protected funding arrangements (now revised), its advertising, its widespread experimentation and its attempt to respond to the breadth and diversity of British culture, has been seen as a new and progressive kind of 'mix' in the organization of broadcasting. It has drawn international attention, sometimes acting as a model for other initiatives where public values are combined with market success and limited subsidy. Harvey places the development of this channel in the context of the British political and cultural changes and contradictions of the 1980s and explores its particular difficulties, which persist despite its record of achievement.

A valuable feature of this account is the way in which it shows a new idea about broadcasting coming to a realization within specific historical and changing circumstances. Having looked at both the kinds of friend and the kinds of enemy which the channel has made, Harvey concludes with some observations on its future within the new conditions for national television in Britain. These observations have relevance for an understanding of the changing shape of television services internationally.

In November 1992, as Channel 4 celebrated its tenth anniversary and its 10 per cent share of the audience, it seemed as though it had always been there, a venerable landmark, taken for granted and helping to shape the contours of contemporary British television.

But, of course, it is a relative newcomer; and its birth was a complex affair. In order to understand its emergence as an institution, we need to unravel some of the complex threads of historical change and development in the relations between British broadcasting and the state; and to have some sense of the relative weight of individual passions, political priorities and economic realities in the unfolding of that relationship. This institution did not drop from the skies in response to a few lines in the British Parliament's Broadcasting Act of 1980. It was pushed into existence by many people, acting sometimes together, sometimes at cross-purposes, and under more or less favourable conditions. Its birth was no accident, its upbringing carefully planned, and its financial needs were secured in advance. It did not always fulfil the hopes and dreams of its progenitors, but a considerable achievement it nonetheless was. It was probably the only television channel in the world with a legislative requirement to *experiment*, to *innovate* and to *complement* the service offered by the existing commercial television channel, and all of this on an income guaranteed in advance by its parliamentary godparents, under the direction of a Conservative government.

THE POLITICAL CONTEXT

The Channel Four Company was incorporated in December 1980 as a wholly owned subsidiary of the Independent Broadcasting Authority (IBA) – the body then charged with regulating commercial radio and television. The date is significant in signalling the birth of a new decade whose social, cultural and economic character is often associated with the values and beliefs of the 'New Right' and of the new Conservative Prime Minister, Margaret Thatcher. One of the continuing problems for British Conservatism in the 1980s was to be that of resolving, or attempting to resolve, a conflict between the values of the 'old' and the 'new' right, between a paternalistic and often authoritarian cultural conservativism, and the demands of economic innovation, of letting the market 'rip'. If the one demanded cultural continuity and respect for heritage and the 'great tradition' (in broadcasting as elsewhere), the other proposed the values of a new enterprise culture, the development of more competitive and cost-effective forms of production, and the absolute sovereignty of individual consumers making choices in the market-place.

This tension between the twin poles of heritage and enterprise can be seen to characterize the formulation of Conservative Party policy in the two Broadcasting Acts (1980 and 1990) that mark the beginning and end of the decade.[1] There is a sense in which Channel 4 bears the marks of both tendencies. The idea of public service and public duty, reaching back well over a century into the ethics of the Victorian civil and colonial services, is manifest in the 1980 public service requirement that the new television channel should serve a variety of audience tastes and interests, encourage innovation in programme making and show a suitable proportion of educational programmes. Such detailed specification of programme categories, and the emphasis on complementarity – that new tastes and interests should be served by the new channel – had become almost a hallmark of British broadcasting policy. Certainly up to and including the 1980 Broadcasting Act there had been support from both the Conservative and Labour parties for careful forward planning to ensure choice of programmes, not just choice of channels. This commitment to 'public service' principles and to the fostering of a cultural heritage had historically overridden demands for a 'free market' in broadcasting, and sharply differentiated the British approach from that of the United States, where channel proliferation within an essentially commercial or free market framework had been the outcome of a different sort of public policy.

The enterprising tendency, on the other hand, is manifested in the mode of production selected: the Channel Four Company was to commission or 'publish' programmes, not to make them itself. Programme-making was to happen predominantly out of house in the new lean, fit and flexible independent sector, called into being as a consequence of this policy. The old 'vertical integration' that had characterized the industry, allowing the same organizations to both produce and broadcast, would no longer be the only model for production. The new independents, it was argued, would have more innovative attitudes to doing business, and lower overheads than the lumbering giants who were their parents: the BBC and ITV companies. The newcomers, motivated by an anxious desire to deliver programmes at competitive prices, would ultimately transform the industry as a whole, replacing permanent contracts with freelance employment, and doing away with 'over-manning', along with the company pension schemes, subsidized canteens and childcare facilities that had indirectly increased the costs of production. From a New Right perspective this newly enterprising sector would (quite apart from the more publicly advanced arguments about freedom and diversity of expression) challenge and ultimately change traditional production practices in television.

BEFORE ANNAN: THE PRE-HISTORY OF CHANNEL 4

The Annan Report of 1977, produced under a Labour government, has been seen as a kind of watershed in the history of Channel 4. It argued the case for a 'third force' in British broadcasting to break the duopoly control then exercised by the BBC and commercial television (ITV). But the outcome of the 20-year battle between those who argued for the creation of an ITV2 and those who wanted something completely different was to be a compromise, formulated by a Conservative government, and expressed in the brief but careful wording of the 1980 Broadcasting Act.

The first major contribution to the debate about a structure for the new channel was made by Anthony Smith. Smith had left the BBC in 1971, and was later to become Director of the British Film Institute and a founding member of the board of Channel 4. In a letter to the *Guardian* in April 1972 he outlined, in brief, his ideas for a National Television Foundation (subsequently worked up as a submission to the Annan Committee).

The Foundation, with a very small staff, would act as a kind of publishing house of the air, buying in and broadcasting programmes from a wide variety of sources. It would be open equally to independent programme makers with fully worked out ideas, and to individuals or organisations who had a particular point that they wished to get across to a larger public. Smith argued that the existing broadcasting institutions had become vast and bureaucratic centres of power, corrosive of creative work, inclined to over-careful self-policing and absorbed in the project of their own institutional survival. Faced with the old-fashioned caution of the duopoly he argued for something completely different: 'What has to be achieved is a form of institutional control wedded to a different doctrine from existing broadcasting authorities, to a doctrine of openness rather than to balance, to expression rather than to neutralization.'[2] Moreover, in a pre-figuring of the language of minority television (or of 'niche marketing' in the terms of advertising), Smith identified the possibility of television going beyond the mass audience and towards the discovery of specialized publics, of particular communities of interest.

The philosophy of the Foundation, with its sharp critique of the perceived inadequacies of contemporary television, acted as a rallying point for many who had become disenchanted with the bland or censorious nature of the medium. However, its address to the issue of funding was regarded as problematic in some quarters, relying as it did upon a mixture of sponsorship, grants from educational and other sources, block advertising and government subvention. Others from within the world of television, and moved by similar concerns, were to develop rather more pragmatic proposals in respect of finance.

In a submission to the Minister in 1973, David Elstein and John Birt (then both at London Weekend Television[3]) argued that the new channel should be developed by the regulator of commercial television: the IBA. The IBA should appoint a programme controller. The existing commercial television contractors, ITV, should then be allowed to sell the advertising airtime for the fourth channel within their own regions, but should not be allowed to control the schedule. They would compete with other independent producers to supply programmes; programme ideas would be selected on merit alone. These would be paid for by a levy on the additional advertising revenue, collected by the IBA. Broadly similar proposals were made by Jeremy Isaacs, then Controller of Features at Thames Television.[4] What Isaacs, Birt and Elstein shared with Anthony Smith was a desire to liberate the creative people in television from the often stifling effects of bureaucracy, and to find a way to ensure – *systematically*, not, as it were, by accident – that new things could be said in new ways. If they lacked the institutional radicalism represented by the National Television Foundation proposal, they none the less shared its aims, and understood some of the practical means required to achieve a greater pluralism and diversity of the airwaves. The best of causes require resources and allies in order to be realized, and their quietly effective memos to the Minister acknowledged two key factors: the importance of advertising revenue for the new endeavour, and the need to seek accommodation with (but not surrender to) the barons of ITV. In the absence of a government with a radical public service bent and money to spend, their pragmatism was ultimately to win the day. [. . .]

The key provisions of the 1980 Broadcasting Act can be briefly summarised (these provisions, with the exception of the IBA ownership arrangements, were carried over almost unchanged into the 1990 Act). The IBA was required to ensure that the Channel 4 service would contain 'a suitable proportion of matter calculated to appeal to tastes and interests not generally catered for by ITV' and a 'suitable proportion of programmes . . . of an educational nature'; it was also to 'encourage innovation and experiment in the form and content of programmes'.[5]

It was left to the IBA to decide upon the appropriate institutional form for Channel

4 and to collect an annual subscription from all the ITV companies to meet its costs. In return, the ITV companies were allowed to sell the advertising airtime on the new channel within their own regions, thus maintaining their monopoly control of airtime sales.

The Act also responded to the vigorous campaigning that had taken place in Wales for the creation of a prime-time Welsh-language channel. A Welsh Fourth Channel Authority was established, Sianel Pedwar Cymru (S4C), and the IBA was to ensure that S4C received an adequate amount of advertising revenue: approximately 20 per cent of the total amount collected from the ITV companies. [. . .]

CHANNEL 4: THE FIRST TEN YEARS

A changing cultural context

Channel 4's parliamentary remit to 'encourage innovation and experiment in the form and content of programmes', together with the view expressed by Jeremy Isaacs, that it should be for 'all of the people some of the time', seemed to provide the basis for a service that was prepared to edge well beyond the previously established limits of broadcasting expression. The first ten years of output can be roughly divided into the periods corresponding to the appointment of the first two Chief Executives: Jeremy Isaacs (1981–87) and Michael Grade (1988–   ). [. . .]

Programme transmissions began in November 1982, the month after the Falklands/Malvinas victory parade and a year after the riots in Brixton and Toxteth. With the wisdom of hindsight, it is possible to see the Falklands victory parade as in some sense a signal for the passing of an old order. No amount of prime ministerial rhetoric about Britain being 'great again' in the wake of this war could stop a growing public recognition that the country had lived through its last days of imperial glory, and needed to discover a new economic centre of gravity and a new role in world affairs.

Channel 4 was to grow in, and try to reflect, a climate of accelerating social and cultural change, with new attitudes to national identity, family life, public services, sex and money. In attempting to pull within the frame of television what had previously been either excluded or treated in a bland or simplistic way, it had to represent (in both factual and fictional programmes) a range of contemporary issues from rising female expectations and a rocketing divorce rate, to a growing number of home owners as well as of homeless people. Its difficult task, with the liberal encouragement of the new Broadcasting Act behind it, was to give a voice to the new pluralism of the 1980s: that explosive mixture of racial hatred with new multi-racial and multi-cultural tolerance, of the quest for sex equality with the consolidation of new forms of male supremacism, of a new tolerance in matters of sexual orientation with outbursts of homophobic hysteria, of a commitment to the welfare state with the argument that its existence was incompatible with the principle of a free market.

The development of the new channel beyond the moment of its legislative conception was to be fashioned by a culture both more pluralistic and more stratified than that of the two preceding decades: a greater variety of ideas and lifestyles, sharper extremes of wealth and poverty, more ferocious political and ideological disagreements, together with a general lessening of public interest in official politics.

In its early days, a greater frankness about the varieties of human sexuality and a more realistic and relaxed representation of everyday speech got Channel 4 into deep trouble with sections of the mass-circulation press. The tabloids attacked the showing of a programme exploring gay lifestyles, *One in Five*, scheduled for New Year's Day 1983, and the *Sun* ran what it called a 'filth count' of the language used in the channel's first month of broadcasting.[6] Subsequently (in 1986), the broadcaster was to experiment with the use of a small red triangle in the corner of the television screen, to indicate material that might be offensive to some. This experiment was discontinued when puritan campaigners persuaded major advertisers to avoid such programmes. But the channel's willingness to engage with its audience's interest in sexual matters, whether in *Out on Tuesday* (1988) or *Sex Talk* (1990), was to expand the horizons of what was possible in television in general. Without its new, often forthright, witty and imaginative approach it would be difficult to imagine the appearance of Carlton's *The Good Sex Guide* on mainstream ITV at the beginning of 1993. In this sense Channel 4 affected the whole ecology of British broadcasting, extending the range of subjects that might be dealt with by television.

In the representation of working life other, less sympathetic cultural and political forces could be seen at work. The programme for trade unionists, *Union World* (1984–5), was to disappear in the course of the 1980s. It was not to be replaced by a similar strand.

In political and ideological debates, in respect of 'balance' and 'impartiality' and in the representation of historical and current affairs material, the channel was also to cause offence to some powerful (and less powerful) people. *The Friday Alternative* (1982–3), which had been set up to provide a critical commentary on the week's news from a variety of viewpoints, was axed after less than a year on the grounds of consistent left-wing bias. Jeremy Isaacs recognised a distinction between 'one-off' opinionated programmes and *series* which consistently advanced the same opinions, and could therefore be taken to undermine the requirement of balance. The first chairman of Channel 4's board, Edmund Dell, was highly critical of *The Friday Alternative* with its irreverent, witty and 'straight to the point' attack on traditional news values and approaches – though, interestingly, one outcome of the cutting of this series and of several bruising encounters between the channel's Chief Executive and its Chairman was the policy assertion by Isaacs that 'We have firmly established the notion that television programmes from a variety of sources may express explicit opinion, without upset to the body politic.'[7] This advocacy and representation of strong opinion was to be furthered through two long-running programme slots: *Opinions*, a 30-minute slot, usually given to well-known speakers, and *Comment*, a three-minute slot after the evening news, given to anyone who had a point of view to put across. One notable blow for opinionated pluralism was struck shortly after the channel went on air, when the socialist historian and anti-nuclear campaigner E.P. Thompson was awarded the *Opinions* platform, having just been turned down for a series of lectures by the BBC.[8]

In other areas too, the taken-for-granted centrism of British televisual life was challenged: in the development of caustic comedy, whether *The Comic Strip Presents . . . The Strike* (1988) or *Crimestrike* (1990); in programmes by women: the original Broadside current affairs series of 1983; or in feature films like *Hush A Bye Baby* (1990) delicately considering the issue of unwanted pregnancy in Catholic Northern Ireland; or *Dream On* (1992) exploring the defiant attitudes of working-class women coping with constant crisis on Tyneside; in positive and witty explorations of gay life, *Out on Tuesday*, 1989; in the presentation of fact and fiction from the 'Third World' (the *Africa on Africa* season of 1984, the series *South* in 1991), and in a rich variety of films by black British film-makers: *Handsworth Songs* (1987), *Playing Away* (1986) and *Looking for Langston* (1990).

Some historical series were highly innovative, and difficult to fault in terms of balance. For example, *Wales: The Dragon Has Two Tongues* (1984), financed by Naomi Sargant, the channel's first Senior Commissioning Editor for Education, was a 13-part series in which two historians, one Marxist and one more conservative, argued over their conflicting interpretations of Welsh history. Another major series, produced by Central for Channel 4, was *Vietnam: A Television History* (1984), exploring, among other things, Britain's difficult and close relationship with the United States. Other 'people's stories', drawing on a rich new vein of oral history in contemporary historiography, accompanied the major series: two examples of this, from Television History Workshop, were *Making Cars* (1983) and *City General* (1984). A far more controversial history, pushing many of the panic buttons of high-level outrage, was *Greece: The Hidden War* (1986); this offered a critical examination of a little-known aspect of recent British history, namely, the highly partisan role played by the British army in relationship to domestic Greek politics, towards the end of the Second World War. Strong complaints were made by powerful figures in the British military establishment.

Isaacs himself offers some useful comments on this novel process whereby entrenched and established views were challenged for the first time *on television*:

> I had never doubted, thinking too much television too unthinking, too bland, that Channel 4 would broadcast programmes that put, as forcibly as possible, a forcible point of view. I had not appreciated, and still find hard to understand, how offensive to some this turned out to be. People had no objection to an opinion strongly expressed in a newspaper, in a railway carriage, in a saloon bar. Why object to opinionated television? Perhaps they only enjoyed reading their own opinions in newspapers, and not the other fellow's at all.[9]

It remains to be seen whether or not the new requirements on 'impartiality', written into the Broadcasting Act of 1990, and the subject of much controversy at the time, are used to stifle the expression of strong opinions. In 1991 the conservative Freedom Association had attempted to take Channel 4 to court over its screening of a programme putting the view of Americans opposed to the war in the Gulf: *Hell, No, We Won't Go* [...]

Programme costs, suppliers and the principle of diversity

Channel 4 might be said to have had two distinct but interrelated purposes: to introduce stylistic and content innovations into British television, and to introduce new industrial structures for the production of programmes. This latter aim was accomplished by the creation of an independent sector, which has grown since the passage of the 1990 Broadcasting Act with its legal requirement that both BBC and ITV commission 25 per cent of their original output from out of house.

A few general observations about costs may be helpful here. First, Channel 4 is a modestly resourced operation. It took around five years to break even (by 1987 the value of the airtime sold on the channel amounted to a little more than its costs). In 1991 its average hourly programme cost was £27,600, and it spent the largest single share of its income on Drama, closely followed by Entertainment, News and Documentaries.[10] By 1991, over half of its originally commissioned programmes were being made in the independent sector (52 per cent as against 48 per cent produced by ITV and ITN), and these were supplied by a total of 668 (mostly small) production companies. [...]

While it is true that Channel 4 provides some opportunities for first-time film-makers and for those who would otherwise have no access to television, the problem for the small independents is 'how to survive' in the face of radical uncertainty about the renewal of production contracts. As the individuals who make up the sector get older, take on domestic commitments and realize the benefits of secure employment, a predictable income, sick pay, paid holidays and properly resourced pensions, their commitment to working in a radically insecure sector inevitably diminishes. It is appropriate, therefore, to ask whose cultural and economic interests are served by the maintenance of this sector and this 'miniature' mode of production. And to what extent are freedom and diversity of expression safeguarded for the television audience by this system of production?

Certainly, many independent producers are experiencing almost intolerable living and working conditions, and yet this sector continues to be the preferred free market policy instrument for implementing the commitment to cultural diversity. There is a tense play-off here between the values of 'heritage' and those of 'enterprise', as discussed at the beginning of this essay. For that variant of broadcasting heritage which involves a commitment to cultural pluralism is underwritten by the 'enterprising' methods of a dependent-independent production sector which may find it difficult to reproduce itself in the long term.

The audience

Across the ten years of its history, from 1982 to 1992, Channel 4's voices of dissent, difference and even alarming experiment have gathered and consolidated audiences across the boundaries of class, race, gender and age. While it remained a minority channel, with its share of the total TV audience rising from 4.7 per cent in 1984 to 9.8 per cent by the end of 1991, it avoided the 'ghetto' trap of always reaching the same small number of people. This is shown by the 'reach' of its programmes, and the number of people who watch it at some time. In its early years some 50 per cent of the television audience viewed something on the channel in any one week; by 1991 that figure had risen to 79 per cent a *week*, and it achieved in the same year a reach of 93 per cent of the population in the course of an average *month*.[11] [...]

In social class terms, as the channel's Annual Reports regularly point out, a good proportion of its audience is within the 'upmarket' socio-economic range ABC1; it also attracts proportionately more younger viewers than ITV.[12] Whether this profile, which is extremely attractive to some advertisers, will ultimately put pressure on the channel to cater principally to the 'upmarket' and youth audiences remains to be seen.

Achievements and future prospects

The 1990 Broadcasting Act preserved some, but not all, of the features established for

Channel 4 by the 1980 Act. The original programming philosophy was retained. The new Act required the channel to encourage 'innovation and experiment in the form and content' of programmes, and to 'appeal to tastes and interests not generally catered for by Channel 3'.

Outright privatization was avoided, though the channel ceased to be a wholly owned subsidiary of the regulatory body. A new corporation was created, whose members were to be appointed by the Independent Television Commission (which replaced the IBA in 1991), and the umbilical link with the ITV companies was broken, as the new corporation was empowered to sell its own advertising. Although this change was designed to inject competition into the sale of airtime (and to end the role of the ITC as 'tax collector' for the channel), nonetheless some element of symbiosis in the relationship between ITV and Channel 4 was retained through the 'safety net' provisions.

Under these arrangements, if the channel's revenue dipped below 14 per cent of total (terrestrial) television advertising revenue, the ITV companies would be required to step in and contribute up to 2 per cent of that total amount. If, however, Channel 4 succeeded in acquiring more than 14 per cent, then any surplus would be divided evenly between itself and the ITV companies. Because of this mechanism the ITV companies have some financial interest in the success of their rival, and this is likely to ameliorate the more savage forms of competition for audiences and for the sale of airtime which might otherwise have occurred.

Separate arrangements for Wales ensure the continuation of S4C. A new Welsh Authority has been created for this purpose, receiving direct government funding of 3.2 per cent of total television advertising revenue each year. This figure is not dependent upon the amount of airtime actually sold by S4C, and the Act commits the Secretary of State to paying this amount out of public funds. If S4C had been made dependent upon the value of its own airtime sales this would have amounted to only a fraction of its costs. In 1991 the value of its airtime was £3.5 million, while the amount which it received through the ITC subscription, then collected from the ITV companies, was £58 million.[13] It is clear that this arrangement is based upon a political recognition of the demands of Welsh cultural nationalism (exemplified by the strong campaign conducted in Wales in 1980) rather than upon free market principles.

In avoiding both a private shareholding solution for Channel 4 and the creation of head-on competition with ITV (for the same audiences at the same time) the long-established public policy principle that audiences should be offered programme choice, not just channel choice, continued to be upheld.

However, it remains to be seen to what extent Channel 4 comes under internal or external pressure to maximize its audience, and to prioritize the kinds of programmes that attract the kinds of viewers that advertisers most want to reach. The presence of airtime sales staff *within* the institution seems likely to affect commissioning and scheduling decisions (how could it not do so since the advertisers pay for the programmes, however indirectly?). It will take considerable managerial skill and a clear cultural vision to hold onto the genuinely pluralistic programming policies established in the 1980s. In recognizing both the practical and political difficulties involved in implementing such policies, and their social importance, it may be worth remembering some comments made by Jeremy Isaacs in 1983:

It is cardinal, surely, to broadcasting in a free, pluralist society, that all sectors of society should be fairly represented on the screen. Tapping those new sources of energy, letting those voices (within an overall obligation to fairness) come through, is both Channel 4's most challenging task, and the practice that evokes most hostility.[14]

NOTES

The dates given for films and programmes in this article are the dates of television transmission, not of production.

1. J. Corner and S. Harvey (eds.), *Enterprise and heritage: cross currents of national culture* (London, Routledge, 1991).
2. A. Smith, 'The National Television Foundation – a plan for the fourth channel', evidence to the Annan Committee on the Future of Broadcasting, December 1974. Reprinted as Appendix II in A. Smith, *The shadow in the cave: a study of the relationship between the broadcaster, his audience and the state* (London, Quartet Books, 1976).
3. Birt was later to become Director-General of the BBC.
4. S. Lambert, *Channel Four: television with a difference?* (London, British Film Institute, 1982), pp. 158–60; J. Isaacs, *Storm over Four: a personal account* (London, Weidenfeld & Nicolson, 1989), pp. 200–2.
5. Broadcasting Act 1980 (London, HMSO, 1980).
6. S. Lambert, 'Isaacs still smiling', *Stills* 6 (1983), pp. 25, 27.
7. Isaacs, *Storm over Four*, pp. 82–6, 88.
8. Isaacs, *Storm over Four*, pp. 53–5.
9. Isaacs, *Storm over Four*, p. 53.
10. Channel 4, *Report and accounts for the year ended 31 December, 1991* (London, Channel 4, 1992), p. 13.
11. Channel 4, *Report and accounts 1991*, p. 10.
12. Channel 4, *Report and accounts 1991*, p. 11.
13. Independent Television Commission, *1991 report and accounts* (London, ITC, 1992), pp. 46, 56.
14. Isaacs, *Storm over Four*, p. 76.

21

Public television: the historical and political context

William Hoynes

From Hoynes, W. 1995: *Public television for sale: media, the market and the public sphere.* Boulder, CO, and Oxford: Westview Press, 1–23, 103–5, 108

Public television was a relatively late arrival on the American scene, established as a result of the 1967 Public Broadcasting Act, a part of President Johnson's 'Great Society' programme. Before this date broadcasting had been privately owned, resolutely commercial and largely advertiser-financed. Federal government was limited to the role of merely allocating frequencies and 'light touch' regulation. Moreover, under the First Amendment to the Constitution, government was clearly probibited from any interference with freedom of speech or of the press; 'free speech' rights had been denied to the cinema but broadcasters were keen to claim them.

In many European countries, by contrast, governments had played a much greater part in setting up and even in running broadcasting stations. In Britain the government had established a compulsory licence fee as early as 1922 and this was to become the exclusive source of finance for the British Broadcasting Corporation, set up as a non-profit institution in 1927. The BBC was supposedly to operate independently of government, though its governors were appointed by the relevant Minister, and it was required to provide a universal service which would 'inform, educate and entertain'. Over the years the BBC has come in for considerable amounts of both political and cultural criticism, and yet its licence fee funding has allowed it to provide a cost-effective service to the population at large, holding on to over 40 per cent of the total television audience and a wide measure of public support well into the 1990s.

Public television in the United States has been managed and financed since 1967 by the Corporation for Public Broadcasting (CPB), which is in turn funded by Congress as part of the annual federal budget appropriations. It has attracted only a very small proportion of the television audience. Arguably it is handicapped (though some see it as a strength) by spreading its already limited production funds across a multitude of small local stations, rather than concentrating its funding centrally and producing a smaller number of well-resourced programmes for a national network. If the BBC might be criticized for being overly centralist, American public television might be seen as the victim of an overly 'localist' strategy and suffering the hard economic and cultural consequences of this.

William Hoynes, in the extracts from his book which are included here, offers a succinct account of the emergence of public television in America, a thoughtful analysis of those social forces and actors who have made it strong or weak, and a vigorous argument about why it might be worth preserving. Hoynes outlines the part played by President Nixon in attacking the CPB as a 'centralist' organization, suggesting that this attack and the 1972 veto on funding was in fact motivated by a fear that public television might become the effective vehicle of liberal ideas. However, the retreat to localism, then seen as a line of defence for public broadcasting, may in fact have provided the basis for its permanent disadvantage, just as underfunding from the public purse led to a strategy of seeking corporate sponsorship finance, thereby limiting its capacity to produce controversial programmes.

Since its inception, American television has been organized by the principles of the free market. Although early regulatory statements suggested that television airwaves are a kind of public utility, and although federal government licenses are necessary to operate a broadcast outlet, television in the United States always has been fundamentally a private industry. In this regard, the United States stands in marked contrast to Europe, where television has been perceived as a scarce public resource, too important to be left simply to market forces. By the 1960s, concerns about the relationship between television, the market, and the quality of public life surfaced in the United States. Critics argued that commercial television's reliance on advertiser revenue and its need to attract a mass audience made it structurally incapable of serving the broader cultural, informational, and educational functions of a democratic mass communication system. In this view, the market orientation of American television was seen as its principal constraint. Rather than fundamentally restructuring the commercial television industry, reformers created a new institution, public television, to help fulfill the communication needs of a democratic citizenry.

In this book, I examine that system of public television, now represented by the Corporation for Public Broadcasting (CPB), the Public Broadcasting Service (PBS), and local public television stations. When a national public television system was first proposed by the Carnegie Commission on Educational Television in its January 1967 report, it was designed as a uniquely American institution, one that would be supported, but not controlled, by the federal government. The Carnegie Commission argued that the new system had a crucial role to play in a democratic society and urged the federal government to act immediately to establish a national public television entity.

SHIFTING POLITICAL PRESSURES: FROM JOHNSON TO REAGAN

In November 1967 President Lyndon Johnson signed the Public Broadcasting Act, which created the Corporation for Public Broadcasting and set the stage for the development of the current system of public broadcasting in the United States. The Public Broadcasting Act, which was first discussed in Congress only nine months before its passage, was one of the final pieces of Johnson's Great Society program – indeed, the only piece of communications legislation that was part of the Great Society. The rapidity with which it moved through the legislative process – now almost unheard of – reflected the firm consensus that the United States needed a healthy, federally funded, noncommercial television system. In the twenty-five years since the passage of the Public Broadcasting Act, the structure of public television has evolved, adapting both to the continuing growth of the public television system and, more dramatically, to changing political pressures.

The history of public broadcasting has been well told elsewhere,[1] and I do not intend to review all of the details. However, in order to understand the current state of public television and the dilemmas and contradictions it now faces, we need to begin with a brief historical overview. Because external political pressure has played such an important role in public television's history, we should be particularly concerned with the changing political climate and how public broadcasters have responded to it.

Since its earliest days, there has been a slow but steady privatization of public television. This trend is partially a result of the fact that fear of political control by the federal government has always outweighed fear of commercialization in public television circles. This attitude should not be surprising, because it reflects the broader political culture in the United States, in which intervention by 'big government' in any arena of community life is immediately suspect.[2] Fears of state involvement, however, were not based simply on abstract popular notions. The formative experiences of many public broadcasters gave them good reason to watch out for government intervention, particularly from the White House.[3]

Rather than model American public television after state television in Europe, the designers of the system sought to avoid state control and suggested an administrative and financial structure to prevent it. The Public Broadcasting Act, however, only set up an administrative structure (CPB),[4] leaving the financing to the federal government's regular appropriations process. As a result, the funding of public broadcasting – even when money is authorized on a three-year basis, two years in advance, as it has been since the late 1970s – has always been a politically charged issue, with partisan debates about 'bias' and 'objectivity' a regular feature of the funding process.

Early proponents suggested that the only way to prevent such a politicization of the funding process was to provide stable, long-term funding for public television.[5] Although President Johnson indicated in 1967 that a long-range funding plan would be worked out in the coming year, his ultimate withdrawal from the 1968 presidential race left public broadcasting without such a plan. The election of Richard Nixon brought new problems for the fledgling public television system. From Nixon's perspective, particularly as the Vietnam War continued to drag on, public television was a home for liberal journalists who produced biased news and public affairs programs with the help of federal funds.

By 1970, the Nixon administration was unhappy with the broadcasting of such documentaries as *Banks and the Poor*,[6] which critically examined banking practices that exacerbated poverty in urban areas and 'closed with a list of 133 senators and congressmen with banking holdings or serving as directors of banks – while the "Battle Hymn of the Republic" played in the background' (Stone, 1985, p. 29). As such, the White House made plans to rein in public television. Federal funding was the weak link in the plan to insulate public television from political pressures, so the administration focused its strategy on the appropriation of money for CPB. On June 30, 1972, President Nixon vetoed CPB's authorization bill, arguing that public television had become too centralized and was becoming a 'fourth network'. In criticizing CPB and the supposed centralization of the system, the administration had hoped to capitalize on the confusion about the evolving relationship between CPB, PBS, and the local stations. In retrospect, it seems clear that Nixon's call for a return to 'the bedrock of localism', as the administration put it, was a cover for the more political problems the administration had with the system – particularly with several members of the CPB board, who were perceived as too liberal and unwilling to work with the administration, and with CPB's relationship to National Educational Television (NET), one of the principal programmers for the young public television system and producer of *Banks and the Poor*. However, as Witherspoon and Kovitz (1987) suggested, the Nixon administration was concerned about the consequences of directly attacking public affairs programs. Its goal of changing the makeup of the CPB board and steering public television away from the production of nationally distributed public affairs programs could be accomplished by focusing on the role of CPB instead of on the particular programs. Such a strategy was intended to shield the White House from the argument that it was interfering politically with public television or that it intended any form of 'censorship'. To a great extent, the strategy worked: over the next two months, the chairman, president, and director of television for CPB resigned. At the end of August, after these resignations had been accepted, Nixon signed a bill authorizing public broadcasting funding for 1973.

The political struggle between Nixon and CPB had three important, and lasting, consequences. First, it showed that public broadcasting was vulnerable to political pressure, particularly from the White House. Its vulnerability came from a predictable source: the fact that the federal government had to regularly approve its funding. Second, it meant that public television had to establish mechanisms to protect itself, as much as possible, from the political pressures it was likely to face in the future. This necessity led to the development of a new, decentralized method for distributing production funds, the Station Program Cooperative (SPC), which would be a central component of the public television programming process from 1974 to 1990.[7] The creation of the SPC was one sign of a broader trend to diffuse the potential targets of political pressure by shifting programming decisions away from CPB. Third, the public television system realized that it needed to look for additional sources of revenue, particularly from the private sector, in order to reduce its dependence on the highly politicized federal appropriations process. Specifically, the Nixon veto led public television producers to turn their attention to corporate underwriting, initially from major oil companies, as a new source of program financing.

These three consequences – vulnerability to presidential political pressure, a reorganization of the relationship between local stations and the national public television system, and the reliance on corporate underwriting dollars – can be seen as a set of recurring issues in the history of public television. The 1972 Nixon veto set the tone, and provided a framework, for the ongoing political contest about the need for, and structure of, the public television system.

In contrast to the Nixon years,[8] Carter's presidency was relatively quiet for public television, which continued to grow. Congressional Democrats had traditionally been supporters of public television (and, for the most part, continue to be), and the lack of tension between public television and the Democratic administration served as a temporary respite from political pressure. When Ronald Reagan became president in 1981, however, public television faced renewed political and economic pressures from the White House. On one level, the hostility to public television was philosophical: the Reagan White House supported wide-ranging deregulation, and it frowned upon a host of federally funded programs. As a result, federally funded public television was, to say the least, not a favored institution in the Reagan administration. On another level the hostility was more partisan, as the old claim of a liberal bias in public television, last heard from the Nixon administration, was once again in the news. Such philosophical differences and partisan political charges did have material consequences. The Reagan administration pushed forward funding reductions for public television through the 1981 Public Broadcasting Amendments Act, and federal funding of public television was under siege again.

The reduction of federal support and the simultaneous deregulation of commercial television were not the only signs of a renewed emphasis on the market orientation of the television industry. In 1984 the Federal Communications Commission (FCC) broadened its guidelines for the identification of corporate underwriter support on public television programs, allowing commercial-like announcements at the beginning and end of programs. Rather than simply allowing 'advertising' on public television, the new regulations, labeled 'enhanced underwriting', permitted 'logos or slogans that identify – but do not promote or compare – locations, value-neutral descriptions of a product line or service, trade names, and product or service listings' (Witherspoon and Kovitz, 1987, p. 56). Not only was the commercial television industry becoming less regulated and therefore less accountable to any measure of the public interest beyond audience ratings, public television itself was – as a result of federal funding cuts and new underwriting codes – becoming more commercial.

THE PRIVATIZATION OF PUBLIC TELEVISION

In the spring of 1992, public television became the subject of national discussion once again. It made newspaper headlines, aroused a great deal of attention on Capitol Hill, and even was the subject of campaign advertisements by one Republican presidential candidate. The attention was not, however, due to the release of another highly acclaimed documentary, such as *Vietnam: A Television History* or *The Civil War*, both of which had catapulted PBS into the national spotlight in previous years. On the contrary, the attention in the first half of 1992 was neither triggered by a particular PBS program nor encouraged by public television executives. It represented, to be sure, the most powerful threat to the survival of a public television system since the 1972 Nixon veto: the growing movement toward the privatization of public institutions.

The process of privatization, as such, does not occur spontaneously, any more than the initial creation of the public sector did. Nor is it simply the product of a particular *zeitgeist*, such as the market fetishism emerging in the post–cold war era in the United States. Privatization must be understood as part of the larger ongoing contest over how societies are to be organized, the social relations of both production and consumption. Occurring at a time in which the collapse of the Soviet Union is taken as the ultimate victory of capitalism – and in which the economic and moral superiority of the free market is celebrated uncritically – the call of privatization must be seen as the work of those social strata, led by corporate America, that have historically had little need for a public sector and will, not surprisingly, benefit most directly from privatization. Although the erosion of the public sector seems to take on a life of its own in a recessionary economic climate – particularly when such an economic climate is combined with a growing perception that some people are 'dependent' upon the public sector and others are not[9] – we must avoid the tendency to forget the actual human agency, in the form of organized political activity, that is the driving force behind movements toward privatization.

This is the context in which public television made headlines in early 1992. At a time when the survival of the National Endowment for the Arts (NEA) appeared in jeopardy and the commitment to public education seemed to be wavering, public television, much to the dismay of its principals, momentarily took center stage in the debate over the future of the public sector. The proximate source of the widespread attention was the organized attack on public television by a coalition of conservative organizations, led by the Heritage Foundation, at a time when Congress was to consider the reauthorization of funding for public broadcasting. The substance of the attack was not new, although its increased vigor gave the impression of being something different. The outcome, at least in the short run, was also reminiscent of previous debates, as a Democrat-controlled Congress passed the reauthorization bill but attached tighter strings. Perhaps the only truly new aspect of this contest was the post–cold war political climate that celebrated the market in a quasi-religious manner, a climate in which the privatization of public television seemed to have become a viable option.

The 1992 debate about public television, much like those that occurred under Nixon and Reagan, illuminates a great deal about the historical tensions, both economic and political, inherent in the public television system in the United States. Since this book [*Public television for sale*] is about the current state of public television – indeed, the very meaning of the term 'public' television – the story of the 1992 conservative attack and its consequences is a particularly useful place to begin.

1992: RENEWED ATTACK ON PUBLIC TELEVISION

The conservative attack on PBS came from two apparently contradictory directions. Any contradiction, however, was superficial; it is more useful to see the two strategies as complementary. Laurence Jarvik, the Bradley Resident Scholar at the Heritage Foundation, was the principal representative of one strategy; David Horowitz of the Committee for Media Integrity was the public face of the second strategy. Jarvik's January 1992 report, 'Making public television public', was distributed by the Heritage Foundation and quoted widely in the mass media; in it, contrary to the title of the report, he argued for the wholesale *privatization* of public television. The rationale for such an argument was twofold: (1) television, in principle, should be a private enterprise, and (2) the particular institutions that make up the public television system had outlived their usefulness. As such, Jarvik's plan for making public television public was to sell the Corporation for Public Broadcasting to the private sector. Ultimately, Jarvik (1992a, p. 12) argued that 'privatization provides the means to clean up the public television mess by creating incentives for excellence, efficiency and accountability. It is time to privatize public television.'[10]

Horowitz, rather than argue for the total privatization of public television, focused his attack on the politics of public television programming. Horowitz's claims of a systematic left-wing bias in public television, based on anecdotal evidence and made in a vituperative tone, made for good newspaper copy and lively talk show debates. His call for Congress to reassert political control over public broadcasting by ensuring 'objectivity' and 'balance' on public television found support among conservatives in the US Senate. Ultimately, Horowitz's assertions of left-wing bias, perhaps more than Jarvik's call for the privatization of public television, framed the congressional debate about public television in the months to follow.

The two positions – one calling for the government to take a more active role in regulating the political content of public television, the other suggesting the complete privatization of public television – may appear antithetical. However, as Jarvik's heavy reliance on Horowitz's argument makes clear, they are two sides of the same coin. What they share is a desire to impose new constraints – in one case political, in the other, economic – on a public television system that has been at least partially removed from such regulation in the past. Moreover, increased state intervention is the centerpiece of an intermediate strategy, one that accepts the short-term existence of public television; the call for privatization is part of a longer-term strategy to eliminate public broadcasting altogether. We can see a similar phenomenon with the attack on the NEA in the early 1990s, where the reassertion of political control may be the first step toward total dissolution.

The combined argument for further state control of public television and total privatization, then, highlights the principal questions for the future of public television: what is the relationship between a *public* television system and both market and state? What, indeed, does it mean to be a *public* institution at a time of rapid privatization? These are ultimately the questions that animate this study of public television. [...]

FUNDING CONTROVERSIAL PROGRAMS

Public television workers have a clear understanding of why corporations fund public television, as well as what they will and will not fund. As such, I heard repeatedly that corporations will not support 'controversial' programming. Several producers noted that they had worked on programs for which corporate dollars were impossible to raise because the programs were 'too controversial'. One producer suggested that 'it is a question of corporate willingness to take risks ... The problem is that whatever program we do, there's probably somebody who's unhappy ... It isn't quite the subject or editorial control or anything like that. I think it has to do with their name associated with something that made somebody unhappy.' Another producer explained why some programs are too controversial for corporations, arguing that the reasons are content-specific. 'It means, practically speaking, that no corporation wants to be identified with that subject. And it means that the corporate funders who are close to the issue worry that you are going to be fair to the controversy and therefore deleterious to their interest.' As a result, any program with potential for controversy is perceived by producers as an unlikely candidate for corporate funding. One staffer suggested that it is not simply programs that are obviously controversial, but public affairs programming in general, for which it is difficult (perhaps even impossible) to bring in corporate underwriters.

This perspective suggests that there are a whole range of programs that do not have access to corporate dollars. This is not to say that only procorporate programming can be produced; clearly, corporate underwriting is only one source of funding for public television. However, it is an important source of funding, one that can be the difference between a program proposal's ending up in production or in a file cabinet.

Nor does this mean that programs that accept corporate dollars become slaves to corporate interests. In fact, my interviews indicate that there is a very strong sense that underwriters must keep their noses out of the production process. As one producer put it, 'more sophisticated funders understand that they can't call the shots'. If an underwriter did try to interfere directly, the attempt would likely backfire, because producers are sensitive to the importance of remaining independent.

The impact of corporate underwriting is much more subtle than direct intervention. The most significant impact of underwriting is that corporate dollars can often be the key variable that determines whether a program will make it on the air. That is, when all other things are equal, the program proposal with access to corporate dollars is more likely to get produced and broadcast. And because controversial programs rarely, if ever, have access to major corporate underwriting dollars, the inevitable result is a narrowing of the range of discourse on public television.

This narrowing operates on two distinct levels. First, major production houses inside the system, in particular WGBH in Boston or WNET in New York, have a limited capacity to raise funds for national programs. They have access to system money (CPB, PBS), foundation grants, corporate underwriting, and some of their own discretionary funds. But there are a limited number of projects that such funding can cover. When producers and managers make calculations about how best to use their time, the funding limits are clearly a factor. Because of the narrow range of programs that corporate funders will support – and according to one of my informants, the National Endowment for the Humanities (NEH) in the late 1980s was similarly narrow in the projects it would fund – potentially controversial programs face an extra obstacle in their pursuit of financial backing. Ultimately, the general understanding of the types of programming corporate underwriters will and will not support influences whether a program proposal will move forward, languish until it disappears, or simply be discarded.

The long-term effects of such a situation may be that the limitations posed by corporate considerations move beyond the realm of rational calculation. As one producer put it, 'people who decide they want to work within the public television structure, they want to make films within this highly bureaucratized organization that really in a way mirrors a corporation. Those people decide to a certain extent they're going to play the game. And so it's a kind of internalized set of understandings about what is and is not acceptable.' Producers have not fully internalized the corporate worldview, and public television is no slave to the corporate agenda. There is no question, however, that the promise of financial support – or the fear of finding no support – not only limits what programs are produced but also limits what programs are even proposed in the first place. [. . .]

Corporate dollars can give programs life and get them on the air; they do not necessarily influence the specific content of particular programs, but they are an important determinant of what viewers ultimately have access to. Potential underwriters make their priorities and interests well known, and PBS and member stations factor this information into their decisionmaking process. Critics who argue that PBS is simply controlled by corporations are missing the more subtle corporate influence that occurs during the idea formation, proposal preparation, and fundraising stages. The fact is that corporate underwriters provide resources for the production and distribution of only a narrow range of programs. [...]

NOTES

1. *See* Witherspoon and Kovitz (1987) for the 'official' history of public broadcasting, a concise report paid for by CPB and distributed by the public broadcasting trade publication *Current*. Rowland (1986) provides a revisionist account of the history of public broadcasting. The 1979 Report of the Carnegie Commission on the Future of Public Broadcasting (known as Carnegie II) also provides a useful early history of public broadcasting. Stone's (1985) analysis of Nixon's relationship to public television includes a detailed history of the years between 1969 and 1974.
2. A large body of recent scholarship has examined the centrality of 'individualism' in American political culture and a corresponding fear of large state structures. *See* Gans (1988), Bellah *et al.* (1985, 1991), and Reinarman (1987) for discussion of these themes.
3. *See* Stone (1985) for an analysis of the Nixon administration's efforts to pressure public television. Lashley (1992) argues that 'executive turnover has profoundly influenced the strategic behavior of public television. Because performance preferences change with each administration, the organizational structure and strategic behavior of this public organization have been adjusted accordingly' (p. 64).
4. We should recognize, however, that even the administrative structure is not totally insulated from the federal government: the president appoints the CPB board.
5. The initial proposal by the Carnegie Commission recommended that an excise tax on the sale of television sets, to be placed in a trust fund specifically for the use of public television, would remove the possibility of politicizing the funding process. Witherspoon and Kovitz note that the idea was a political nonstarter: 'Legislators dislike excise taxes because they are hard to control; economists dislike them because there may not be a connection between the amount of money raised and the amount needed' (1987, p. 14). A more cynical reading is that legislators opposed the excise tax precisely because it would have created a federally funded public television system that was, at the same time, financially autonomous of the federal government.
6. *See* Witherspoon and Kovitz (1987) and Stone (1985) for discussions of the reaction to this particular documentary.
7. Under the SPC, local stations, which received most of CPB's money through community service grants, would decide which programs to support through a complex process of voting. *See* Reeves and Hoffer (1976) and Campbell and Campbell (1978) for a more thorough description of the SPC. Reeves and Hoffer also provide a content analysis of the SPC's first year. They found that '[t]he stations purchased two kinds of proposals: those that were cheap and those already on the air. The first criterion was understandable; there was little money to spend. The second is difficult to reconcile with the lofty statements made by PBS officials and the Carnegie Commission regarding the necessity of risk-taking by public broadcasters. The SPC ventured and gained little' (p. 562). In 1990 the SPC was abolished and the program funding process was centralized under the leadership of PBS's new programming chief, Jennifer Lawson.
8. In 1974, public television was thrust into the middle of national politics again, as it broadcast live the entire set of Watergate hearings. *See* Fletcher (1977) for a discussion of the audience for PBS's coverage and Stone (1985) for a discussion of what he calls the 'poetic symmetry' of public television's broadcasts of the hearings that brought down its nemesis.

9. *See* Coontz (1992) for a thoughtful analysis of the myths associated with the discourse on 'dependence'.
10. *See* Jarvik (1992a, 1992b) and Horowitz (1991) for fuller versions of their own arguments. A variety of critics have responded directly to the substance of these arguments. *See*, for example, Daniel (1992), Grossman (1992), Schone (1992), FAIR (1992), and Ouelette (1991) for analysis and criticism of the conservative mobilization against PBS.

REFERENCES

BELLAH, R.N., MADSEN, R., SULLIVAN, W.M., SWIDLER, A. and TIPTON, S.M. 1985: *Habits of the heart*. Berkeley: University of California Press.

BELLAH, R.N., MADSEN, R., SULLIVAN, W.M., SWIDLER, A. and TIPTON, S.M. 1991: *The good society*. New York: Knopf.

CAMPBELL, D.C. and CAMPBELL, J.B. 1978: Public television as a public good. *Journal of Communication* 28, 52–62.

CARNEGIE COMMISSION ON THE FUTURE OF PUBLIC BROADCASTING 1979: *A public trust*. New York: Bantam.

COONTZ, S. 1992: *The way we never were: American families and the nostalgia trap*. New York: Basic Books.

DANIEL, J. 1992: Uncivil wars: the conservative assault on public broadcasting. *The Independent*, August/September.

FAIRNESS AND ACCURACY IN REPORTING (FAIR) 1992: 'PBS' missing voices. *Extra!*, June.

FLETCHER, J.E. 1977: Commercial versus public television audiences: public activities and the Watergate hearings. *Communication Quarterly* 25(4), 13–16.

GANS, H. 1988: *Middle American individualism*. New York: Free Press.

GANS, H. 1979: *Deciding what's news*. New York: Vintage.

GROSSMAN, L.K. 1992: PBS funding mix helps keep it uniquely free. *Boston Sunday Globe*, 17 May, 84.

HOROWITZ, D. 1991: The politics of public television. *Commentary* 92 (December) 25–32.

JARVIK, L. 1992a: Making public television public. Washington, DC: The Heritage Foundation.

JARVIK, L. 1992b: What price PBS? *Boston Sunday Globe*, 10 May, 73.

LASHLEY, M. 1992: *Public television: panacea, pork barrel, or public trust?* New York: Greenwood Press.

OUELETTE, L. 1991: Right wing vs. public TV. *Media Culture Review* 1, 1.

REEVES, M.G. and HOFFER, T.W. 1976: The safe, cheap and known: a content analysis of the first (1974) PBS program cooperative. *Journal of Broadcasting* 20(4), 549–65.

REINARMAN, C. 1987: *American states of mind*. New Haven, CT: Yale University Press.

ROWLAND, W.D., Jr 1986: Continuing crisis in public broadcasting: a history of disenfranchisement. *Journal of Broadcasting and Electronic Media* 30(3), 251–74.

SCHONE, M. 1992: The Jarvik mart. *Village Voice*, 25 February, 46–7.

STONE, D.M. 1985: *Nixon and the politics of public television*. New York/London: Garland.

WITHERSPOON, J. and KOVITZ, R. 1987: *The history of public broadcasting*. Washington, DC: Current.

22

Globo village: television in Brazil

Roberto Mader

From Dowmunt, T. (ed.) 1993: *Channels of resistance: global television and local empowerment*. London: British Film Institute in Association with Channel 4 Television, 67–89

Brazil is the giant of Latin America with a population of 161 million, and an economy which in terms of per capita output is richer than Poland or Russia and has achieved just over half the level of wealth of its erstwhile European colonizer, Portugal. A study of its television system makes a useful contribution to the 'media imperialism' debate since it seems to provide an exception to the general rule of the export dominance of the countries of the northern hemisphere over those of the south.

Mader's article was written for a book which accompanied a thematic season of programmes: *Channels of Resistance*, broadcast on Britain's Channel 4 in 1993. This season looked at the tendency towards international concentration of media ownership and at alternative examples of vigorous local and indigenous work. The article should be seen in the context of a larger debate, developed principally through the United Nations' cultural organization, UNESCO, which tried to link the principle of political independence from the old colonial powers to the issue of cultural independence. The 1980 MacBride Report, *Many voices, one world*, supported the concept of a 'New World Information and Communications Order' (NWICO), and challenged the dominance of Western news values and sources, and associated inequalities in the field of information and culture. The governments of Britain and the United States responded with considerable hostility to the NWICO proposals, withdrawing their membership and financial support for UNESCO in the mid-1980s.

Mader's analysis approaches the issue of cultural independence from a new and interesting angle, offering an account of the emergence and success of Globo Television. Globo is the major indigenous producer of Brazilian programmes (although the country still imports around 39 per cent of total broadcasting requirements) and has around a 70 per cent share of the national audience. It has attained its dominance, Mader suggests, as a result of three factors: the absence of any historical commitment from the state to the principles of public service broadcasting (little money is spent on educational or factual programming); widespread personal investment by politicians in commercial broadcasting; and the predominance of advertising as a source of revenue. Its near-monopoly control was achieved through a judicious mix of co-operation with the military government after the coup of 1964, the development of popular fictional entertainment programmes (the *tele-novelas*), and the strategic attraction of North American investment which allowed the company to upgrade both its management skills and its technologies.

In a country where more than a quarter of the adult population is illiterate Globo has succeeded not only in dominating the national market but also in creating a significant export market. However, its achievements have been predominantly in the entertainment genre and it has been increasingly criticized both for political bias during election periods and for failing to provide the sort of factual and investigative work that might contribute to the growth of a democratic culture. Mader's article points to the possible conclusion that where commercial broadcasting is entertainment rich, information poor and subject to accusations of political bias, the result is a kind of benign internal imperialism which blocks the attainment of cultural independence and the fostering of cultural and political pluralism.

Brazilian television is one of the most developed systems in the world. It also provides some of the most outrageous examples of the effects deregulation can have. State-run channels are almost non-existent and have insignificant audiences; private networks control the market and dictate the rules. The main network, Globo Television, is well managed and achieves high standards of broadcasting quality, producing 80 per cent of Brazil's programming and employing nearly 15,000 people. It is the fourth largest commercial television network in the world – following ABC, NBC, CBS in the United States – and only in the last few years has it experienced occasional threats to its dominance of the ratings.

Globo penetrates 99.93 per cent of Brazil's territory (as large as Europe without the former Soviet Union), and is the main communication channel for 150 million people. A quarter of Brazilian adults are illiterate and millions more are semi-literate. The country has 40 million TV sets, six national TV networks (one state-run) and two regional networks. There are 247 TV stations – 227 commercial and 20 educational – of which Globo controls 79. Globo's audience share never dips below an average of 45 per cent in any state and the nationwide average hovers around 70 per cent.

What circumstances made this private monopoly possible? A realistic portrait of television in Brazil would include three basic characteristics. First, there has never been any notion of public service broadcasting, and private networks are free to broadcast whatever they find will attract the largest audience and therefore advertisers. Insignificant amounts are spent on quality programmes such as educational material or investigative journalism. TV Cultura, a state-run channel in São Paulo, is exceptional in terms of its high quality but its ratings are not encouraging. Second, licences for broadcasting have been bargaining instruments in the hands of politicians, who also own most of the channels. Approximately 20 per cent of Brazilian members of Parliament, and fourteen senators out of seventy-five, own shares in at least one radio or TV station. Regulation of media ownership is vague and not respected. In 1988 the former president, José Sarney, bargained for a wider mandate in exchange for franchise concessions to 1,250 radio and TV stations. The third significant characteristic of television in Brazil is that advertising is the *raison d'être* of every channel, except the weak state-run channels. Advertising comes before, during and after every programme, without any warning or rational regulation. In addition, news items can be sponsored, which paves the way for many different sorts of censorship.

I will consider here the problems these features have caused and examine some of the solutions attempted so far, such as alternative video production, which has flourished since the early 1980s but which still has very limited distribution, and the radical review of state policy on television, which is gathering support from a growing number of organisations and social groups which see the control of the media by democratic institutions as a major step towards a democratic society.

DYNASTY: FAMILY CONTROL

The history of television in Brazil is one of powerful families running regional services. The chaos and the lack of concern for public service broadcasting which characterises Brazilian television is rooted in the development of a system of political favours that has benefited powerful businessmen and influential politicians since television started with TV Tupi in São Paulo in September 1950. By 1953 there were also Tupi Rio, Radio Televisão Paulista and TV Record Rio, all concentrated in Rio and São Paulo. Tupi, the first television station to be established in Latin America, was owned by Assis Chateaubriand, an early media baron who controlled a thick slice of the communications market. Later his group would control thirty-six radio stations, thirty-four newspapers and eighteen television channels. Industry in Brazil was still virtually non-existent, so equipment and technical assistance came from General Electric and RCA.

Commercial considerations have been fundamental to Brazilian television from the start, and financial, as well as technological, models derive from the United States. Initially few advertisers were attracted, but agencies working in Brazil saw the potential in a medium reaching the well-off who could then afford a television set, which cost at that time not much less than a car. Advertising campaigns were launched to encourage consumers to buy TV sets, with the argument that they needed to play their role in 'modernising the country'. Trying to popularise the new medium, Chateaubriand himself ordered some TV sets to be installed in city squares for public viewing, and more popular programming such as soap operas and variety programmes was squeezed between programmes aimed at an elitist audience: classical theatre, dance and music, and many US-produced documentaries.

The sponsoring model for programming set up at that time indicates the regulatory chaos that has always marked television in Brazil. The whole production process was totally dependent on sponsors who retained the ownership of programmes. If they were not happy it could mean the end of the programme, no matter what the TV station or the audience thought. TV stations only provided the studios and equipment and broadcast the programme. These productions were usually named after the sponsor, like *Cine Max Factor*, *Mappin Movietone*, *Teatro Walita*, *Espetaculos Tonelux* and *Reporter Esso* from TV Tupi, adapted from radio and broadcast on television from 1952 to 1970. *Reporter Esso* was entirely produced outside Tupi, by an advertising company using the services of United Press International (UPI), and it contained hardly any national news. The first advertisement filmed was produced by J. Walter Thompson, working for Ford, which sponsored *Telenoticias Panair*, one of the first televised news bulletins on TV Tupi in 1952.[1] It was not until 1961 that the government limited advertising breaks to three minutes; before then nobody could say how long each commercial break would last. Sponsors also controlled the main artists, who would be moved, along with their programmes, from one station to another if it was thought they could reach a larger audience.

During the 1950s technical limitations and the lack of an administrative structure in the Brazilian broadcasting industry meant that TV was entirely a regional phenomenon. However, in 1955 the newly elected president Juscelino Kubitschek promised to make Brazil achieve fifty years of growth within five years with his National Industrial Development Plan. Television was seen as a centrepiece for capitalism's expansion in the country, importing foreign ideas and spreading values which would gradually create a more urban society. Starting from Rio and São Paulo, the expansion of this cultural industry stimulated industrial development on a national scale.[2] Kubitschek was also the first politician to use television as a mass medium in Brazil: the inauguration of his government was broadcast live.

In the 1960s, with expanding industries and markets and the arrival of videotape and cheaper TV sets making advertising on a national scale more attractive, programming at a national level began to be standardised. Programmes, once produced with a different cast in each region, were now centrally produced in Rio or São Paulo and then distributed to the regions, which lost ground in both cultural and labour markets as a result. Videotape, besides facilitating programme production in the economic centres, encouraged commercialisation of programmes and opened the market to foreign productions such as US-made series. North American values started to penetrate Brazilian television, which had relied on the hitherto cheaper alternatives of home-made products. [. . .]

TELEJOURNALISM

In 1971 General Medici, the third military president, said:

> I feel happy when every evening I turn on the television to watch the news. While there is news of strikes, agitations, crimes and conflicts all over the world, Brazil is peacefully marching towards development. It is as if I had taken a tranquilliser, after a day's work.

Two years previously 100,000 people had been in the streets protesting against the regime. The government, having declared an open war against left-wing guerrilla groups fighting the military's 'revolution', took total dictatorial control. Parliament was shut and pre-censorship of the media was established.

During the military period there were hijacks, kidnaps, institutionalised torture, robberies, and anti-communist death squads bombing newspapers, theatres and universities. But the war between left and right was totally ignored by television. This was the result of both institutional and self-censorship, as Walter Clark, Globo's top executive from 1965 to 1977, admitted:

> We would have been awarded medals for any act of courage but it would have cost the existence of the network. We hired a professional censor to anticipate possible clashes with the regime. We would prefer to decide what we were broadcasting rather than hearing it from the military's censors.[3]

Globo was heavily censored, as were the other stations. But to say that self-censorship was due solely to pressure from the regime is to forget that the company openly supported the government. It is more of an excuse now in more democratic times. The military have gone but their anti-democratic heritage remains. Television coverage for peak-time news bulletins, especially those involving delicate political issues, still conforms to the interests of TV owners and to their relations with the government. The larger the audience, the heavier the pressures. Globo was the slowest network to follow the course of political openness when contradictions within society began to be more openly debated, at least in the streets. Armando Nogueira, head of Globo's journalism during the military years, complains that 'the job of informing people is more difficult when television stations are afraid of losing their concessions. It is even worse when we return to democracy and people know the official censorship has finished, but we are still not corresponding to expectations.'[4]

The situation is in fact far more complicated than it appears. Globo pays the best salaries and employs some of the best journalists, who are often sharp critics of the government. Beth Costa, president of the Rio de Janeiro journalists' trade union, works for Globo and tells the local joke: 'People say the high payment here is not salary any more. It is a bribe to cope with this journalism.'[5] Costa explains that Globo's journalism is built on half-truths, softening the impact of bad news and not showing the real Brazil. 'The orders come from above.' From personal experience I know it is not an easy task to keep your integrity as a journalist in one of the main Brazilian television networks. Having worked for two of them – Manchete and Bandeirantes – I know that in one way or another you are always serving the interests of sponsors or TV station owners. I experienced several occasions when the audience had to live without information which might have damaged the sponsors' businesses. And whether it is sponsorship by the state or by a private company makes little difference. There is no formal rule. You simply know that some issues are not to be spoken of in particular ways on that network. Some topics are taboo on all networks, agrarian reform for instance: rural workers are simply ignored most of the time because media barons own significant pieces of land. More than once I received instructions from above to be careful with the questions I was going to ask Antonio Carlos Magalhaes, the former Communications Minister. I was told that he simply asks the network to fire 'inconvenient' reporters. For my colleagues from Globo the situation was worse: they would be fired on the network's own initiative.

Some networks follow the prejudices of their owners. At Manchete, after making numerous vox-pops with a wide range of people, I was told, 'You shouldn't bother about interviewing black people. Mr Bloch doesn't like it.' I kept wasting tapes. Still, at Manchete I experienced an unusual situation. An increasing awareness of Globo's bias against trade unions meant that at one point strikers would not allow their crews to cover the rallies but other networks, like Manchete, were welcomed. Manchete did not exactly support the strikes, but it took a slightly less biased approach.

The censorship practised by the Brazilian media in the last few years leaves the country with some gaps in its contemporary history and, sadly, the words of TV journalists are taken as gospel. By 1983 Globo's national TV news bulletin had the largest audience in Brazil, and today, in a country where more than a quarter of the adult population is illiterate, 80 per cent of the population watch the slick *Jornal Nacional* every evening for thirty minutes. The following cases show how Globo has ignored some of the democratic changes which have taken place in Brazil.

- In 1975 the left-wing journalist Vladimir Herzog, head of news at São Paulo Educational TV station, was killed after hours of interrogation and torture in the offices of the military police. The news of his death was reported by the press in the first major act of resistance against censorship. Globo only mentioned the fact later, reading an official communiqué which tried to prove that Herzog had committed suicide.

- The late 1970s saw the first post-coup strikes, organised by metal workers from a new trade union movement in São Paulo. Thousands of workers gathered for rallies and their leaders were arrested under national security legislation. Globo showed they were only prepared to cover the strikes on their terms: no sound tracks for shots of rallies, and no interviews with strike leaders, only with the bosses.

- The social democratic Leonel Brizola returned from exile to run for governor of the state of Rio de Janeiro in 1982. Popular in Rio since before the coup, Brizola had always been feared by the military, who had their own candidate, 'coincidentally' supported by Globo. Even before the elections the network was predicting Brizola's defeat. While the official results were not announced – they were slow in coming and constantly postponed – Globo television was releasing partial results and their own projections which showed Brizola would be defeated. The official explanation is that the computers were first registering the votes from less urban areas with more conservative tendencies. Brizola's version is that Globo was preparing public opinion for a major fraud that would take victory away from its most famous enemy. Brizola was elected and is still boycotted by Globo.

- In 1984, Globo ignored for months a broad-based political movement which drew thousands of people to the streets demanding that the president once again be elected by direct popular vote. The first time Globo gave this any notice was when 500,000 people demonstrated in São Paulo. Even so, the event was minimised and muddled with a celebration of São Paulo's anniversary. When a million people took to the streets of Rio, Globo finally broadcast the demonstration live (winning the highest ratings) and for the first time tried to distance itself from the unpopular government.

- The most recent example of Globo's partial journalism came with the elections in November and December 1989. After a month-long campaign – with party political broadcast times proportionately distributed according to parties' representations in Congress – two candidates went forward to the second round. Surprisingly, one of them was Lula (Workers' Party), the main trade union leader of the late 1970s strikes. Collor, a conservative state governor with a moralistic anti-corruption campaign, was Lula's opponent. Despite the free broadcasting time, Lula was disadvantaged by the media's boycott of the ordinary election coverage. Collor's family just happens to own the Globo affiliate in the north-eastern state he was governing.

In the second round there were two nationally televised debates. In the eyes of the public, Lula had won the first and he seemed likely to eliminate Collor's lead in the opinion polls. For the second debate, Collor improved his performance and before people had the chance to express their opinion at the ballot box, Globo prepared a special summary of the debate for the main news bulletin. The summary was watched by more people than the unedited version had been and was broadcast two days before the election with no free broadcast time left to allow an answer. Collor was given more time than Lula in the summary, and the editing enhanced his good performance since his best moments were intercut with the poorest parts of Lula's performance. Earlier that day a different and fairer version of the summary had been broadcast. Vianey Pinheiro supervised the editing of the first version and protested against the changes made for the later summary, which he called an 'advertising piece'. He was fired. Collor was elected and now has people he trusts commanding Globo's journalism. Ironically, at the time of writing (1992) he is in danger of being impeached for corruption, the 'evil' which he campaigned so vigorously against in the election. [He has since resigned.]

TELE-NOVELAS

Soap operas, or *tele-novelas*, are the most valuable product Globo has to offer advertisers, and careful planning partly explains their success. The network won the absolute lead in the ratings when it started planning the schedules and which advertisements should accompany each programme. Through its competent administration of advertising income, Globo was able to invest in drama and attract leading professionals not only from television but also from theatre and cinema, which simply cannot pay as well.

The first *novelas* were melodramas in traditional Latin American style, but it was not long before they were refined to modern television genre patterns. From 1964 to 1989 Globo produced 155 *novelas*, comprising more than 22,000 episodes. Three different *novelas* are shown in prime time six days a week for an average of six months when, unlike American soaps, they reach a conclusion. The main news bulletin at eight o'clock is sandwiched by two sixty-minute *novelas*. One guarantees the audience for the other. Episodes are written just a few days before being broadcast, which gives the writers the chance to play with current issues, very often weaving political analogies within what is sometimes a loose adaptation of a classic novel. Audience researchers advise on the plot and the development of characters to maximise ratings.

Some television experts credit the success of *novelas* to this openness. The former communist Dias Gomes, one of the main *tele-novela* writers (whose work has occasionally had the astonishing audience share of 100 per cent), believes the genre has developed in a particular way in Brazil.[6] In 1975 his *Rogue Santeiro* (a sharp and critical analogy of Brazilian society) was censored after Globo had invested US$500,000 in the first twenty episodes. It was finally broadcast ten years later. Gomes still thinks the *novelas* were the only form of popular art to develop during the dictatorship, and that they did not suffer as much as theatre or cinema. Nevertheless, *novelas* have been criticised for their folkloric poverty, for the easy solutions they offer to complex problems, and for their capacity to depoliticise information in a country where the education system is weak and illiteracy rife.[7]

Novelas have become more complex over the last two decades, and the latest examples have tended to include a wide range of characters who are not representative of the reality of Brazil since they are still predominantly urban and middle-class. Aesthetic standards, accents and cultural trends come from Rio, more precisely from the southern part of Rio, inhabited by the middle class. In regional *novelas*, artists from the main urban centres struggle to imitate regional accents. Rio's middle-class way of life was first exported to the rest of the country, including remote villages in the Amazon, thanks to satellite and to the standardisation of programming that has slowly inhibited regional cultures. Globo then became interested in foreign markets, and in 1973 *O bem amado*, the first colour soap – based on a regional romance written by Jorge Amado – was its first programme to be sold profitably abroad.

Globo's income from international sales rose from under US$300,000 in 1977 to US$14 million in 1985. This success took Rio's accent to Portugal, where it has begun to affect the former coloniser's speech patterns: a sweet historical revenge [...]

ALTERNATIVES

Over the last few years, TV Globo has been faced with competition in parts of the television schedules. This threat comes mainly from stations that are simply Globo clones, offering less glossy versions of the same. Neither market expansion nor the recent opening up of UHF broadcasting have led to significant changes; and since once again the groups in control of the new media are the same as those controlling the main networks, the so-called segmentation of the market (with channels broadcasting only sport, journalism, music or movies) is unlikely to democratise Brazilian television.

Within the main channels in Brazil the one exception in terms of programming comes from TV Cultura. Run by an independent foundation but financed by the state of São Paulo, it carries an emphasis on high-quality educational and cultural programmes but does not have a competitive share of the audience – it hardly ever has more than 1 per cent of the ratings. In Rio, the channel funded by the government has improved journalistic standards over the last few years, after a long period of subordination to politicians. However, low ratings are again the main obstacle to success.

Alternative groups have been trying to penetrate the mainstream market since the early 1980s, when video technology became accessible to a wide range of social groups and organisations. With rare exceptions television networks closed their doors to independent producers, arguing that they did not meet broadcasting standards.

Election times offer political parties rare chances to penetrate the defences of commercial television. In campaigns that last months, with political parties sharing airtime proportional to their representation in Congress, more radical political groups have their opportunity to air their points of view. They can criticise not only the government but also the media monopolies. The social democrat leader Leonel Brizola frequently uses his airtime to attack Globo's monopoly, and the campaign broadcasts by the Workers' Party in the last presidential election were a major boost for Lula's campaign. The 'People's Network', as it is called, produced parodies of politicians, denunciations and serious proposals. It parodied Globo's style at the same technical standard (many of Globo's employees also worked on a voluntary basis for Lula's campaign).

Young film- and video-makers, individuals and alternative organisations have been responsible for a huge amount of material not usually seen on the Brazilian small screen. The areas covered have been varied: educational, ecological, scientific, training, domestic, social, touristic. Video has also become popular among artists and video-art groups have spread. Political organisations such as trade unions, women's groups, tenants' associations and ethnic minorities have benefited from the new medium, even though distribution has always been a major problem. Local and First World non-governmental organisations contribute funding to productions of this kind.

This grass roots video movement created an alternative to traditional ways of covering current affairs and brought to some screens faces hardly seen before. TV Viva in Recife is an outstanding example of alternative production in Brazil, having for many years produced a wide variety of videos screened in different town squares in the centre or the outskirts of this northeastern area. In simple, sharp language they rediscover the 'grass roots'. All they need to attract enthusiastic audiences is their van with a large screen and a few actors who also perform in their videos. The live performance and interviews with the audience will later be part of the follow-up work, in a continuous process of debate. Their style and language have gradually been incorporated by other groups and even mainstream programmes like *Casseta e Planeta* from Globo. In Santarem, in Amazonia, the 'Circo Saude-Alegria' have used a video-boat to circulate educational video-letters about health issues, at the same time recording the visits. TV Maxambomba from Centro de Criação de Imagem Popular (CECIP) in Nova Iguacú (Rio de Janeiro) works with what is now known as 'video-process' in a similar way. In the north, the Projeto Video Nas Aldeias (video in the tribes project) is co-ordinated by the Centro de Trabalho Indigenista, who work with Indian tribes, advising on politics, law and economics in the hope that Indians will find their own images and eventually recover their cultural identity through video production. The technology is handed over to the tribes, who now record traditional events and ceremonies, music, dance, legends and celebrations, and their contact with urban white society.

Other political movements have developed through the use of video. In Recife, the women's group Sos Corpo produces programmes for TV Viva on issues like birth control, sexuality and abortion. In São Paulo the Coletivo Feminista Sexualidade e Saude produces feminist videos. The black movements of Rio, Salvador and São Luis use videos in their campaigns, as does the movement of street kids in Fortaleza. In the industrialised state of São Paulo, powerful trade unions acquired professional TV equipment which enabled them to portray their movement – strikes, rallies, conferences – from a different perspective. Apart from the usual alternative circuit (taking the videos to the factories), TV Dos Trabalhadores (Workers' TV) can produce cheaper material for alternative organisations or parties which cannot afford airtime on the main TV stations; their work was crucial for the Workers' Party campaign in the last presidential elections. Some unions now advertise rallies on TV. Other examples of trade union videos are TV Sinitel in Rio Grande do Sul, Minas and Rio, and TV Do Trio in Campinas.

As a result of this video boom, several associations were set up in Latin America to co-ordinate the exchange of material and experience between grass roots producers around the continent. In Brazil in 1987, the ABVP (an association for grass roots videos) pioneered the difficult task of cataloguing and distributing the work of thousands of organisations. They also run courses and encourage production. But how will they ever extend beyond the alternative circuit?

Brazil's 1989 constitution consolidated the privilege of the few and powerful media groups which had a strong lobby in the Constituent Assembly. Revision of the broadcasting franchises was made extremely difficult. However, on franchise matters power has now been transferred from the executive to the Congress, and there are opportunities for legislation to make significant changes. Different segments of Brazilian society, as well as alternative video-makers and television professionals, have sought to effect changes in the broadcasting scenario. Access to video production facilities with restricted distribution is no longer enough. There is a broad demand for the democratisation of all communications in Brazil. Lasting reform of the Brazilian media will necessarily mean a profound revision of state policies on the concession of television franchises and on programming regulations. If media ownership and programme content remain subject to market forces, many social groups will stay marginalised and misrepresented.

Today, the concentration of capital and technology around television is accepted as inevitable. The challenge is to create democratic mechanisms to provide the necessary social control over the media. Only a wide range of properly represented social groups can guarantee real power of choice for the audience, and allow room for diversity and conflict. The creation of a Social Communication Council to represent these groups and advise the Congress on franchise matters is therefore at the top of their agenda. Most groups favour maintaining the commercial system, but in order to avoid monopolies and oligopolies they would like to see statutory limitations on the production capacity of TV networks, and the encouragement of competition based on quality rather than economic or political power. Decisions would also have to be made as to which frequencies would be allowed to carry advertisements, which would be guaranteed for non-state public service stations and which non-commercial stations could be controlled by communities, cultural and ethnic groups, trade unions, educational groups or political parties. A tax would have to be introduced whereby commercial TV stations would finance the non-commercial ones. A guaranteed minimum of broadcast hours would have to be agreed for local and regional programmes, and independent productions encouraged.

These objectives may take a long time to achieve and may not arrive in the expected form, given the power of the organisations involved. However, encouraging steps have been taken towards a more democratic environment in Brazilian communications. If changes cannot come from within the broadcasting organisations, they will certainly occur through the steady growth of alternative production.

In 1986, I worked on a documentary series called *Movimento*, which portrayed grass roots communities around Brazil. They had their problems, but they also showed the audience their creative solutions, based on hard work and organisation. The series was optimistic and stimulating, even though it dealt with some of the poorest areas of the country. After a few months, the sponsors (in this case the federal government) withdrew funding for the series. Perhaps those smiling faces were too disturbing for them, or didn't suit their political propaganda. But I still dream about the day we will fill our small screens with those subversive smiles.

NOTES

1. G. Richeri and C. Lasagni, 'Precocious broadcasting', *Intermedia*, 15(3) (1987), p. 23.
2. S. Caparelli, *Televisão e capitalismo no Brasil* (Porto Alegre, L&PM, 1982), p. 21.
3. W. Clark, *O campeao de audiencia* (São Paulo, Editora Nova Cultural, 1991), p. 253.
4. A. Nogueira, from an interview for the programme *Beyond Citizen Kane* (Large Door Productions for Channel 4, 1991).
5. B. Costa, interview for *Beyond Citizen Kane*.
6. D. Gomes, interview for *Beyond Citizen Kane*.
7. M. R. Kehl, interview for *Beyond Citizen Kane*.

Section V

INDUSTRY DOCUMENTS

Introduction

In the section which follows we have excerpted documents from British and American sources. The selection is designed to illuminate a number of regulatory and policy issues on both sides of the Atlantic.

Extracts (a), (b) and (d) are taken from papers issued by the British regulatory body, the Independent Television Commission. These deal with issues of diversity and quality in programme content, advertising directed at children, and procedures for ensuring impartiality in the production of programmes. Extract (c) is taken from the European Community's 1989 Directive on broadcasting and concerns advertising and sponsorship.

Extracts (e) and (f) are taken from guidelines issued by British broadcasting organizations (BBC and ITV) concerning the treatment of factual issues on television in the areas both of news and drama.

The following pieces, (g) and (h), offer brief but pointed introductions to the issues of regulation and public interest in American broadcasting, prepared by Newton Minow, a former Chair of the Federal Communications Commission. Extract (i) is from the US Communications Act and deals with the requirements for reporting during election periods. Finally, extracts (j) and (k) come from papers issued by the US Federal Communications Commission and deal with the operation and subsequent suspension of the 'Fairness Doctrine'.

(a) Diversity and quality in television (ITC)

From the *Invitation to apply for a Channel 3 licence*. London: Independent Television Commission, 1991, extracts from paragraphs 103, 104, 105, 106

DIVERSITY IN THE SERVICE

In addition to specific mandatory strands of programming, the ITC is required to ensure that (taken as a whole) the programmes in the applicant's proposed service are calculated to appeal to a wide variety of tastes and interests. In considering the diversity of the proposed service, the ITC will have regard to the programme range in the present ITV schedule. The ITV service is required to maintain a high general standard and a wide range in its subject matter. The strands and sub-strands of programmes provided on ITV are as follows:

1. *Drama*, including
   - *single plays* and *anthologies of single plays* transmitted as a series, and *feature films*.
   - *drama series*, with a dramatic narrative running over a limited number of episodes or separate stories sharing common characters.
   - *drama serials*, running over an unlimited number of episodes.
2. *Entertainment*, including comedy and satire, game and quiz shows, chat shows, variety and music.
3. *Sport*, including coverage of events, magazine and news programmes.
4. *News*, including newscasts and news flashes, news magazines and weather forecasts.
5. *Factual programmes*, including
   - *current affairs*, defined as programming which contains explanation and analysis of current events and issues, including material dealing with political or industrial controversy or with current public policy.
   - *general factual*, defined as documentary and feature material (other than news, current affairs, religion, education, sport, and arts).
6. *Education*, including
   - *adult education*, usually backed by specially prepared literature advertised on screen and in other appropriate ways.
   - *social action*, covering programmes which reflect social needs or promote individual or community action.
7. *Religion*, including acts of worship and programmes examining religious issues and reflecting faith and belief.

8. *Arts*, consisting of theatre, music, dance, cinema, visual arts, photography and literature, presented and reviewed in relays of performance or exhibitions, documentaries or special features.
9. *Children's*, including
   - drama
   - information
   - entertainment.

Strands 1–8 exclude children's programmes.

The ITC considers that there should be some programming in each of the nine strands defined above. An applicant may consider that the exclusion from the proposed service of non-mandated elements of programming *within* strands is justified, for example by the characteristics of the audience which he intends to serve. If so, the ITC will expect these conclusions to be demonstrated. Applicants should note that a service with a more limited range than is indicated here is unlikely to pass the quality threshold.

HIGH-QUALITY PROGRAMMES

The ITC considers that the categorisation of programmes as of high quality is a matter which cannot be reduced to a single formula. They may be programmes which have a special one-off character or programmes of marked creative originality, or programmes, from any category, of exceptionally high production standards, or any combination of these factors. Programmes of high quality may not be regarded as mainly or exclusively of minority appeal, and it is important that programmes of wide audience appeal should also be of high quality. High quality cannot be guaranteed by any particular combination of talent and resources, although both are normally crucial elements. Moreover those who seek to achieve high quality in one of the ways mentioned above may not always succeed even in their own terms. It would be wrong to penalise them for making the attempt.

The ITC will expect the applicant to support his proposals for the service with a statement of the thinking behind the service which he intends to supply, explaining *inter alia* how he proposes to secure a range of high-quality programmes and to encourage and sustain the professionalism and creative talent needed for this. The statement should take into account the size, special characteristics and earning potential of the region concerned.

(b) Advertising and children (ITC)

From the *Code of advertising standards and practice*. London: Independent Television
Commission, 1993, Appendix 1, paragraphs 1–11

The child audience

1. At times when large numbers of children are likely to be viewing, no product or
   service may be advertised, and no method of advertising may be used which
   might result in harm to them physically, mentally or morally, and no method of
   advertising may be employed which takes advantage of the natural credulity and
   sense of loyalty of children. For the purposes of this Code, unless otherwise stated,
   the Commission normally regards as children those aged 15 years and under.

Misleadingness

2. Children's ability to distinguish between fact and fantasy will vary according to
   their age and individual personality. With this in mind, no unreasonable
   expectation of performance of toys and games may be stimulated by, for example,
   the excessive use of imaginary backgrounds or special effects.
3. Advertisements for toys, games and other products of interest to children must not
   mislead, taking into account the child's immaturity of judgement and experience.
   In particular:
   (a) The true size of the product must be made easy to judge, preferably by
       showing it in relation to some common object by which it can be judged. In
       any demonstration it must be made clear whether the toy can move
       independently or only through manual operation.
   (b) Treatments which reflect the toy or game seen in action through the child's
       eyes or in which real life counterparts of the toy are seen working must be
       used with due restraint. There must be no confusion as to the noise produced
       by the toy – e.g. a toy racing car and its real life counterpart.
   (c) Where advertisements show results from a drawing, construction, craft or
       modelling toy or kit, the results shown must be reasonably attainable by the
       average child and ease of assembly must not be exaggerated.

Competitions

4. If there is to be a reference to a competition for children in an advertisement, the

published rules must be submitted in advance to the licensee. The value of the prizes and the chances of winning one must not be exaggerated.

Direct exhortation

5. Advertisements must not exhort children to purchase or to ask their parents or others to make enquiries or purchases.

Appeals to loyalty

6. No advertisement may imply that unless children themselves buy or encourage other people to buy a product or service they will be failing in some duty or lacking in loyalty.

Inferiority

7. No advertisement may lead children to believe that if they do not have or use the product or service advertised they will be inferior in some way to other children or liable to be held in contempt or ridicule.

Direct response

8. No advertisement may invite children to purchase products by mail or telephone.

Restriction on times of transmission

9.

(a) Advertisements for the following must not be transmitted during children's programmes or in the advertisement breaks immediately before or after them – alcoholic drinks, liqueur chocolates, matches, medicines, vitamins or other dietary supplements, 15 and 18 rated film trailers.

(b) Except in circumstances approved by the Commission, the following will be acceptable only after 9 p.m.:

(i) advertisements in which children are shown having any medicine, or vitamin or other dietary supplement administered to them;

(ii) advertisements for medicines, or vitamins or other dietary supplements which use techniques that are likely to appeal particularly to children, such as cartoons, toys or characters of special interest to children.

(c) Children must not be shown self-administering medicines or vitamins or other dietary supplements unless prior permission is given by the Commission.

Notes to 9b and 9c

(i) *For the purposes of this rule 'medicines' are classified as products which carry a product licence. 'Dietary supplements' are classified as isolated or highly purified or concentrated products sold in forms resembling medicines, e.g. vitamins, minerals and amino acids.*

    (ii) *In the case of a product which cannot easily be distinguished from a medicine, or where the advertising itself contributes to such a lack of distinguishability, particularly with regard to very young children (those five years old and under), Rule 9(a), (b) and (c) above should be applied.*

    (iii) *Where an exemption is sought under this rule it is likely to be granted only in relation to products such as those for oral hygiene, skin preparations including acne treatments and externally-applied decongestants. The exemption will be granted only if the Commission is fully satisfied that harm is unlikely to arise as a result of very young children's responses to the advertisements.*

(d)   Advertisements in which personalities, or other characters (including puppets etc) who appear regularly in any children's television programme, present or positively endorse products or services of particular interest to children must not be transmitted before 9 p.m. This does not apply to public service advertisements or to characters specially created for advertisements.

(e)   Advertisements for merchandise based on children's programmes must not be broadcast in any of the two hours preceding or succeeding transmission of the relevant programme or of episodes or editions of the relevant programme.

(f)   Advertisements which contain material which might frighten or cause distress to children must be subject to appropriate restrictions on times of transmission designed to minimise the risk that children in the relevant age group will see them. Trailers for 15 or 18 rated films must not be shown in or around children's programmes and, depending on content, may require more rigorous timing restrictions.

Prices

10. Except in the case of services carrying advertising directed exclusively at audiences outside the UK, advertisements for expensive toys, games and similar products must include an indication of their price.

(a)   A product will not be regarded as expensive if it is reasonably widely available at a retail price below that specified by the Commission from time to time.

(b)   Where a range of products is featured in a single advertisement only the most expensive item need be priced.

(c)   Where more than one item is priced, each price must clearly refer to a particular item.

(d)   When parts, accessories or batteries which a child might reasonably suppose to be part of a normal purchase are available only at extra cost, this must be made clear.

(e)   The cost must not be minimised by the use of words such as 'only' or 'just'.

Health and hygiene

11.

(a)   Advertisements must not encourage children to eat frequently throughout the day.

(b) Advertisements must not encourage children to consume food or drink (especially sweet, sticky foods) near bedtime.

(c) Advertisements for confectionery or snack foods must not suggest that such products may be substituted for balanced meals.

(c) Advertising and sponsorship (EU)

From the EEC Directive on the pursuit of broadcasting in member states 1989 (89/552/EEC), published in the *Official Journal of the European Communities* L298/29 1989, Chapter IV, articles 10–18

Article 10

1. Television advertising shall be readily recognizable as such and kept quite separate from other parts of the programme service by optical and/or acoustic means.
2. Isolated advertising spots shall remain the exception.
3. Advertising shall not use subliminal techniques.
4. Surreptitious advertising shall be prohibited.

Article 11

1. Advertisements shall be inserted between programmes. Provided the conditions contained in paragraphs 2 to 5 of this Article are fulfilled, advertisements may also be inserted during programmes in such a way that the integrity and value of the programme, taking into account natural breaks in and the duration and nature of the programme, and the rights of the rights holders are not prejudiced.
2. In programmes consisting of autonomous parts, or in sports programmes and similarly structured events and performances comprising intervals, advertisements shall only be inserted between the parts or in the intervals.
3. The transmission of audiovisual works such as feature films and films made for television (excluding series, serials, light entertainment programmes and documentaries), provided their programmed duration is more than 45 minutes, may be interrupted once for each complete period of 45 minutes. A further interruption is allowed if their programmed duration is at least 20 minutes longer than two or more complete periods of 45 minutes.
4. Where programmes, other than those covered by paragraph 2, are interrupted by advertisements, a period of at least 20 minutes should elapse between each successive advertising break within the programme.
5. Advertisements shall not be inserted in any broadcast of a religious service. News and current affairs programmes, documentaries, religious programmes, and children's programmes, when their programmed duration is less than 30 minutes, shall not be interrupted by advertisements. If their programmed duration is of 30 minutes or longer, the provisions of the previous paragraphs shall apply. [...]

Article 12

Television advertising shall not:
  (a) prejudice respect for human dignity;
  (b) include any discrimination on grounds of race, sex or nationality;
  (c) be offensive to religious or political beliefs;
  (d) encourage behaviour prejudicial to health or to safety;
  (e) encourage behaviour prejudicial to the protection of the environment.

Article 13

All forms of television advertising for cigarettes and other tobacco products shall be prohibited.

Article 14

Television advertising for medicinal products and medical treatment available only on prescription in the Member State within whose jurisdiction the broadcaster falls shall be prohibited.

Article 15

Television advertising for alcoholic beverages shall comply with the following criteria:
  (a) it may not be aimed specifically at minors or, in particular, depict minors consuming these beverages;
  (b) it shall not link the consumption of alcohol to enhanced physical performance or to driving;
  (c) it shall not create the impression that the consumption of alcohol contributes towards social or sexual success;
  (d) it shall not claim that alcohol has therapeutic qualities or that it is a stimulant, a sedative or a means of resolving personal conflicts;
  (e) it shall not encourage immoderate consumption of alcohol or present abstinence or moderation in a negative light;
  (f) it shall not place emphasis on high alcoholic content as being a positive quality of the beverages.

Article 16

Television advertising shall not cause moral or physical detriment to minors, and shall therefore comply with the following criteria for their protection:
  (a) it shall not directly exhort minors to buy a product or a service by exploiting their inexperience or credulity;
  (b) it shall not directly encourage minors to persuade their parents or others to purchase the goods or services being advertised;
  (c) it shall not exploit the special trust minors place in parents, teachers or other persons;
  (d) it shall not unreasonably show minors in dangerous situations.

Article 17

1. Sponsored television programmes shall meet the following requirements:
    (a) the content and scheduling of sponsored programmes may in no circumstances be influenced by the sponsor in such a way as to affect the responsibility and editorial independence of the broadcaster in respect of programmes;
    (b) they must be clearly identified as such by the name and/or logo of the sponsor at the beginning and/or the end of the programmes;
    (c) they must not encourage the purchase or rental of the products or services of the sponsor or a third party, in particular by making special promotional references to those products or services.
2. Television programmes may not be sponsored by natural or legal persons whose principal activity is the manufacture or sale of products, or the provision of services, the advertising of which is prohibited by Article 13 or 14.
3. News and current affairs programmes may not be sponsored.

Article 18

1. The amount of advertising shall not exceed 15% of the daily transmission time. However, this percentage may be increased to 20% to include forms of advertisements such as direct offers to the public for the sale, purchase or rental of products or for the provision of services, provided the amount of spot advertising does not exceed 15%.
2. The amount of spot advertising within a given one-hour period shall not exceed 20%.
3. Without prejudice to the provisions of paragraph 1, forms of advertisements such as direct offers to the public for the sale, purchase or rental of products or for the provision of services shall not exceed one hour per day.

(d) Impartiality (ITC)

From *The Independent Television Commission programme code*. London: Independent Television Commission, 1995, extracts from sections 3.2, 3.3, 3.5 and 3.8

DUE IMPARTIALITY

The Broadcasting Act requires the ITC to do all that it can to secure 'that due impartiality is preserved on the part of the person providing the service as respects matters of political or industrial controversy or relating to current public policy'.

The term 'due' is significant; it should be interpreted as meaning adequate or appropriate to the nature of the subject and the type of programme. While the requirement of due impartiality applies to all areas of controversy covered by the Act, it does not mean that 'balance' is required in any simple mathematical sense or that equal time must be given to each opposing point of view, nor does it require absolute neutrality on every issue. Judgment will always be called for. The requirement will also vary with the type of programme; the considerations applying to drama, for example, are different from those applying to current affairs programmes. News and personal view programmes are also different in kind and bound by separate sets of rules. Similarly, the choice of participants in a research-led investigative report will be determined by the need to be fair to the subject matter, while participants in a political discussion programme will normally be chosen more with a view to reflecting the principal opposing viewpoints.

The provision that due impartiality must be preserved 'on the part of the person providing the service' is also significant. It puts the burden for compliance on licensees rather than individual programme-makers. Subject to the safeguards contained in this Code, the provision allows for individual contributors to put forward what may be a personal or subjective view, or for such views to be reflected in a programme. It is for each licensee, acting through the executives who commission and schedule programmes, to ensure the service they provide deals fairly with matters of political or industrial controversy, or current public policy.

EDITORIALISING

The avoidance of editorialising on the part of licensees is integral to the preservation of due impartiality in the service they provide. So while individual contributors may be commissioned to broadcast personal view programmes on controversial matters covered by the Act, licensees may not use programmes to put forward their own views on such matters.

The Act places the additional duty on the ITC to do what it can to secure the exclusion of the licensee's views and opinions on controversial matters other than the provision of programme services. If, in a programme included in a licensed service, a director or officer of a licensee does express an opinion on a controversial matter other than the provision of programme services, it must be in a context which makes clear that the opinion expressed is not that of the licensee. Speeches in Parliament are exempt from this provision.

IMPARTIALITY OVER TIME

There are times when licensees will need to ensure that the principal opposing viewpoints are reflected in a single programme or programme item, either because it is not likely that the licensee will soon return to the subject, or because the issues involved are of current and active controversy. At other times, a narrower range of views may be appropriate within individual programmes. The ITC recognises that such issues call for editorial judgement based on the particular circumstances and that an impartial programme service does not necessarily have to ensure that in a single programme, or programme item, all sides have an opportunity to speak. [...]

NEWS

In addition to the general requirements relating to matters of political or industrial controversy or current public policy, the Act requires that any news, given in whatever form, must be presented with due accuracy and impartiality.

Reporting should be dispassionate and news judgments based on the need to give viewers an even-handed account of events. In reporting on matters of industrial or political controversy, the main differing views on the matter should be given their due weight in the period during which the controversy is active. Editorial discretion will determine whether a range of conflicting views is included within a single news item or whether it is acceptable to spread them over a series of bulletins. [...]

CONDUCT OF INTERVIEWS

[...] On occasion, proposed interviewees will be unable or unwilling to accept an invitation to participate in a programme. This need not prevent the programme going ahead, but in order to achieve impartiality, care must be taken to give an impartial account of the subject under discussion, particularly when this is one of controversy or public policy covered by the Act.

Reference to the absence of such a spokesman should be made in as detached and factual a manner as possible. [...]

EDITING OF INTERVIEWS

Impartiality applies equally to the editing of interviews as to their conduct. Editing to shorten recorded interviews must not distort or misrepresent the known views of the interviewee.

Interviews held on library tapes should be checked before use to see whether the views expressed are still valid, and where necessary captioned to show the date they were originally recorded.

INTERVIEWS WITH POLITICIANS

Appearances by politicians in news and current affairs programmes, when they take part as spokesmen for their party, or for their own political point of view, are governed by the requirements of due impartiality.

In programmes dealing with political issues the participants do not necessarily have to be spokesmen for the main political parties. The obligation to ensure due impartiality relates to issues, not to parties, and some important issues do not divide opinion along existing party lines. Indeed there are occasions when it is preferable to confine discussion to the spokesmen of only one party; the opportunity can be taken to investigate a particular approach to an issue in depth, provided that overall in a series of programmes impartiality is maintained. On the other hand there are many issues on which the attitudes of the parties are clear cut and distinct, recognisably part of the current political debate. In those cases spokesmen of known party allegiance should be chosen by the broadcasters.

(e) BBC producers' guidelines

From the *Producers' guidelines* (1993) of the British Broadcasting Corporation,
Chapter 8, section 6 (subsections 6.1–6.11) and Chapter 13, sections 1, 2, 3, 4 and 6

THE NORTHERN IRELAND BROADCASTING RESTRICTIONS

A wide range of programmes is affected by the restrictions in the Notice which came into force on 19 October 1988 when it was served on the BBC and the IBA (now the ITC and the Radio Authority) by the Home Secretary. The Notice bans British broadcasters from transmitting the voices of Northern Ireland terrorists, members of paramilitary groups and of other organisations specifically listed, when they are speaking in that capacity. It also bans directly voiced expressions of support for such groups, whoever makes them. The listed groups include the IRA, INLA, UVF, Sinn Fein and the UDA. (The full text of the Notice, the text of a letter from the Home Office explaining it, and the list of organisations affected are given at the end of this chapter.)

Who the law affects

The Notice – or the Northern Ireland ban as it is often called – affects two categories of people: those who represent or purport to represent the Northern Ireland organisations named, and those who speak words of support for any of the organisations whether they represent them or not.

What the effect is

The effect is that any person who represents one of the organisations cannot be heard in a programme in that capacity. This is so even if the individual would have talked on a non-violent topic. People who in some situations represent one of the organisations may appear in other capacities: a local government councillor elected on a Sinn Fein ticket could, for instance, represent the council or one of its committees, or may be heard as a spokesman for his or her constituency or ward talking about constituency or ward matters. Such people may also be heard at times speaking in a personal capacity, for instance as an eye witness to an incident.

Anyone at all who expresses support for one of the organisations cannot be heard in a programme expressing that support unless the comments are made in Parliament at Westminster or by a person involved in an election campaign in the United Kingdom. The ban applies even to an MP speaking outside the House of Commons. The spoken words of ordinary members of the public are similarly restricted. The individual speaking the words does not offend the Notice; the BBC would do so if it were to broadcast a voice in circumstances forbidden by the ban.

Reported speech allowed

Anyone, including representatives of the organisations, can be quoted in reported speech. Pictures of the individual speaking can be shown with the words spoken in voice-over by someone else or shown in caption.

Pictures without words

Television could show pictures of demonstrators waving banners of support for one of the organisations affected, but the sound would have to be cut if they chanted support for the organisation. [...]

Alerting the audience

When a programme or programme item is materially affected by the Notice it is right to alert the audience to the fact. The form of words used should be clear and as specific as possible about the effect: e.g. 'Because of government restrictions we cannot let you hear the voice of ...' or some such.

Text of the Notice served on the BBC by the Home Secretary on 19th October 1988

1. In pursuance of clause 13(4) of the Licence and Agreement made between Her Majesty's Secretary of State for the Home Department and the British Broadcasting Corporation on 2 April 1981, I hereby require the said Corporation to refrain at all times from sending any broadcast matter which consists of or includes any words spoken, whether in the course of an interview or discussion or otherwise, by a person who appears or is heard on the programme in which the matter is broadcast where:
    (a) the person speaking the words represents or purports to represent an organisation specified in paragraph 2 below, or
    (b) the words support or solicit or invite support for such an organisation, other than any matter specified in paragraph 3 below.
2. The organisations referred to in paragraph 1 above are:
    (a) any organisation which is for the time being a proscribed organisation for the purpose of the Prevention of Terrorism (Temporary Provisions) Act 1984 or the Northern Ireland (Emergency Provisions) Act 1978; and
    (b) Sinn Fein, Republican Sinn Fein and the Ulster Defence Association.
3. The matter excluded from paragraph 1 above is any words spoken:
    (a) in the course of proceedings in Parliament, or

(b)   by or in support of a candidate at a parliamentary, European Parliamentary or local election pending that election.

Signed:

DOUGLAS HURD
One of Her Majesty's Principal Secretaries of State

Text of a letter from the Home Office to the BBC dated 24 October 1988

As you know, when I met BBC officials on 20 October to discuss the Notice which the Home Secretary sent to the BBC the previous day, a number of points were raised concerning its interpretation on which the BBC had doubts. We explained the Home Office approach to the drafting on these points and the scope of the restrictions which it was intended should be imposed on broadcast programmes. I promised to put what we said in writing so that the BBC would be left in no doubt as to the effect of the Notice.

It was asked whether the Notice applied only to direct statements by representatives of the organisations or their supporters or whether it applied also to reports of the words they had spoken. We confirmed, as the Home Secretary has made clear in Parliament, that the correct interpretation (and that which was intended) is that it applies only to direct statements and not to reported speech, and that the person caught by the Notice is the one whose words are reported and not the reporter or presenter who reports them. Thus the Notice permits the showing of a film or still picture of the initiator speaking the words together in paraphrase or verbatim. We confirmed that programmes involving the reconstruction of actual events, where actors use the verbatim words which had been spoken in actuality, are similarly permitted.

For much the same reason, we confirmed that it was not intended that genuine works of fiction should be covered by the restrictions, on the basis that the appropriate interpretation of 'a person' in paragraph 1 of the Notice is that it does not include an actor playing a character.

The BBC also asked whether a member of an organisation or one of its elected representatives could be considered as permanently representing that organisation so that all his words, whatever their character, were covered by the Notice. We confirmed that the Home Office takes the view that this is too narrow an interpretation of the word 'represents' in paragraph 1(a) of the text. A member of an organisation cannot be held to represent that organisation in all his daily activities. Whether at any particular instance he is representing the organisation concerned will depend upon the nature of the words spoken and the particular context. Where he is speaking in a personal capacity or purely in his capacity as a member of an organisation which does not fall under the Notice (for example, an elected Council), it follows, from that interpretation, that paragraph 1(a) will not apply. Where it is clear, from context and the words, that he is speaking as a representative of an organisation falling under the Notice, his words may not be broadcast directly, but (as mentioned above) can be reported. (He may, of course, come within the scope of paragraph 1(b), if his words contain support for the organisation.) Although there may be borderline occasions when this distinction will require a careful exercise of judgement, we believe that the great majority of broadcast material will fall clearly within one case or the other.

We confirmed that direct broadcast coverage of statements in court would be subject to the present Notice, but that this did not raise practical issues since broadcast coverage of court proceedings is not currently permitted in this country. Statements falling within the Notice that were made in court proceedings in countries where direct broadcast coverage was permitted could not be broadcast directly here, but, again, the words could be fully reported. Similarly, the exemption under paragraph 3(a) of the Notice applies only to proceedings in Parliament at Westminster, and not to the European Parliament or Parliaments in other countries.

I hope that this statement, which constitutes what the Home Office believes to be the correct interpretation of the Notice and which represents the Home Secretary's intentions in issuing it, will be of help to you in providing advice to the Corporation's staff.

This letter has been seen and approved by the Home Secretary. I am sending a copy of it, for information, to the Secretary to the IBA.

Signed:

C. L. SCOBLE
Broadcasting Department

The BBC opposes the continuation of the Notice because it believes that the ban deprives audiences of the right to hear and judge the representatives of organisations which have a profound effect on life in Northern Ireland, and because it enables those organisations more easily to avoid taking responsibility for the consequences of their actions.

While the Notice remains in force it is necessary to observe its provisions but it is also vital that we do not extend its scope unnecessarily. BBC journalists must ensure that they continue to seek, question, and report the views of all significant parties and organisations in accordance with providing full, responsible coverage of the Northern Ireland situation and in accordance with the other provisions of these Guidelines.

[*Editor's Note*: The Notice referred to in the above section was cancelled by the Home Secretary in 1994.]

GENERAL

The BBC has a responsibility to serve all sections of society. Its domestic service programmes should aim to reflect and represent the composition of the nation accurately. Programme makers must always be aware of the sensitivities of groups in society who feel unjustly treated or discriminated against.

Producers should be careful that BBC programmes overall do not perpetuate myths, reinforce stereotypes or cause needless offence to minorities or groups. Those who feel they are misrepresented or neglected by society in general should feel that they are dealt with, and portrayed, fairly and accurately by the BBC.

This guideline applies in full force to factual programmes of all kinds. They should aim to be exemplary.

Creative programmes have greater freedom. They may be provocative and explore taboos. Comedy and fiction may sometimes include or explore prejudice. But that does not mean that anything is acceptable. There are boundaries to be respected. Creative freedom must be wisely used. Challenging material should not be excessive, gratuitous, overly cruel or used with intent to harm a person or a group.

Chief Adviser Editorial Policy is available to offer advice and support to programme-makers on the whole range of issues involved in portrayal.

COMMON CONCERNS

Some concerns are common to all groups who feel inadequately portrayed in programmes:

- under-representation on air: people from all groups should be represented in the full range of our programmes. Programmes should draw their participants or casts from a broad range, and not concentrate unreasonably on able-bodied white men. The BBC has specialist programmes, programme departments and a range of equal opportunity databases which can be used to widen the field.
- hurtful or inaccurate stereotypes: it is important that BBC programmes should not regularly categorise black people as criminals, women as housewives, disabled people as victims, gay people as ineffectual, old people as incapable, or people of any particular profession, vocation or walk of life as inevitable figures of fun. People should appear in the full range of roles that reflect reality.

We must be careful not to perpetuate stereotypes by thoughtless use of material which associates groups with particular patterns of behaviour. Repeated use of pictures of immigrants at an airport to illustrate the theme of drugs, or of women in supermarkets to illustrate food prices, or of transvestites or drag artists to illustrate gay issues – all serve to reinforce images which are of dubious validity.

While avoiding stereotypes and portraying the full range of roles we must beware the danger of depicting a society that does not exist. The BBC is not in the business of social engineering. Where prejudice and disadvantage exist we may need to report and reflect them in our programmes. But we should do nothing to perpetuate them.

WOMEN

They are the majority. In spite of laws and changing attitudes women are still discriminated against in certain respects and are often under-represented in programmes.

Casting women in narrow or secondary roles for no good reason can annoy and offend. Fewer than five percent of UK households consist of a working husband with wife at home looking after school-age children. Women do many jobs. Remember too that increasing numbers of men go shopping, look after children and have jobs like nursing or secretarial work.

Terminology

In many cases, gender is irrelevant. The aim of non-sexist language is to avoid giving offence to the individuals we describe and to avoid creating through repetition the impression that certain activities are the preserve of one sex only.

We need to avoid using words that date back to days when women were barred from many types of work (busmen, policemen, taxmen, newsmen, manning). There are nearly always comfortable alternatives which are not sexist (bus-drivers, police officers, tax inspectors, journalists, staffing).

Some people are uncomfortable at the use of some non-sexist terms. It is always possible to re-write a sentence to avoid both sexism and political correctness. But we should normally respect people's wishes about how we refer to them. If someone calls himself or herself the 'Chair' of an organisation it is not for us to make them Chairman or Chairwoman.

ETHNIC MINORITIES

It is narrow-minded to identify people only by ethnic origin or colour when they have a host of other characteristics. Colour should be mentioned only when it is relevant. Ask yourself each time: would you say 'white' in similar circumstances?

Terminology

When ethnic origin is considered relevant geographic origin rather than colour of skin is often preferable ... 'from Bangladesh', 'Asian', 'Jamaican', 'West Indian' and so on. The more specific the better.

'Black' should not normally include Asians. BBC programmes should refer to 'black and Asian people' or 'Asian, African and Caribbean people'. We should never say 'Non-whites', just as we do not say 'Non-blacks'. Some African and Caribbean people prefer to be called black British. Use the term 'black people' rather than 'blacks'. 'Coloured' is usually inappropriate and offensive. A good rule of thumb is to ask how people describe themselves: there have to be good reasons for our calling them something different.

Wrong images

Most ethnic minority people living in Britain are British nationals. A large proportion were born here. Few are immigrants and many have known no other home. They are an integral part of British society.

Black and Asian people suffer considerably from negative stereotypes. Programmes must not allow offensive assumptions or generalisations in scripted material, and interviewees who express them need to be challenged.

SEXUAL ORIENTATION

BBC programmes must not be vehicles for prejudice. Lesbians and gay men can be particularly subject to thoughtless and offensive stereotyping. The fact that many people keep their sexuality hidden makes it particularly difficult for programme makers to portray the incidence of homosexuality accurately, but we must try.

Gay and lesbian people, and those who are bi-sexual, make up a significant minority entitled to be served and treated fairly by the BBC. Programme makers should remember that homosexuals experience the same range of emotions as heterosexuals, and they play the full range of roles in society. They have the right to see that range truthfully portrayed.

Wrong images

Stereotyping is a particular danger if the gay characters we portray are present only because of their sexuality or if their sexuality is their main distinguishing characteristic. Remember that sexual orientation may be an incidental characteristic. We must not confuse homosexuality with transvestism or trans-sexualism, neither of which relates specifically to a person's sexuality. Programmes must not allow offensive assumptions or generalisations in scripted material, and interviewees who express them need to be challenged with vigour.

Acknowledging sexuality

When appropriate, there should be straightforward reference to the publicly acknowledged homosexuality of well-known people and their acknowledged partners. This might occur, for example, in profiles, obituaries and other contexts where it is strictly relevant or where heterosexual relationships would be considered relevant. However, it is not for the BBC to force matters of sexuality into the open. We have a strong regard for privacy in this as in other matters.

Terminology

Be sensitive to the effect of language. 'Homosexual' has wide currency. 'Gay and lesbian' is often preferred and is certainly acceptable. There is no place in factual programmes for our use of words like 'queer', 'dyke', 'fairy' or 'poof': when contributors use them they should be challenged. When they are used by characters in drama programmes they are just as sensitive as racial abuse and should be considered accordingly.

(f) Guidelines for drama-documentary (ITV Network Centre)

From the *Statement of best practice: factual drama on television*. London: Independent Television Network Centre, 1994

ITV is proud of its record in factual drama. Programmes such as *Who Bombed Birmingham*, *Shoot to Kill*, *The Life and Death of Phillip Knight* and *Fighting for Gemma* have used journalistic methods and drama techniques to bring important issues of public policy to the widest audiences. Series such as *Crime Story* and *In Suspicious Circumstances* in part fulfil a documentary tradition of throwing light on the human condition, as well as presenting popular programming.

ITV producers are keen to minimise the risk that viewers will be confused about a programme's intentions, or that they may have cause to suspect that drama techniques have misrepresented real events. This statement sets out best practice within which ITV produces factual drama, and is intended to supplement the ITC Programme Code. The statement does not cover acquired programmes.

We deal with two strands of programming within ITV's factual drama. The first, *drama-documentary*, has a matter of public policy as its subject and has journalism as its prime purpose. The second, *dramatisation of a true story*, shares some of the same characteristics as drama-documentary but has as its main purpose the recounting of an arresting or illuminating story.

NB: There is a third category, dramas based on a true story, which remains the exclusive province of producers and writers whose purpose is primarily creative and dramatic rather than journalistic. These programmes are not covered by this statement.

Producers of all ITV factual drama endorse the following:
1. Audiences are entitled to know what degree of accuracy is claimed for factual drama programmes. *Drama-documentary* makes bold claims for detail and accuracy while *dramatisation of a true story* may not.

    ITV producers will inform viewers of the nature of programmes in advance of transmission. This may be in pre-publicity and in promotion but will always be made clear in introductions to such programmes.
2. The same standards of accuracy, due impartiality and journalistic rigour will be demanded of *drama documentaries* as those demanded of other documentary or current affairs programmes. No version of events or conclusions will be offered as definitive if it cannot be sustained through responsible journalistic methods.

3. Producers of *drama-documentaries* on ITV will not depict individual scenes which have no basis in reality. Producers will do so in *dramatisations of a true story* only when they have informed viewers in advance.

4. As in traditional drama or documentary, it is necessary for producers of factual drama to adjust chronology in order to achieve clarity for viewers. Where appropriate ITV producers will inform viewers of any such adjustments, at least in general terms, in advance. Such techniques will be used in *drama-documentary* only with the utmost care, and not in a way which misleads the audience about any material aspect of the story.

5. It is sometimes necessary in factual drama to change names or alter the identity of characters. This may be, for example, to avoid placing real people in danger. When this happens with principal named characters in a *drama-documentary* production, ITV producers will inform viewers in advance.

6. Equally, sometimes several real people who play minor roles in a real story might be represented in a factual drama by a single actor. For example, twenty nameless officials behind a desk might be composited into one or two. This will be done on ITV only where it makes no material difference to the substance of the story being told.

7. ITV producers will be sensitive to the depiction of real people and will use best endeavours to portray them fairly. For example, an actor will not be shown drinking, smoking, using offensive language or engaging in any type of sexual activity, unless it has been established that the person being depicted acted in such a manner.

8. Producers of all factual drama on ITV will use the greatest care when reconstructing incidents of violence. Violent incidents will be depicted only where there is a clear journalistic purpose, and always with the greatest restraint consistent with that purpose.

9. Dramatisations of true stories will frequently involve depictions of people who have innocently or unwittingly become involved in a traumatic experience. Where ITV programmes are depicting named people in such circumstances, producers undertake to use all reasonable endeavours to contact them and to take into account their perspectives on the production.

10. Where principal characters depicted in ITV factual drama have died or it has not been possible to trace them, producers will use all reasonable endeavours to contact members of their immediate family and will take into account their perspectives on the production. ITV producers will use best endeavours to inform such people of the times of intended transmission of programmes and programme trails.

11. ITV producers may sometimes use genuine news footage or news bulletins to illustrate developments in their story. However, they will not edit together real footage with reconstructed footage in a manner which leads to an interpretation of events which is not sustainable by traditional journalistic methods.

(g) The Federal Communications Commission and American broadcast regulation (Newton Minow)

From the Introduction to Krasnow, E.G. and Longley, L.D. 1973: *The politics of broadcast regulation*. New York: St Martin's Press

The Federal Communications Commission is one of the most important and least understood government agencies. Issues of momentous concern to every citizen come to the FCC, but its responsibilities, limitations, and processes are followed closely only by a small segment of the press, the bar, and the engineering fraternities. True, it is accountable directly to the Congress and there are frequent Congressional reviews of its decisions and deliberations. True, the courts are constantly reviewing – and reversing – its decided cases and regulations. True, the President appoints the Commissioners, thereby having some supervisory control. But, despite these continuing links with all three branches of the federal government, citizen familiarity with the FCC remains dim and distant. [. . .]

Now, Erwin G. Krasnow, an active member of the FCC bar who has also had legislative experience on Capitol Hill, and Lawrence D. Longley, a political scientist with expertise in interest-group politics, have pooled their talents to carry the analysis more specifically into the record of one agency – the FCC.

Their efforts have produced a useful book which gets down to hard cases. By focusing on the very real case histories of regulation – of FM broadcasting, of UHF television, of proposed limits on broadcast commercial time, and of license renewal policies – the authors have shown us how the regulatory process actually works, how it is influenced by political realities, and how decisions are really made.

Pressures are intense in the regulation of broadcasting. The industry is strong, vocal, and has many powerful friends. Citizens' groups, a latecomer to the scene, are beginning to acquire some muscle and sophistication in the ways of the regulatory world. The White House is becoming more concerned about regulatory decisions because it is now aware that FCC decisions have not only national but also international implications. And the Congress and courts have the last word.

Let me give but one example from personal experience. When I was at the FCC, I was one of a few Commissioners who wanted to place some limits on the amount of commercial time on radio and television. We strongly believed that some rules were long overdue. We proposed that the commercial time rules established by the broadcasters themselves in the National Association of Broadcasters be enforced. I finally mustered a majority of the Commission to support this proposal. After I left, my successor, Bill Henry, was besieged by the industry. The Congress reacted almost immediately, and, as described in detail in Chapter 7, the House of Representatives made it clear to the FCC that it should stay out of the area. Thus, we remain the only nation in the world which has no limits on how many commercials a broadcaster may run, and our best broadcasters are reduced to the law of the jungle in this area. Yet the FCC is blamed as a spineless tool of the broadcasting lobby, when in fact, its efforts to regulate were frustrated by the Congress.

Authors Krasnow and Longley document similar examples in their work. They conclude, quite properly, that while the FCC may initiate policy, the fate of such policy is often determined by others. A good example which I know something about is the creation of policy in the early 1960s concerning international communication satellites. Here, we succeeded in getting Comsat launched and thus preserved American leadership in the world. But we succeeded only because the FCC was willing to compromise with various competing economic interests and theories, governmental and private agencies, and because we turned to the President and the Congress for the final word. This required an understanding of the political process; the essence of that process will almost always require compromise. Sometimes, compromise will not necessarily be the best service to the public interest – but under our system of government, I do not know a better alternative.

I commend the authors for digging beneath the surface to give their readers an accurate understanding of how the regulation of broadcasting really works. The idea of active practitioners like Erwin Krasnow working in harness with academic authorities like Lawrence Longley is a good one. The union of their efforts is in the best interests of their readers.

How do I know? I can best answer by quoting a favorite poem of President Kennedy's. It is a poem written by a bullfighter, Domingo Ortega, as translated by Robert Graves:

> Bullfight critics ranked in rows
> Crowd the enormous Plaza full;
> But he's the only one who knows –
> And he's the one who fights the bull.

NOTE

Newton Minow became Chairman of the Federal Communication Commission in 1961.

(h) Public interest and American broadcasting (Newton Minow)

From Minow, N. 1964: *Equal time: the private broadcaster and the public interest,* edited by L. Laurent. New York: Atheneum, vii–x

Before he became President, John F. Kennedy once told a group of broadcasters:

> You are aware that a private industry which utilizes public airwaves and TV channels – and which is necessarily regulated by public agencies – has a tremendous responsibility for public service.
>
> The public service broadcaster and the public servant – we have a great deal more in common than we might at first realize. In the last analysis, we are both dependent in large measure on the same factor: public approval. The broadcaster who offers shows that are neither seen nor heard is not offering a public service, no matter how high the quality of his show. The politician whose indifference to public opinion costs him his seat will no longer be able to perform effective public service, no matter how high-principled his courage or independence might have seemed.
>
> We both need, in short, public approval – not necessarily instant, or unanimous, or easily identified – but enough in the long run to keep us on our course.
>
> The question facing us both is: will that desire for public approbation become dominant? Will Gresham's law operate in the broadcasting and political worlds wherein the bad inevitably drive out the good? Will the politician's desire for reelection – and the broadcaster's desire for ratings – cause both to flatter every public whim and prejudice – to seek the lowest common denominator of appeal – to put public opinion at all times ahead of the public interest?
>
> For myself, I reject that view of politics, and I urge you to reject that view of broadcasting ...

Because I deeply agree with President Kennedy's analysis, I was honored to accept his appointment as Chairman of the Federal Communications Commission in 1961.

I had some strong convictions, not about the FCC, but about television, one of the industries which the FCC regulates. With many millions of other citizens, I was an avid television viewer, and so were my wife and children. And I often wondered about the effect television might be having on other Americans.

I believe television is the most powerful instrument ever created to reach the minds and hearts of man; an instrument which any President or dictator, any Congress or army, must reckon with forevermore.

I believe that the future of this nation – of the democratic ideal – and the world depends on an enlightened electorate, on an informed citizenry. And I believe that nothing in the history of man approaches the potential of television for information and misinformation, for enlightenment and obfuscation, for sheer reach and sheer impact.

Stalin once said: 'If I could control the medium of the American motion picture, I would need nothing else in order to convert the entire world to Communism.' What might he have said of the more pervasive and dominating medium of television?

A television channel is America's most scarce natural resource. As many as a dozen applicants plead for the privilege of using one channel. And because television channels are so scarce, because they can be used by such a small percentage of those who would like to have channels entrusted to them, their allocation and the supervision of their use rests with the federal government. Thus the government, not by choice but by absolute necessity, is ultimately responsible for the effect this medium has on the public. What is this effect? Boredom? Escape? Wisdom? Understanding? Inspiration? Condescension? Tolerance? Indifference? All of these? None of these?

I took on the assignment as Chairman of the FCC because I care about these things. I had the disturbing feeling that this elevating medium was on the way to being debased and demeaned. I had an equally uneasy belief that the FCC was not doing enough to halt this gradual debasement.

I was sure that the sad by-products of this debasement – the payola and the quiz scandals and the influence peddling – could be reversed by FCC action. I wasn't sure that the good things about American television could be encouraged and stimulated by a governmental agency.

But I was determined to try.

My motives were neither unusual nor complicated. Our country had been generous to my family and to me. With unbounded respect for President Kennedy, and in total agreement with his conviction that it is better to light a single candle than curse the darkness, we made the move to Washington.

Very early I decided that of all the routes I might take to the best performance of my job, the most effective and the wisest road in the long run was to speak out in the hope of influencing public opinion about television. I knew that the people were generally unaware that broadcasting was a public trust, and most of them did not know the extent of their rights to this public resource. I felt that many broadcasters, who naturally had a vested interest in the medium, had, in the flush of enormous financial success, too quickly grown complacent and closed their eyes to their responsibilities and trust. I decided to disturb their sleep – and to encourage these trustees to entertain and yet to inform, to make us laugh but also to make us think.

Hopefully, I tried also to awaken the public mind. [. . .]

NOTE

Newton Minow became Chairman of the Federal Communications Commission in 1961.

(i) The Communications Act, USA. Candidates for public office

From Section 315 of the Communications Act, 47 USC 315

If any licensee shall permit any person who is a legally qualified candidate for any public office to use a broadcasting station, he shall afford equal opportunities to all other such candidates for that office in the use of such broadcasting station; *Provided,* That such licensee shall have no power of censorship over the material broadcast under the provisions of this section. No obligation is imposed under this subsection upon any licensee to allow the use of its station by any such candidate. Appearance by a legally qualified candidate on any

1. bona fide newscast,
2. bona fide news interview,
3. bona fide news documentary (if the appearance of the candidate is incidental to the presentation of the subject or subjects covered by the news documentary), or
4. on-the-spot coverage of bona fide news events (including but not limited to political conventions and activities incidental thereto),

shall not be deemed to be use of a broadcasting station within the meaning of this subsection. Nothing in the foregoing sentence shall be construed as relieving broadcasters, in connection with the presentation of newscasts, news interviews, news documentaries, and on-the-spot coverage of news events, from the obligation imposed upon them under this chapter to operate in the public interest and to afford reasonable opportunity for the discussion of conflicting views on issues of public importance. [...]

(j) The Fairness Doctrine and procedures to be used in filing Fairness Doctrine complaints (FCC)

From Federal Communications Commission, 1983: Mass Media Bureau Publication 83304–FD, 1983

In general, broadcasters are treated very much like the editors of newspapers. As you may know, newspaper content is not regulated by any government agency. Broadcasters, like newspaper editors, decide what is to be presented and the format used. Specific program judgments by broadcasters are not reviewed by the Commission because of restraints placed on it by the United States Constitution and a provision of the Communications Act that prohibits censorship by this agency. Unlike newspapers, broadcasters are subject to a general policy known as the Fairness Doctrine. In administering the Fairness Doctrine, the Commission must still be very concerned about the constitutional and legal limits placed on it in connection with the content of programming. Because of these restrictions, the requirements of the Fairness Doctrine and procedures for filing complaints are not simple. What follows is our best attempt to summarize this complicated area of law in a way that we hope will be understood by most people. The material is in two main sections: (1) information about the Fairness Doctrine and (2) procedures for filing complaints.

THE FAIRNESS DOCTRINE

1. *Question*: What is the Fairness Doctrine?

Answer: The Fairness Doctrine has two parts. The first part requires that broadcasters present controversial issues that are of importance to the public. The second part of the Fairness Doctrine requires that when a broadcast station presents one side of a controversial issue of public importance, it has an obligation to afford a reasonable opportunity for the presentation of contrasting points of view in its *overall* programming.

2. *Question*: Let's be more specific. As to the first part of the Fairness Doctrine, do broadcasters have to cover every controversial issue of public importance?

Answer: No. It is in this area that broadcasters have the widest discretion to select what issues they will or will not cover. Inquiry by the Commission in such matters is rare. We have no intention of becoming involved in the selection of issues to be discussed, and we do not expect broadcasters to cover each and every important issue which may arise in their communities.

3. *Question*: The second part of the Fairness Doctrine is more complex. What is a 'controversial issue'?

Answer: By controversial, we generally mean that the issue is the subject of vigorous debate, with substantial elements of the community in opposition to one another.

4. *Question*: When is an issue of public importance?

Answer: Three factors are considered when deciding whether an issue is of public importance: (1) the amount of broadcast or newspaper coverage the issue has received; (2) the amount of attention the issue has received from government and other community leaders; and, most important, (3) the impact the issue is likely to have on the community at large.

5. *Question*: Does the Fairness Doctrine apply if the issue is controversial but not of public importance? Or if the issue is of public importance but not controversial?

Answer: No. The Fairness Doctrine applies only if the issue is both controversial *and* of public importance.

6. *Question*: Is it safe to assume that any story covered in the news or on a public affairs program triggers Fairness Doctrine obligations?

Answer: No. Many things are broadcast that are newsworthy, but may not be of public importance or controversial.

7. *Question*: A station is broadcasting statements about a person that put him in a bad light. That isn't fair. Does the person have a right to respond under the Fairness Doctrine?

Answer: Probably not. The Fairness Doctrine refers to the fairness of how an *issue* is covered, not to treating people fairly. Unless the person's conduct, such as that of a public official, is itself a controversial issue of public importance, no Fairness Doctrine obligation is imposed on the broadcaster. Broadcasters may be sued in local courts (but not before the Commission) if they defame individuals. (There is a very narrow area where a person who is attacked on the air may be entitled to a reasonable time on a station to respond under the personal attack rule. The rule applies only to attacks made during the discussion of controversial issues of public importance, and the attack must be on a person's honesty, integrity, or similar characteristics. The rule does not apply to attacks made during news programs. [. . .]

8. *Question*: Does a 'reasonable opportunity' for presenting contrasting views mean 'equal time'?

Answer: No. 'Equal time' applies only to candidates for public office, not to the Fairness Doctrine. What is a 'reasonable opportunity' depends primarily on three factors: (1) the total time afforded to each differing view; (2) the frequency of announcements or programs afforded to the differing views; and (3) the relative size of the audience when announcements or programs are broadcast. In some cases where an issue must be resolved by a certain date, such as a vote on a bond issue or action by a city council, the nearness of the programming to that date will also be a factor.

9. *Question*: If I find that a station has not fully met its Fairness Doctrine obligations, can I insist that the station give me time to present a contrasting view?

Answer: No. The purpose of the Fairness Doctrine is to inform the listener or viewer of the contrasting views, not to give anyone a right of access to a microphone or camera. So if you bring a valid Fairness Doctrine complaint to a station's attention, its obligation is to present contrasting views, but not necessarily by you.

10. *Question*: I watched a news program one evening. It presented only one side of an issue that I believe is controversial and of public importance. Is that the basis for a complaint?

Answer: No. The Fairness Doctrine applies to *overall* programming. The station may have already presented, or planned to present, contrasting views on other news programs, on public affairs programs or on other kinds of programs.

11. *Question*: Who decides whether an issue is of public importance and controversial, and whether the broadcaster has afforded reasonable opportunity for the presentation of contrasting views?

Answer: In the first instance, the broadcaster decides. The Commission will not review complaints on the grounds that it agrees or disagrees with the broadcaster. Rather, the Commission will act only if it finds that the broadcaster acted unreasonably or in bad faith. [...]

NOTE

The Federal Communications Commission is the key national agency for American broadcast regulation.

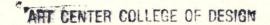

(k) General Fairness Doctrine obligations of broadcast licensees (FCC)

From *Federal Register* 50(169), Friday, 30 August, 1985, 35418–19

INTRODUCTION

1. Before the Commission for consideration are the matters raised by the *Notice of Inquiry* in the ... proceeding in which the Commission solicited comments on the statutory, constitutional, and policy implications underlying this fairness doctrine. Specifically, the Commission questioned whether the doctrine is constitutionally permissible under current marketplace conditions and First Amendment jurisprudence. Moreover, as a policy matter, the Commission inquired whether the doctrine remains necessary to further the governmental interest in an informed electorate and solicited comment on whether or not the doctrine, in operation, has an impermissible 'chilling' effect on the free expression of ideas. Finally, the Commission queried whether the fairness doctrine is codified either by Section 315 or by the general public interest standard embodied in the Communications Act.

2. More than one hundred parties submitted formal comments and reply comments in this proceeding. Many other persons participated in this proceeding through the submission of informal comments. In addition, the Commission, *en banc*, on February 7 and 8, 1985, heard oral presentations on the issues raised by the *Notice*.

3. The fairness doctrine, as developed by the Commission, imposes upon broadcasters a two-pronged obligation. Broadcast licensees are required to provide coverage of vitally important controversial issues of interest in the community served by the licensees and to provide a reasonable opportunity for the presentation of contrasting viewpoints on such issues. An examination of the genesis of the fairness doctrine reveals an evolutionary process, spanning a considerable period of time, and marked by a considerable uncertainty as to the proper approaches to insure that licensees operate in the public interest. This inquiry is a further step in a continuing process in evaluating the fairness doctrine. In undertaking this reexamination, we will first determine the purposes underlying promulgation of the fairness doctrine and then assess, in light of current marketplace conditions, whether or not its retention is consistent with the public interest.

4. Our past judgment that the fairness doctrine comports with the public interest was predicated upon three factors. First, in light of the limited availability of broadcast frequencies and the resultant need for government licensing, we concluded that the licensee is a public fiduciary, obligated to present diverse viewpoints representative of the community at large. We determined that the need to effectuate

the right of the viewing and listening public to suitable access to the marketplace of ideas justifies restrictions on the rights of broadcasters. Second, we presumed that a governmentally imposed restriction on the content of programming is a viable mechanism – indeed the best mechanism – by which to vindicate this public interest. Third, we determined, as a factual matter, that the fairness doctrine, in operation, has the effect of enhancing the flow of diverse viewpoints to the public.

5. On the basis of the voluminous factual record compiled in this proceeding, our experience in administering the doctrine and our general expertise in broadcast regulation, we no longer believe that the fairness doctrine, as a matter of policy, serves the public interest. In making this determination, we do not question the interest of the listening and viewing public in obtaining access to diverse and antagonistic sources of information. Rather, we conclude that the fairness doctrine is no longer a necessary or appropriate means by which to effectuate this interest. We believe that the interest of the public in viewpoint diversity is fully served by the multiplicity of voices in the marketplace today and that the intrusion by government into the content of programming occasioned by the enforcement of the doctrine unnecessarily restricts the journalistic freedom of broadcasters. Furthermore, we find that the fairness doctrine, in operation, actually inhibits the presentation of controversial issues of public importance to the detriment of the public and in degradation of the editorial prerogative of broadcast journalists.

6. We believe that the same factors which demonstrate that the fairness doctrine is no longer appropriate as a matter of policy also suggest that the doctrine may no longer be permissible as a matter of constitutional law. We recognize that the United States Supreme Court, in *Red Lion Broadcasting Co.* v. *FCC,* upheld the constitutionality of the fairness doctrine. But in the intervening sixteen years the information services marketplace has expanded markedly, thereby making it unnecessary to rely upon intrusive government regulation in order to assure that the public has access to the marketplace of ideas. In addition, the compelling evidence adduced in this proceeding demonstrates that the fairness doctrine, in operation, inhibits the presentation of controversial issues of public importance; this fact impels the dual conclusion that the doctrine impedes the public's access to the marketplace of ideas and poses an unwarranted intrusion upon the journalistic freedom of broadcasters.

NOTE

The Federal Communications Commission is the key national agency for American broadcast regulation. The Fairness Doctrine was suspended in 1987.

Index